Encryption for Digital Content

Advances in Information Security

Sushil Jajodia
Consulting Editor
Center for Secure Information Systems
George Mason University
Fairfax, VA 22030-4444
email: jajodia@gmu.edu

The goals of the Springer International Series on ADVANCES IN INFORMATION SECURITY are, one, to establish the state of the art of, and set the course for future research in information security and, two, to serve as a central reference source for advanced and timely topics in information security research and development. The scope of this series includes all aspects of computer and network security and related areas such as fault tolerance and software assurance.

ADVANCES IN INFORMATION SECURITY aims to publish thorough and cohesive overviews of specific topics in information security, as well as works that are larger in scope or that contain more detailed background information than can be accommodated in shorter survey articles. The series also serves as a forum for topics that may not have reached a level of maturity to warrant a comprehensive textbook treatment.

Researchers, as well as developers, are encouraged to contact Professor Sushil Jajodia with ideas for books under this series.

For other titles in this series, go to
www.springer.com/series/5576

Aggelos Kiayias • Serdar Pehlivanoglu

Encryption for Digital Content

Springer

Dr. Aggelos Kiayias
National and Kapodistrian
University of Athens
Department of Informatics
and Telecommunications
Panepistimiopolis, Ilisia,
Athens 15784 Greece
aggelos@kiayias.com

Dr. Serdar Pehlivanoglu
Division of Mathematical Sciences
School of Physical and
Mathematical Sciences
Nanyang Technological University
SPMS-MAS-03-01, 21 Nanyang Link
Singapore 637371
Email: spehlivan38@gmail.com

ISSN 1568-2633
ISBN 978-1-4614-2721-6 ISBN 978-1-4419-0044-9 (eBook)
DOI 10.1007/978-1-4419-0044-9
Springer New York Dordrecht Heidelberg London

Printed on acid-free paper

Springer is part of Springer Science+Business Media (www.springer.com)

Preface

Today human intellectual product is increasingly — and sometimes exclusively — produced, stored and distributed in digital form. The advantages of this capability are of such magnitude that the ability to distribute content digitally constitutes a media revolution that has deeply affected the way we produce, process and share information.

As in every technological revolution though, there is a flip-side to its positive aspects with the potential to counteract it. Indeed, the quality of being digital is a *double-edged* sword; the ease of production, dissemination and editing also implies the ease of misappropriation, unauthorized propagation and modification.

Cryptography is an area that traditionally focused on secure communication, authentication and integrity. In recent times though, there is a wealth of novel fine-tuned cryptographic techniques that sprung up as cryptographers focused on the specialised problems that arise in digital content distribution. This book is an introduction to this new generation of cryptographic mechanisms as well as an attempt to provide a cohesive presentation of these techniques that will enable the further growth of this emerging area of cryptographic research.

The text is structured in five chapters. The first three chapters deal with three different cryptographic techniques that address different problems of digital content distribution.

- Chapter 1 deals with fingerprinting codes. These mechanisms address the problem of *source identification* in digital content distribution : how is it possible to identify the source of a transmission when such transmission originates from a subset of colluders that belong to a population of potential transmitters. The chapter provides a formal treatment of the notion as well as a series of constructions that exhibit different parameter tradeoffs.
- Chapter 2 deals with broadcast encryption. These mechanisms address the problem of *distribution control* in digital content distribution : how is it possible to restrict the distribution of content to a targeted set of

recipients without resorting to reinitialising each time the set changes. The chapter focuses on explicit constructions of broadcast encryption schemes that are encompassed within the subset cover framework of Naor, Naor and Lotspiech. An algebraic interpretation of the framework is introduced that characterises the fundamental property of efficient revocation using tools from partial order theory. A complete security treatment of the broadcast encryption primitive is included.
- Chapter 3 deals with traitor tracing. These mechanisms address the problem of source identification in the context of decryption algorithms; among others we discuss how it is possible to reverse engineer "bootlegged" cryptographic devices that carry a certain functionality and trace them back to an original leakage incident. Public-key mechanisms such as those of Boneh-Franklin are discussed as well as combinatorial designs of Chor, Fiat and Naor. A unified model for traitor tracing schemes in the form of a tracing game is introduced and utilized for formally arguing the security of all the constructions.

These first three chapters can be studied independently in any order. Based on the material laid out in these chapters we then move on to more advanced mechanisms and concepts.

- Chapter 4 deals with the combination of tracing and revocation in various content distribution settings. This class of mechanisms combines the functionalities of broadcast encryption of Chapter 2 and traitor tracing schemes of Chapter 3 giving rise to a more wholesome class of encryption mechanisms for the distribution of digital content. A formal model for trace and revoke schemes is introduced that extends the modeling of chapter 3 to include revocation games. In this context, we also address the *propagation* problem in digital content distribution : how is it possible to curb the redistribution of content originating from authorised albeit rogue receivers. The techniques of all the first three chapters become critical here.
- Chapter 5 deals with a class of attacks against trace and revoke schemes called pirate evolution. This type of adverse behavior falls outside the standard adversarial modeling of trace and revoke schemes and turns out to be quite ubiquitous in subset cover schemes. We illustrate pirate evolution by designing attacks against specific schemes and we discuss how thwarting the attacks affects the efficiency parameters of the systems they apply to.

The book's discourse on the material is from first principles and it requires no prior knowledge of cryptography. Nevertheless, a level of reader maturity is assumed equivalent to a beginning graduate student in computer science or mathematics.

The authors welcome feedback on the book including suggestions for improvement and error reports. Please send your remarks and comments to:

`book@encryptiondc.com`

A web-site is maintained for the book where you can find information about its publication, editions and any errata:

`www.encryptiondc.com`

The material found in this text is partly based on the Ph.D. thesis of the second author. Both authors thank Matt Franklin for his comments on a paper published by the authors that its results are presented in this text (Chapter 5). They also thank Juan Garay for suggesting the title of the text.

Athens and Singapore,
August, 2010

Aggelos Kiayias
Serdar Pehlivanoglu

Contents

List of Figures

1

Fingerprinting Codes

In the context of digital content distribution, an important problem is tracking the origin of an observed signal to one out of many possible sources. We are particularly interested in settings where no other help is available for achieving this tracking operation except the mere access to the signal itself. We take a quite liberal interpretation of the notion of a signal : it may correspond to data transmission or even to a content related functionality. For instance, it might correspond to the decryption function of a decoder owned by a user where the population of users is defined by the keys they have access to. In another setting, it might be the retransmission of a certain content stream where the copies licensed to each user have the capacity to uniquely identify them.

An immediate application of such tracking capability is a leakage deterrence mechanism : by linking an incident of exposure of content back to the event of licensing the content, it is possible that willful content leaking can be deterred.

The problem of tracking can be addressed through "fingerprinting" : a one-to-one mapping from the set of users to a set of objects of equivalent functionality. Ideally there will be as many objects as the number of users and each object, even if slightly manipulated, it will still be capable of distinguishing its owner from others. Unfortunately it is the case that it can be quite expensive or even infeasible to generate a high number of variations of a certain functionality. Consider, for instance, in the context of encryption, assigning each user an independently generated key; this trivial solution would make it easy to distinguish a certain user but in order to maintain identical functionality among users a linear blowup in the complexity of encryption would be incurred.

A solution approach for solving the fingerprinting problem that is consistent with digital content distribution is the expansion of the object set to the set of sequences of objects of certain lengths. In this way, if at least two variations are feasible at the object level, say 0 and 1, then it is possible to assign to each user one sequence out of exponentially many that corresponds to a

A. Kiayias and S. Pehlivanoglu, *Encryption for Digital Content*, Advances in Information Security 52, DOI 10.1007/978-1-4419-0044-9_1,

unique bitstring. This type of assignment gives rise to the concept of fingerprinting codes where not only different strings correspond to different users, but also it is possible to identify a user who contributes to the production of a valid object sequence that is produced as a combination of a number of assigned user sequences. Fingerprinting codes will prove to be an invaluable tool for digital content distribution. In this chapter we will provide a formal treatment of this primitive and we will put forth a number of constructions.

1.1 Preliminaries

In this chapter and throughout the book we use standard notation. For $n \in \mathbb{N}$ we denote by $[n]$ the set $\{1, \ldots, n\}$. Vectors are denoted by $\mathsf{x}, \mathsf{y}, \mathsf{z}, \ldots$ and we write $\mathsf{x} = \langle \mathsf{x}_1, \ldots, \mathsf{x}_\ell \rangle$ for a vector x of dimension ℓ.

We next introduce some preliminary facts about random variables and probability distributions that will be frequently used in this chapter and elsewhere. Unless noted otherwise we use capital letters $X, Y, Z, \ldots$ to denote random variables. We use the notation $\mathbf{Prob}[R(X)]$ to denote the probability the event $R(X)$ happens where $R(\cdot)$ is a predicate that has domain equal to the range of X.

We will frequently utilize the exponentially decreasing bounds on the tails of a class of related distributions commonly referred to as Chernoff bounds. We will skip the proofs of these inequalities as they are out of the scope of this book and we refer the reader to e.g., Chapter 4 of [85] for a detailed discussion.

Theorem 1.1 (The Chernoff Bound). *Let* $\mathrm{X}_1, \ldots, \mathrm{X}_n$ *be independent Poisson trials such that* $\mathbf{Prob}(\mathrm{X}_i) = p_i$. *Let* $\mathrm{X} = \sum_{i=1}^{n} \mathrm{X}_i$ *and* $\mu = \mathsf{E}[\mathrm{X}]$, *then the following hold:*

1. *For any* $\delta > 0$, $\mathbf{Prob}[\mathrm{X} \geq (1+\delta)\mu] < \left(\frac{e^\delta}{(1+\delta)^{1+\delta}}\right)^\mu$
2. *For any* $0 < \delta \leq 1$, $\mathbf{Prob}[\mathrm{X} \geq (1+\delta)\mu] \leq e^{-\mu\delta^2/3}$
3. *For any* $R \geq 6\mu$, $\mathbf{Prob}[\mathrm{X} \geq R] \leq 2^{-R}$
4. *For any* $0 < \delta < 1$, $\mathbf{Prob}[\mathrm{X} \leq (1-\delta)\mu] \leq \left(\frac{e^{-\delta}}{(1-\delta)^{1-\delta}}\right)^\mu$
5. *For any* $0 < \delta < 1$, $\mathbf{Prob}[\mathrm{X} \leq (1-\delta)\mu] \leq e^{-\mu\delta^2/2}$

Often, the following two-tailed form of the Chernoff bound, which is derived immediately from second and fifth inequalities above, is used for $0 < \delta < 1$:

$$\mathbf{Prob}[|\mathrm{X} - \mu| \geq \delta\mu] \leq 2e^{-\mu\delta^2/3} \tag{1.1}$$

More generally it holds for $\delta > 0$,

$$\mathbf{Prob}[|\mathrm{X} - \mu| \geq \delta\mu] \leq 2e^{-\mu\delta^2/(2+\delta)} \tag{1.2}$$

It is possible to obtain stronger bounds for some special cases:

Theorem 1.2. *Let* $\mathrm{X}_1, \ldots, \mathrm{X}_n$ *be independent variables with* $\mathbf{Prob}(\mathrm{X}_i = 0) = \mathbf{Prob}(\mathrm{X}_i = 1) = \frac{1}{2}$ *for* $i = 1, \ldots, n$. *We then have for* $\mathrm{X} = \sum_{i=1}^{n} \mathrm{X}_i$*:*

1. *For any* $a > 0$, $\mathbf{Prob}[\mathrm{X} \geq n/2 + a] \leq e^{-2a^2/n}$.
2. *For any* $0 < a < n/2$, $\mathbf{Prob}[\mathrm{X} \leq n/2 - a] \leq e^{-2a^2/n}$.

Note that in settings where much less information is known about the distribution of a non-negative random variable X we can still utilize Markov's inequality to obtain a crude tail bound as follows for any positive constant a,

$$\mathbf{Prob}[X \geq a] \leq \mathbf{E}[X]/a \tag{1.3}$$

In a number of occasions we will also use the following handy lemma.

Lemma 1.3 (The coupon collector problem). *Suppose that there are* $n \in \mathbb{N}$ *coupons, from which coupons are being collected with replacement. Let* $\beta > 0$ *and* F_β *be the event that in* $k \geq \beta n \ln n$ *trials there exists a coupon that has not been drawn. It holds that* $\mathbf{Prob}[F_\beta] \leq n^{1-\beta}$.

Proof. The probability that a certain coupon is not drawn in k trials is $(1 - 1/n)^k$. It follows that the probability of the event F_β will be bounded by $n(1 - 1/n)^k$ by applying the union bound. Using the inequality $1 + x \leq e^x$ we have that $\mathbf{Prob}[F_\beta] \leq ne^{-\beta \ln n}$ from which we draw the conclusion of the lemma. ■

1.2 Definition of Fingerprinting Codes

A codeword x of length ℓ over an alphabet Q is an ℓ-tuple $\langle \mathsf{x}_1, \ldots, \mathsf{x}_\ell \rangle$ where $\mathsf{x}_i \in Q$ for $1 \leq i \leq \ell$. We call a set of codewords $\mathcal{C} \subseteq Q^\ell$ with size n, a (ℓ, n, q)-code given that the size of the alphabet is q, i.e. $|Q| = q$.

Given an (ℓ, n, q)-code $\mathcal{C}$, each codeword $\mathsf{x} \in \mathcal{C}$ will be thought of as the unique fingerprint of a user. The user accesses an object that is somehow fingerprinted with this codeword. Furthermore, we suppose that any other object corresponding to an arbitrary codeword in Q^ℓ is equally useful. Given those assumptions, we think of an adversary (which is also called a *pirate*) that corrupts a number of users (which are sometimes called *traitors*) and retrieves their codewords. The pirate then runs a **Forging** algorithm that produces a "pirate" codeword $\mathsf{p} \in Q^\ell$. In the adversarial formalization, the **Forging** algorithm will be subject to a *marking assumption* which forces the pirate to produce a codeword that is correlated to the user codewords that the pirate has corrupted. The simplest form of the marking assumption that will prove to be relevant in many settings is the following :

Definition 1.4 (Marking assumption). *We say a* **Forging** *algorithm satisfies the* marking assumption *for a set of codewords* $\mathcal{C} = \{\mathsf{c}^1, \ldots, \mathsf{c}^n\}$ *where* $\mathsf{c}^j \in Q^\ell$ *for* $j \in [n]$, *if for any set of indices* $\mathsf{T} \subseteq [n]$, *it holds that* **Forging**

on input $\mathcal{C}_\mathsf{T} = \{\mathsf{c}^j \mid j \in \mathsf{T}\}$ *outputs a codeword* p *from the descendant set* $\mathsf{desc}(\mathcal{C}_\mathsf{T})$ *that is defined as follows:*

$$\mathsf{desc}(\mathcal{C}_\mathsf{T}) = \{\mathsf{x} \in Q^\ell : \mathsf{x}_i \in \{\mathsf{a}_i : \mathsf{a} \in \mathcal{C}_\mathsf{T}\}, 1 \leq i \leq \ell\}$$

where $\mathsf{x}_i, \mathsf{a}_i$ *are the i-th symbols of the related vectors.*

In the context of fingerprinting codes, the set $\mathsf{desc}(\mathcal{C}_\mathsf{T})$ is the set of codewords that can be produced by a pirate using the codewords of the set $\mathcal{C}_\mathsf{T}$. Therefore in an (ℓ, n, q)-code $\mathcal{C}$, forging would correspond to producing a pirate codeword $\mathsf{p} \in Q^\ell$ out of the codewords available to a traitor coalition T. A q-ary fingerprinting code is a pair of algorithms $(\textbf{CodeGen}, \textbf{Identify})$ that generates a code for which it is possible to trace back to a traitor for any pirate codeword. Formally we have,

- **CodeGen** is an algorithm that given input 1^n, it samples a pair $(\mathcal{C}, tk) \leftarrow \textbf{CodeGen}(1^n)$ where $\mathcal{C}$ is an (ℓ, n, q)-code defined over an alphabet Q with ℓ as a function of n and q, and the identifying key tk is some auxiliary information to be used by **Identify** that may be empty. We may use ℓ as a superscript in the notation $\textbf{CodeGen}^\ell$, to emphasize the fact that **CodeGen** produces output a set of strings of length ℓ that might be a function of n, q and other parameters if such are present.
- **Identify** is an algorithm that on input the pair $(\mathcal{C}, tk) \leftarrow \textbf{CodeGen}(1^n)$ and the codeword $\mathsf{c} \in Q^\ell$, it outputs a codeword-index $t \in [n]$ or it fails.

Remark. Note that **CodeGen** can be either deterministic or probabilistic and we will name the fingerprinting code according to the properties of the underlying **CodeGen** procedure. Each codeword can be considered as the unique identifier of the corresponding user. If c is constructed by a traitor coalition, the objective of the **Identify** algorithm is to identify a codeword that was given to one of the traitors who took role in the forgery.

Definition 1.5. *We say a q-ary fingerprinting code* $\langle\textbf{CodeGen}, \textbf{Identify}\rangle$ *is* (α, w)*-identifier if the following holds :*

- *For any* **Forging** *algorithm that satisfies the* marking assumption *and* $(tk, \mathcal{C}) \leftarrow \textbf{CodeGen}(1^n)$ *it holds that*

$$\forall \mathsf{T} \subseteq [n] \;\; s.t. \; |\mathsf{T}| \leq w \quad \textbf{Prob}[\emptyset \not\subseteq \textbf{Identify}(tk, \mathsf{p}) \subseteq \mathsf{T}] \geq 1 - \alpha$$

where $\mathcal{C} = \{\mathsf{c}^1, \ldots, \mathsf{c}^n\}$ *is an* (ℓ, n, q)*-code and* $\mathsf{p} \in Q^\ell$ *is the output of the* **Forging** *algorithm on input* $\mathcal{C}_\mathsf{T} = \{\mathsf{c}^j \mid j \in \mathsf{T}\}$.

The probability is taken over all random choices of **CodeGen** and **Identify** algorithms when appropriate. We say the fingerprinting code is *w-identifier* if the failure probability $\alpha = 0$. The above definition supports identification for traitor coalitions of size up to w, and thus such fingerprinting codes will be called w-collusion resistant codes. By expanding the choice of T in the property of the **Identify** algorithm to run over any subset, we obtain a fully collusion resistant code.

We also note that the above definition leaves open the possibility for a secret scheme where the **Forging** algorithm has no access to the whole-code $\mathcal{C}$ generated by the **CodeGen** algorithm. While keeping the code secret will prove to be advantageous for the purpose of identifying a traitor as the traitor coalition has less information in constructing the pirate codeword, there are many cases where in an actual deployment of fingerprinting codes one would prefer an *open fingperinting code*, i.e. having the code publicly available (or even fixed - uniquely determined by n). A variant of the above definition where the **Forging** algorithm is not only given the traitor codewords $\mathcal{C}_\mathsf{T} = \{\mathsf{c}^j \mid j \in \mathsf{T}\}$ but also the code $\mathcal{C}$ as input gives rise to open fingerprinting codes. Taking this a bit further, a one may additionally provide the key tk to the attacker as well; this would be termed a *public fingerprinting code.*

1.3 Applications to Digital Content Distribution

Fingerprinting codes play an important role in the area of encryption mechanisms for digital content distribution. Encryption mechanisms can be designed to take advantage of a fingerprinting code by having a key-space for encryption that is marked following a fingerprinting code. In such case, a user codeword in the code describes the particular sequence of keys that are assigned to the user. The encryption of the content is then designed in such a way so that the recovery of the content requires a valid key sequence. Assuming it is possible to figure out what keys are stored in a pirate decoder this would provide a pirate codeword at the code level and the identification of a traitor user would be achieved by calling the identification algorithm of the underlying fingerprinting code.

The integration of a fingerprinting code with the encryption mechanism requires three independent and orthogonal tasks: (i) Designing the content encryption mechanism so that the key-space is distributed among the receivers according to a fingerprinting code. (ii) Detecting the keys used in the pirate decoder. (iii) Applying the identification algorithm of the underlying fingerprinting code.

Still, this is not the only way we may apply fingerprinting codes in our setting. To see another possible scenario consider an adversarial scenario where the pirate is entirely hiding the keys it possesses and rebroadcasts the clear text content after decrypting it. This would entirely numb any attempt to catch a traitor on the basis of a decryption key pattern. A different approach to address this issue that also utilizes fingerprinting codes would apply watermarking to the content itself. Naturally, to make the detection of a traitor possible, the watermarking should be robust, i.e. it should be hard to remove or modify the embedded marks of the content without substantial decrease in the quality or functionality of the distributed content. In this setting the identification algorithm of the fingerprinting codes will be applied on the marked digital content stream that is emitted by the adversary.

To make the above a bit more concrete in this section willintroduce these two adversarial models as well as comment further on how fingerprinting codes are utilized in each scenario.

Pirate Decoder Attacks. In this scenario, the secret information of a user is embedded in a decoder so that decryption of the content is available to the user through this decoder. Each decoder is equipped with a different set of keys so that the key-assignment reflects the fingerprinting code. The pirate, in this particular adversarial setting, publishes a pirate decoder that is constructed by the traitor keys embedded in the decoders available to the pirate.

The detection of the keys embedded in the pirate decoder requires an interaction with the device. In the non-black box model, the assumption is that the keys used in the pirate decoder become available through reverse-engineering. When only black-box interaction is permitted the setting is more challenging as the keys are not available but rather require the observation of the input/output of the decoder when subjected to some forensic statistical analysis. After detecting the keys responsible for the piracy, those keys are projected into the corresponding pirate codeword. The identification of a traitor is then achieved by employing the **Identify** algorithm of the underlying fingerprinting code.

The marking assumption of Definition 1.4 is enforced due to the security of the underlying encryption system that is embedded in the user decoders. Any adversary will only be able to use the traitor keys available to her, and the security properties of the underlying encryption mechanisms should prevent her to compute or receive other keys. We will return to these issues in much more detail when we discuss traitor tracing in Chapter 3.

Pirate Rebroadcast Attacks. In this adversarial model, the pirate instead of publishing the pirate decoder, it rebroadcasts the content in cleartext form. To achieve a similar type of identification, watermarking the content can be useful. Creating variations of a content object with different marks is something that should be achieved robustly and is a content specific task. It is not the subject of the present exposition to address such mechanisms. Still we will be concerned with achieving the most possible at the combinatorial and algorithmic level while requiring the minimum variability possible from the underlying marking scheme.

We consider the sequence of content segments with each part marked following a suitable watermarking technique. The variations of a particular segment correspond to the alphabet of the fingerprinting code. The length of the content sequence of segments should match the length of the fingerprinting code. Any codeword of the code amounts to a "path" over the segment variations with exactly one marked segment for each position in the content-sequence. Each receiver is able to receive a unique path in such content sequence.

In this setting, the marking assumption of definition 1.4 will be enforced by a robustness condition of the underlying watermarking technique so that the pirate neither removes the mark nor alters it into another variation which is not available to that pirate. For the sake of concreteness we will define the type of watermarking that would be useful to us. A watermark embedding algorithm is used to embed marks in the objects that are to be distributed. In a certain setting where arbitrary objects $\mathcal{O}$ are distributed, the robustness condition is defined as a property of a watermarking embedding function **Emb** that postulates that it is impossible for an attacker, that is given a set of marked objects derived from an original object, to generate an object that is similar to the original object whose mark cannot be identified as one of the marks that were embedded in the objects given to the adversary. Specifically we formalize the above property as follows:

Definition 1.6. *A watermarking embedding* **Emb** $: \{1, \ldots, q\} \times \mathcal{O} \rightarrow \mathcal{O}$ *satisfies the* robustness condition *with respect to a similarity relation* $\mathsf{Sim} \subseteq \mathcal{O} \times \mathcal{O}$, *alphabet size* q *and security parameter* $\lambda = \log(\frac{1}{\varepsilon})$ *if there exists a watermark reading algorithm* **Read** *such that for any subset of* $\mathsf{A} \subseteq [q]$ *the following holds for any probabilistic polynomial time adversary* $\mathcal{A}$ *and for any object* $\mathsf{a} \in \mathcal{O}$,

$$\mathbf{Prob}[\mathcal{A}(\{\mathbf{Emb}(a, \mathsf{a}) \mid a \in \mathsf{A}\}) = \mathsf{e} \wedge (\mathsf{e}, \mathsf{a}) \in \mathsf{Sim} \wedge \mathbf{Read}(\mathsf{e}) \notin \mathsf{A}] \leq \varepsilon$$

Note that it is assumed that $(\mathbf{Emb}(a, \mathsf{a}), \mathsf{a}) \in \mathsf{Sim}$ for all objects $\mathsf{a} \in \mathcal{O}$) and symbols $a \in [q]$.

The robustness condition would enforce the marking assumption and thus enable us to apply the identification algorithm of the fingerprinting code.

1.4 Constructions

1.4.1 Combinatorial Constructions

Combinatorial Properties of the Underlying Codes.

Consider an (ℓ, n, q)-code. A pirate codeword can be any codeword of length ℓ over the same alphabet Q. Based on the marking assumption, a pirate codeword $\mathsf{p} \in Q^\ell$ will be related to a set of user-codewords which are capable of producing this pirate codeword through combination of their components. Based on our formalization in Section 1.2, we express this relation by stating $\mathsf{p} \in \mathsf{desc}(\mathcal{C}_\mathsf{T})$, where $\mathcal{C}_\mathsf{T} = \{\mathsf{c}^i \mid i \in \mathsf{T}\}$ is defined as the total set of codewords available to the traitor coalition specified by the traitor user set T.

Traitor identification, in some sense, amounts to evaluating similarities between the pirate codeword and the user codewords. However it might be impossible through such calculations to identify a traitor. To illustrate such an impossibility, consider two disjoint set of codewords $\mathcal{T}_1, \mathcal{T}_2 \subseteq \mathcal{C}$ such that $\mathcal{T}_1 \cap \mathcal{T}_2 = \emptyset$, and further suppose that their descendant sets contain a common codeword p, i.e. $\mathsf{p} \in \mathsf{desc}(\mathcal{T}_1) \cap \mathsf{desc}(\mathcal{T}_2)$. Provided that the pirate codeword observed is the codeword p, no traitor identification can be successful in this unfortunate circumstance. This is the case, since p is possibly constructed by a pirate who has given the codeword set $\mathcal{T}_1$ or the set $\mathcal{T}_2$ and it is impossible to distinguish between these two cases.

In order to rule out such problems and obtain positive results, a useful measure is to bound the coalition size; without specifying an upper bound on the size of sets T_1 and T_2, it can be quite hard to avoid the above failures in some cases (nevertheless we will also demonstrate how it is possible to achieve unbounded results - later in this chapter). Hence, we will start discussing some necessary requirements that are parameterized with a positive integer w. This parameter specifies the upper bound on the size of the traitors corrupted by the pirate, or in other terms the size of the traitor coalition. For a code $\mathcal{C}$, we define the set of w-descendant codewords of $\mathcal{C}$, i.e. the set of codewords that could be produced by the pirate corrupting at most w traitors, denoted by $\mathsf{desc}_w(\mathcal{C})$ as follows:

$$\mathsf{desc}_w(\mathcal{C}) = \bigcup_{\mathsf{T} \subseteq [n], |\mathsf{T}| \leq w} \mathsf{desc}(\mathcal{C}_\mathsf{T})$$

We, now, formally define a set of combinatorial properties of codes that are related to the task of achieving identification:

Definition 1.7. *Let* $\mathcal{C} = \{\mathsf{c}^1, \ldots, \mathsf{c}^n\}$ *be an* (ℓ, n, q)*-code and* $w \geq 2$ *be an integer.*

1. *$\mathcal{C}$ is a w-FP (frameproof) q-ary code if for any* $\mathsf{x} \in \mathsf{desc}_w(\mathcal{C})$ *the following holds: Given that* $\mathsf{x} \in \mathsf{desc}(\mathcal{C}_\mathsf{T}) \cap \mathcal{C}$ *with* $\mathsf{T} \subseteq [n], |\mathsf{T}| \leq w$*, then it holds that* $\mathsf{x} = \mathsf{c}^i$ *for some* $i \in \mathsf{T}$*; i.e. for any* $\mathsf{T} \subseteq [n]$ *that satisfies* $|\mathsf{T}| \leq w$*, we have* $\mathsf{desc}(\mathcal{C}_\mathsf{T}) \cap \mathcal{C} \subseteq \mathcal{C}_\mathsf{T}$.
2. *$\mathcal{C}$ is a w-SFP (secure-frameproof) q-ary code if for any* $\mathsf{x} \in \mathsf{desc}_w(\mathcal{C})$ *the following holds: Given that* $\mathsf{x} \in \mathsf{desc}(\mathcal{C}_{\mathsf{T}_1}) \cap \mathsf{desc}(\mathcal{C}_{\mathsf{T}_2})$ *for* $\mathsf{T}_1 \neq \mathsf{T}_2$ *with* $|\mathsf{T}_1|, |\mathsf{T}_2| \leq w$*, it holds that* $\mathsf{T}_1 \cap \mathsf{T}_2 \neq \emptyset$.
3. *$\mathcal{C}$ is a w-IPP (identifiable parent property) q-ary code if for any* $\mathsf{x} \in \mathsf{desc}_w(\mathcal{C})$*, it holds that*

$$\bigcap_{\{\mathsf{T}: \mathsf{x} \in \mathsf{desc}(\mathcal{C}_\mathsf{T}) \wedge |\mathsf{T}| \leq w\}} \mathcal{C}_\mathsf{T} \neq \emptyset$$

4. *$\mathcal{C}$ is a w-*TA (traceability) q-ary code if for any $\mathsf{T} \subseteq [n]$ with $|\mathsf{T}| \leq w$ and for any $\mathsf{x} \in \mathsf{desc}(\mathcal{C}_\mathsf{T})$, there is at least one codeword $\mathsf{y} \in \mathcal{C}_\mathsf{T}$ such that $\mathsf{I}(\mathsf{x}, \mathsf{y}) > \mathsf{I}(\mathsf{x}, \mathsf{z})$ holds for any $\mathsf{z} \in \mathcal{C} \setminus \mathcal{C}_\mathsf{T}$ where we define $\mathsf{I}(\mathsf{a}, \mathsf{b}) = |\{i : \mathsf{a}_i = \mathsf{b}_i\}|$ for any $\mathsf{a}, \mathsf{b} \in Q^\ell$.

The implications of the above definitions in terms of identification is as follows:

- For any pirate codeword in a w-frameproof code $\mathcal{C}$, that is produced by a codeword coalition of size at most w, the pirate codeword is identical to a user-codeword if and only if that user is involved in piracy. This means that the marking assumption makes it impossible to trace an innocent user.
- If two different sets of coalitions with size less than w are capable of producing the same pirate codeword, then w-secure frameproof code implies that these two coalitions are not disjoint. While this property is necessary for absolute identification it is not sufficient : it is possible for example to have three different sets with their descendant sets having a non-empty intersection while themselves share only elements pairwise. In such case, it would still be impossible to identify a traitor codeword. This motivates the next property called the identifiable parent property.
- If any number of different coalitions with size less than w are capable of producing the same pirate codeword, then the w-identifiable parent property implies that there is at least one common user codeword in all of the coalitions. Under such circumstance on input a pirate codeword, an identification algorithm becomes feasible as follows: all possible sets of coalitions which produces the given pirate codeword are recovered. The w-identifiable parent property implies the existence of at least one codeword that is contained in the intersection of all those sets. This is the output of the algorithm (note that this algorithm is not particularly efficient but it achieves perfect correctness - we provide a formal description below).
- For any pirate codeword in a w-traceability code, that is produced by a codeword coalition of size at most w, there exists a simple procedure that is linear in n and recovers at least one traitor. This procedure simply considers all codewords z as possible candidates and calculates the function $\mathsf{I}(\mathsf{x}, \mathsf{z})$ with the pirate codeword x. The codewords with the highest value are the traitor codewords.

The above properties are hiearachical; in fact, it is quite easy to observe that identifiable parent property implies the secure frameproof property which in turn also implies the frameproof property. Here, we will give the proof for the first link which states that the traceability property implies the identifiable parent property.

Theorem 1.8. *If an (ℓ, n, q)-code $\mathcal{C}$ over an alphabet Q is w-TA q-ary code, then the code satisfies the w-identifiable parent property.*

Proof of Theorem 1.8: Suppose that a code $\mathcal{C} = \{\mathsf{c}^1, \ldots, \mathsf{c}^n\}$ over an alphabet Q is w-TA. Now pick $\mathsf{x} \in \mathsf{desc}_w(\mathcal{C})$. There is some T' such that $\mathsf{x} \in \mathsf{desc}(\mathcal{C}_{\mathsf{T}'})$ and $\mathsf{T}' \subseteq [n]$ with $|\mathsf{T}'| \leq w$. Due to the w-TA property there exists a user codeword $\mathsf{y} \in \mathcal{C}_{\mathsf{T}'}$ such that

$$\mathsf{I}(\mathsf{x},\mathsf{y}) > \mathsf{I}(\mathsf{x},\mathsf{z}) \tag{1.4}$$

holds for any $\mathsf{z} \in \mathcal{C} \setminus \mathcal{C}_{\mathsf{T}'}$. Given that there can be many codewords y with this property we choose one that maximizes the function $\mathsf{I}(\mathsf{x},\cdot)$. We claim that for this codeword the following holds:

$$\{\mathsf{y}\} \subseteq \bigcap_{\{\mathsf{T}:\mathsf{x}\in\mathsf{desc}(\mathcal{C}_{\mathsf{T}})\wedge|\mathsf{T}|\leq w\}} \mathcal{C}_{\mathsf{T}} \tag{1.5}$$

Provided that the above claim hold then the code satisfies the identifiable parent property since the above equation holds for any x that belongs to the set $\mathsf{desc}_w(\mathcal{C})$.

Suppose that Equation 1.5 does not hold. In other terms there exists some T^* with $|\mathsf{T}^*| \leq w$ for which $\mathsf{x} \in \mathsf{desc}(\mathcal{C}_{\mathsf{T}^*})$ but $\mathsf{y} \notin \mathcal{C}_{\mathsf{T}^*}$.

On the other hand, the traceability property of the code ensures the existence of a user codeword $\mathsf{y}^* \in \mathcal{C}_{\mathsf{T}^*}$ for which $\mathsf{I}(\mathsf{x},\mathsf{y}^*) > \mathsf{I}(\mathsf{x},\mathsf{z})$ for any $\mathsf{z} \in \mathcal{C}\setminus\mathcal{C}_{\mathsf{T}^*}$; given that $\mathsf{y} \notin \mathcal{C}_{\mathsf{T}^*}$ we obtain $\mathsf{I}(\mathsf{x},\mathsf{y}^*) > \mathsf{I}(\mathsf{x},\mathsf{y})$.

Now in case $\mathsf{y}^* \notin \mathcal{C}_{\mathsf{T}'}$ from Equation 1.4, we obtain $\mathsf{I}(\mathsf{x},\mathsf{y}) > \mathsf{I}(\mathsf{x},\mathsf{y}^*)$ which is a contradiction. Therefore it follows that $\mathsf{y}^* \in \mathcal{C}_{\mathsf{T}'}$. Nevertheless, now given that $\mathsf{I}(\mathsf{x},\mathsf{y}^*) > \mathsf{I}(\mathsf{x},\mathsf{y})$ we derive a contradiction on the choice of y which was assumed to maximize $\mathsf{I}(\mathsf{x},\cdot)$. This contradiction suggests our claim in Equation 1.5 holds, i.e., the identifiable parent property is proven. ■

An important observation relates the size q of the code-alphabet and the size w of the traitor coalition for which the code is resistant:

Theorem 1.9. *If an (ℓ, n, q)-code $\mathcal{C}$ over an alphabet Q is w-IPP then it holds that $w < q$.*

Proof of Theorem 1.9: We will prove the statement by contradiction. Suppose that a code $\mathcal{C} = \{\mathsf{c}^1, \ldots, \mathsf{c}^n\}$ over an alphabet Q is w-IPP while at the same time $w \geq q = |Q|$.

Consider now a traitor coalition $\mathsf{T} = \{t_1, \ldots, t_w\} \subseteq [n]$ with $w \geq q$, and a receiver-index $u \in [n] \setminus \mathsf{T}$, denote the set $\mathsf{T}_i = \mathsf{T} \setminus \{t_i\} \cup \{u\}$ for $i = 1, \ldots, w$, and also say $\mathsf{T}_0 = \mathsf{T}$.

We will now consider a specific pirate codeword $\mathsf{m}_{\mathsf{T},u}$ that is constructed by picking the the symbols most frequent for each position, i.e., $\mathsf{m}_{\mathsf{T},u} = \langle \mathsf{m}_1, \ldots, \mathsf{m}_\ell \rangle$ where $\mathsf{m}_i = b \in Q$ such that b is the element with a maximal $|\{j \in \mathsf{T} \cup \{u\} : \mathsf{c}_i^j = b\}|$ (ties are broken arbitrarily). Since $w \geq q$, and the size of the set $\mathsf{T} \cup \{u\}$ is $w + 1$, for each $i = 1, \ldots, \ell$ we have

$$|\{j \in \mathsf{T} \cup \{u\} : \mathsf{c}_i^j = \mathsf{m}_i\}| \geq 2 \tag{1.6}$$

Observe now that $\mathsf{m}_{\mathsf{T},u} \in \mathsf{desc}(\mathcal{C}_{\mathsf{T}_j})$ holds for each $j = 0, 1, \ldots, w$. Indeed, 1.6 ensures that no matter what $j \in \{0, 1, \ldots, w\}$, the i-th symbol m_i of the pirate codeword $\mathsf{m}_{\mathsf{T},u}$ is descendant of the codewords of the coalition T_j.

The identifiable parent property implies that the intersection of all these sets is not empty, while on the other hand, it is obvious that $\bigcap_{j=0}^{w} \mathsf{T}_j = \emptyset$. This contradiction concludes the proof of the statement of the theorem. ■

Combinatorial Fingerprinting Codes

Among the properties of codes listed above, the w-IPP property is necessary and sufficient to produce a perfect identification of a traitor, and hence, as we see here, we can obtain a fingerprinting code based on an IPP code. It should be noted though that the corresponding **Identify** algorithm may take exponential amount of time (but is guaranteed to succeed always).

IPP Identifying Algorithm. We will now describe the straightforward identifying algorithm $\mathbf{Identify}^{\mathbf{w}}_{\mathbf{IPP}}$ that is associated with an IPP code. The algorithm is given a pirate codeword $\mathsf{p} \in Q^\ell$, with $|Q| = q$, and the (ℓ, n, q) code $\mathcal{C}$, it outputs an index $t \in [n]$. It first computes the user coalitions $\mathsf{S} \subseteq [n]$ for which $\mathsf{p} \in \mathsf{desc}(\mathcal{C}_\mathsf{S})$ and $|\mathsf{S}| \leq w$, i.e. the set S is a possible traitor coalition that is responsible for producing the pirate codeword p. The time-complexity of this algorithm is proportional to $\binom{n}{w}\ell$.

Listing the collection of all such traitor coalitions by

$$\mathcal{T}_\mathsf{p} = \{\mathsf{S} \subseteq [n] \mid \mathsf{p} \in \mathsf{desc}(\mathcal{C}_\mathsf{S}), |\mathsf{S}| \leq w\}$$

The algorithm returns $\bigcap_{\mathsf{S} \in \mathcal{T}_\mathsf{p}} \mathsf{S}$ if such set is non-empty or it exists or fails.

Theorem 1.10. *Provided that* $\mathbf{CodeGen}(1^n)$ *generates a w-IPP code for all $n \in \mathbb{N}$, the q-ary fingerprinting code* $\langle \mathbf{CodeGen}, \mathbf{Identify}^{w}_{IPP} \rangle$ *is w-identifier.*

Proof. Based on the condition of the theorem, when $(\mathcal{C}, tk) \leftarrow \mathbf{CodeGen}(1^n)$, we assume without loss of generality that the identifying key $tk = \epsilon$ is empty and $\mathcal{C} = \{\mathsf{c}^1, \ldots, \mathsf{c}^n\}$ is a w-IPP q-ary code.

For any $\mathsf{x} \in \mathsf{desc}_w(\mathcal{C})$ we define $\mathcal{T}_\mathsf{x}$ by $\{\mathsf{S} \subseteq [n] \mid \mathsf{x} \in \mathsf{desc}(\mathcal{C}_\mathsf{S}), |\mathsf{S}| \leq w\}$; the identifiable parent property implies that

$$\forall \mathsf{x} \in \mathsf{desc}_w(\mathcal{C}) \qquad \bigcap_{\mathsf{S} \in \mathcal{T}_\mathsf{x}} \mathsf{S} \neq \emptyset \tag{1.7}$$

Consider now a **Forging** adversary that is subject to the marking assumption that is given in Definition 1.4. Consider a traitor coalition with index-set T which satisfies $|\mathsf{T}| \leq w$. The adversary is given the traitor codewords $\mathcal{C}_\mathsf{T} = \{\mathsf{c}^j \mid j \in \mathsf{T}\}$ and outputs a pirate codeword $\mathsf{p} \in \mathsf{desc}(\mathcal{C}_\mathsf{T})$.

Due to the fact that the code is w-IPP, the pirate codeword p satisfies the equation in 1.7; hence, the identifying algorithm $\mathbf{Identify}^{w}_{IPP}(\mathcal{C}, \mathsf{p})$ returns an user-index that belongs to the intersection $\bigcap_{\mathsf{S} \in \mathcal{T}_\mathsf{p}} \mathsf{S} \neq \emptyset$.

This concludes the fact that no matter the strategy of the forging algorithm, on input traitor set $\mathsf{T} \subseteq [n]$ with $|\mathsf{T}| \leq w$, outputs a pirate codeword p it holds that $\mathbf{Prob}[\emptyset \neq\subseteq \mathbf{Identify}^{w}_{IPP}(\mathcal{C}, \mathsf{p}) \subseteq \mathsf{T}] = 1$, i.e. the fingerprinting code $\langle \mathbf{CodeGen}, \mathbf{Identify}^{w}_{IPP} \rangle$ is w-identifier provided that $\mathbf{CodeGen}(1^n)$ generates a w-IPP code. ■

TA Identifying Algorithm The class of w-IPP codes can be paired with an exponential time algorithm; naturally this is not very useful and more efficient solutions are to be sought. In contrast with general w-IPP codes, the subclass of w-TA codes can be paired with an algorithm that has computation time linear in the product of the size and the length of the code. The idea is to score each of receiver according to the number of overlaps between its codeword and the pirate codeword; the receiver with the highest score would be necessarily among the traitors assuming that the traitor coalition has size less than w (compare this also with the proof of Theorem 1.8).

We will, now, define an identifying algorithm $\mathbf{Identify_{TA}}$ that given a pirate codeword $\mathsf{p} \in Q^\ell$, with $|Q| = q$, and an (ℓ, n, q) code $\mathcal{C} = \{\mathsf{c}^1, \dots, \mathsf{c}^n\}$, it outputs an index $t \in [n]$. The algorithm first computes the score s_j for each codeword index $j \in [n]$ as follows:

$$s_j = |\{i : \mathsf{p}_i = \mathsf{c}_i^j\}|$$

The algorithm returns the index for which the score is maximal; i.e. the index corresponding to the score $\max_{j\in[n]}\{s_1, \dots, s_n\}$. Observe that the score of a user with index $j \in [n]$ is equal to $\mathsf{I}(\mathsf{p}, \mathsf{c}^j)$.

Theorem 1.11. *Provided that* ($\mathbf{CodeGen}(1^n)$ *generates a* w*-TA code for all* $n \in \mathbb{N}$*; the* q*-ary fingerprinting code* $\langle \mathbf{CodeGen}, \mathbf{Identify}_{TA} \rangle$ *is* w*-identifier.*

Proof of Theorem 1.11: Based on the condition of the theorem, when $(\mathcal{C}, tk) \leftarrow \mathbf{CodeGen}(1^n)$, we assume without loss of generality that the identifying key $tk = \epsilon$ is empty and $\mathcal{C} = \{\mathsf{c}^1, \dots, \mathsf{c}^n\}$ is a w-TA q-ary code. The traceability property of the code implies the following:

$$\begin{aligned} &\forall \mathsf{T} \subseteq [n] \text{ with } |\mathsf{T}| \leq w \text{ and } \forall \mathsf{x} \in \mathsf{desc}(\mathcal{C}_\mathsf{T}) \\ &\qquad \exists \mathsf{y} \in \mathcal{C}_\mathsf{T} \forall \mathsf{z} \in \mathcal{C} \setminus \mathcal{C}_\mathsf{T} \text{ s.t. } \mathsf{I}(\mathsf{x}, \mathsf{y}) > \mathsf{I}(\mathsf{x}, \mathsf{z}) \end{aligned} \tag{1.8}$$

Consider now a **Forging** adversary that is subject to the marking assumption as given in Definition 1.4. The adversary chooses a traitor coalition with index-set T which satisfies $|\mathsf{T}| \leq w$. The adversary is given the traitor codewords $\mathcal{C}_\mathsf{T} = \{\mathsf{c}^j \mid j \in \mathsf{T}\}$ and finally outputs a pirate codeword $\mathsf{p} \in \mathsf{desc}(\mathcal{C}_\mathsf{T})$.

Due to the fact that the code is w-TA, the pirate codeword p satisfies the equation in 1.8; hence, the identifying algorithm $\mathbf{Identify}_{TA}(\mathcal{C}, \mathsf{p})$ returns the user index with a maximum score that belongs to the traitor coalition T. Recall that the score of a user with index $j \in [n]$ is equal to $\mathsf{I}(\mathsf{p}, \mathsf{c}^j)$.

This concludes the fact that no matter what the strategy of the forging algorithm, on input traitor set $\mathsf{T} \subseteq [n]$ with $|\mathsf{T}| \leq w$, outputs a pirate codeword p it holds that $\mathbf{Prob}[\emptyset \neq\subseteq \mathbf{Identify}_{TA}(\mathcal{C}, \mathsf{p}) \subseteq \mathsf{T}] = 1$, i.e. the fingerprinting code $\langle \mathbf{CodeGen}, \mathbf{Identify}_{TA} \rangle$ is w-identifier provided that $\mathbf{CodeGen}(1^n)$ generates a w-TA code. ■

Instantiating Traceability Codes

It is possible to generate a w-TA code out of an error correcting code that has a suitably high distance. We first define the error correcting codes.

Definition 1.12. *An* $[\ell, n, d]_q$ error-correcting code $\mathcal{C}$ *is a set of* n *vectors from the set* Q^ℓ, *where* $|Q| = q$, *with the following condition: for all* $\mathsf{x}, \mathsf{y} \in \mathcal{C}$, $\mathsf{distance}(\mathsf{x}, \mathsf{y}) \geq d$ *where* $\mathsf{distance}(\mathsf{x}, \mathsf{y}) = |\{i : \mathsf{x}_i \neq \mathsf{y}_i\}|$, *and* $\mathsf{x}_i \in Q$ *is the* i*-th element of vector* x.

If the condition $\ell > w^2(\ell - d)$ holds $\mathcal{C}$ then $\mathcal{C}$ is a w-TA code, (recall Definition 1.7).

Theorem 1.13. *If* $\mathcal{C}$ *is an* $[\ell, n, d]_q$ *error-correcting that satisfies* $d > \ell(1 - \frac{1}{w^2})$, *then* $\mathcal{C}$ *is a* w*-TA* (ℓ, n, q) *code.*

Proof of Theorem 1.13: $\mathcal{C}$ is a linear error correcting code with distance d. Since $\mathsf{I}(\mathsf{x}, \mathsf{y}) = |\{i : \mathsf{x}_i = \mathsf{y}_i\}|$ is the complement of the function $\mathsf{distance}(\cdot, \cdot)$, i.e., their sum equals to the length of the code ℓ, we obtain:

$$\forall \mathsf{x}, \mathsf{y} \in \mathcal{C} \quad \mathsf{I}(\mathsf{x}, \mathsf{y}) \leq \ell - d < \ell - \ell(1 - \frac{1}{w^2}) = \frac{\ell}{w^2} \tag{1.9}$$

We will now prove that $\mathcal{C}$ is a w-TA code by showing the following: for any $\mathsf{T} \subseteq [n]$ with $|\mathsf{T}| \leq w$ and for any $\mathsf{x} \in \mathsf{desc}(\mathcal{C}_\mathsf{T})$,

$$\exists \mathsf{y} \in \mathcal{C}_\mathsf{T} \;\; s.t. \;\; \forall \mathsf{z} \in \mathcal{C} \setminus \mathcal{C}_\mathsf{T} \quad \mathsf{I}(\mathsf{x}, \mathsf{y}) > \mathsf{I}(\mathsf{x}, \mathsf{z}) \tag{1.10}$$

Towards proving the existence of such codeword, first observe the following: for any $\mathsf{T} \subseteq [n]$ with $|\mathsf{T}| \leq w$, and any $\mathsf{x} \in \mathsf{desc}(\mathcal{C}_\mathsf{T})$, the sum $\sum_{\mathsf{v} \in \mathcal{C}_\mathsf{T}} \mathsf{I}(\mathsf{x}, \mathsf{v}) \geq \ell$. Hence, if we denote the codeword within $\mathcal{C}_\mathsf{T}$ that has maximal overlap with the codeword x by $\mathsf{y}_{\mathsf{x},\mathsf{T}} = \max_{\mathsf{v} \in \mathcal{C}_\mathsf{T}}(\mathsf{I}(\mathsf{x}, \mathsf{v}))$, we have that satisfies $\mathsf{I}(\mathsf{x}, \mathsf{y}_{\mathsf{x},\mathsf{T}}) \geq \ell/w$.

We claim that for any $\mathsf{z} \in \mathcal{C} \setminus \mathcal{C}_\mathsf{T}$ it holds that $\mathsf{I}(\mathsf{z}, \mathsf{x}) < \ell/w$. Due to the fact that $\mathsf{x} \in \mathsf{desc}(\mathcal{C}_\mathsf{T})$ we obtain $\mathsf{I}(\mathsf{x}, \mathsf{z}) \leq \sum_{\mathsf{v} \in \mathcal{C}_\mathsf{T}} \mathsf{I}(\mathsf{z}, \mathsf{v})$. Since we have 1.9, it holds that $\mathsf{I}(\mathsf{x}, \mathsf{z}) \leq w \cdot \ell/w^2$. Finally, we have $\mathsf{I}(\mathsf{x}, \mathsf{z}) < \ell/w$.

This completes the proof, since the codeword $\mathsf{y}_{\mathsf{x},\mathsf{T}}$ satisfies the condition given in 1.10 with ℓ/w being the actual threshold. ■

Reed-Solomon codes can be used to construct w-TA codes in the fashion suggested in the theorem above. A Reed-Solomon code over a finite field $Q := \mathbb{F}_q$ includes all vectors of the form $\langle p(f_1), \ldots, p(f_{q-1}) \rangle$ where $p(\cdot)$ is a polynomial of degree $r - 1$ in the field, and $f_i \in \mathbb{F}_q$ for $i = 1, \ldots, q - 1$. This yields a w-TA code with $w \leq \sqrt{(q-1)/(r-1)}$ and q^r codewords. One would notice the immediate downside in this construction in its high lower bound on the alphabet size : it should grow at least quadratically with the collusion threshold w and even if $q = O(w^2)$ the number of users that can be accommodated can be rather small. We will improve in this situation in section 1.4.2 where we will show that we can reduce alphabet size much closer to w. For smaller alphabet values though we will stumble upon the following limitation.

Limitations on Combinatorial Constructions

Although, w-IPP (especially efficient w-TA) codes are good for identification purposes, the alphabet size bounds the coalition size as illustrated in Theorem 1.9. This in turn imposes a limitation on designing w-identifier fingerprinting codes:.

Theorem 1.14. *Provided that $w \geq q$, there is no q-ary fingerprinting code* (**CodeGen**, **Identify**) *that is w-identifier.*

Proof of Theorem 1.14: We will prove the statement by contradiction. Provided that $w \geq q$ we assume the existence of a q-ary fingerprinting code (**CodeGen**, **Identify**) that is w-identifier. The algorithm **CodeGen** samples an (ℓ, n, q) code $\mathcal{C} = \{\mathsf{c}^1, \ldots, \mathsf{c}^n\}$ and an identifying key tk. Recall the definition for w-identifier: For any **Forging** algorithm that satisfies the *marking assumption*, it holds that

$$\forall \mathsf{T} \subseteq [n] \text{ s.t } |\mathsf{T}| \leq w \quad \mathbf{Prob}[\emptyset \not\subseteq \mathbf{Identify}(tk, \mathsf{p}) \subseteq \mathsf{T}] = 1$$

where $\mathsf{p} \in Q^\ell$ is the output of the **Forging** algorithm on input $\mathcal{C}_\mathsf{T} = \{\mathsf{c}^j \mid j \in \mathsf{T}\}$.

First, observe that, the code $\mathcal{C}$ is not w-IPP. Indeed, otherwise Theorem 1.9, i.e. $w < q$, would be effective which contradicts with the fact that $w \geq q$. Given that $\mathcal{C}$ is not w-IPP, then there exists a codeword $\mathsf{x} \in \mathsf{desc}_w(\mathcal{C})$ for which we have

$$\bigcap_{\{\mathsf{T}:\mathsf{x}\in\mathsf{desc}(\mathcal{C}_\mathsf{T})\wedge|\mathsf{T}|\leq w\}} \mathcal{C}_\mathsf{T} = \emptyset \tag{1.11}$$

The **Identify** algorithm, on input x, will return an index $j \in [n]$. The equation 1.11 implies that there exists a set T' with size less than w such that $j \notin \mathsf{T}'$. Hence, consider the case where the **Forging** algorithm of an adversary has corrupted T' and produces the pirate codeword x. In such case, the **Identify** algorithm fails to identify the traitor correctly, hence there is a possibility of error that contradicts with the statement that the q-ary fingerprinting code (**CodeGen**, **Identify**) is w-identifier. ■

As we will see later, we can overcome the limitation of the above theorem by allowing some failure probability in the identification process (see the constructions of Sections 1.4.3 and 1.4.4).

1.4.2 The Chor-Fiat-Naor Fingerprinting Codes

In this section we will consider two basic variants of this class of codes. The first variant is an open code, i.e., the adversary is allowed to have access to the code. Moreover, given that the tracing key is the code itself this amounts to a public fingerprinting code (cf. see the discussion on these notion after

Definition 1.5). The second variant is secret code and hence the adversary is not privy to the code; it achieves better efficiency parameters.

Code Generation. Given the number of users n, the $\mathbf{CodeGen}^{\ell}_{CFN}$ algorithm is parameterized by the length ℓ which is a function of n and q; we write $(\mathcal{C}, tk = \mathcal{C}) \leftarrow \mathbf{CodeGen}^{\ell}_{CFN}(1^n)$. The (ℓ, n, q)-code $\mathcal{C}$ is constructed by sampling n codewords uniformly and randomly from the codeword space Q^{ℓ}.

Analysis. An easy observation is that if the resulting code turns out to be a w-TA code then we can employ the identifying algorithm $\mathbf{Identify}_{TA}$ for which the resulting fingerprinting code is w-identifier as it is shown in theorem 1.11.

Theorem 1.13 presents a sufficient but a stronger condition on a code to satisfy the requirements of a traceability code. More specifically, an approach might be checking if the the output of the $\mathbf{CodeGen}^{\ell}_{CFN}$ is an $[\ell, n, d]_q$ error-correcting code such that $d > \ell(1 - \frac{1}{w^2})$. This is quite easy but takes time quadratic in the size of code to verify if the generated code is an $[\ell, n, d]_q$ error-correcting code, by examining all the pairs of codewords (x, y) and checking if $\mathsf{I}(\mathsf{x}, \mathsf{y}) \leq \frac{\ell}{w^2}$. A question in this context becomes what would be a suitable length so that the event that this happens is relatively high. This would be required to calculate the number of samplings from the $\mathbf{CodeGen}^{\ell}_{CFN}$ algorithm that are needed to get such an $[\ell, n, d]_q$ error-correcting code.

Relaxing the above strong condition we recall the necessary condition on the output of $\mathbf{CodeGen}^{\ell}_{CFN}$ to be a w-TA code: for the descendant set of any coalition of w traitor codewords, any codeword from the descendant set shall not share more than $\frac{\ell}{w}$ positions with any other codeword in the code generated by $\mathbf{CodeGen}^{\ell}_{CFN}$. This, indeed, would be satisfactory as it happens that there exists a traitor for any descendant codeword that shares at least ℓ/w positions.

In the open code scenario, we assume that the adversary has access to the code $\mathcal{C}$ generated by $\mathbf{CodeGen}^{\ell}_{CFN}$. Hence, the adversary is allowed to choose a descendant codeword that shares the most with any of the other codewords if they wish. Towards calculating the probability of having a w-TA code we first present a general lemma over a number of strings sampled independently and randomly from each other.

Lemma 1.15. *Supppose $w+1$ strings of length ℓ over an alphabet Q are sampled uniformly and independently. Denote the strings by $\mathsf{f}^0, \mathsf{f}^1, \ldots, \mathsf{f}^w$. Provided that $|Q| = q = 2w^2$ and $\ell \geq 4w \log(1/\varepsilon)$ it holds that*

$$\mathbf{Prob}\left[\left|\{i \mid \exists j \in [w] \ s.t. \ \mathsf{f}^0_i = \mathsf{f}^j_i\}\right| \geq \frac{\ell}{w}\right] \leq \varepsilon$$

where the probability is taken over all the choices of the vectors.

Proof of Lemma 1.15: Let X_i, for $i = 1, \ldots, \ell$, be the random variable such that $\mathrm{X}_i = 1$ if the i-th symbol in f^0 matches with one of the i-th symbols of the subsequent codewords, i.e. if $\exists j \in [w]$ s.t. $\mathsf{f}_i^0 = \mathsf{f}_i^j$. The probability of this happening for any position i would be $\frac{w}{q}$. Since the random variables X_i, for $i = 1, \ldots, \ell$, are independent from each other by employing the Chernoff bound (see Theorem 1.1) we have for $\delta > 0$:

$$\mathbf{Prob}[\sum_{i=1}^{l} \mathrm{X}_i \geq (1+\delta) \cdot \frac{\ell \cdot w}{q}] < \left(\frac{e^\delta}{(\delta+1)^{\delta+1}}\right)^{\frac{\ell \cdot w}{q}}$$

Substituting $\delta = 1$ and $q = 2w^2$, we get:

$$\begin{aligned} \mathbf{Prob}[\textstyle\sum_{i=1}^{l} \mathrm{X}_i \geq 2 \cdot \frac{\ell \cdot w}{2w^2}] &< \left(\frac{e}{4}\right)^{\frac{\ell \cdot w}{2w^2}} \\ \mathbf{Prob}[\textstyle\sum_{i=1}^{l} \mathrm{X}_i \geq \frac{\ell}{w}] &< \left(\frac{e}{4}\right)^{\frac{\ell}{2w}} \\ \mathbf{Prob}[\textstyle\sum_{i=1}^{l} \mathrm{X}_i \geq \frac{\ell}{w}] &< \left(\frac{e^2}{16}\right)^{\frac{\ell}{4w}} \\ \mathbf{Prob}[\textstyle\sum_{i=1}^{l} \mathrm{X}_i \geq \frac{\ell}{w}] &< \left(2^{-1}\right)^{\frac{\ell}{4w}} \end{aligned}$$

We choose $\ell \geq 4w \log \frac{1}{\varepsilon}$ so that the above probability is bounded by ε. ■

Theorem 1.16. *The* $\mathbf{CodeGen}^{\ell}_{CFN}(1^n)$ *algorithm generates a* w*-TA* (ℓ, n, q) *code with probability at least* $1 - \varepsilon$ *if* $\ell \geq 4w \log(\frac{n^{w+1}}{\varepsilon})$ *and* $q = 2w^2$.

Proof of Theorem 1.16: Let $(\mathcal{C}, \varepsilon) \leftarrow \mathbf{CodeGen}^{\ell}_{CFN}(1^n)$ where $\mathcal{C}$ is an (ℓ, n, q) code for $\ell > 4w \log \frac{n^w}{\varepsilon}$ and $q = 2w^2$. The sufficient condition on code $\mathcal{C}$ to be a w-TA code is as follows: for any $\mathsf{T} \subseteq [n]$ with $|\mathsf{T}| \leq w$ for all $\mathsf{p} \in \mathsf{desc}(\mathcal{C}_\mathsf{T})$, there exists $u \in \mathsf{T}$ such that $\mathsf{I}(\mathsf{c}^u, \mathsf{p}) > \mathsf{I}(\mathsf{c}^j, \mathsf{p})$ for any $j \in [n] \setminus \mathsf{T}$. We will now argue the probability of obtaining a w-TA code.

Observe that regardless of choice of T and $\mathsf{p} \in \mathsf{desc}(\mathcal{C}_\mathsf{T})$ there exists some $u \in \mathsf{T}$ such that $\mathsf{I}(\mathsf{c}^u, \mathsf{p}) \geq \frac{\ell}{w}$.

We will now compute the probability for existence of T and some $\mathsf{p} \in \mathsf{desc}(\mathcal{C}_\mathsf{T})$ such that there exists some $j \in [n] \setminus \mathsf{T}$ with $\mathsf{I}(\mathsf{c}^j, \mathsf{p}) \geq \frac{\ell}{w}$. If we can bound such probability, this would also be an upper bound on the failure of generating a w-TA code.

Consider a fixed coalition $\mathsf{T}' \subseteq [n]$ of size $\leq w$ and a receiver index $j' \in [n] \setminus \mathsf{T}'$; the corresponding $w + 1$ codewords are actually strings of length ℓ over an alphabet Q that are sampled uniformly and independently. Lemma 1.15 suggests that regardless of the traitor strategy in constructing a pirate codeword p to increase the number of positions that agree with $\mathsf{c}^{j'}$, we obtain $\mathsf{I}(\mathsf{c}^{j'}, \mathsf{p}) \geq \frac{\ell}{w}$ with probability at most $\frac{\varepsilon}{n^{w+1}}$. Considering all possible coalitions of size w and all receiver indices, the overall failure probability will be bounded by $n \cdot \binom{n}{w} \cdot \frac{\varepsilon}{n^{w+1}} \leq \varepsilon$. ■

Another approach is to employ the $\mathbf{Identify}_{TA}$ algorithm but regardless of whether the code that is sampled satisfies the w-TA property or not. This approach would suggest some failure probability in identification.

Recall that the $\textbf{Identify}_{TA}$ algorithm accuses a codeword that will share at least $\frac{\ell}{w}$ positions with the pirate codeword, indeed there exists a traitor codeword who has a score at least $\frac{\ell}{w}$. We will now discuss the success probability of a forging algorithm in producing a pirate codeword that frames a user, i.e. the maximum score, at least $\frac{\ell}{w}$, belongs to an innocent user. The probability is taken over all traitor coalitions and the framed user-index and the code randomization. A critical component of the analysis below is that the resulting code is not open, i.e., the adversary has no access to the code while preparing the descendant codeword. We start with a preparatory lemma.

Lemma 1.17. *Let σ be a mapping that, on input a set of strings $\mathcal{T} \subseteq 2^{Q^\ell}$ with $|\mathcal{T}| \leq w$, it outputs a string of the same length from $\mathsf{desc}(\mathcal{T})$. Given a vector $\mathsf{f} \in Q^\ell$ the following holds:*

$$\textbf{Prob}\left[\left|\{i \mid \mathsf{f}_i = \sigma(\mathcal{T})_i\} \geq \frac{\ell}{w}\right|\right] \leq \varepsilon$$

for $\ell \geq 4w\log(\frac{1}{\varepsilon})$ and $|Q| = q = 2w$ where the probability is taken over random choices of σ and $\mathcal{T} \subseteq 2^{Q^\ell}$ with $|\mathcal{T}| \leq w$.

Proof of Lemma 1.17: Let X_i, for $i = 1, \ldots, \ell$, be the random variable such that $\mathrm{X}_i = 1$ if the i-th symbol in the user codeword matches with the i-th symbol of the pirate codeword that is the output of the adversarial strategy σ, i.e. if $\mathsf{f}_i = \sigma(\{\mathsf{c}^j\}_{j \in \mathsf{C}})_i$. The mean value for any position would be $\frac{1}{q}$ given that the strategy is independent of the choice of f. Applying the Chernoff bound (see Theorem 1.1) for $\delta > 0$ we have :

$$\textbf{Prob}[\sum_{i=1}^{l} \mathrm{X}_i \geq (1+\delta)\cdot\frac{\ell}{q}] < \left(\frac{e^\delta}{(\delta+1)^{\delta+1}}\right)^{\frac{\ell}{q}}$$

Setting $\delta = 1$ and $q = 2w$ we get:

$$\begin{aligned}
\textbf{Prob}[\textstyle\sum_{i=1}^{l} \mathrm{X}_i \geq 2\cdot\frac{\ell}{2w}] &< \left(\tfrac{e}{4}\right)^{\frac{\ell}{2w}} \\
\textbf{Prob}[\textstyle\sum_{i=1}^{l} \mathrm{X}_i \geq \frac{\ell}{w}] &\leq \left(\tfrac{e^2}{16}\right)^{\frac{\ell}{4w}} \\
\textbf{Prob}[\textstyle\sum_{i=1}^{l} \mathrm{X}_i \geq \frac{\ell}{w}] &\leq \left(2^{-1}\right)^{\frac{\ell}{4w}}
\end{aligned}$$

Provided we choose $\ell \geq 4w\log\frac{1}{\varepsilon}$ the above probability is bounded by ε and the theorem is proven. ■

Based on the lemma we can now put forth the following theorem on the secret Chor-Fiat-Naor code:

Theorem 1.18. *The q-ary secret fingerprinting $(\textbf{CodeGen}^{\ell}_{CFN}, \textbf{Identify}_{TA})$ is (ε, w)-identifier provided that $\ell \geq 4w\log(\frac{n}{\varepsilon})$ and $q = 2w$.*

Proof of Theorem 1.18: Recall that $(\mathcal{C}, tk = \mathcal{C}) \leftarrow \mathbf{CodeGen}^{\ell}_{CFN}(1^n)$, and $\mathcal{C} = \{\mathsf{c}^1, \ldots, \mathsf{c}^n\}$ is an (ℓ, n, q) code with $q = 2w$.

Consider now a **Forging** adversary that is subject to the marking assumption as is described in Definition 1.4. The adversary chooses a traitor coalition with index-set T which satisfies $|\mathsf{T}| \leq w$. The adversary is given the traitor codewords $\mathcal{C}_{\mathsf{T}} = \{\mathsf{c}^j \mid j \in \mathsf{T}\}$ and finally outputs a pirate codeword $\mathsf{p} \in \mathsf{desc}(\mathcal{C}_{\mathsf{T}})$.

Regardless of the choice of T and $\mathsf{p} \in \mathsf{desc}(\mathcal{C}_{\mathsf{T}})$ there exists some $u \in \mathsf{T}$ such that $\mathsf{I}(\mathsf{c}^u, \mathsf{p}) \geq \frac{\ell}{w}$. We will now compute the probability for the existence some $j \in [n] \setminus \mathsf{T}$ such that $\mathsf{I}(\mathsf{c}^j, \mathsf{p}) \geq \frac{\ell}{w}$ (which would cause ambiguity in identification). If we can bound such probability, this would also be an upper bound on the failure of identification. Indeed, if there does not exist any such j then the identification algorithm $\mathbf{Identify}_{TA}$ will return an index from T as it happens that $u \in \mathsf{T}$ already satisfies $\mathsf{I}(\mathsf{c}^u, \mathsf{p}) \geq \frac{\ell}{w} > \mathsf{I}(\mathsf{c}^j, \mathsf{p})$ for any $j \in [n] \setminus \mathsf{T}$.

We consider a fixed coalition $\mathsf{T}' \subseteq [n]$ of size at most w and a receiver index $j' \in [n] \setminus \mathsf{T}'$; the corresponding $w + 1$ codewords are strings of length ℓ over the alphabet Q that are sampled uniformly and independently. Lemma 1.17 suggests that independently of the adversary strategy that is employed for constructing a pirate codeword p it happens that $\mathsf{I}(\mathsf{c}^{j'}, \mathsf{p}) \geq \frac{\ell}{w}$ with probability at most $\frac{\varepsilon}{n}$. Given that we would like this to hold true for all receiver indices, the overall failure probability will be bounded by $n \cdot \frac{\varepsilon}{n} \leq \varepsilon$. ∎

So we showed in this section that we can get quite close to the optimal alphabet for fingerprinting codes as suggested in Theorem 1.14 via a probabilistic construction. Nevertheless an alphabet proportional to w is still quite high for many reasonable settings. In the coming section we show how the w barrier can be broken and constant alphabets can be achieved.

1.4.3 The Boneh-Shaw Fingerprinting Codes

Code Generation. Given an integer n, the length of the code is determined as $\ell = d \cdot (n-1)$ where $d = 2n^2(\lambda + \ln 2n)$ for some $\lambda = \log(1/\varepsilon)$ that will be relatedto the failure probability in the identification algorithm. The $\mathbf{CodeGen}^{\ell}_{BS}$ algorithm, where $\ell = d \cdot (n-1)$, first constructs a master-matrix $\mathbf{M}_d$ of size $n \times d(n-1)$ such that $\mathbf{M}_d(i,j) = 1$ if $j > (i-1)d$ and $\mathbf{M}_d(i,j) = 0$ otherwise (see Figure 1.1). The code generation algorithm, then, samples a permutation $\pi \in_R \mathsf{Perm}(d(n-1))$ and permutes the columns of $\mathbf{M}_d$ according to the permutation π. The resulting matrix $\mathbf{M}_{d,\pi}$ would satisfy the following: $\mathbf{M}_{d,\pi}(i,j) = 1$ if $\pi^{-1}(j) > (i-1)d$ and $\mathbf{M}_{d,\pi}(i,j) = 0$ otherwise. A codeword w^i for $1 \leq i \leq n$ is defined as an $d(n-1)$-tuple where $\mathsf{w}^i_j = \mathbf{M}_{d,\pi}(i,j)$. The $\mathbf{CodeGen}^{\ell}_{BS}$ algorithm outputs the tracing key $tk = \pi$ as well as the $(d(n-1), n, 2)$-code $\mathcal{C} = \{\mathsf{w}^1, \ldots, \mathsf{w}^n\}$.

Identifying Algorithm. Given a pirate codeword $\mathsf{p} \in \{0,1\}^{d(n-1)}$ and π, it first applies the inverse permutation π^{-1} on p so that the resulting vector

M	$1 \ldots d$	$d+1 \ldots 2d$	$\ldots$	$(n-2)d+1 \ldots (n-1)d$
1	$1 \ldots 1$	$1 \ldots 1$	$\ldots$	$1 \ldots 1$
2	$0 \ldots 0$	$1 \ldots 1$	$\ldots$	$1 \ldots 1$
2	$0 \ldots 0$	$0 \ldots 0$	$\ldots$	$1 \ldots 1$
$\vdots$	$\vdots$	$\vdots$	$\vdots$	$\vdots$
n	$0 \ldots 0$	$0 \ldots 0$	$\ldots$	$0 \ldots 0$

Fig. 1.1. The master matrix of the Boneh-Shaw codes.

$\mathsf{x} \in \{0,1\}^{d(n-1)}$ satisfies $\mathsf{x}_i = \mathsf{p}_{\pi(i)}$. The $\mathbf{Identify}^{\ell}_{BS}$ algorithm will then partition x into $n-1$ blocks of length d. Let's denote B_i as the i-th block. The identifying procedure calculates the weight k_i which is the Hamming weight of x projected onto the to the block B_i. The algorithm finally outputs an integer from $[n]$ as follows:

1. if $k_1 > 0$ then return 1.
2. if $k_{n-1} < d$ then return n.
3. if $k_{s-1} < \frac{k_{s-1}+k_s}{2} - \sqrt{\frac{(k_{s-1}+k_s)(\lambda+\ln 2n)}{2}}$ then return s for $s = 2, \ldots, n-1$.
4. Otherwise fail.

Analysis. As we will see the Boneh-Shaw fingerprinting code is fully-collusion resistant, i.e., it works for any coalition size, and the length of the code affects the failure probability of underlying identification algorithm. We, first, would like to find a sufficient condition that makes the $\mathbf{Identify}^{\ell}_{BS}$ algorithm to output an index from the set $[n]$.

Lemma 1.19. *If $d \geq 2n^2(\lambda + \ln 2n)$, then $\mathbf{Identify}^{\ell}_{BS}$ always outputs an index from the set $[n]$.*

Proof of Lemma 1.19: Towards proving the lemma we first claim the following: If the algorithm fails, i.e. no user-index is returned, then it holds that

$$k_s \leq 2s^2(\lambda + \ln 2n) \text{ for } s \in \{1, \ldots, n-1\}$$

We will prove the above claim by induction.

BASE CASE: As the algorithm fails, it does not return 1. This is possible only when we have $k_1 = 0$, hence the base case satisfies the claim.

INDUCTION ASSUMPTION: For some $2 \leq s \leq n-1$, suppose that $k_i \leq 2 \cdot i^2 \cdot (\lambda + \ln 2n)$ for all $i = 1, \ldots, s-1$.

INDUCTION STEP: We will now show that $k_s \leq 2s^2(\lambda + \ln 2n)$:

(1) From the induction assumption we have $k_{s-1} \leq 2(s-1)^2(\lambda + \ln 2n)$.

(2) Given the fact that the output of the algorithm is not s, we also know that

$$k_{s-1} \geq \frac{k_{s-1}+k_s}{2} - \sqrt{\frac{(k_{s-1}+k_s)(\lambda+\ln 2n)}{2}}$$

By combining the above two, we will have:

$$\begin{aligned}\tfrac{k_s}{2} &\leq \tfrac{k_{s-1}}{2} + \sqrt{\tfrac{(k_{s-1}+k_s)(\lambda+\ln 2n)}{2}} \\ &\leq (s-1)^2(\lambda+\ln 2n) + \sqrt{\tfrac{(2(s-1)^2(\lambda+\ln 2n)+k_s)(\lambda+\ln 2n)}{2}}\end{aligned}$$

Suppose that $k_s = 2r^2(\lambda + \ln 2n)$ holds for some positive r.

$$\begin{aligned}\tfrac{2r^2(\lambda+\ln 2n)}{2} &\leq (s-1)^2(\lambda+\ln 2n) + \\ &\quad \sqrt{\tfrac{(2(s-1)^2(\lambda+\ln 2n)+2r^2(\lambda+\ln 2n))(\lambda+\ln 2n)}{2}} \\ r^2(\lambda+\ln 2n) &\leq (s-1)^2(\lambda+\ln 2n) + (\lambda+\ln 2n)\sqrt{(s-1)^2+r^2} \\ r^2 &\leq (s-1)^2 + \sqrt{r^2+(s-1)^2} \\ (r-s+1)(r+s-1) &\leq \sqrt{r^2+(s-1)^2} \\ (r-s+1)(r+s-1) &\leq r+s-1 \\ r-s+1 &\leq 1 \\ r &\leq s\end{aligned}$$

It follows that $k_s \leq 2s^2(\lambda + \ln 2n)$ for all $s = 1, \ldots, n-1$. Now we return to the statement of the theorem. Suppose that the $\mathbf{Identify}^{\ell}_{BS}$ algorithm fails to return a user index. In such case $k_{n-1} \geq d \geq 2n^2(\lambda + \ln 2n)$ holds since there is no output, but on the other hand, the above inductive claim implies that $k_{n-1} \leq 2(n-1)^2(\lambda + \ln 2n)$. This two statements contradict hence the algorithm will not fail. ■

We will now state the basic theorem on the effectiveness of the Boneh-Shaw fingerprinting code.

Theorem 1.20. *The Boneh-Shaw binary fingerprinting code* ($\mathbf{CodeGen}^{\ell}_{BS}$, $\mathbf{Identify}^{\ell}_{BS}$) *is* (ε, n)*-identifier for* $\ell \geq 2n^2(n-1)(\ln(\frac{1}{\varepsilon}) + \ln 2n)$.

Proof of Theorem 1.20: Let $\lambda = \ln \frac{1}{\varepsilon}$. The given length implies that the $\mathbf{Identify}^{\ell}_{BS}$ algorithm outputs a user due to Lemma 1.19. If that user is the first or the last, the marking assumption ensures that these users are indeed traitors.

Otherwise, $k_{s-1} < \frac{k_{s-1}+k_s}{2} - \sqrt{\frac{(k_{s-1}+k_s)(\lambda+\ln 2n)}{2}}$ holds for some $s \in \{2, \ldots, n-1\}$, and so the user assigned the codeword w^s is considered to be a traitor. Suppose to the contrary that the s-th user is innocent.

If the user-codeword w^s is not available to the traitor coalition, then the traitors will not be able to differentiate the blocks B_{s-1} and B_s. Hence, $|k_{s-1} - k_s|$ is expected to be close to 0, in other terms k_{s-1} cannot be substantially different than the expectation $\frac{k_{s-1}+k_s}{2}$. We will, now, compute the probability of k_{s-1} to be less than $\frac{k_{s-1}+k_s}{2} - \sqrt{\frac{(k_{s-1}+k_s)(\lambda+\ln 2n)}{2}}$.

Let the total Hamming weight of the pirate codeword as projected on the blocks B_{s-1} and B_s be k (after the application of π^{-1}). Denote the random variable X that is the weight k_{s-1} conditioning on the event that the total Hamming weight is k. The probability that $X = r$ equals:

$$\mathbf{Prob}[X = r] = \frac{\binom{d}{r}\binom{d}{k-r}}{\binom{2d}{k}}$$

Consider a random variable Y which is a binomial distribution of k successive experiments with success probability $1/2$, hence $\mathbf{Prob}[Y = r] = \frac{\binom{k}{r}}{2^k}$. It is easy to see the following(just substitute and do regular computation):

$$\mathbf{Prob}[X = r] \leq 2 \cdot \mathbf{Prob}[Y = r]$$

Note that $E[Y] = k/2$. By applying the Chernoff bound(see Theorem 1.2) we have the following for some $0 < \alpha < k/2$.

$$\mathbf{Prob}[Y < k/2 - \alpha] \leq e^{-2\alpha^2/k}$$

Substituting $\alpha = \sqrt{\frac{k(\lambda+\ln 2n)}{2}}$, we will see with what probability a pirate codeword puts a weight $\leq k/2 - \sqrt{\frac{k(\lambda+\ln 2n)}{2}}$ on block B_{s-1} while at the same time user s is innocent.

$$\begin{aligned}\mathbf{Prob}[X \leq k/2 - \sqrt{\tfrac{k(\lambda+\ln 2n)}{2}}] &\leq 2 \cdot \mathbf{Prob}[Y \leq k/2 - \sqrt{\tfrac{k(\lambda+\ln 2n)}{2}}] \\ &\leq 2 \cdot e^{\frac{-2}{k} \cdot \frac{k(\lambda+\ln 2n)}{2}} \\ &= 2 \cdot (\frac{e^{-\lambda}}{2n}) \\ &= \frac{e^{-\lambda}}{n}\end{aligned}$$

Summing the above failure probability for each user will result to an upper bound of $e^{-\lambda} = \varepsilon$ on framing one of the innocent users. This completes the proof of Theorem 1.20 ■

1.4.4 The Tardos Fingerprinting Codes

Code generation. The Tardos code generation uses a distribution of values p over $[0, 1]$ that is based on a parameter $t \in (0, \frac{1}{2})$ and is defined as follows: $p = \sin^2(r)$ where r is a random variable uniformly distributed over $[t', \pi/2 - t']$ where $t' = \arcsin(\sqrt{t})$. Note that the range of p as defined is $[t, 1-t]$.

Given the number of users n, the length of the code ℓ is determined (the choice will be made explicit in the analysis) as a function of the bound on coalition size w and the security parameter $\lambda = \log(\frac{1}{\epsilon})$. The values $p_1, \ldots, p_\ell$ are sampled independently as defined above and subsequently the code $\mathcal{C} =$

$\{c^{(1)},\ldots,c^{(n)}\}$ is formed so that $c_i^{(j)}$ is generated by tossing a p_i-coin for $j=1,\ldots,n$ and $i=1,\ldots,\ell$.

The tracing key contains $\mathcal{C}$, the values p_i as well as a parameter $Z \in \mathbb{R}$ that will be determined in the analysis.

Identifying Algorithm. Given a codeword $c^* \in \mathsf{desc}(\mathcal{T}_C)$ for some $C \subseteq [n]$ the tracing proceeds as follows: a user $j \in \{1,\ldots,n\}$ with codeword $c_i^{(j)}$ is assigned a score for a column i according to the table:

c_i^*	$c_i^{(j)}$	score
0	0	$+1/q_i$
0	1	$-q_i$
1	0	$-1/q_i$
1	1	$+q_i$

where $\mathsf{q} = \mathsf{q}(p)$ is a function of p equal to $\sqrt{(1-p)/p}$ and we set $q_i = \mathsf{q}(p_i)$. Based on the above table, the total score accumulated by the user j can be expressed as follows

$$S_j = \sum_{i=1}^{\ell}(2\cdot c_i^* - 1)\cdot \mathsf{C}_{p_i}(c_i^{(j)})$$

where the function $\mathsf{C}_p : \{0,1\} \to \mathbb{R}$ is defined as $\mathsf{C}_p(x) = q\cdot x - (1-x)/q$. The **Identify**$_T^\ell$ algorithm returns all user-indices $j \in \{1,\ldots,n\}$ for which it holds that $S_j \geq Z$.

We next state the effectiveness of the Tardos fingerprinting code as follows:

Theorem 1.21. *The Tardos binary fingerprinting code* (**CodeGen**$_T^\ell$, **Identify**$_T^\ell$) *with accusation threshold Z is (ϵ, n)-identifier for $\ell = 108\cdot w^2\cdot\log(\frac{2n}{\epsilon})$ and $Z = 24\cdot w\cdot\log(\frac{2n}{\epsilon})$.*

Analysis: Proof of The Theorem 1.21. We will first consider the requirement of accusing at least one guilty user, i.e. that there is a non-empty intersection between the output of the tracing algorithm and the guilty subset users. This will impose a lower bound on the length of the code ℓ. In general we make no assumptions regarding how the coalition places its digits, except of course the adherence to the marking assumption of producing a codeword in the descendant set of the given codewords. The coalition lacks knowledge of the values $p_1,\ldots,p_\ell$, but observe that the codewords possessed by the guilty coalition enable a rough estimation of these values. Given the set of codewords the coalition will produce a codeword $c^* \in \mathsf{desc}(\mathcal{T}_C)$ following a strategy σ.

We formalize the coalition strategy σ as follows. We denote by X the $w\times\ell$ matrix that contains all codewords available to the coalition, i.e., X_{ji} is a random 0/1 variable distributed according to p_i. Given such X we will denote by x_i the Hamming weight of the i-th column, $i=1,\ldots,\ell$. The strategy σ is a function in $(\{0,1\}^{w\times\ell} \to \{0,1\}^{\ell})$; we denote $\sigma_i(X)$ the i-th symbol of $\sigma(X)$. Based on the marking assumption, the strategy σ must satisfy the following constraints (i) if $x_i = 0$ it holds that $\sigma_i(X) = 0$, (ii) if $x_i = w$ it holds that $\sigma_i(X) = 1$.

In the analysis we will use the notation $\mathsf{C}_p(w,x) = x\cdot\mathsf{C}_p(1)+(w-x)\cdot\mathsf{C}_p(0)$ with $w \in \mathbb{N}, x \in \{0,\dots,w\}$. We next determine the random variable that corresponds to the cumulative score assigned to a coalition of w users. We have

$$S_\sigma = \sum_{i=1}^{\ell}(2\cdot\sigma_i(X)-1)\cdot\mathsf{C}_{p_i}(w,x_i)$$

Consider now some parameter $\alpha \in \mathbb{R}^+$; we are interested in an upper bound of the expectation

$$\mathbf{E}[e^{-\alpha S_\sigma}] = \mathbf{E}\Big[\prod_{i=1}^{\ell} e^{-\alpha(2\cdot\sigma_i(X)-1)\cdot\mathsf{C}_{p_i}(w,x_i)}\Big]$$

$$= \sum_{X\in\{0,1\}^{w\times\ell}}\prod_{i=1}^{\ell}\mathbf{E}[p^{x_i}(1-p)^{w-x_i}e^{-\alpha(2\cdot\sigma_i(X)-1)\cdot\mathsf{C}_p(w,x_i)}]$$

where the above follows from the fact that the columns are selected independently.

We next provide a simplification on the domain of possible adversarial strategies. Consider the equivalence class over the set of all matrices $X \in \{0,1\}^{w\times\ell}$ such that $X \sim X'$ if and only if X and X' share the same column Hamming weights. Consider now two matrices $X \neq X'$ that satisfy $X \sim X'$ and a strategy σ for which it holds that $\sigma_i(X) \neq \sigma_i(X')$ for some location $i \in \{1,\dots,\ell\}$. We call such strategies "unorthodox." On the other hand if $\sigma_i(X) = \sigma_i(X')$ for all X, X' with $X \sim X'$ and all locations $i \in \{1,\dots,\ell\}$ we call the strategy "orthodox."

Given a possibly unorthodox strategy σ we construct an orthodox strategy σ' as follows: for each equivalence class Q of $\sim$ we consider the value:

$$\max_{X\in Q}\Big\{\prod_{i=1}^{\ell}\mathbf{E}[p^{x_i}(1-p)^{w-x_i}e^{-\alpha(2\cdot\sigma_i(X)-1)\cdot\mathsf{C}_p(w,x_i)}]\Big\}$$

If $X_Q^{\max}$ is a class representative that matches the above maximal value, we define for all $X \in \{0,1\}^{w\times\ell}$ the new strategy $\sigma'(X) = \sigma(X_Q^{\max})$ where Q is the equivalence class of X.

Lemma 1.22. *For any $\alpha \in \mathbb{R}^+$, given any coalition strategy σ, the strategy σ' defined above is an orthodox strategy that satisfies $\mathbf{E}[e^{-\alpha S_\sigma}] \le \mathbf{E}[e^{-\alpha S_{\sigma'}}]$.*

Proof. It is easy to see that σ' is orthodox as for any X it returns σ evaluated on a single representative of the class of X. The bound on the expectation follows easily from the choice of the class representative made. ∎

Consider now an arbitrary strategy σ. Recall that S_σ is the cumulative score that the whole coalition will amass; we will show that S_σ with very high probability will be greater than $w \cdot Z$ and thus at least one guilty user will be included in the list of users returned by the tracing algorithm **Identify**.

We consider the random variable $e^{-\alpha S_\sigma}$ for a suitable parameter α to be determined below and we will provide an upper bound on its expectation. In the light of lemma 1.22 we can restrict ourselves in bounding the expectation for orthodox strategies. In particular,

$$\mathbf{E}[e^{-\alpha S_\sigma}] = \sum_{X\in\{0,1\}^{w\times\ell}} \prod_{i=1}^{\ell} \mathbf{E}[p^{x_i}(1-p)^{w-x_i} \cdot e^{-\alpha\cdot(2\sigma_i(X)-1)\cdot \mathsf{C}_p(w,x_i)}] \quad (1.12)$$

where $\sigma(\cdot)$ depends only on the column weights of X. Recall that $\mathsf{C}_p(w,x) = (q\cdot x - (w-x)/q)$ and $q = \sqrt{(1-p)/p}$. Note that in the above expression the matrix X determines $x_1,\ldots,x_n$. Moreover, the likelihood of a particular matrix X is only dependent on the values $x_1,\ldots,x_\ell$ and the number of 1's in the i-th column follows a Binomial distribution with success probability p where p is distributed independently for each column i.

Given that we want to quantify over all possible (orthodox) strategies, it will be helpful to introduce some notations to be used as upper bounds on the expectations. We define the following for all values $w \in \mathbb{N}$, $x = 0,\ldots,w$, $\alpha \in \mathbb{R}^+$,

$$\begin{aligned}
Z_x &= \mathbf{E}[p^x(1-p)^{w-x}] \\
H_x &= \mathbf{E}[p^x(1-p)^{w-x}\cdot \mathsf{C}_p(w,x)] \\
Q_x &= \mathbf{E}[p^x(1-p)^{w-x}\cdot (\mathsf{C}_p(w,x))^2] \\
U_x^\alpha &= \mathbf{E}[p^x(1-p)^{w-x}\cdot e^{-\alpha\cdot \mathsf{C}_p(w,x)}] \\
P_x^\alpha &= \mathbf{E}[p^x(1-p)^{w-x}\cdot e^{\alpha\cdot \mathsf{C}_p(w,x)}]
\end{aligned}$$

$$M_x^\alpha = \begin{cases} \max\{U_x^\alpha, Z_x, P_x^\alpha\} & x\in\{1,\ldots,w-1\} \\ P_0^\alpha & x = 0 \\ U_c^\alpha & x = w \end{cases}$$

We make first the following handy observation: For any $\alpha \in \mathbb{R}^+$, $w \in \mathbb{N}$, we have $U_x^\alpha = P_{w-x}^\alpha$ for $x \in \{0,1,\ldots,w\}$. Similarly, $Z_0 = Z_w$. This follows from the symmetry of the range of p. Note that $P_{w-x}^\alpha = \mathbf{E}[p^{w-x}(1-p)^x \cdot e^{\alpha \mathsf{C}_p(w,w-x)}]$. We have that $\mathsf{C}_p(w,w-x) = q(w-x) - x/q = -\mathsf{C}_{1-p}(w,x)$ and given that $p \in [t, 1-t]$ we obtain the desired result by substituting p for $1-p$.

Using the above notations and the fact that the strategy σ is orthodox (i.e., it depends only on column Hamming weights) we can bound the summation of equation (1.12) by a sum over all column counts (as opposed to matrices X):

$$\mathbf{E}[e^{-\alpha S_\sigma}] \leq \sum_{x_1,\ldots,x_\ell=0}^{w} \Big(\prod_{i=1}^{\ell} \binom{w}{x_i} M_{x_i}^{\alpha}\Big) \tag{1.13}$$

From this we obtain the following:

$$\mathbf{E}[e^{-\alpha S_\sigma}] \leq \Big(\sum_{x=0}^{w} \binom{w}{x} M_x^{\alpha}\Big)^{\ell} \tag{1.14}$$

We will next bound the summation on the right-hand-side. We first prove some helpful lemmas. The first lemma deals with the expectation and variance of $\mathsf{C}_p(X)$ when X is a p-coin. We show that the score expectation is 0 and the variance equals 1.

Lemma 1.23. *Consider X to be a p-coin where $p = \sin^2(r)$ and r is uniform over $[t', \frac{\pi}{2} - t']$ with $t' = \arcsin(\sqrt{t})$ and $t \in (0, \frac{1}{2})$. Then, we have that* $\mathbf{Var}[\mathsf{C}_p(X)] = 1$ *and for any $p \in [t, 1-t]$,* $\mathbf{E}[\mathsf{C}_p(X) \mid p] = 0$.

Proof. We first show the result regarding the expectation. Recall that $\mathsf{C}_p(x) = q \cdot x - (1-x)/q$. We have $\mathbf{E}[\mathsf{C}_p(X) \mid p] = \mathbf{E}[Xq - (1-X)/q \mid p] = pq - (1-p)/q = 0$, given that $q = \sqrt{(1-p)/p}$. Regarding the variance, we have $\mathbf{Var}[\mathsf{C}_p(X)] = \mathbf{E}[(\mathsf{C}_p(X))^2] - (\mathbf{E}[C_p(X)])^2$. Given that for any p, $\mathbf{E}[\mathsf{C}_p(X) \mid p] = 0$ we only need to calculate $\mathbf{E}[(\mathsf{C}_p(X))^2] = \mathbf{E}[\mathbf{E}[(\mathsf{C}_p(X))^2 \mid p]]$. We have $\mathbf{E}[(\mathsf{C}_p(X))^2 \mid p] = \mathbf{E}[q^2X^2 + (1-X)^2/q^2 + 2X(1-X) \mid p] = \mathbf{E}[pq^2 + (1-p)/q^2) \mid p] = \mathbf{E}[1 - p + p \mid p] = 1$. ■

Lemma 1.24. *Let $\mathsf{C}_p(w,x) = x\mathsf{C}_p(1) + (w-x)\mathsf{C}_p(0)$. Suppose that for some distribution of p, it holds that $\mathbf{E}[\mathsf{C}_p(X)|p] = 0$ for all p, and $\mathbf{Var}[\mathsf{C}_p(X)] = 1$. Then we have*

$$\sum_{x=0}^{w} \binom{w}{x} \cdot \mathbf{E}[p^x(1-p)^{w-x} \cdot (\mathsf{C}_p(w,x))^2] = w$$

Proof. Consider $X_1, \ldots, X_w$ independent Bernoulli trials of probability p. Given the lemma's condition we have that:

$$\begin{aligned}\mathbf{E}\Big[\Big(\textstyle\sum_{j=1}^{w} \mathsf{C}_p(X_j)\Big)^2\Big] &= \mathbf{E}[\mathsf{C}_p(X_1)^2 + \ldots + \mathsf{C}_p(X_w)^2 + 2\textstyle\sum_{i<j} \mathsf{C}_p(X_i)\mathsf{C}_p(X_j)] \\ &= w\end{aligned} \tag{1.15}$$

To see why this holds observe that (i) $\mathbf{E}[\mathsf{C}_p(X_j)^2] = 1$ for all $j = 1, \ldots, w$, and (ii) $\mathbf{E}[\mathsf{C}_p(X_i) \cdot \mathsf{C}_p(X_j)] = \mathbf{E}[\mathbf{E}[\mathsf{C}_p(X_i)\mathsf{C}_p(X_j) \mid p]]$ and as X_i, X_j conditioned on p are independent flips we have $\mathbf{E}[\mathsf{C}_p(X_i)\mathsf{C}_p(X_j) \mid p] = \mathbf{E}[\mathsf{C}_p(X_i) \mid p]\mathbf{E}[\mathsf{C}_p(X_j) \mid p] = 0$. Now, expanding the expectation on the left hand side of equation (1.15) we have

$$\begin{aligned}&\mathbf{E}\Big[\textstyle\sum_{x_1,\ldots,x_w \in \{0,1\}} \prod_{\ell=1}^{w} p^{x_\ell}(1-p)^{1-x_\ell} \cdot (\sum_{j=1}^{w} \mathsf{C}_p(x_j))^2\Big] \\ &= \mathbf{E}\Big[\textstyle\sum_{x=0}^{w} \binom{w}{x} p^x(1-p)^{w-x}(\mathsf{C}_p(w,x))^2\Big]\end{aligned} \tag{1.16}$$

By combining equations (1.15) and (1.16) we obtain

$$\sum_{x=0}^{w} \binom{w}{x} \cdot \mathbf{E}[p^x(1-p)^{w-x} \cdot (\mathsf{C}_p(w,x))^2] = w \tag{1.17}$$

This completes the proof of the lemma. ■

The following lemma is quite critical and its proof is the one that primarily accounts for the particular choice of the p distribution.

Lemma 1.25. *For any $w \in \mathbb{N}$ and $x \in \{0, 1, \ldots, w\}$, and $p = \sin^2(r)$ where r is uniform over $[t', \pi/2 - t']$ with $t' = \arcsin(\sqrt{t})$ and $t \in (0, \frac{1}{2})$, it holds that*

$$\begin{aligned} H_x &= \mathbf{E}[p^x(1-p)^{w-x} \cdot \mathsf{C}_p(w,x)] \\ &= \tfrac{1}{\pi - 4t'} \cdot ((1-t)^x t^{w-x} - t^x(1-t)^{w-x}) \end{aligned}$$

Proof. By definition we have

$$\begin{aligned} &\mathbf{E}[p^x(1-p)^{w-x} \cdot (xq - (w-x)/q))] \\ &\quad = \tfrac{1}{\pi/2 - 2t'} \cdot \int_{t'}^{\pi/2 - t'} \sin^{2x} r \cos^{2(w-x)} r (x \cot r - (w-x) \tan r) dr \\ &\quad = \tfrac{1}{\pi/2 - 2t'} \cdot [\tfrac{1}{2} \sin^{2x} r \cos^{2(w-x)} r]_{t'}^{\pi/2 - t'} \end{aligned}$$

from which the statement of the lemma follows easily. ■

We next proceed to provide a bound for $\sum_{x=0}^{w} \binom{w}{x} M_x^\alpha$. Given that $e^u \leq 1 + u + u^2$ for any $u < 1.7$, assume that α is selected so that $-\alpha \mathsf{C}_p(w,x) < 1.7$ for all feasible choices of p, x. It follows that:

$$e^{-\alpha \cdot \mathsf{C}_p(w,x)} \leq 1 - \alpha \cdot \mathsf{C}_p(w,x) + \alpha^2 \cdot (\mathsf{C}_p(w,x))^2$$

under the condition that

$$\alpha \cdot \max_{p,w} \mathsf{C}_p(w,x) < 1.7 \Longleftarrow \alpha < \frac{1.7\sqrt{t}}{w} \tag{1.18}$$

Based on this we obtain that for $x \in \{1, \ldots, w-1\}$,

$$M_x^\alpha \leq \max\{Z_x \pm \alpha \cdot H_x + \alpha^2 Q_x\} \leq Z_x + \alpha \cdot |H_x| + \alpha^2 Q_x$$

while,

$$M_0^\alpha \leq Z_0 + \alpha \cdot H_0 + \alpha^2 \cdot Q_0 \quad \text{and} \quad M_w^\alpha \leq Z_w - \alpha \cdot H_w + \alpha^2 \cdot Q_w$$

It follows that

$$\sum_{x=0}^{w} \binom{w}{x} M_x^\alpha \leq \sum_{x=0}^{w} Z_x - \alpha \cdot (H_w - H_0 - \sum_{x=1}^{w-1} |H_x|) + \alpha^2 \cdot \sum_{x=0}^{w} Q_x$$

Next observe that $\sum_{x=0}^{w} Z_x = 1$ independently of the distribution of p and by applying lemma 1.24 and lemma 1.25, as well as the fact that $|a-b| \leq a+b$ for positive a, b we have

$$\begin{aligned}\textstyle\sum_{x=0}^{w} \binom{w}{x} M_x^{\alpha} &\leq 1 - \alpha\Big(2\gamma \cdot (2(1-t)^w - 2t^w - 1) - \alpha \cdot w\Big) \\ &\leq e^{-\alpha(2\gamma(2(1-t)^w - 2t^w - 1) - \alpha \cdot w)}\end{aligned} \tag{1.19}$$

where $\gamma = \frac{1}{\pi - 4t'}$. We apply the above inequality 1.19 to the bound of equation 1.14 to obtain:

$$\mathbf{E}[e^{-\alpha S_\sigma}] \leq \exp\Big(- \alpha \cdot \ell \cdot \underbrace{(2\gamma \cdot (1 - 2wt - 2t^w) - \alpha \cdot w)}_{\rho}\Big)$$

Next we constrict α, t to show that the expression ρ has a positive lower bound. In particular, under the conditions:

$$\alpha \leq \frac{1}{6w} \tag{1.20}$$

$$t \leq \frac{1}{300w} \tag{1.21}$$

we obtain that $2\gamma(1 - 2wt - 2t^w) \geq 1/2$ and $\alpha \cdot w \leq 1/6$. Utilizing the fact that $\gamma \geq \frac{1}{4}$ we obtain that under the conditions placed on α, t we have that $\rho \geq 1/3$ which implies that:

$$\mathbf{E}[e^{-\alpha S_\sigma}] \leq e^{-\alpha\ell/3}$$

We are now ready to obtain an upper bound on the probability that the malicious coalition accumulates a score of at most wZ.

$$\mathbf{Prob}[S_\sigma \leq wZ] = \mathbf{Prob}[e^{-\alpha S_\sigma} \geq e^{-\alpha w Z}] \leq \mathbf{E}[e^{-\alpha S_\sigma}]/e^{-\alpha w Z} \leq e^{-\alpha\ell/3 + \alpha w Z}$$

where the penultimate inequality follows from Markov's inequality. Bounding the probability by ϵ we have to select ℓ, Z so that they satisfy

$$\ell \geq 3 \cdot \Big(\frac{\log(\frac{1}{\epsilon})}{\alpha} + wZ\Big) \tag{1.22}$$

It follows that if ℓ, Z are selected so that the above lower bound on ℓ holds we have that with probability at least $1 - \epsilon$ the output of the tracing algorithm will contain at least one member of the traitor coalition.

We next turn our attention to the requirement that the output of the tracing algorithm does not contain any innocent users. This will provide another condition on ℓ, Z, an upper bound on ℓ. We will take advantage of the fact that, given that the code $\mathcal{C}$ is private, the codeword assigned to any innocent user can be assumed to be selected after the traitor coalition is formed.

In order to simplify the analysis of this section we will assume that the exact values $p_1, \ldots, p_\ell$ are known to the adversary. Moreover we will impose no restriction on how the adversarial coalition decides to output a value $\{0,1\}$ as the i-th letter of a descendant codeword.

Observe that the i-th position of the codeword of an innocent user is determined by a p-biased coin. For this case, we can determine the following useful expectation relating to the random variable $\mathsf{C}_p(X)$ (where $\beta \in \mathbb{R}^+$ to be determined below and X is a p-biased $0/1$ random variable). Suppose that the coalition digit is $y \in \{0,1\}$; we have:

$$\mathbf{E}[e^{\beta\cdot(2y-1)\cdot\mathsf{C}_p(X)}|y] = \mathbf{E}[e^{\beta(2y-1)(Xq-(1-X)/q)}|y] \le e^{\beta^2}$$

The above is justified as follows: first observe that $e^u \le 1+u+u^2$ provided that $u < 1.7$. We have that for any $x \in \{0,1\}$, it holds that $\beta \cdot \mathsf{C}_p(x) \le \beta q \le \beta/\sqrt{t}$ and thus by constraining β to satisfy

$$\beta < 1.7 \cdot \sqrt{t} \tag{1.23}$$

for the case $y \in \{0,1\}$ we can apply the bound on the exponential and lemma 1.23 to obtain

$$\mathbf{E}[e^{\beta(2y-1)\mathsf{C}_p(X)}|y] \le 1 \pm \beta\mathbf{E}[\mathsf{C}_p(X) \mid y] + \beta^2\mathbf{E}[\mathsf{C}_p(X)^2 \mid y] = 1 + \beta^2 \le e^{\beta^2}$$

We next observe that the score accumulated by an innocent user will be equal to $S = \sum_{i=1}^{\ell}(2y_i - 1)\mathsf{C}_{p_i}(X_i)$ where $y_i \in \{0,1\}$. Based on the above we have the following bound on the expectation for any strategy of the adversary:

$$\mathbf{E}[e^{\beta\cdot S}] \le e^{\beta^2\cdot\ell}$$

We are interested in obtaining an upper bound on the probability that $S \ge Z$, i.e., the event that an innocent user is accused. We have the following:

$$\mathbf{Prob}[S \ge Z] = \mathbf{Prob}[e^{\beta S} \ge e^{\beta Z}] \le e^{\beta^2\ell - \beta Z}$$

To bound the above by ϵ, it suffices to choose Z, ℓ that satisfy

$$\ell \le \frac{Z}{\beta} - \frac{\log(\frac{1}{\epsilon})}{\beta^2} \tag{1.24}$$

By combining the upper bound on ℓ, equation (1.24) with the lower bound on ℓ, equation (1.22) we obtain the bound on Z,

$$Z \ge (1 - 3\cdot w\beta)^{-1}\Big(3\cdot\frac{\beta}{\alpha} + \frac{1}{\beta}\Big)\log(\frac{1}{\epsilon}) \tag{1.25}$$

which requires the upper bound on β as follows:

$$\beta < \frac{1}{3w} \tag{1.26}$$

Choosing ℓ, Z to be the smallest value allowed by the above constraints, we can set

$$\ell = 3 \cdot (1 - 3w\beta)^{-1} \cdot \left(\frac{1}{\alpha} + \frac{w}{\beta}\right) \cdot \log(\frac{1}{\epsilon}) \tag{1.27}$$

Instantiating the construction. We find $t, \alpha, \beta, \ell, Z$ that satisfy the bounds given in (1.18),(1.20), (1.21), (1.23) and (1.26). Below for illustration purposes we provide a possible choice:

$$\alpha = \frac{1}{12w^2} \quad \beta = \frac{1}{6w} \quad t = \frac{1}{300w}$$

Which allows determining the basic parameters as follows:

$$Z = 24 \cdot w \cdot \log(\frac{1}{\epsilon})$$

$$\ell = 108 \cdot w^2 \cdot \log(\frac{1}{\epsilon})$$

We note finally that the analysis of framing an innocent user was performed for a single user and thus in order to accommodate a number of n users as well as the two error summants in the bound calculation, the error parameter in the above expressions can be set to $\log(2n/\epsilon)$. This completes the proof of theorem 1.21.

1.4.5 Code Concatenation

As illustrated in the results of this section the challenge in the design of fingerprinting codes is to support many reasonably long codewords while maintaining a small alphabet size. Code concatenation is a technique utilized extensively in coding theory and is proven effective in reducing alphabet size in code designs. The technique is also useful in the context of fingerprinting codes yielding valuable trade-offs in the efficiency parameters of a fingerprinting code. We investigate this further in this section.

Code concatenation entails the composition of two codes: an "inner" code with an "outer" code. The composition is feasible as long as the codes adhere to a suitable structural characteristic. The end effect is that the codewords of the inner code substitute the alphabet symbols of the outer code. In more details we have the following.

Code Generation for a q-ary Concatenated Code. Given the number of users n, an intermediate value n_1 is chosen as a function of q and n. The technique, then, employs two fingerprinting codes as follows:

- An inner q-ary fingerprinting code ($\mathbf{Codegen}_{in}, \mathbf{Identify}_{in}$) over an alphabet Q_{in}. This inner fingerprinting code is chosen to be collusion resistant against any traitor coalition size, with possibly some failure probability; the code generation will be executed on input 1^{n_1}, i.e., produce n_1 codewords.

- An outer n_1-ary fingerprinting code ($\mathbf{CodeGen}_{out}, \mathbf{Identify}_{out}$) over an alphabet Q_{out}; the code generation of the outer code will be executed on input 1^n, i.e., produce n codewords.

The code generation of the concatenated code will apply the above fingerprinting codes to produce an inner and outer code as follows:
(i) $(C_{in}, tk_{in}) \leftarrow \mathbf{CodeGen}_{in}(1^{n_1})$ where $C_{in} = \{\mathsf{i}^1, \ldots, \mathsf{i}^{n_1}\}$ is an (ℓ_1, n_1, q) inner code.
(ii) $(C_{out}, tk_{out}) \leftarrow \mathbf{CodeGen}_{out}(1^n)$ where $C_{out} = \{\mathsf{o}^1, \ldots, \mathsf{o}^n\}$ is an (ℓ_2, n, n_1) outer code.

Consider a bijection f from C_{in} to Q_{out}. The resulting code would be the $(\ell_1 \cdot \ell_2, n, q)$ code $C_{con} = \{\mathsf{c}^1, \ldots, \mathsf{c}^n\}$ where c^j is an $\ell_1 \cdot \ell_2$ tuple over the alphabet Q_{in}, defined as follows:

$$\mathsf{c}^j = \mathsf{f}^{-1}(\mathsf{o}_1^j)||\mathsf{f}^{-1}(\mathsf{o}_2^j)|| \ldots ||\mathsf{f}^{-1}(\mathsf{o}_{\ell_2}^j)$$

Identification Algorithm. On a pirate codeword $\mathsf{p} \in Q_{in}^{\ell_1 \cdot \ell_2}$, the identification algorithm $\mathbf{Identify}_{con}$ proceeds as follows:

First chop the pirate codeword $\mathsf{p} = \langle \mathsf{p}_1, \ldots, \mathsf{p}_{\ell_1 \ell_2} \rangle$ into ℓ_2 blocks of size ℓ_1, and denote the j-th block as $\mathsf{p}^j = \langle \mathsf{p}_{\ell_1(j-1)+1}, \mathsf{p}_{\ell_1(j-1)+2}, \ldots, \mathsf{p}_{\ell_1(j-1)+\ell_1} \rangle$.

Observe that $\mathsf{p}^j \in Q_{in}^{\ell_1}$ is a valid codeword in the inner-code domain. The identification operates on two levels:

(1) For each $j = 1, \ldots, \ell_2$, compute $\mathbf{Identify}_{in}(tk_{in}, \mathsf{p}^j) = ind_j \in [n_1]$ and denote the symbol $\mathsf{f}(\mathsf{i}^{ind_j}) \in Q_{out}$ by q_j. Construct the codeword $\mathsf{p}^* = \langle q_1, q_2, \ldots, q_{\ell_2} \rangle$ within the outer-code domain.

(2) Compute, now, $\mathbf{Identify}_{out}(tk_{out}, \mathsf{p}^*) = t \in [n_2]$, and output t.

If any of the underlying identification algorithms fails in outputting an index for some reason, the identification algorithm for the concatenated code fails as well.

Analysis. We will now discuss how the underlying fingerprinting codes affect the efficiency of the concatenated code:

Theorem 1.26. *Provided that the q-ary fingerprinting code* ($\mathbf{CodeGen}_{in}$, $\mathbf{Identify}_{in}$) *is fully-collusion resistant with failure probability ε_1 and the n_1-ary fingerprinting code* ($\mathbf{CodeGen}_{out}, \mathbf{Identify}_{out}$) *is (ε_2, w)-identifier, then the concatenated q-ary code presented above is $(\varepsilon_2 + \ell_2\varepsilon_1, w)$-identifier.*

Proof of Theorem 1.26: We have $(C_{in}, tk_{in}) \leftarrow \mathbf{CodeGen}_{in}(1^{n_1})$ where $C_{in} = \{\mathsf{i}^1, \ldots, \mathsf{i}^{n_1}\}$ is an (ℓ_1, n_1, q) inner code for which the $\mathbf{Identify}_{in}$ algorithm satisfies the following:

$$\forall \mathsf{T}_1 \subseteq [n_1] \;\; \mathbf{Prob}[\emptyset \not\subseteq \mathbf{Identify}_{in}(tk_{in}, \mathsf{p}_{in}) \subseteq \mathsf{T}_1] \geq 1 - \varepsilon_1 \qquad (1.28)$$

where $\mathsf{p}_{in} \in Q_{in}^{\ell_1}$ is an output of any probabilistic polynomial depth **Forging** adversary, that is bounded by the marking assumption of Definition 1.4, given the set of codewords $(C_{in})_{\mathsf{T}_1}$.

We also have $(\mathcal{C}_{out}, tk_{out}) \leftarrow \mathbf{CodeGen}_{out}(1^n)$ where $\mathcal{C}_{out} = \{\mathsf{o}^1, \ldots, \mathsf{o}^n\}$ is an (ℓ_2, n, n_1) outer code for which $\mathbf{Identify}_{out}$ satisfies the following:

$$\forall \mathsf{T}_2 \subseteq [n_1] \text{ s.t. } |\mathsf{T}_2| \leq w \;\; \mathbf{Prob}[\emptyset \not\subseteq \mathbf{Identify}_{out}(tk_{out}, \mathsf{p}_{out}) \subseteq \mathsf{T}_2] \geq 1 - \varepsilon_2 \tag{1.29}$$

where $\mathsf{p}_{out} \in Q_{out}^{\ell_2}$ is an output of any probabilistic polynomial time **Forging** adversary, that is bounded by the marking assumption of Definition 1.4, given the set of codewords $(\mathcal{C}_{out})_{\mathsf{T}_2}$.

Let $\mathsf{T} \subseteq [n]$ be a traitor coalition with size less than or equal to w, and suppose that the **Forging** algorithm, on input $(\mathcal{C}_{con})_\mathsf{T}$, outputs $\mathsf{p} \in Q_{in}^{\ell_1 \cdot \ell_2}$. According to the identification algorithm for the concatenated code, we chop the pirate codeword $\mathsf{p} = \langle \mathsf{p}_1, \ldots, \mathsf{p}_{\ell_1 \ell_2} \rangle$ into ℓ_2 blocks of size ℓ_1, and denote the j-th block as $\mathsf{p}^j = \langle \mathsf{p}_{\ell_1(j-1)+1}, \mathsf{p}_{\ell_1(j-1)+2}, \ldots, \mathsf{p}_{\ell_1(j-1)+\ell_1} \rangle$. We will prove that $\mathbf{Identify}_{con}$ returns an index from T with a failure probability at most $\varepsilon_2 + \ell_2\varepsilon_1$.

Due to the code concatenation, a user receives an inner-codeword for each block. Hence, the traitor coalition T amounts to a different set of traitor coalitions for each block within the formalization of inner fingerprinting code. For each block $j = 1, \ldots, \ell_2$ we define $\mathsf{T}_j = \{v \in [n_1] : \exists u \in \mathsf{T} \text{ s.t. } \mathsf{i}^v = \mathsf{f}^{-1}(\mathsf{o}_j^u)\}$. It further holds that $\mathsf{p}^j \in \mathsf{desc}((\mathcal{C}_{in})_{\mathsf{T}_j})$.

Equation 1.28 ensures that, with a failure probability at most ε_1, it holds $\mathbf{Identify}_{in}(tk_{in}, \mathsf{p}^j) = ind_j \in [n_1]$ and the symbol $q_j = \mathsf{f}(\mathsf{i}^{ind_j}) \in \{a \in Q_{out} \mid \exists u \in \mathsf{T} \text{ s.t. } a = \mathsf{o}_j^u\}$.

Summing the error probability over $j \in \{1, \ldots, \ell_2\}$ we obtain the fact that $\mathsf{p}^* = \langle q_1, \ldots, q_{\ell_2} \rangle \in \mathsf{desc}(\mathcal{C}out_\mathsf{T})$ with probability at least $1 - \ell_2\varepsilon_1$.

Finally, 1.29 ensures that $\mathbf{Identify}(tk_{out}, \mathsf{p}^*) \in \mathsf{T}$ with probability at most $1 - \varepsilon_2$.

The proof completes with a failure probability at most $\varepsilon_2 + \ell_2\varepsilon_1$. ∎

An example of concatenating fingerprinting codes. As the concatenation asks for a fully-collusion resistant inner code, we can either employ the Boneh-Shaw fingerprinting code $(\mathbf{CodeGen}_{BS}^{\ell}, \mathbf{Identify}_{BS}^{\ell})$ or the Tardos fingerprinting code $(\mathbf{CodeGen}_T, \mathbf{Identify}_T)$. Both of these codes are over binary alphabets which suits the purpose of code concatenation, i.e., an inner code with a smaller alphabet. On the other hand, the traceability codes based on error correcting codes or Chor-Fiat-Naor construction can be used in the place of the outer code. None of those combinations provides asymptotically good results. Still, an interesting combination is the application of a Boneh-Shaw inner code with length $\ell_2 \geq 2w^2(w-1)\ln(\frac{2w}{\varepsilon_1})$ for some parameters w, ε_1 with an outer Chor-Fiat-Naor secret fingerprinting code with length $4w\log(\frac{2n}{\varepsilon})$ and alphabet $2w$. By choosing $\varepsilon_1 = \frac{\varepsilon}{8w\log(2n/\varepsilon)}$ we can produce a binary concatenated code that is (ε, w) identifier and has length $\ell = O(w^4\log(\frac{n}{\varepsilon})(\log\frac{w}{\varepsilon} + \log\log n))$. This fingerprinting code is binary and may have reasonable length for some applications; it is of course outperformed by the Tardos code that has length almost the square root of ℓ.

1.5 Bibliographic Notes

The concept of fingerprinting codes was first studied in [120]. An early work is by Blakley et al. [15] presented a construction resilient against larger coalitions. Fingerprinting codes were implicit in the work of [28] that focused on combinatorial tools in the design of traitor tracing schemes (cf. the extended version of this work in [29]). Subsequent works on improving the code constructions have been very much related to the concept of traitor tracing. Still the two notions, of fingerprinting and traitor tracing, are distinct and are presented separately here. We also opted to use the term "Identify" to name one of the essential algorithms of fingerprinting instead of "tracing" that has been used occasionally in the literature due to the relation to traitor tracing [28].

The formalization of the problem of designing fingerprinting codes is due to Boneh and Shaw [23] who also introduced the first family of fingerprinting codes over a binary alphabet that is collusion-resistant against any coalition size. In following works an improvement in the length code — but not asymptotically – was made by Lindkvist [81] and an efficient implementation was designed by Yacobi [126]. A restricted case lower bound was given in [93].

Tardos's collusion-secure probabilistic fingerprinting codes were presented in [115, 116]) along with a matching lower bound. In this chapter we described the Tardos' codes distribution with a slightly modified "symmetric" variant of the accompanying tracing algorithm where both 0's and 1's account in the penalty function (Tardos originally employs only 1's for this purpose). We note that asymptotically there is no difference in the performance of the original tracing procedure and the present variant; still the presentation and analysis is somewhat differently laid out. Tardos codes use a continuous probability distribution for codeword generation which can lead to difficulties in an implementation. Obviously in practice only approximations can be achieved that would affect the security and efficiency aspects of the code. In [92] a related code distribution was shown that is discretized.

Fingerprinting codes in this chapter were shown under the marking assumption. Enforcing the marking assumption in practice can be achieved through methods related to watermarking see e.g., [30]. Still, the assumption can be problematic at times depending on the underlying content that is marked. If the marking assumption collapses then the fingerprinting system that relies on the assumption would collapse as well, i.e., it will be unable to identify the source of a signal or possibly present wrongful accusations.

We note that attacks against the marking assumption in the context of watermarking have been shown in practice, see e.g., the work of Kirovski and Petitcolas [73]. To address such issues various extensions of the marking assumption have been identified in specific contexts. For example, Guth and

Pfitzmann [52], put forth that reading errors in the code may cause failure of the system to facilitate the marking assumption. Kiayias and Yung [70], identify marking assumption collapse in the context of traitor tracing schemes and propose the use of all-or-nothing transforms of [98] to deal with it in this particular context. Safavi-Naini and Wang [101] consider the problem in terms of shortening as well as corrupting the object and present some related constructions.

In the same context, Boneh and Naor [21] deal with this issue in traitor tracing schemes and extend the marking assumption with the notion of δ-robustness. This extension of the marking assumption allows the adversary to adaptively corrupt a δ-fraction of the codeword they produce. This fraction can account for corrupting elementary objects by padding them with elementary objects of low utility or otherwise unreadable. This relaxation gives rise to δ-robust fingerprinting codes. An optimal up to logarithmic factors construction of such codes appears in [20].

The combinatorial properties of the subclasses of fingerprinting codes that were treated in this chapter were discussed in [111]. A number of works, including [54, 100, 111, 114, 113], investigated further these properties and proposed explicit constructions.

2

Broadcast Encryption

A broadcast channel enables a sender to reach many receivers in a very effective way. Broadcasting, due to its very nature, leaves little room for controlling the list of recipients N — once a message is put on the channel any listening party can obtain it. This may very well be against the objectives of the sender. In such case, encryption comes in mind as a potential way to solve the problem: it can be employed to deny eavesdroppers free access to the content that is broadcasted. Nevertheless, the use of encryption raises the issue of how to do key management. Enabled receivers should be capable of descrambling the message while eavesdroppers should just perceive it as noise. It follows that receivers that are enabled for reception should have access to the decryption key, while any other party should not. The major problem that springs up in this scenario is that receivers might get corrupted and thus become cooperative with the adversary. As a result one cannot hope that a party that owns a key will not use it to the fullest extend possible, i.e., for as long as such key allows descrambling which can be the moment that a global rekey operation takes place. Moreover, such a key can even be shared with more than a single listening party and thus enable the reception of the transmission for a multitude of rogue receivers. If a traditional encryption scheme is used then a single corrupted receiver is enough to bring forth such undesired effects. The subject of this chapter, *broadcast encryption* deals with solving the above problem in an effective way.

Based on the above, a path to effective broadcast encryption that avoids rekeying is that all recipients should have different but related keys. Taking advantage of the structure of the key space, the sender should be capable of choosing on the fly any set R of revoked receivers to be excluded from a transmission, and given such R prepare an encryption that can only be decrypted by the set of receivers $\mathsf{N} \setminus \mathsf{R}$.

We can classify broadcast encryption schemes in two major categories. The first one, that can be called *combinatorial*, is characterized as follows : the key-space contains cryptographic keys suitable for a standard encryption scheme. Each user receives a subset of those keys according to some assign-

A. Kiayias and S. Pehlivanoglu, *Encryption for Digital Content*, Advances in Information Security 52, DOI 10.1007/978-1-4419-0044-9_2,

ment mapping. In the setting of combinatorial schemes, we can think that each key corresponds to a set of users. The transmission problem then becomes a type of a set-cover problem: given the set of enabled users $\mathsf{N} \setminus \mathsf{R}$ find the best way to cover it using the subsets that correspond to the assigned keys. Combinatorial schemes can be constructed by employing probabilistic techniques or with explicit constructions. The second category of broadcast encryption, that can be called *structured*, assumes that the key-space has some structure that enables the preparation of ciphertexts that are decipherable only by the enabled users. For example a polynomial function can be used as a master key and each user can own a point of this polynomial. Messages can be encrypted under a point of a related polynomial and successful decryption can be achieved by the ability to interpolate the related polynomial.

In this chapter we will focus on explicit combinatorial schemes. An important characteristic of such schemes is that they are suitable for efficient implementation as they can be readily paired with an efficient underlying block-cipher such as the Advanced Encryption Standard[1] to yield very effective broadcast encryption in the symmetric key setting. The explicitness of such constructions guarantees that there is no error probability in the expression of their efficiency and security guarantees. Moreover, for such schemes, as we will illustrate, there is a way to express sufficient requirements for effective broadcast encryption in a compact algebraic fashion.

We note that most broadcast encryption schemes incur an overhead in the transmission that makes them unsuitable for the delivery of long plaintexts due to efficiency degradation. This issue is fairly common with cryptographic functions with special properties with the most prominent example being public-key encryption that includes schemes such as ElGamal and RSA. The way this is dealt in practice is through a hybrid approach. In particular two levels of encryption are used: at the first layer, the encryption is employed to encrypt a one-time key. Next, at the second layer, an efficient block or stream cipher is employed in combination with the one-time key. In this chapter we will assume that this approach is taken for the deployment of a broadcast encryption scheme.

2.1 Definition of Broadcast Encryption

A broadcast encryption scheme $\mathtt{BE}$ is a triple $(\mathbf{KeyGen}, \mathbf{Encrypt}, \mathbf{Decrypt})$ of algorithms. The parameter of the scheme is n, the number of receivers and is associated with three sets $\mathsf{K}, \mathsf{M}, \mathsf{C}$ corresponding to the sets of keys, plaintexts and ciphertexts respectively. We describe the I/O of these algorithms below:

- **KeyGen**. It is a probabilistic algorithm that on input 1^n, it produces $(ek, sk_1, \ldots, sk_n)$. The decryption key sk_i is to be assigned to the i-th user

[1] The Advanced Encryption Standard [32] is a symmetric encryption scheme adopted by the National Institute of Standards and Technology, USA in 2002.

while ek is the encryption key. The algorithm also produces a membership test for a language $\mathcal{L}$. The language $\mathcal{L}$ encodes all possible revocation instructions for the encryption function.

- **Encrypt**. It is a probabilistic algorithm that on input $m \in \mathsf{M}$, a string $\psi \in \mathcal{L}$ and ek, it outputs a ciphertext $c \in \mathsf{C}$. We write $c \leftarrow \mathbf{Encrypt}(ek, m, \psi)$ to denote that c is sampled according to the distribution of the encryptions of the plaintext m based on the revocation instruction ψ.
- **Decrypt**. It is a deterministic algorithm that on input c sampled from $\mathbf{Encrypt}(ek, m, \psi)$ and a user-key $sk_i \in \mathsf{K}$ where $(ek, sk_1, \ldots, sk_n) \leftarrow \mathbf{KeyGen}(1^n)$, it either outputs m or fails. Note that **Decrypt** can also be generalized to be a probabilistic algorithm but we will not take advantage of this here.

A broadcast encryption scheme BE can be in the public or symmetric key setting by signifying that the encryption key ek is either public or secret respectively. In case of public encryption this would enable any party to use the broadcast encryption to distribute content to the receiver population. A natural generalization of the above definition (which we will not consider in this chapter) is to accept a vector of messages $M = \langle m_1, \ldots, m_s \rangle \in \mathsf{M}^s$ so that **Decrypt** either outputs m_i for some $i \in [s]$ or fails. We call such scheme an s-ary broadcast encryption.

Regarding the language of revocation instructions we will require that it contains at least the descriptions of some subsets $\mathsf{R} \subseteq [n]$. The way a certain subset R is described by a revocation instruction varies and there can even be many different revocation instructions resulting in the same set of revoked users R. Depending on the scheme it might be the case that any subset of indices R can be encoded in $\mathcal{L}$ or there are only some specific subsets that are included, e.g., all subsets up to a certain size.

Next we define the correctness properties that are required from a broadcast encryption scheme.

Definition 2.1. ***Correctness.*** *We say an s-ary broadcast encryption scheme is correct if for any $\psi \in \mathcal{L}$ that encodes a subset $\mathsf{R} \subseteq [n]$ and for all $M = \langle m_1, \ldots, m_s \rangle \in \mathsf{M}^s$ and for any $u \in [n] \setminus \mathsf{R}$, it holds that*

$$\mathbf{Prob}[\mathbf{Decrypt}(\mathbf{Encrypt}(ek, M, \psi), sk_u) \in \{m_1, \ldots, m_s\}] = 1$$

where $(ek, sk_1, \ldots, sk_n)$ is distributed according to $\mathbf{KeyGen}(1^n)$. *Naturally one may generalize the above definition to have decryption fail with some small probability.*

The correctness definition ensures that the **Decrypt** algorithm does not fail as long as the index u is not removed from the list of enabled users.

Efficiency Parameters.

The efficiency of a broadcast encryption scheme is evaluated according to the following parameters.

1. Key-Storage: This refers to the size of the information required for each receiver to store so that the decryption operation is enabled.
2. Decryption Overhead: This refers to the computation time required by a receiver in order to perform the recovery of the plaintext.
3. Encryption Overhead: This refers to the computation time the sender is supposed to invest in order to parse the given revocation instruction and sample the ciphertext that disables all users that are meant to be excluded from the transmission and produce the ciphertext.
4. Transmission Overhead. This refers to the actual length of the ciphertexts (or the maximum such length if it varies).

The above parameters will have a functional dependency in the number of users n, as well as on possibly other parameters such as the number of users that the revocation information instructs to be excluded.

Adversarial Model.

The goal of an adversary in the broadcast encryption setting is to circumvent the revocation capability of the sender. In a setting where the hybrid encryption approach is employed, the content distribution operates at two levels: first, a one-time content key k is selected and encrypted with the broadcast encryption mechanism. Second, the actual message will be encrypted with the key k and will be broadcasted alongside the encrypted key. It follows that a minimum requirement would be that the scheme $\mathtt{BE}$ should be sufficiently secure to carry a cryptographic key k. As an encryption mechanism this is known in the context of public key cryptography as a "Key Encapsulation Mechanism". The security model we present in this section will take this formalization approach, i.e., it will focus on the type of security that needs to be satisfied by a broadcast encryption scheme in order to be used as a key encapsulation mechanism. We note that for simplicity we adopt the syntax of an encryption scheme, i.e., the message is given as an input to the encryption algorithm, while the security property will capture the case where the message is uniformly random as in key encapsulation. Later on in the chapter, the plaintext m in the definition of broadcast encryption schemes will be used to mean the one-time content key k unless otherwise noted.

The adversarial scenario that we envision for broadcast encryption is as follows. The adversary is capable of corrupting a set of users so that the adversary has access to the key material of the users in the corrupted set T. Subsequently, the adversary, given a pair (c, m), tries to distinguish if the pair is an actual plaintext ciphertext pair where m is sampled uniformly at random, i.e., the adversary attempts to see whether c is an encryption of m or m has been sampled in a manner independent of c. If indeed the adversary has no means of distinguishing a valid encryption key pair from an invalid one, then the encryption mechanism would be sufficiently strong to be used for the distribution of cryptographic keys.

The adversary may have at its disposal the following resources that can be thought of as oracles it can query and obtain a response.

1. Chosen Plaintext. The adversary can obtain valid plaintext-ciphertext pairs. In the case that broadcast encryption is used only for cryptographic key distribution the adversary may not be able to influence the distribution of plaintext - nevertheless allowing this capability only makes the security property stronger. When the adversary requests an encryption it will also be allowed to specify the set of revoked users or even choose the revocation information ψ that is passed to the encryption algorithm.
2. Chosen Ciphertext. The adversary can obtain output about how a certain uncorrupted user responds to a decryption request. The query may not necessarily contain a valid ciphertext but rather it can be an arbitrary bitstring created by the adversary to see how a user reacts in decryption.
3. User Corruption. In the static corruption setting, the adversary obtains the key material of all users in a set $\mathsf{T} \subseteq [n]$. In the adaptive corruption setting, the adversary corrupts each user one by one after performing other operations as allowed in the course of the attack.

The security of a broadcast encryption scheme will be defined using a game between the adversary and the challenger. We say the adversary has broken the scheme when the revocation list contains all of the corrupted users, but the adversary, still, is capable of distinguishing a valid plaintext-ciphertext pair from a pair where the plaintext is independent of the ciphertext and uniformly random. In figure 2.1 we present the security game that captures the security for key-encapsulation that we require from a broadcast encryption scheme in order to be useful in a hybrid encryption setting.

EncryptOracle(m, ψ)	DecryptOracle(c, u)	CorruptOracle(u)
retrieve ek;	retrieve sk_u;	$\mathsf{T} \leftarrow \mathsf{T} \cup \{u\}$
$c \leftarrow \mathbf{Encrypt}(ek, m, \psi)$;	return $\mathbf{Decrypt}(c, sk_u)$;	retrieve sk_u;
return c;		return sk_u;

Experiment $\mathbf{Exp}_{\mathcal{A}}^{rev}(1^n)$

$(ek, sk_1, \ldots, sk_n) \leftarrow \mathbf{KeyGen}(1^n)$; $\mathsf{T} \leftarrow \emptyset$
$\psi \leftarrow \mathcal{A}^{\mathsf{EncryptOracle}(),\mathsf{DecryptOracle}(),\mathsf{CorruptOracle}()}(1^n)$
$M_0, M_1 \stackrel{R}{\leftarrow} \mathsf{M}^s$; $b \stackrel{R}{\leftarrow} \{0,1\}$; $c \leftarrow \mathbf{Encrypt}(ek, M_1, \psi)$
$b' \leftarrow \mathcal{A}^{\mathsf{EncryptOracle}()}(\{sk_i\}_{i \in \mathsf{T}}, M_b, c)$
return 1 if and only if $b = b'$ and
ψ excludes all members of T.

Fig. 2.1. The security game for key encapsulation.

In the definition below we introduce the notion of ε-insecurity that captures the advantage the adversary may have in distinguishing valid plaintext ciphertext pairs from those that are independently chosen.

Definition 2.2. *We say an s-ary broadcast encryption* BE *is ε-insecure if for any probabilistic polynomial-time adversary $\mathcal{A}$, it holds that*

$$\mathbf{Adv}_{\mathcal{A}}^{rev}(1^n) = |\mathbf{Prob}[\mathbf{Exp}_{\mathcal{A}}^{rev}(1^n) = 1] - \frac{1}{2}| \leq \varepsilon$$

where the experiment is defined as in figure 2.1. It is also possible to extend the definition to accept a vector of messages $M = \langle m_1, \ldots, m_s \rangle \in \mathsf{M}^s$ as an input; it will be considered to be correct if **Decrypt** *returns m_i for some $i \in [s]$.*

We note that ε in general is not supposed to be a function n, i.e., the security property should hold for any $\mathcal{A}$ i.e., independently of the number of users n.

2.2 Broadcast Encryption Based on Exclusive-Set Systems

In this section we will focus on concrete combinatorial broadcast encryption schemes. These are also the only such schemes that are currently widely deployed in commercial products (a notable example of such deployment is the AACS[2]). Recall that in combinatorial schemes there is a pool of cryptographic keys for an underlying encryption scheme such as a block cipher. The message m to be broadcasted is encrypted with some of these keys. In order to receive it, the user will need to either possess or be able to derive at least one of these keys.

Given that the keys in the pool are shared by many users, we can obtain a correspondence between such keys and subsets so that a key would correspond to the set of users who possess that key. Hence, the set of keys corresponds to a collection of subsets of users, who without loss of generality are subsets of $[n]$. This collection defines a set system over the user population. The set of keys that are used in a certain transmission of a plaintext is mapped to a set of subsets from the collection that we call the "broadcast pattern" or simply pattern of the transmission. Hence, encryption in this case involves the problem of finding a set of subsets, i.e. a broadcast pattern, that covers the enabled set of receivers.

The reader should observe that the choice of the set system that underlies the assignment of cryptographic keys will play a crucial role in the effectiveness of revocation. As it is quite clear, not any set system would provide a feasible way to revoke any subset of receivers. We will start the investigation of this topic by formally defining exclusive set systems, that are instances of set systems useful for broadcast encryption.

---

[2] The Advanced Access Content System (AACS, see [1]) is a standard for content distribution and digital rights management, intended to restrict access to and copying of optical discs such as Blu-Ray disks.

Definition 2.3. *Consider a family of subsets* $\Phi = \{\mathsf{S_j}\}_{\mathsf{j} \in \mathcal{J}}$ *defined over* $[n]$ *where* $\mathcal{J}$ *denotes the set of encodings for the elements in* Φ *over an alphabet* Σ *with length of at most* $\mathsf{l}(n)$ *for some length function* $\mathsf{l}(\cdot)$. *We say* Φ *is* (n, r, t)*-exclusive if for any subset* $\mathsf{R} \subseteq [n]$ *with* $|\mathsf{R}| \leq r$, *we can write* $[n] \setminus \mathsf{R} = \cup_{i=1}^{s} \mathsf{S}_{\mathsf{j}_i}$ *where* $s \leq t$ *and* $\mathsf{S}_{\mathsf{j}_i} \in \Phi$ *for* $1 \leq i \leq s$.

Having defined exclusive-set systems, we will now give a construction for broadcast encryption schemes based on exclusive-set systems. We note that the recovery of $\mathsf{j}_1, \ldots, \mathsf{j}_s$ given R should be done efficiently for a system to be useful. For this reason when one proposes a set system it is imperative to include a description of how the covering algorithm would work (that is at the heart of the revocation algorithm). The goal of this algorithm would be to produce the indices j_i, $i = 1, \ldots, s$ of the subsets that cover the set of enabled users $[n] \setminus \mathsf{R}$. A trivial covering algorithm for revocation that works with any set system would be to search for the pattern in a brute force manner. Given that in an exclusive set system the target pattern is postulated to exist, the exhaustive search algorithm is guaranteed to find a solution. Nevertheless this will not lead to an efficient implementation for any but entirely trivial set systems. In the rest of the chapter we will be concerned with the design of exclusive set systems with efficient revocation algorithms and in fact we will present a generic revocation algorithm given any set system that satisfies a simple algebraic property.

In Figure 2.2 we present a template for a broadcast encryption system based on exclusive set systems. We assume a family of exclusive set systems indexed by n as well as an underlying symmetric encryption scheme $(\mathtt{E}, \mathtt{D})$ that uses as keys elements of K.

The characteristics of the scheme given in figure 2.2 that make it a template are as follows:

1. The exclusive set system Φ is not explicitly specified but used in a black-box fashion. It is assumed that an exclusive set system can be found for any number of users n. To specify this we may use the notation $\{\Phi_n\}_{n \in \mathbb{N}}$ to denote the collection of exclusive set systems produced for each number of users n, or simply write Φ overloading the set-system notation (in such case there an implicit reference to the number of users n will be assumed).
2. The exact mechanism that **KeyGen** uses to sample the keys $\{k_\mathsf{j}\}_{\mathsf{j} \in \mathcal{J}}$ is not specified. The only restriction is that each key belongs to the set K.
3. The underlying encryption scheme $(\mathtt{E}, \mathtt{D})$ is not specified but used in a black box fashion.

Comments on the Template Construction.

For any exclusive set system Φ and an encryption scheme $(\mathtt{E}, \mathtt{D})$ we can instantiate the template of Figure 2.2 by having the **KeyGen** procedure sample the keys $\{k_\mathsf{j}\}_{\mathsf{j} \in \mathcal{J}}$ independently at random from the set of keys for the encryption scheme $(\mathtt{E}, \mathtt{D})$. We will refer to this scheme as : $\mathtt{BE}^{\Phi}_{\mathtt{basic}}$. As we will see later

Combinatorial broadcast encryption template.

- **KeyGen**. Given 1^n it chooses an (n, r, t)-exclusive set system $\Phi = \{\mathsf{S_j}\}_{\mathsf{j}\in\mathcal{J}}$. The algorithm then generates a collection of keys $\{k_\mathsf{j}\}_{\mathsf{j}\in\mathcal{J}} \subseteq \mathsf{K}$. For any $u \in [n]$, define $\mathcal{J}_u := \{\mathsf{j} \mid u \in \mathsf{S_j}\}$ and $\mathsf{K}_u = \{k_\mathsf{j} \mid \mathsf{j} \in \mathcal{J}_u\}$. Set $ek = \langle \Phi, \{k_\mathsf{j}\}_{\mathsf{j}\in\mathcal{J}}\rangle$ and set $sk_u = (\mathcal{J}_u, \mathsf{K}_u)$ for any $u \in [n]$.
  The language $\mathcal{L}$ consists of the descriptions of those elements of 2^Φ such that $\mathcal{P} = \{\mathsf{S}_{\mathsf{j}_1}, \ldots, \mathsf{S}_{\mathsf{j}_s}\} \in \mathcal{L}$ if and only if $s \leq t$ and the set $\mathsf{R} = [n] \setminus \cup_{i=1}^{s} \mathsf{S}_{\mathsf{j}_i}$ satisfies $|\mathsf{R}| \leq r$; in such case we say that $\mathcal{P}$ encodes R.
- Encrypt. Given $\mathcal{P} \in \mathcal{L}$ and a message m, say $\mathcal{P} = \{\mathsf{S}_{\mathsf{j}_1}, \ldots, \mathsf{S}_{\mathsf{j}_s}\}$ where $\mathsf{j}_i \in \mathcal{J}$ for $i \in \{1, \ldots, s\}$. Then the set of keys $\{k_\mathsf{j} \mid \mathsf{j} \in \mathcal{J}$ and $\mathsf{S_j} \in \mathcal{P}\}$ is selected from $\{k_\mathsf{j}\}_{\mathsf{j}\in\mathcal{J}}$. By employing the encryption scheme $(\mathtt{E}, \mathtt{D})$ the ciphertext is computed as follows:
$$c \leftarrow \langle \mathsf{j}_1, \ldots, \mathsf{j}_s, \mathtt{E}_{k_{\mathsf{j}_1}}(m), \ldots, \mathtt{E}_{k_{\mathsf{j}_s}}(m)\rangle$$
- Decrypt. Given the key-pair $sk_u = (\mathcal{J}_u, \mathsf{K}_u)$ for some $u \in [n]$ and a ciphertext of the form
$$c = \langle \mathsf{j}_1, \ldots, \mathsf{j}_s, c_1, \ldots, c_s\rangle$$
  it first searches for an encoding j_i that satisfies $\mathsf{j}_i \in \mathcal{J}_u$ and then returns $\mathtt{D}_{k_{\mathsf{j}_i}}(c_i)$. If no such encoding is found it returns $\perp$.

Fig. 2.2. The construction template for broadcast encryption using an exclusive set system.

on in this chapter there are substantial advantages to be gained by exploiting the particular structure of the exclusive set system and packing the information in the sets $(\mathcal{J}_u, \mathsf{K}_u)$ in a more compact form than simply listing all their elements. In this way we will derive much more efficient schemes compared to $\mathtt{BE}^{\Phi}_{\mathtt{basic}}$. This gain will come at the expense of introducing additional cryptographic assumptions in the security argumentation.

The three procedures in the template broadcast encryption scheme BE play the following role in an actual system instantiation. The **KeyGen** procedure produces a set system Φ which corresponds to the set of keys in the system and the collection of sets $\mathcal{I}_u$ which determines the key assignment for each user u. The procedure **Encrypt**, given the revocation instructions and a message m to be distributed, produces the ciphertext by choosing the corresponding keys from the set of possible keys. This is done by computing the encryption of the plaintext m under the key assigned to the subset S for all subsets that are specified in the revocation instruction. The Decrypt procedure will decrypt the content transmission by using the set of user keys in a straightforward manner : it will parse the transmitted ciphertext sequence for a ciphertext block that it can decrypt and then it will apply the correponding key to it to recover m.

The efficiency of the above construction template depends on the characteristics of the underlying set system and the way **KeyGen** works. Key storage is bounded from above by the number of keys in K_u it can be decreased in favor of increasing the decryption overhead. Such tradeoffs will be possible by either variating the underlying set system or employing a computational key derivation that makes it possible to compress the information in $sk_u = (\mathcal{J}_u, \mathsf{K}_u)$, cf. section 2.3.3. The encryption overhead is also related to the efficacy of the algorithm that accompanies the set system and produces the revocation instruction given the set of users that need to be revoked. This is part of the challenge of the design of good set systems to be used in the above basic construction. Finally, the transmission overhead, i.e., the ciphertext length, is linear in number of subsets that is specified in the revocation instruction. We note that for the exclusive set systems we will see this will be a function of $r = |\mathsf{R}|$ and n where R is the set of revoked users. Intuitively the size of the broadcast pattern as a function of r depends on how dense the set system is.

There are two trivial instantiations of the above basic construction exhibiting a wide tradeoff between the efficiency parameters. In the first trivial instantiation, the set system consists merely of singletons for each receiver, i.e., $\Phi = \{\{1\}, \ldots, \{n\}\}$. Subsequently the encryption overhead would be linear in number of enabled receivers $n - r$. While this solution is optimal from the key-storage point of view, it wastes a lot of bandwidth and exhausts the broadcast center in the preparation of the transmission. In the second trivial instantiation, the set system Φ is the power set of the receiver population so that each receiver possesses the keys for all subsets it belongs to. In this case the ciphertext has minimal length (no larger than $r \cdot \log n + \lambda$ where λ is the ciphertext length of the underlying encryption scheme) but each receiver is required to store 2^{n-1} keys which is exponential in the number of users n. We will discuss combinatorial properties of the set systems that support efficient revocation in Section 2.4.2 and discuss a number of constructions that enjoy non-trivial tradeoffs in Section 2.5.

Next we prove the correctness of the template scheme following Definition 2.1.

Proposition 2.4. *Any broadcast encryption scheme that matches the template of Figure 2.2 satisfies correctness (cf. Definition 2.1).*

Proof. Let any $\mathcal{P} \in \mathcal{L}$ that encodes a set of revoked users R. Then we have that $\mathcal{P} = \{\mathsf{S}_{\mathsf{j}_1}, \ldots, \mathsf{S}_{\mathsf{j}_s}\}$ with $s \leq t$ and $[n] \setminus \cup_{i=1}^{s} \mathsf{S}_{\mathsf{j}_i} = \mathsf{R}$. It follows that any user $u \in [n] \setminus \mathsf{R}$ belongs to a set $\mathsf{S}_{\mathsf{j}_{i'}}$ for some $i' \in \{1, \ldots, s\}$. For user u, the input of the decryption function is some c such that $c \leftarrow \mathbf{Encrypt}(ek, m, \mathcal{P})$ as well as $sk_u = \langle \mathcal{J}_u, \mathsf{K}_u \rangle$ where $\mathcal{J}_u = \{\mathsf{j} \in \mathcal{J} \mid u \in \mathsf{S}_\mathsf{j}\}$ and $\mathsf{K}_u = \{k_\mathsf{j} \mid \mathsf{j} \in \mathcal{J}_u\}$. It follows that u will discover the index i' and apply the key $k_{\mathsf{j}_{i'}}$ to the i'-th component of the ciphertext c to recover the plaintext m correctly always.

2.2.1 Security

In this section we will focus on proving the security of the template construction of broadcast encryption based on exclusive set systems. We will follow the security modeling as expressed by Definition 2.2. The overall security of the scheme is based on the security of the underlying encryption scheme $\mathtt{E}_k, \mathtt{D}_k$ as indexed by a key k as well as the properties of the key assignment, i.e., the way that the keys of user u are sampled by the **KeyGen** algorithm.

Key Encapsulation Mechanisms.

We require the broadcast encryption scheme to be capable of transmitting a cryptographic key. We will ask that this same requirement should also be satisfied by the underlying cryptographic primitive $(\mathtt{E}, \mathtt{D})$, i.e., a cryptographic key should be encapsulated safely by the underlying encryption primitive.

We formalize the security requirement as the following game: for a random choice of the key k, the adversary $\mathcal{A}$ can adaptively choose plaintexts and see how $\mathtt{E}_k$ encrypts them; similarly, is capable of observing the output of decryption procedure $\mathtt{D}_k$. The adversary is challenged with a pair (c, m) for which it holds that either $c \leftarrow \mathtt{E}_k(m)$ or $c \leftarrow \mathtt{E}_k(m')$ where m, m' are selected randomly from the message space. The goal of the adversary is to distinguish between the two cases. This models a CCA1 type of encryption security, or what is known as a security against lunch-time attacks.

Experiment $\mathbf{Exp}_{\mathcal{A}}^{kem}$

Select k at random.
$aux \leftarrow \mathcal{A}^{\mathtt{E}_k(), \mathtt{D}_k()}()$
$m_0, m_1 \stackrel{R}{\leftarrow} \mathsf{M}$; $b \stackrel{R}{\leftarrow} \{0,1\}$; $c = \mathtt{E}_k(m_1)$
$b' \leftarrow \mathcal{A}^{\mathtt{E}_k()}(aux, c, m_b)$
return 1 if and only if $b = b'$;

Fig. 2.3. The security game of CCA1 secure key encapsulation for an encryption scheme.

Definition 2.5. *We say the symmetric encryption scheme* $(\mathtt{E}, \mathtt{D})$ *is* ε*-insecure if it holds that for any probabilistic polynomial-time* $\mathcal{A}$

$$\mathbf{Adv}_{\mathcal{A}}^{kem} = |\mathbf{Prob}[\mathbf{Exp}_{\mathcal{A}}^{kem} = 1] - \frac{1}{2}| \leq \varepsilon$$

Observe that the above requirement is weaker that one would typically expect from an encryption scheme that may be desired to protect the plaintext even if it is arbitrarily distributed. We note though that the key encapsulation security requirement will still force the encryption function to be probabilistic: indeed, in the deterministic case, the adversary can easily break security by encrypting m_b and testing the resulting ciphertext for equality to c. Further, since we are only interested in key encapsulation we can require the encryption oracle to only return encryptions of random plaintexts (as opposed to have them adaptively selected by the adversary).

Key-indistinguishability.

To ensure the security of the broadcast encryption scheme based on an exclusive set system, we have to perform the key-assignment in an appropriate way, i.e., a user should not be able to extract any information on a key of a subset that it does not belong to. Recall that for a set system Φ, where $\Phi = \{\mathsf{S}_\mathsf{j}\}_{\mathsf{j}\in\mathcal{J}}$, the **KeyGen** procedure generates a collection of keys $\{k_\mathsf{j}\}_{\mathsf{j}\in\mathcal{J}}$, one for each subset in Φ. Any user $u \in [n]$ is provided with a key assignment that is determined by the pair of sets $\langle \mathcal{J}_u, \mathsf{K}_u \rangle$ where $\mathcal{J}_u = \{\mathsf{j} \in \mathcal{J} \mid u \in \mathsf{S}_\mathsf{j}\}$ and $\mathsf{K}_u = \{k_\mathsf{j} \mid \mathsf{j} \in \mathcal{J}_u\}$. The key-indistinguishability property ensures that any coalition of users are not able to distinguish the key $k_{\mathsf{j}'}$ of a subset $\mathsf{S}_{\mathsf{j}'}$ they do not belong to from a random key. We will formalize the key-indistinguishability requirement through the following security-game.

EncryptOracle(m, j)	DecryptOracle(c, j)
retrieve $k_\mathsf{j}, \mathsf{j}_0$;	retrieve $k_\mathsf{j}, \mathsf{j}_0$;
return $c \leftarrow \mathtt{E}_{k_\mathsf{j}}(m)$;	return $\mathtt{D}_{k_\mathsf{j}}(c)$

Experiment $\mathbf{Exp}_{\mathcal{A}}^{key-ind}(1^n)$

$b \xleftarrow{R} \{0,1\}$; $\quad \mathsf{j}_0 \leftarrow \mathcal{A}(\Phi)$
if $b = 0$ then $(\Phi, \{k_\mathsf{j}\}_{\mathsf{j}\in\mathcal{J}}) \leftarrow \mathbf{KeyGen}(1^n)$
else $(\Phi, \{k_\mathsf{j}\}_{\mathsf{j}\in\mathcal{J}}) \leftarrow \mathbf{KeyGen}^{\mathsf{j}_0}(1^n)$
$b' \leftarrow \mathcal{A}^{\mathsf{EncryptOracle}(),\mathsf{DecryptOracle}()}(\langle \mathcal{J}_u, \mathsf{K}_u \rangle_{u \notin \mathsf{S}_{\mathsf{j}_0}})$
return 1 if and only if $b = b'$

Fig. 2.4. The security game for the key-indistinguishability property.

Definition 2.6. *We say that the broadcast encryption* BE *based on an exclusive set system satisfies the key indistinguishability property with distinguishing probability ε if there exists a family of key generation procedures $\{\mathbf{KeyGen}^\mathsf{j}\}_{\mathsf{j}\in\mathcal{J}}$ with the property that for all* j, $\mathbf{KeyGen}^\mathsf{j}$ *selects the* j*-th key independently at random and it holds that for any probabilistic polynomial-time $\mathcal{A}$, $\mathbf{Adv}_{\mathcal{A}}^{key-ind}(1^n) = |\mathbf{Prob}[\mathbf{Exp}_{\mathcal{A}}^{key-ind}(1^n) = 1] - \frac{1}{2}| \leq \varepsilon$, where the experiment is defined as in figure 2.4.*

The definition of key indistinguishability suggests the following : the key generation algorithm **KeyGen** makes such a selection of keys that it is impossible for an adversary to distinguish with probability better than ε the key of subset S_j from a random key, even if it is given access to the actual keys of all users that do not belong to S_j as well as arbitrary encryption and decryption capability within the key system.

An easy way to satisfy the property of key indistinguishability is to have all keys of subsets selected randomly and independently from each other as is done in the broadcast encryption scheme $\mathtt{BE}^{\Phi}_{\mathtt{basic}}$. Indeed, we have the following proposition.

Proposition 2.7. *The basic broadcast encryption scheme* $\mathtt{BE}^{\Phi}_{\mathtt{basic}}$ *(refer to Figure 2.2 and comments below) satisfies the key indistinguishability property with distinguishing probability* 0.

Proof. It is easy to see that the choice k_{j_0} by the **KeyGen** algorithm is identically distributed to the random selection of k_1 from K. Based on this it is easy to derive that the scheme $\mathtt{BE}^{\Phi}_{\mathtt{basic}}$ satisfies key indistinguishability.

We, now, come to the point we can state the security theorem for the template broadcast encryption as defined in Figure 2.2. The requirements for security are the key-indistinguishability property and the use of an encryption that is suitable for key encapsulation.

Theorem 2.8. *Consider a broadcast encryption scheme* $\mathtt{BE}$ *that fits the template of Figure 2.2 over an* (n, r, t)*-exclusive set system* Φ *and satisfies (1) the key indistinguishability property with distinguishing probability* ε_1*, (2) its underlying encryption scheme* $(\mathtt{E}, \mathtt{D})$ *is* ε_2*-insecure in the sense of Definition 2.5. Then, the broadcast encryption scheme* $\mathtt{BE}$ *is* ε*-insecure in the sense of Definition 2.2 where* $\varepsilon \le 2t \cdot |\Phi| \cdot (2\varepsilon_1 + \varepsilon_2)$.

Proof. We will prove the above argument by structuring the proof as a sequence of indistinguishable games all operating over the same underlying probability space. Starting from the actual attack scenario, we consider a sequence of hypothetical games. In each game, the adversary's view is obtained in different ways, but the probability of success will be related in a predictable fashion. Let us start writing the original game $\mathbf{Exp}_0 = \mathbf{Exp}^{rev}_{\mathcal{A}}(n)$ explicitly in Figure 2.5:

Experiment $\mathbf{Exp}^v_1$. This experiment, for $v = 0, \ldots, t$, is identical to $\mathbf{Exp}_0$, with two slight modifications. The first modification is in the encryption on line 5. The experiment of type v, $\mathbf{Exp}^v_1$, is one where the encryption is computed so that the first v subset keys are over a random plaintext while the remaining subsets encode the correct message. More specifically, the 5th line in the experiment would look as follows :

$$c = \langle \mathsf{j}_1, \ldots, \mathsf{j}_s, E_{k_{\mathsf{j}_1}}(R_1), \ldots, E_{k_{\mathsf{j}_v}}(R_v), E_{k_{\mathsf{j}_{v+1}}}(m_1), \ldots, E_{k_{\mathsf{j}_s}}(m_1) \rangle$$

where R_i is a random string of the same length as the message m_1 for $i = 1, \ldots, v$. Note that if $v > s$ all plaintexts are selected independently at random.

The second modification of the experiment $\mathbf{Exp}^v_1$ is the choice of a uniformly random variable $w \in \{1, \ldots, |\Phi|\}$. Consider an enumeration for the key encodings, i.e. $\mathcal{J} = \{\mathsf{j}[1], \ldots, \mathsf{j}[|\Phi|]\}$. The experiment $\mathbf{Exp}^1_v$ is modified in the

EncryptOracle(m, ψ)	DecryptOracle(c, u)	CorruptOracle(u)
retrieve ek;	retrieve sk_u;	$\mathsf{T} \leftarrow \mathsf{T} \cup \{u\}$
$c \leftarrow \mathbf{Encrypt}(ek, m, \psi)$;	return $\mathbf{Decrypt}(c, sk_u)$;	retrieve sk_u;
return c;		return sk_u;

Experiment $\mathbf{Exp}_{\mathcal{A}}^{rev}(1^n)$

$\langle(\Phi, \{k_{\mathsf{j}}\}_{\mathsf{j} \in \mathcal{J}}), (\mathcal{J}_1, \mathsf{K}_1), \ldots, (\mathcal{J}_n, \mathsf{K}_n)\rangle \leftarrow \mathbf{KeyGen}(1^n)$; $\mathsf{T} \leftarrow \emptyset$
$ek = (\Phi, \{k_{\mathsf{j}}\}_{\mathsf{j} \in \mathcal{J}})$; $sk_u = (\mathcal{J}_u, \mathsf{K}_u)$ for $u = 1, \ldots, n$
$\psi^* \leftarrow \mathcal{A}^{\mathsf{EncryptOracle}(),\mathsf{DecryptOracle}(),\mathsf{CorruptOracle}()}(\Phi)$
$m_0, m_1 \stackrel{R}{\leftarrow} \mathsf{M}$; $b \stackrel{R}{\leftarrow} \{0, 1\}$;
$c = \langle \mathsf{j}_1, \ldots, \mathsf{j}_s, \mathsf{E}_{k_{\mathsf{j}_1}}(m_1), \ldots, \mathsf{E}_{k_{\mathsf{j}_s}}(m_1)\rangle \leftarrow \mathbf{Encrypt}(ek, m_1, \psi^*)$
$b' \leftarrow \mathcal{A}^{\mathsf{EncryptOracle}()}(\{sk_i\}_{i \in \mathsf{T}}, m_b, c)$
return 1 if and only if $b = b'$ and
ψ^* is an instruction that excludes all members of T.

Fig. 2.5. The initial security game $\mathbf{Exp_0}$.

output line to behave as follows: if it happens that the index of $(v+1)$-th subset in the challenge ciphertext in line 5 does not match $\mathsf{j}[w]$ then a random coin flip is returned as the output of the experiment. If it happens that $v + 1 > s$ the s-th subset is used in the test.

Let p_1^v be the probability that experiment $\mathbf{Exp}_1^v$ returns 1 and similarly let p_0 be the probability that the experiment $\mathbf{Exp}_0$ returns 1. Observe that in the case $v \geq s$, the sequence of encryptions no longer contains any information on b, and the same is true for all other information given to the adversary. It follows that the adversary's view is independent of b and therefore it is easy to see that $p_1^t = \frac{1}{2}$.

On the other hand, let us assume that the adversary has advantage of at least ε in being succesful on the original experiment $\mathbf{Exp}_0$, i.e., without loss of generality, $p_0 \geq 1/2 + \varepsilon$. This suggests that

$$p_1^0 \geq 1/2 + \frac{\varepsilon}{|\Phi|}$$

It follows there is a gap of $\varepsilon/|\Phi|$ between p_1^0, p_1^t and by applying the triangular inequality we obtain that there must exist some $0 < v' \leq t$ such that

$$| \, p_1^{v'-1} - p_1^{v'} \, | \geq \frac{\varepsilon}{t \cdot |\Phi|}$$

Experiment $\mathbf{Exp}_2^v$. This experiment, for $v = 0, \ldots, t$ is identical to $\mathbf{Exp}_1^v$, except that one of the keys is replaced with a random key, i.e., the way the normal key generation algorithm **KeyGen** works in line 1 of the game is modified. Specifically, in the modified game we employ the alternative key generation $\mathbf{KeyGen}^{\mathsf{j}[w]}$. In case a user owning this key gets corrupted the experiment fails and returns a random coin flip. We denote by p_2^v the probability the experiment returns 1.

We claim that for any $v = 0, \ldots, t$

$$|p_1^v - p_2^v| \leq 2\varepsilon_1$$

We next prove the claim. Consider the following key indistinguishability adversary for some parameter v. $\mathcal{B}_1$ follows the structure of the experiments $\mathbf{Exp}_1^v, \mathbf{Exp}_2^v$. It first provides as output the index $\mathsf{j}[w]$; this would be the key that will be attacked for key indistinguishability. Following the game-based definition, $\mathcal{B}_1$ receives the keys of all users that are outside of $\mathsf{S}_{\mathsf{j}[w]}$ as well as it is given oracle access to encryption and decryption for any key j that corresponds to a subset of $\mathsf{S}_{\mathsf{j}[w]}$. $\mathcal{B}_1$ proceeds to simulate the challenger and the adversary $\mathcal{A}$ as in $\mathbf{Exp}_2^v$. Based on the key material that is available to $\mathcal{B}_1$, it can perform the simulation without difficulty except when the adversary decides to corrupt a user $u \in \mathsf{S}_{\mathsf{j}[w]}$. In such case $\mathcal{B}_1$ fails and returns 0. This completes the description of $\mathcal{B}_1$. Based on our assumption about key indistinguishability we know that $|\mathbf{Prob}[\mathbf{Exp}_{\mathcal{B}_1}^{key-ind}(1^n)] - 1/2| \leq \varepsilon_1$.

We observe that $\mathbf{Prob}[\mathbf{Exp}_{\mathcal{B}_1}^{key-ind}(1^n)|b = 0] = 1 - p_1^v$. This holds as the only seeming difference between the way $\mathcal{B}_1$ operates in the conditional space $b = 0$ and the experiment $\mathbf{Exp}_1^v$ is the event when a party in $\mathsf{S}_{\mathsf{j}[w]}$ is corrupted. In this case $\mathcal{B}_1$ returns 0. For the same event in the experiment $\mathbf{Exp}_1^v$ we observe that the end condition will force also a 0 output. In a similar fashion it holds that $\mathbf{Prob}[\mathbf{Exp}_{\mathcal{B}_1}^{key-ind}(1^n)|b = 1] = p_2^v$. Based on this we obtain the proof of the claim.

We next claim that for any $v = 1, \ldots, t$,

$$|p_2^{v-1} - p_2^v| \leq 2\varepsilon_2$$

We prove the claim. Consider the following CCA1 key encapsulation adversary with a parameter v. $\mathcal{B}_2$ follows the structure of the experiment $\mathbf{Exp}_2^v$. To break the security claim of the underlying symmetric encryption scheme $(\mathtt{E}, \mathtt{D})$, $\mathcal{B}_2$, is given access to encryption-decryption oracle of the primitive. $\mathcal{B}_2$ has also access to the decryption/encryption under a key k that is unknown to her. She is then challenged with plaintext-ciphertext pair (c, m_1) for which either $c = \mathtt{E}_k(m_1)$ or $c = \mathtt{E}_k(m)$ for some random message m that has the same length with m_1. She is asked to test if the pair is a correct plaintext-ciphertext pair.

$\mathcal{B}_2$ will simulate the experiment $\mathbf{Exp}_2^v$. $\mathcal{B}_2$ will focus its attack on the key of the $\mathsf{j}[w]$-th subset. In the initial stage it will simulate $\mathcal{A}$ as in the experiment $\mathbf{Exp}_2^v$ by answering all queries except those that involve the $\mathsf{j}[w]$-th subset that will be answered by the encryption and decryption oracle available to $\mathcal{B}_2$. In the second stage, $\mathcal{B}_2$ will be given the challenge (c, m) where either m is the proper plaintext of c or it is randomly selected. $\mathcal{B}_2$ will prepare a challenge for $\mathcal{A}$ in the security game $\mathbf{Exp}_2^v$ by setting the v-th location of the challenge ciphertext with c and the remaining positions from $v+1, \ldots, s$ with the appropriate encryptions of m as dictated in the revocation instruction ψ^*

that is selected by $\mathcal{A}$ in its first stage. The simulation of the second stage of $\mathcal{A}$ within experiment $\mathbf{Exp}_2^v$ can be carried out by $\mathcal{B}_2$ without problem by resorting to its encryption oracle whenever needed.

Based on the assumption on the underlying encryption scheme we have that $\mathbf{Prob}[\mathbf{Exp}_{\mathcal{B}_2}^{kem}(1^n)]-1/2| \leq \varepsilon_2$. We observe that in the key encapsulation attack of $\mathcal{B}_2$ in the conditional space $b=0$, the adversary $\mathcal{B}_2^{kem}(1^n)$ operates identically to the experiment $\mathbf{Exp}_2^{v-1}$ while in the conditional space $b=1$ it operates identically to the experiment $\mathbf{Exp}_2^v$. Based on this derive the proof of the claim.

We are now ready to give the proof of the theorem. First recall from our first claim that there is a $v' \in \{1,\ldots,t\}$ such that

$$| p_1^{v'-1} - p_1^{v'} | \geq \frac{\varepsilon}{t \cdot |\Phi|}$$

From our second claim we know that $|p_1^{v'} - p_2^{v'}| \leq 2\varepsilon_1$ as well as $|p_1^{v'-1} - p_2^{v'-1}| \leq 2\varepsilon_1$. We know that for any a,b,c,d,e, $|a-b| \geq d$ and $|b-c| \leq e$ implies $|a-c| \geq d-e$. By combining this with the above facts we have $|p_2^{v'-1} - p_2^{v'}| \geq \varepsilon/(t \cdot |\Phi|) - 4\varepsilon_1$. Now based on our third claim we have that $|p_2^{v'-1} - p_2^{v'}| \leq 2\varepsilon_2$. From this we obtain $\varepsilon \leq 2t \cdot |\Phi| \cdot (2\varepsilon_1 + \varepsilon_2)$ which completes the proof.

2.2.2 The Subset Cover Framework

Among set systems, *fully-exclusive set systems* are of interest due to their support for revocation for any number of receivers. The subset cover framework class of fully-exclusive set systems to be used in broadcast encryption template given in Figure 2.2. We can list the requirements of a set system Φ to be considered in the framework as follows:

1. The set system Φ is fully-exclusive, i.e. Φ is (n,n,t)-exclusive where Φ is defined over a set of size n, and t is a function of the size r of the revoked set.
2. The set system is accompanied with an efficient revocation algorithm **Revoke** that produces the indices $\mathsf{j}_i, i = 1,\ldots,s$ of the subsets that cover the set of enabled users $[n] \setminus \mathsf{R}$. We require the efficiency in the following sense: (i) The time required to compute the pattern is efficient, i.e. polylog in the number of receivers (ii) The output pattern consists of minimal number of subsets that is a function of n and $r = |\mathsf{R}|$.
3. The set system Φ supports "bifurcation property": it should be possible to split any subset $\mathsf{S} \in \Phi$ into two roughly equal sets, i.e. that there exists $\mathsf{S}_1, \mathsf{S}_2 \in \Phi$ such that $\mathsf{S} = \mathsf{S}_1 \cup \mathsf{S}_2$ and $|\mathsf{S}_1|/|\mathsf{S}_2|$ is bounded above from a constant. In some cases, although the first split might not hold the above property, it is also acceptable if the relative size of the larger subset in consecutive split operations converges to the bound quickly.

The last property is required to defend against traitors leaking their key materials which we will discuss more in Chapter 4.

In general, we will represent a subset-cover scheme by a pair $\langle \Phi, \mathbf{Revoke} \rangle$ where $\Phi = \{\mathsf{S_j}\}_{\mathsf{j} \in \mathcal{J}}$ is a fully-exclusive set system defined over $[n]$ that satisfies the above properties. Later in this chapter, we will start designing fully-exclusive set systems that are accompanied with an efficient revocation algorithm. We found imperative to see the set system as a partial order over a 'subset' relation. This will enable us to define a generic revocation algorithm for set systems that satisfy the necessary requirements we put forth. Section 2.4.2 will elaborate on the actual algorithm after we build the necessary notions and definitions in the following section.

2.3 The Key-Poset Framework for Broadcast Encryption

In this section we will introduce an algebraic perspective for the study of broadcast encryption based on exclusive set systems that we call the Key-Poset (KP) framework. Recall that every key in the construction template for broadcast encryption in Figure 2.2 can be viewed as a set of users (the users that own it or can derive it) and thus the set of keys forms a partially ordered set (or poset) which is a sub-poset of the powerset of $\{1, \ldots, N\}$, the set of all users. This is based on the fact that if a user owns (or can derive) a key corresponding to a set of users S it should own (or be able to derive) all keys that dominate S in the key poset.

The rest of the section is structured as follows. In section 2.3.1 we discuss some basic elements of partial order theory that we need. Next we introduce a more careful formalization of the representation of exclusive set families in section 2.3.2. Finally we discuss how the **KeyGen** algorithm can be modified to compress the information in the secret key-material sk_u available to each user $u \in [n]$. We will provide a generic key compression technique over the key-poset in Section 2.3.3 that satisfies the key indistinguishability property described in Definition 2.6.

2.3.1 Viewing Set Systems as Partial Orders

A partial order set (or poset) is a set Φ equipped with a relation $\leq$ that is reflexive, antisymmetric and transitive. A nonempty subset A of a partially ordered set $(\Phi, \leq)$ is called a *directed set* if for any two elements $a, b \in \mathsf{A}$, there exists c in A such that $a \leq c$ and $b \leq c$. It is called a *lower set* if for every $x \in \mathsf{A}$, $y \leq x$ implies that y is in A. An *atom* in a poset Φ is an element that is minimal among all elements. A poset would be called *atomistic* if $x \nleq y$ implies that there is an atom a such that $a \leq x$ and $a \nleq y$.

A nonempty subset I of a partially ordered set $(\Phi, \leq)$ is called an *ideal* if I is lower and directed. The smallest ideal that contains a given element p if it exists is called a principal ideal and p is said to be a principal element of the ideal in this case. The principal ideal $\downarrow p$ for a principal p is thus given by $\downarrow p = \{x \in P \mid x \leq p\}$.

The dual notion of ideal, the one obtained in the reverse partial order, is called a *filter*. We define $\mathsf{F}(x)$ as the set of elements $\{a \in \Phi : x \leq a\}$. It is not hard to prove that $\mathsf{F}(x)$ constitutes a filter. We call $\mathsf{F}(x)$ an *atomic filter* if x is an atom. We also denote by P_x the complement of $\mathsf{F}(x)$ in $(\Phi, \leq)$, i.e., $\mathsf{P}_x = \Phi \setminus \mathsf{F}(x)$.

A useful observation is the following :

Lemma 2.9. *For any atom u in a poset Φ it holds that P_u is a lower set.*

Proof. Let $x, y \in \Phi$ with $y \in \mathsf{P}_u$ and $x \leq y$. Suppose that $x \notin \mathsf{P}_u$, i.e., it must be the case that $x \in \mathsf{F}(u)$, i.e., $u \leq x$. By transitivity we have that $u \leq y$ and as a result $y \in \mathsf{F}(u)$, a contradiction. It follows $x \in \mathsf{P}_u$. ■

The following definition will be an essential tool in our exposition.

Definition 2.10. *Given a nonempty subset A of a finite atomistic partially ordered set $(\Phi, \leq)$ that is a lower set, we say $\langle \mathsf{M}_1, \mathsf{M}_2, \ldots, \mathsf{M}_k \rangle$ is a* lower-maximal partition *of A if*

1. *$\emptyset \neq \mathsf{M}_i \subseteq \mathsf{A}$ is a lower set for $i = 1, \ldots, k$.*
2. *for all i, i', $(i \neq i') \rightarrow \mathsf{M}_i \not\subseteq \mathsf{M}_{i'}$.*
3. *M_i is maximal with respect to A, i.e., for all $a \in \mathsf{M}_i$ if $\exists b \in \mathsf{A}$ s.t $a \leq b$, then $b \in \mathsf{M}_i$.*
4. *k is the largest integer such that all the above hold.*

The order of a lower set A is defined as the size of its lower-maximal partition. We denote the order by $\mathsf{ord}(\mathsf{A})$.

We next prove some properties of the lower-maximal partition of a lower set; we start with a preparatory lemma.

Lemma 2.11. *Let A be a lower set. The set of all subsets of A that are lower and maximal with respect to A is closed under intersection and set subtraction. Specifically, if $\mathsf{M}_1, \mathsf{M}_2 \subseteq \mathsf{A}$ are two lower sets that are maximal with respect to A then the sets $\mathsf{M}_1 \cap \mathsf{M}_2$, $\mathsf{M}_1 \setminus \mathsf{M}_2$ are also lower and maximal with respect to A.*

Proof. Consider the set $\mathsf{M}_1 \cap \mathsf{M}_2$. It is easy to see that it is a lower set as an intersection of lower sets. Further, if there is some $b \in \mathsf{A}$ with $a \in \mathsf{M}_1 \cap \mathsf{M}_2$ and $a \leq b$ it follows that b must belong to both M_1 and M_2 due to the maximality of those sets with respect to A. As a result $\mathsf{M}_1 \cap \mathsf{M}_2$ is also maximal with respect to A. Now consider $\mathsf{D} = \mathsf{M}_1 \setminus \mathsf{M}_2$. Let $b \in \mathsf{D}$ and $a \in \Phi$ such that $a \leq b$. We will show that $a \in \mathsf{D}$. First observe that due to the fact that M_1 is lower we have that $a \in \mathsf{M}_1$. Second, if $a \in \mathsf{M}_2$ then it follows that $b \in \mathsf{M}_2$ by the maximality of M_2 with respect to A. This is a contradiction as a result $a \in \mathsf{D}$. This proves that D is a lower set.

We next show that D is maximal with respect to A. Let $a \in \mathsf{D}$ and some $b \in \mathsf{A}$ with $a \leq b$. We will show that $b \in \mathsf{D}$. First observe that $b \in \mathsf{M}_1$ due to the maximality of M_1. On the other hand, if it is the case that $b \in \mathsf{M}_2$ we would have that $a \in \mathsf{M}_2$ due to the fact that M_2 is lower, a contradiction. It follows that that $b \in \mathsf{D}$ and as a result D is maximal with respect to A. ■

Proposition 2.12. *For any lower set* A, *the sets* $\mathsf{M}_1, \ldots, \mathsf{M}_k$ *in the lower-maximal partition of* A *form a* partition *of* A, *i.e., they are disjoint and their union covers* A.

Proof. Regarding disjointness, suppose, without loss of generality, that $\mathsf{M}_1 \cap \mathsf{M}_2$ is a non-empty proper subset of M_1 and M_2. Consider, now, the collection $(\mathsf{M}_1 \cap \mathsf{M}_2), \mathsf{M}_1 \setminus \mathsf{M}_2, \mathsf{M}_2 \setminus \mathsf{M}_1, \mathsf{M}_3 \setminus (\mathsf{M}_1 \cap \mathsf{M}_2), \ldots, \mathsf{M}_k \setminus (\mathsf{M}_1 \cap \mathsf{M}_2)$; observe that all these sets are lower and maximal with respect to A in the light of lemma 2.11. It is easy to see that this collection of subsets also satisfies the requirements of the lower-maximal partition and it is a contradiction as it has $k+1$ elements.

Consider now $a \in \mathsf{A}$ an atom. Suppose that no set in the lower-maximal partition $\mathsf{M}_1, \ldots, \mathsf{M}_k$ contains it. We will derive a contradiction.

We define a *zig-zag* path towards a to be a vector of elements $\langle x_1, \ldots, x_t \rangle$ from A such that $x_1 = a$, and $x_1 \leq x_2, x_2 \geq x_3, x_3 \leq x_4, \ldots$. Consider the set $\mathsf{M} = \{x \mid \exists \text{ zig-zag path } \langle x_1, \ldots, x_t \rangle : (x_1 = a) \wedge (x_t = x)\}$. This set is lower : suppose $x \leq y$ with $y \in \mathsf{M}$. Note that $x \in \mathsf{A}$ due to the fact that A is lower. Consider the zig-zag path, $\langle y_1, \ldots, y_t \rangle$ with $y_1 = a$ and $y_t = y$. If $y_{t-1} \leq y_t = y$ then x can extend the zig-zag path and thus $x \in \mathsf{M}$. If $y_{t-1} \geq y_t$ we have by transitivity that also $y_{t-1} \geq x$ and thus $\langle y_1, \ldots, y_{t-1}, x \rangle$ is a zig-zag path that shows $x \in \mathsf{M}$.

Consider some $y \in \mathsf{A}$ with $x \leq y$ and $x \in \mathsf{M}$. As before, given the zig-zag path $\langle x_1, \ldots, x_t = x \rangle$ we have that if $x_{t-1} \geq x$ we can extend the zig-zag path to y. On the other hand, if $x_{t-1} \leq x$ we have by transitivity that $x_{t-1} \leq y$ and again we obtain a zig-zag path to y. This shows that $y \in \mathsf{M}$ and that M is maximal with respect to A.

Obviously M is non-empty (it contains at least a) and it is a subset of A. Moreover, it cannot be the subset of any of $\mathsf{M}_1, \ldots, \mathsf{M}_k$ (that as none of these sets contain a). Suppose now that for some i it holds that $\mathsf{M}_i \subseteq \mathsf{M}$. This means that for any $b \in \mathsf{M}_i$ we can find a zig-zag path to a, i.e., there is $\langle x_1, \ldots, x_t \rangle$ with $x_1 = a$ and $x_t = b$. Suppose that $b = x_t \geq x_{t-1}$. Due to the fact that M_i is lower we obtain that $x_{t-1} \in \mathsf{M}_i$. On the other hand, if $b = x_t \leq x_{t-1}$ we have that due to the fact that M_i is maximal with respect to A it holds that $x_{t-1} \in \mathsf{M}_i$. Repeating this argument along the zig-zag path shows that $a \in \mathsf{M}_i$ which is a contradiction. It follows that it cannot be the case that M_i is covered with M.

Based on the above we conclude that $\mathsf{M}, \mathsf{M}_1, \ldots, \mathsf{M}_k$ satisfies the properties of a lower maximal partition with length longer than k, a contradiction. Therefore all the atoms of A are included in the union of $\mathsf{M}_1, \ldots, \mathsf{M}_k$. ■

The lower-maximal partition of a lower set is uniquely determined as we show next.

Theorem 2.13. *Any lower set* A *of poset* $(\Phi, \leq)$ *has a unique lower-maximal partition.*

Proof. Theorem 2.13 Suppose that A has two different lower-maximal partitions, i.e. $\langle \mathsf{M}_1, \ldots, \mathsf{M}_k \rangle = \langle \mathsf{M}'_1, \ldots, \mathsf{M}'_{k'} \rangle$ are satisfying the conditions listed in Definition 2.10. Note first that it must be $k = k'$ due to the fact that k, k' are both the largest integers that satisfy the first three conditions, thus the order of A is unique.

Suppose now that there is a set M'_j that is not equal to any of $\mathsf{M}_1, \ldots, \mathsf{M}_k$. Without loss of generality let us consider $j = 1$. Consider the sets $\mathsf{L}_i = \mathsf{M}_i \cap \mathsf{M}'_1$ and $\mathsf{D}_i = \mathsf{M}'_1 \setminus \mathsf{M}_i$. If there is some i for which it holds that both $\mathsf{L}_i, \mathsf{D}_i$ are non empty then we derive a contradiction as we could form a lower-maximal partition longer than k. Indeed, say this holds for $i = 1$, then the collection $\mathsf{L}_1, \mathsf{D}_1, \mathsf{M}'_2 \setminus \mathsf{L}_1, \ldots, \mathsf{M}'_k \setminus \mathsf{L}_1$ satisfies the properties (1-3) of a lower-maximal partition and has $k + 1$ subsets.

It follows that for all i, either there is no intersection between M_i and M'_1 or M'_1 is a strict subset of M_i. Suppose that there is an i for which M'_1 is a strict subset of M_i. This means that there is some atom $a \in \mathsf{M}_i$ for which it holds that it is not in M'_1. Indeed, for the sake of contradiction, suppose that all atoms of M_i are in M'_1. Then if $x \in \mathsf{M}_i$, by the fact that M_i is lower, we can build a chain connecting x to an atom of M_i, which is also an atom of M'_1 and by the fact that M'_1 is maximal with respect to A we have that $x \in \mathsf{M}'_1$, i.e., $\mathsf{M}'_1 = \mathsf{M}_i$, a contradiction to the fact that the former is a strict subset. We derive from this that there is some other set M'_j that includes those atoms of M_i that are excluded from M'_1. Then, it follows that $\mathsf{M}'_j \cap \mathsf{M}_i$ is a strict non-empty subset of M_i and we can apply the same reasoning as before to derive a longer lower-maximal partition. This is a contradiction and as a result it cannot be that there is some i for which M'_1 is a strict subset of M_i. It follows that for all i, M'_1 has no intersection with M_i which is also a contradiction as some overlap is guarranteed by the fact that M'_1 is a non-empty lower set that must contain at least one atom of A. This contradiction is against our initial assumption that there is a set among $\mathsf{M}'_1, \ldots \mathsf{M}'_k$ that is not equal to any of $\mathsf{M}_1, \ldots, \mathsf{M}_k$. From this we derive the equality of the two lower-maximal partitions. ∎

In the context of broadcast encryption we will restrict our attention to finite and atomistic posets. In this domain it is easy to see that all ideals have a single maximal element and thus are principal. Further observe that for any ideal I it holds that $\mathsf{ord}(\mathsf{I}) = 1$. Indeed, if it happens that we have a lower maximal partition $\mathsf{M}_1, \ldots, \mathsf{M}_k$ of I with $k > 1$, for any two elements $a \in \mathsf{M}_1, b \in \mathsf{M}_2$ it holds that $a \leq m$ and $b \leq m$ where m is the maximal element of I. Due to the maximality of $\mathsf{M}_1, \mathsf{M}_2$ with respect to I we also obtain that $m \in \mathsf{M}_1 \cap \mathsf{M}_2$. But due to the fact that M_2 is lower it also holds that

$a \in \mathsf{M}_2$. It follows $\mathsf{M}_1 \subseteq \mathsf{M}_2$ a contradiction. It follows that I has as a lower maximal partition just itself.

It is interesting to note though that $\mathsf{ord}(\mathsf{A}) = 1$ is not a sufficient condition to make A an ideal. This is due to the fact that the directed property is not implied by $\mathsf{ord}(\mathsf{A}) = 1$.

In the definition below we define the set of maximal elements of a subset A of a poset.

Definition 2.14. *Given a nonempty subset* A *of a partially ordered set* $(\Phi, \leq)$ *we say* $\langle \mathtt{m}_1, \ldots, \mathtt{m}_k \rangle$ *is the set of* maximal-elements *of* A *if the following holds:*

1. $\mathtt{m}_i \in \mathsf{A}$ *for* $i = 1, \ldots, k$.
2. *For any* $\mathtt{a} \in \mathsf{A}, i \in \{1, \ldots, k\}$, *it holds that either* $\mathtt{a} \leq \mathtt{m}_i$ *or it is not possible to compare* $\mathtt{a}$ *with* $\mathtt{m}_i$.

We will denote the number of maximal-subsets of a lower set A *by* $\mathsf{maxnum}(\mathsf{A})$ *(the maximal-order of* A*).*

We next prove an important property elaborating on the relations between the maximal elements of a lower set with an order 1 : a maximal element in such a lower set can not be disjoint from other maximal elements.

Lemma 2.15. *Given that* $\langle \mathtt{m}_1, \ldots, \mathtt{m}_k \rangle$ *is the set of maximal elements of a lower set* A *that satisfies* $\mathsf{ord}(\mathsf{A}) = 1$, *for each* $\mathtt{m}_i$ *there exists another maximal element* $\mathtt{m}_j$ *that they share a common atom, i.e. there exists an atom* $a \in \mathsf{A}$ *such that* $a \leq \mathtt{m}_i$ *and* $a \leq \mathtt{m}_j$ *hold.*

Proof. of Lemma 2.15: Consider now a maximal element $\mathtt{m}_i$ and suppose that $\mathtt{m}_i$ does not share a common atom with any other maximal element. We will derive a contradiction.

We denote the set of atoms dominated by $\mathtt{m}_i$ by A_i. Consider the set $\mathsf{D} = \{\mathtt{b} \in \mathsf{A} \mid \exists a \in A_i \text{ s.t. } a \leq \mathtt{b}\}$.

The set D is lower: suppose $x \leq y$ with $y \in \mathsf{D}$. We will first prove that $y \leq \mathtt{m}_i$. Suppose the converse is true, $y \not\leq m_i$ and recall that atomicity implies that there exists an atom a with $a \leq y$ and $a \not\leq \mathtt{m}_i$. We know that there exists a maximal element $\mathtt{m}_j$ such that $y \leq \mathtt{m}_j$. Hence, we obtain $\mathtt{m}_j \in \mathsf{D}$ which is a contradiction with the fact that $\mathtt{m}_i$ shares no common element with any other maximal element. Given now that $y \leq m_i$, we have by transitivity that also $x \leq \mathtt{m}_i$. This implies that there is an atom $a \in A_i$ such that $a \leq x$, i.e. $x \in \mathsf{D}$.

We next show that the set D is maximal with respect to A. Consider some $y \in \mathsf{A}$ with $x \leq y$ and $x \in \mathsf{D}$. Since $x \in \mathsf{D}$ then there exists an atom $a \in A_i$ with $a \leq x$ and by transitivity we have $a \leq y$. This shows that $y \in \mathsf{D}$ and thus D is maximal with respect to A.

Now it holds that trivially, A is lower and maximal with respect to itself and thus by Lemma 2.11 we have that $\mathsf{A} \setminus \mathsf{D}$ is a lower set and maximal with respect to set A. Then, the pair $\langle \mathsf{D}, \mathsf{A} \setminus \mathsf{D} \rangle$ satisfies the properties (1-3) of a lower maximal partition which contradicts with the fact that $\mathsf{ord}(\mathsf{A}) = 1$. ■

The following proposition sets the stage for our investigation of fully exclusive set systems as posets.

Proposition 2.16. *Any fully-exclusive set system $\Phi \subseteq 2^{[n]}$ forms a finite atomistic poset ordered by subset inclusion whose ideals are all principal.*

Proof. Proposition 2.16 Suppose that $\Phi = \{\mathsf{S_j}\}_{\mathsf{j} \in \mathcal{J}}$. Φ indeed forms a poset ordered by subset inclusion as the reflexive, antisymmetric and transitive properties hold for subset inclusion. This poset would be atomistic due to the fact that Φ is a fully-exclusive set system, i.e. any user, itself, should be a valid subset in the set system which is equivalent to a corresponding atom. Consider any lower-directed set (an ideal) I of Φ, this ideal would have a single maximal element. This maximal element, itself, is a subset S in Φ, and the ideal I would be the smallest ideal that contains S. Hence, any ideal I turns out to be a principal ideal. ■

A useful observation we make finally is that in a fully exclusive set system disjoint ideals are made out of disjoint sets of atoms.

Lemma 2.17. *Consider any two disjoint ideals $\mathsf{I}_1, \mathsf{I}_2$ of a fully exclusive set system Φ. It holds for any $\mathsf{S}_1 \in \mathsf{I}_1$ and $\mathsf{S}_2 \in \mathsf{I}_2$ that $\mathsf{S}_1 \cap \mathsf{S}_2 = \emptyset$.*

Proof. Lemma 2.17 Suppose the converse; i.e. $u \in \mathsf{S}_1 \cap \mathsf{S}_2$. Because Φ forms a finite atomistic poset, there exists an atom corresponding to the element u. That atom is subset of both S_1 and S_2, thus, it is an element of both ideals due to the lower property. This contradicts with the definition of being disjoint. ■

In general we may use the notation Φ to refer the corresponding poset $(\Phi, \subseteq)$ interchangeably depending on the context. Similarly, we use the term "subset" in a set system interchangeably with the term "node" or member in the poset. When drawing diagrams of posets, we will always draw the transitive-reduction of the key-poset unless stated otherwise.

2.3.2 Computational Specification of Set Systems

So far we have avoided explaining what is the exact data structure that represents a set system Φ. While it is possible to think of a representation of Φ as a collection of sets this is not the most efficient way that an algorithm can interact with Φ. Representing an explicit data structure that packages Φ will help in the design as well as the exact complexity analysis of the algorithms that operate on a set system.

The formal specification of a set system Φ that we lay out below is comprised by six basic functions. Henceforth it will be possible to design algorithms that employ these basic functions in black-box fashion and hence they can be "family-independent."

Definition 2.18. *A collection of families Φ parameterized by n is defined by six algorithms* (**tst**, **mbr**, **slo**, **sbs**, **cvr**, **spt**) *and a constant* **cvm**, *a finite alphabet and a length function* $\mathsf{l}(\cdot)$. *Each element of Φ is encoded over the alphabet with length of at most $\mathsf{l}(n)$ where n is the number of users, and we denote the set of encodings by $\mathcal{J}$. Below the input s is thought to be a string of length at most $\mathsf{l}(N)$. The algorithms are defined as follows.*

1. **tst**: *(Encoding Testing); given s, returns 1 if s is a valid encoding of a member of Φ or 0 otherwise, i.e. returns 1 if $s \in \mathcal{J}$ or 0 otherwise.*
2. **mbr**: *(Membership Testing); given (s, u) returns 1 if u belongs to the set encoded by s, 0 otherwise.*
3. **slo**: *(Outside Selection); given a list of $\{s_1, s_2, \ldots s_r\} \subseteq \Phi$ it returns an element u outside of the union of the sets encoded by $\{s_1, s_2, \ldots s_r\}$ or $\perp$ if no such element exists.*
4. **sbs**: *(Inclusion Testing); given (s, s') returns 1 if and only if s is a subset of s'.*
5. **cvr**: *(Parent Finding); given (s, i) for $i \leq$ **cvm**, it returns a parent s' of s, i.e., an s' such that $sbs(s, s') = 1$ and there exists no s'' such that $\mathbf{sbs}(s, s'') = \mathbf{sbs}(s'', s') = 1$ holds. There are possibly up to* **cvm** *parents of s; the index i refers to a specific parent according to some order.*

   We also assume that $\mathbf{cvr}(s, j) = \perp$ if no j-th parent of s exists. For convenience we will also assume if $\mathbf{cvr}(s, i), \mathbf{cvr}(s, j)$ are both defined it holds $|\mathbf{cvr}(s, i)| \geq |\mathbf{cvr}(s, j)|$ for $i \leq j$, i.e., the parents are ordered from larger to smaller.
6. **spt**: *(Split Finding); given s it returns a pair (s', s'') such that the union of the subsets represented by s', s'' is equal to the subset represented by s and s', s'' are disjoint. If s is an atom it returns $\perp$.*

We say that a family Φ is efficient if $\mathsf{l}(n)$ is polylogarithmic in n and the above six algorithms are polynomial-time.

The split finding algorithm cited above is not needed for the purpose of broadcast encryption but it will become handy for traitor tracing something we will elaborate on in Chapter 4. In some set systems we note that splitting may return more than 2 subsets. We give the computational specification of various collections Φ for existing subset cover schemes in Section 2.5.

2.3.3 Compression of Key Material

In this section we will focus on the issue of key assignment and perform a closer examination of how **KeyGen** can be designed to improve its key storage characteristics. This is an important aspect that also has a bearing in the design of the underlying set systems. So far we have considered $\mathsf{BE}^{\Phi}_{\mathtt{basic}}$, where each subset in the set system has a unique key selected independently. This means that for each user u, for which we have $\mathsf{K}_u = \{k_\mathsf{j} \mid \mathsf{j} \in \mathcal{J}_u\}$ and $\mathcal{J}_u := \{\mathsf{j} \mid u \in \mathsf{S}_\mathsf{j}\}$, the user needs to store all the k_j keys in a resulting key vector of length $|\mathcal{J}_u|$. This approach provides the key-indistinguishability property perfectly as we have seen in Proposition 2.7.

Nevertheless, there are advantages in employing large set systems that exhibit tradeoffs betwen the communication overhead and the number of subsets a user belongs to. In such case, it can easily become very uneconomical to follow the independent key assignment approach above. For this reason we will see alternative strategies that enable the receiver to compress the key material. The compression mechanisms we are interested in should facilitate the selective decompression of the needed keys on the fly.

In this section, we will give a general key material compression technique that works for any set system. In a nutshell, the technique works as follows: some "select" subsets are assigned keys independently while the keys of the remaining subsets are derivable through computations employing the keys of the select subsets. The challenge that immediately springs up with this methodology is to ensure that key-indistinguishability is preserved.

Next we describe the compression technique in more detail. We will split the key poset into a *forest* $\mathcal{F}$ of "upward" looking trees so that the root of any tree is the smallest subset compared to the other subsets in its tree in the poset partial order. Hence, keys in each tree of $\mathcal{F}$ are supersets of the root and any path of the tree from root to leaf is a chain of the underlying poset Φ. In each tree the keys will be dependent and in particular any key that corresponds to a node in a tree would be derivable from the key of any ancestral node.

From the receiver perspective, a receiver u should be capable of computing the keys of the subsets in the filter $\mathsf{F}(u)$, i.e., all those subsets that contain u. It follows that u would need to store all the keys of the roots of the trees in the intersection forest $\mathcal{F} \cap \mathsf{F}(u)$ (by slightly abusing notation whenever $\mathcal{F}$ is a forest and A is a set of nodes, we denote $\mathcal{F} \cap A$ as the forest that is derived from $\mathcal{F}$ after removing any node that is not in A). It is clear that u will be able to derive any key in its filter from the keys given to it. But to preserve key-indistinguishability, we need to employ a suitable cryptographic primitive for deriving keys. We define this next.

Definition 2.19. *Let* K *be a key space and* $c \in \mathbb{N}$. *We say that the function* $\mathsf{f}_c : \mathsf{K} \mapsto \mathsf{K}^c$ *is a c-fold key-extender with* ε*-insecurity if any polynomial-time test exhibits statistical distance at most* ε *between the distribution* $\mathsf{f}_c(k)$ *and the distribution* $\langle k_1, \ldots, k_c\rangle$ *where* $k, k_1, \ldots, k_c$ *are random variables uniformly distributed over* K.

Note that K would be typically the set of all bitstrings of a particular length so a key-extender in such case would be a *pseudorandom bit sequence generator* that extends its seed by a multiplicative factor of c.

We next give the definition of a *key-forest* which is a partition of the set system Φ in a set of trees, i.e., a forest.

Definition 2.20. *Given a set system Φ, we say that $\mathcal{F} = \{\mathsf{F}_1, \ldots, \mathsf{F}_v\}$ is a key-forest of Φ if*

1. *F_i is a rooted directed tree for $i = 1, \ldots, k$ following the superset relation. Specifically if S_1 is a descendant of S_2 in F_i, it holds that $\mathsf{S}_1 \subset \mathsf{S}_2$; further, F_i is connected and there are no cycles in F_i, i.e., there are no nodes $\mathsf{S}_1, \mathsf{S}_2, \mathsf{S}_3, \mathsf{S}_4 \in \mathsf{F}_i$ with $\mathsf{S}_1 \subset \mathsf{S}_2$, $\mathsf{S}_1 \subset \mathsf{S}_3$ and $\mathsf{S}_2 \subset \mathsf{S}_4$, $\mathsf{S}_3 \subset \mathsf{S}_4$.*
2. *Any subset $\mathsf{S} \in \Phi$ belongs to exactly one tree F_i for some $i \in \{1, \ldots, k\}$.*

We say the key-forest $\mathcal{F}_\Phi$ is of degree c if it consists of trees whose nodes have degree strictly less than c.

We next give the definition for the broadcast encryption scheme $\mathsf{BE}^{\Phi}_{\mathcal{F},\mathsf{f_c}}$ that demonstrates the key compression strategy that employs a key-forest $\mathcal{F}$ of degree c and a key-extender $\mathsf{f_c} : \mathsf{K} \mapsto \mathsf{K}^c$. We use the notation $\mathsf{f}^i_{\mathsf{c}}(k)$ to denote the i-th block of $\mathsf{f_c}(k)$ for $0 < i \leq c$.

Definition 2.21. *The scheme $\mathsf{BE}^{\Phi}_{\mathcal{F},\mathsf{f_c}}$ where $\mathcal{F}$ is a key-forest $\langle \mathsf{F}_1, \ldots, \mathsf{F}_v \rangle$ and $\mathsf{f_c}$ is a key-extender follows the template of Figure 2.2 with the following modifications:*

1. *Each subset $\mathsf{S_j} \in \Phi$ is associated with a local $l_\mathsf{j} \in \mathsf{K}$ as well as a key k_j. It holds that $k_\mathsf{j} = \mathsf{f}^c_{\mathsf{c}}(l_\mathsf{j})$.*
2. *If it happens that $\mathsf{S_{j_1}}$ is the v-th child of $\mathsf{S_{j_0}}$ in a tree F_i it holds that $l_{\mathsf{j_1}} = \mathsf{f}^v_{\mathsf{c}}(l_{\mathsf{j_0}})$.*
3. *During the execution of* **KeyGen** *only the values l_j for which $\mathsf{S_j}$ is a tree-root in are selected independently at random from K. The remaining values determined based on $\mathsf{f_c}$ as defined in item 2.*
4. *The secret-key sk_u is defined as $(\mathcal{J}^{\mathcal{F}}_u, \mathsf{K}^{\mathcal{F}}_u)$ where $\mathcal{J}^{\mathcal{F}}_u$ contains those indices j that are tree roots in the intersection forest $\mathcal{F} \cap \mathsf{F}(u)$. $\mathsf{K}^{\mathcal{F}}_u = \{k_\mathsf{j} \mid \mathsf{j} \in \mathcal{J}^{\mathcal{F}}_u\}$.*
5. *During decryption a user will need to recover the key of some subset $\mathsf{S} \in \mathsf{F}(u)$. If it happens that S is a tree-root in $\mathcal{F} \cap \mathsf{F}(u)$ then u has the key. Otherwise it can derive it as follows. Denote the path to S from the root as follows $(\mathsf{S_{j_0}}, \mathsf{S_{j_1}}, \ldots, \mathsf{S_{j_m}} = \mathsf{S})$ for some integer m. Assume that $\mathsf{S_{j_i}}$ is the c_i-th child of the subset $\mathsf{S_{j_{i-1}}}$ for $1 \leq i \leq m$. The local l_{j_m} assigned to the subset S can be derived from $l_{\mathsf{j_0}}$ by successive applications of $\mathsf{f_c}(\cdot)$. More specifically, $l_{\mathsf{j}_m} = \mathsf{f}^{c_m}_{\mathsf{c}}(\mathsf{f}^{c_{m-1}}_{\mathsf{c}} \ldots \mathsf{f}^{c_1}_{\mathsf{c}}(l_{\mathsf{j_0}}))$. Finally the key k_{j_m} can be computed as $\mathsf{f}^c_{\mathsf{c}}(l_{\mathsf{j}_m})$.*

Obviously the above methodology will impact the time required to derive any key that is assigned to a subset that a user belongs to. The compression technique defined above has a computational overhead that is bounded by the height of the underlying key-forest. Indeed, in the worst case, any user would have to compute as many applications of $\mathsf{f_c}$ as the height of the tallest tree to derive a key at the leaf-level. The maximum key-storage on the other hand is the number of trees in the forest $\max_{u\in[n]}(|\mathcal{F}\cap \mathsf{F}(u)|)$ and thus it depends on the structure of the key-poset and the choice of $\mathcal{F}$.

Note that, if the key-forest of a set system consists of single nodes, i.e. any node in the key-poset defines a tree of size 1, the key compression procedure defined above would yield an independent key for each subset, i.e. all subsets are assigned unique keys randomly and independently from each other (and in essence no compression would be achieved in this case).

Illustration.

Below we present an illustration of our key-compression strategy. Consider the set system Φ of figure 2.6(a). In this system that applies to 4 users there is a total of 11 encryption key (one for each subset) and it is possible to transmit to any subset of users using just two ciphertexts. Following an independent key assignment as the one suggested in the basic scheme $\mathsf{BE}^{\Phi}_{\mathtt{basic}}$ we will require from each user the storage of 5 keys. Consider now the forest $\mathcal{F}$ given in figure 2.6(b). This forest has 5 trees (two of height 2 and 3 of height 0); it is a degree 3 forest. Using the key assignment of $\mathsf{BE}^{\Phi}_{\mathcal{F},\mathsf{f}_c}$ we have that each user would need to store at most 3 keys.

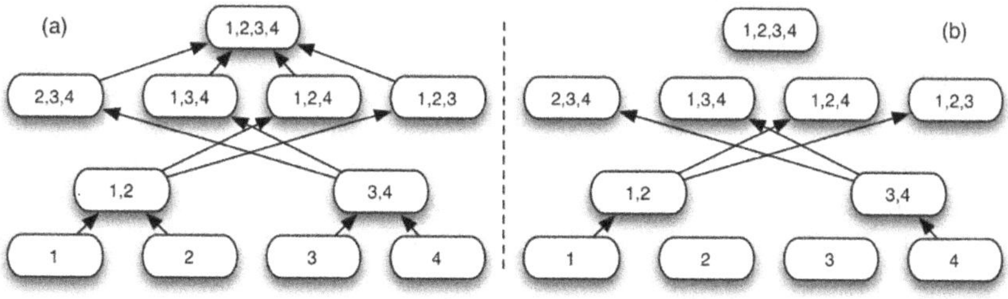

Fig. 2.6. An illustration of the key-compression strategy.

More specifically, observe that based on the key compression strategy on the given forest, we will choose at random the labels $l_{\{1\}}, l_{\{2\}}, l_{\{3\}}, l_{\{4\}}, l_{\{1,2,3,4\}}$. The remaining labels will be calculated based on a key-extender function f_3. User 2, for example, will receive the following data as her key material $l_{\{2\}}, l_{\{1,2\}} = f_3^1(l_{\{1\}}), l_{\{1,2,3,4\}}$. It is easy to see that user 2 based on her information can recover all necessary keys. For example the key of the subset $\{1,2,3\}$ is calculated as $k_{\{1,2,3\}} = f_3^3(f_3^2(l_{\{1,2\}}))$.

We will next prove the key-indistinguishability property (see Definition 2.6) of the key compression technique as given above in Definition 2.21.

Theorem 2.22. *The broadcast encryption* $\mathsf{BE}^{\Phi}_{\mathcal{F},\mathsf{f}_c}$ *satisfies the key indistinguishability property with distinguishing probability* $h_{\mathcal{F}} \cdot \varepsilon$ *where* $\mathcal{F}$ *is a key* *forest over Φ and f_c is a key extender with insecurity ε and $h_{\mathcal{F}}$ is the height of the forest $\mathcal{F}_\Phi$ plus one.*

Proof. We will first show the existence of a family of key generation procedures $\{\mathbf{KeyGen}^{\mathsf{j}}\}_{\mathsf{j}\in\mathcal{J}}$ with the property that for all j, $\mathbf{KeyGen}^{\mathsf{j}}$ selects the j-th key independently at random and it holds that for any probabilistic polynomial-time adversary $\mathcal{A}$, $\mathbf{Adv}_{\mathcal{A}}^{key-ind}(1^n) = |\mathbf{Prob}[\mathbf{Exp}_{\mathcal{A}}^{key-ind}(1^n) = 1] - \frac{1}{2}| \leq h_{\mathcal{F}} \cdot \varepsilon$, where the experiment is defined as in figure 2.4.

We consider a sequence of key generation $\mathbf{KeyGen}_i^{\mathsf{j}}$ procedures that are successive modifications of the way key generation works in the scheme $\mathsf{BE}^{\Phi}_{\mathcal{F},\mathsf{f}_c}$ for $i = 0, \ldots, l$. We first set $\mathbf{KeyGen}_0^{\mathsf{j}}$ to be exactly the key generation $\mathbf{KeyGen}$. The procedure $\mathbf{KeyGen}_1^{\mathsf{j}}$ modifies $\mathbf{KeyGen}_0^{\mathsf{j}}$ by substituting the labels of all level 1 children of the key tree F_j with random values from K while respecting the key derivation method for all remaining keys. Based on the property of the key extender f_c this incurs a distance of at most ε in distinguishing these two key generation algorithms. We continue in the same fashion for procedures $i = 2, \ldots, l, l+1$, following the path from the tree root of F_j to S_j. At each level we incur a distance of at most ε. At procedure $\mathbf{KeyGen}_l^{\mathsf{j}}$ the key k_{j} has been substituted by a random element of K. At last in the final modification, for $l+1$, we substitute the labels of all children of the subset S_j with random values to obtain $\mathbf{KeyGen}^{\mathsf{j}}$. Finally, we have the value k_{j} selected independently at random.

Based on this we derive that the distribution $\mathbf{KeyGen}$ of the scheme $\mathsf{BE}^{\Phi}_{\mathcal{F},\mathsf{f}_c}$ has a distance of at most $h_{\mathcal{F}} \cdot \varepsilon$, from the distribution $\mathbf{KeyGen}^{\mathsf{j}}$ for any j. This proves the fact that for any key indistinguishability adversary $\mathcal{A}$ against the broadcast encryption $\mathsf{BE}^{\Phi}_{\mathcal{F},\mathsf{f}_c}$ where $\mathcal{F}$ is a key forest over Φ and f_c is a key extender with insecurity ε, It holds that $\mathbf{Adv}_{\mathcal{A}}^{key-ind} \leq h_{\mathcal{F}} \cdot \varepsilon$ where $h_{\mathcal{F}}$ is the height of the forest $\mathcal{F}_\Phi$ plus one and $\mathbf{KeyGen}^{\mathsf{j}}$ is defined as above. ■

2.4 Revocation in the Key-Poset Framework

In order for a set system to be suitable for the design template of Figure 2.2 it should have an efficient covering algorithm that can be used for revocation. It follows that any proposal for a set system should be accompanied by a description of how the revocation algorithm works. Instead of treating the design of a fully-exclusive set systems with an efficient revocation algorithm on a case-by-case basis, in this chapter we will introduce an algebraic property that implies the existence of a revocation algorithm that optimally works for any set system that satisfies the property.

This section is structured as follows. In section 2.4.1 we will formalize the revocation problem in the key-poset framework and we will show its relation to a basic problem for a poset called `PatternCover`. We show that revocation is interreducible to `PatternCover` through an algebraic manipulation of the underlying key poset that we introduce called *chopping filters*. This observation is advantageous since in case we can solve `PatternCover` optimally we also have an optimal solution for the revocation problem.

In section 2.4.2, we introduce the property of *factorizability* for posets that characterizes a wide class of key posets for which we can optimally solve `PatternCover`. Specifically, we first observe that if a poset satisfies a property we call *separable* then `PatternCover` can be solved optimally. Building on this simple observation we then define factorizability for posets and we show that the operation of chopping filters when applied to a factorizable poset results to a separable poset. This provides the design of an optimal and efficient revocation algorithm.

2.4.1 Revocation in the key-poset framework: Definitions

Let Φ be a set system over the set $[n]$. Note that since Φ is a fully-exclusive set system, there exists a trivial revocation algorithm that searches for a broadcast pattern that covers $[n] \setminus \mathsf{R}$ in a brute-force manner. Moreover, if one does not wish to spend the time required to brute-force the optimal solution, there is a way to find a feasible cover that consists simply of all the individual elements in the set $[n] \setminus \mathsf{R}$; this is due to the fact that Φ is fully exclusive and thus all singletons should be present in Φ. Clearly these two approaches are undesirable as either inefficient or grossly wasteful in terms of communication overhead. In this section we will be interested in finding the shortest pattern in an efficient way. We will next define the revocation problem formally as the problem of finding a broadcast pattern for a set of enabled users that is minimal in size.

Definition 2.23. `Revocation` *Problem (Optimization Version).*
Input: A fully-exclusive set system Φ over set $[n]$ and a set of users R
Output: A minimal sized set $\mathcal{P} = \{\mathsf{S}_{\mathsf{j}_1}, \ldots, \mathsf{S}_{\mathsf{j}_m}\}$ of disjoint subsets in Φ, such that $[n] \setminus \mathsf{R} = \bigcup_{i=1}^{m} \mathsf{S}_{\mathsf{j}_i}$.

As we will show the revocation problem is a natural extension to the problem of `PatternCover` that we define next. `PatternCover` is the problem of finding an optimal cover for a family Φ.

Definition 2.24. `PatternCover` *Problem (Optimization Version).*
Input: A fully-exclusive set system Φ over set $[n]$
Output: A minimal sized set $\mathcal{P} = \{\mathsf{S}_{\mathsf{j}_1}, \ldots, \mathsf{S}_{\mathsf{j}_m}\}$ of disjoint subsets in Φ, such that $[n] = \bigcup_{i=1}^{m} \mathsf{S}_{\mathsf{j}_i}$.

Hardness of Pattern Cover for General Families.

We next discuss the hardness of `PatternCover` problem in the general case, something that shows that without imposing any special structure on the family there is no way to solve this problem efficiently (and the same would be true for the revocation problem). Specifically we show that `PatternCover` is NP-hard with a reduction from the the Set Cover problem. The difference between the two problems lies on the requirement that the instances of `PatternCover` are fully-exclusive (as opposed to arbitrary in the case of the Set Cover problem) and that they should admit the data structure specification of definition 2.18.

Theorem 2.25. `PatternCover` *is* NP-*hard.*

Proof. We recall that `SetCover` problem is NP-hard, because it is a special case of the `VertexCover` problem which itself is dual to `Clique`. It should be noted that `VertexCover` remains NP-complete even in graphs with node degree at most 3, see [48]. We next outline a reduction of `VertexCover` with node degree at most 3 to `PatternCover` thereby establishing its NP-hardness. Given a graph $G = (V, E)$ with node degree at most 3, Vertex Cover requires a minimal set of vertices $V' \subseteq V$ such that each edge in E is incident to at least one vertex in V'. The decisional version of Vertex Cover is a set of instances of the form $\langle G(V, E), b\rangle$ such that G is a graph with node degree at most 3 and there exists b vertices in V for which any edge in E is incident to one of these b vertices. From such a graph, we construct a fully-exclusive set system Φ over the set of edges E. A subset in Φ consists of edges for which there exists a vertex such that all edges are incident to it. Since nodes in G have degree at most 3, the maximum possible number of subsets in Φ would be $4|V| + |E|$ where each edge itself defines a subset and for any vertex we have at most 4 additional subsets, i.e. all three edges (if exist) incident to this vertex constitute a subset and all three combinations of two out of three edges define another three subsets. It is easy to see that Φ is a fully-exclusive set system. Further, we can describe an algorithmic specification according to Definition 2.18 by enumerating the vertices and defining a $\leq$ relation between the edges according to the vertex enumeration. Finally, we conclude that an optimal solution of the `VertexCover` problem would be interchangeable to an optimal cover in Φ over the set of users E. ■

Chopping Filters.

Despite the fact that revocation appears to be more general than `PatternCover`, we show that the two problems are interreducible. A reduction of `PatternCover` to `Revocation` is immediate (by simply considering $\mathsf{R} = \emptyset$). The other direction is the interesting one. Let us say a user u should be revoked; observe that any subset of Φ that contains u should not be in the cover of the set $\mathsf{N} \setminus \{u\}$. In other terms, finding a cover in Φ for $\mathsf{N} \setminus \{u\}$ is equivalent to finding a cover for $\mathsf{N}' = \mathsf{N} \setminus \{u\}$ in a new family Φ' where Φ' is constructed by deleting all supersets of $\{u\}$ in Φ which amounts to removing from Φ the filter $\mathsf{F}(u)$. To capture this we introduce formally the operation of chopping filters:

Definition 2.26. *Given the family* $\Phi = \{\mathsf{S_j}\}_{\mathsf{j}\in\mathcal{J}}$ *and* $\mathsf{j}_1, \ldots, \mathsf{j}_m \in \mathcal{J}$, *we define the new family* $\mathbf{Chop}(\Phi, \{\mathsf{j}_1, \ldots, \mathsf{j}_m\}) = \Phi \setminus \cup_{i=1}^{m} \mathsf{F}(\mathsf{S}_{\mathsf{j}_i})$; *the specification of its six algorithms is given in Figure 2.7.*

Chop(`Subset Collection` Φ, `list of encodings` $\{\mathsf{j}_1, \ldots, \mathsf{j}_m\}$)
set **cvm** $= \Phi$.**cvm**
return descriptions of (**tst**, **mbr**, **slo**, **sbs**, **cvr**, **spt**) as follows:

Ctst(s)
if (Φ.**tst**(s)=1)
  if (Φ.**sbs**(j_1, s) $= 1 \vee \ldots \vee$ Φ.**sbs**(j_m, s) $= 1$)
    return 0
  else return 1
else 0

Cmbr(s, u)
return Φ.**mbr**(s, u)

Cslo($s_1, \ldots, s_r$)
Let $U = \{u_1, \ldots, u_t\}$ such that $u \in U$ if and only if
u is an atom and there is some $1 \leq i \leq k$, such that $\mathsf{S}_{\mathsf{j}_i} = \{u\}$.
return Φ.**slo**($s_1, \ldots, s_r, u_1, \ldots, u_t$)

Csbs(s, s')
return Φ.**sbs**(s, s')

Ccvr(s, i)
$s' = \Phi$.**cvr**(s, i)
if (**Ctst**(s') $= 1$)
  then output s'
else return $\perp$

Cspt(s)
return Φ.**spt**(s)

Fig. 2.7. The computational description of a chopped family Φ.

It is easy to verify that the transformation pointed above from the family Φ to Φ' can be done in polynomial-time. Moreover if it happens that $\mathsf{S}_{\mathsf{j}_1}, \ldots, \mathsf{S}_{\mathsf{j}_m}$ are atoms, i.e., $\mathsf{S}_{\mathsf{j}_i} = \{u_i\}$ for some $u_i \in [n]$ for each $i = 1, \ldots, m$, it is easy to see that Φ' is fully exclusive over $[n] \setminus \mathsf{R}$ where R is equal to $\{u_1, \ldots, u_m\}$. Consider now an instance $\langle \Phi, [n], \mathsf{R} \rangle$ of the `Revocation` problem; note first that the optimal solution would be covering the set $[n] \setminus \mathsf{R}$. Note also that any subset in the optimal solution is also an element of the subset collection $\Phi' = \Phi \setminus \{\mathsf{S} \in \Phi \mid \mathsf{S} \cap \mathsf{R} \neq \emptyset\}$. Thus, the optimal solution is an optimal solution for the instance $\langle \Phi', [n] \setminus \mathsf{R} \rangle$ of `PatternCover` for the chopped collection Φ'.

Lemma 2.27. *The* `Revocation` *problem is polynomial-time interreducible to the* `PatternCover` *problem.*

Proof. Lemma 2.27 First consider an instance of the `PatternCover` problem, i.e., a fully exclusive set system Φ. We can form an instance of the `Revocation` problem by setting $\mathsf{R} = \emptyset$. It is clear that an optimal solution of this instance translates immediately to an optimal solution of the original `PatternCover` problem.

On the other hand, suppose that we have an instance of the `Revocation` problem, i.e., a fully exclusive set system Φ as well as a set of users R for revocation. We define the chopped family $\Phi' = \Phi \setminus \{\mathsf{S} \in \Phi \mid \mathsf{S} \cap \mathsf{R} \neq \emptyset\}$ as in figure 2.7. The set system Φ' is fully exclusive over $[n] \setminus \mathsf{R}$. An optimal solution of the `PatternCover` instance Φ' would immediately provide an optimal solution of the original `Revocation` problem.

In the next section, we will characterize sufficient algebraic properties of the underlying family Φ for solving the revocation problem optimally.

2.4.2 A sufficient condition for optimal revocation

In this subsection, we will characterize a simple sufficient algebraic property for the underlying set system Φ to have an efficient optimal revocation solution.

We will first focus on solving the `PatternCover` problem. It is easy to see an optimal solution of `PatternCover` problem defined for a set system Φ would consist of maximal subsets in the collection. The set of all maximal subsets might be overlapping, but if the maximal subsets of Φ are disjoint then an optimal solution could be easily found for such set systems. Since each subset has a corresponding principal ideal, we want to formalize the case when there are disjoint maximal subsets in Φ in terms of ideals. We introduce the following notion:

Definition 2.28. *We say a lower set* A *of a poset* Φ *is* separable *if in the lower-maximal partition* $\langle \mathsf{M}_1, \ldots \mathsf{M}_k \rangle$ *of* A *it holds that* M_i *is ideal for* $i = 1, \ldots, k$.

We show next that in a separable family Φ we can easily define an optimal solution for `PatternCover`. Indeed, since all ideals of Φ are principal, finding ideals is equivalent to finding the maximal subsets in Φ. In Figure 2.8 we present an optimal solution for a separable collection Φ; the intuition behind the algorithm is to build one chain for each ideal and use the basic algorithms of the collection to recover the ideals in the lower-maximal partition of Φ.

Theorem 2.29. *Assuming that* Φ *is separable, the algorithm in Figure 2.8 outputs an optimal solution to* `PatternCover` *problem which is of size* $\mathsf{ord}(\Phi)$.

`PatternCover`(Subset Collection Φ)
$\mathcal{P} = \emptyset$
Repeat the following steps until break.
  $u = \Phi.\mathbf{slo}(\mathcal{P})$, let $s = \{u\}$
  if $u = \perp$ then output $\mathcal{P}$ and break.
  Repeat the following steps until s does not change.
    Find $y = \Phi.\mathbf{cvr}(s, i)$ for minimal $i \leq \Phi.\mathbf{cvm}$ such that $y \neq \perp$
     if it exists.
    if $y \neq \perp$ then $s = y$
  $\mathcal{P} = \mathcal{P} \cup s$

Fig. 2.8. A `PatternCover` algorithm that works optimally for separable set systems.

Proof. Theorem 2.29 Note that the algorithm in Figure 2.8, starts from an atom in the poset of subset collection Φ and "grows" the current element until it hits the top of the ideal the selected atom was in. In the next iteration, another atom is selected outside the ideals so far included in the broadcast pattern. These ideals are actually the ones that make up the lower-maximal partition of the set system Φ. Overall, the algorithm will return the set of upper bounds from each ideal, i.e., their principal elements, which result in, of course, the optimal solution with size $\mathsf{ord}(\Phi)$. This is because, the optimal solution requires at least one element from each ideal necessarily. ■

The running time of the algorithm in Figure 2.8 is bounded by the sum of the chains followed by $\Phi.\mathbf{cvr}()$ in each of the ideals that comprise the lower maximal partition of Φ. Typical collections (see next section) have chains of polylogarithmic length in the number of users and thus the running time of the algorithm is quite efficient. The parent finding procedure $\mathbf{cvr}(\cdot, \cdot)$ of the set system plays an important role in this algorithm. Note that the `PatternCover` algorithm looks for a parent with a maximal size out of at most $\Phi.\mathbf{cvm}$ possible choices.

Factorizable Families.

We next introduce a basic property regarding the ideals of a family Φ that will play an important role in solving optimally the revocation problem. Intuitively the factorizable property mandates that the complements of the atomic filters in $(\Phi, \subseteq)$ share some similar properties to prime ideals over rings. We use the notation (S) to denote the principal ideal of $\mathsf{S} \in \Phi$.

Definition 2.30. *A fully-exclusive set system Φ is called* factorizable *if the poset, itself, is separable and for any subset $\mathsf{S} \subseteq \Phi$ and any atom u, it holds that $(\mathsf{S}) \cap \mathsf{P}_u$ is a separable set.*

In the following lemma we present some useful facts about the P_u sets and the factorizable property.

Lemma 2.31. *Let Φ be a factorizable fully exclusive set system defined over $[n]$.*

1. *For any $\mathsf{S} \in \Phi$, it holds that $(\mathsf{S}) = \cap_{u \in [n] \setminus \mathsf{S}} \mathsf{P}_u$.*
2. *For any $\mathsf{S} \in \Phi$, it holds that $\Phi \setminus \mathsf{F}(\mathsf{S}) = \cup_{u \in \mathsf{S}} \mathsf{P}_u$.*
3. *For any $\mathsf{S} \in \Phi$, (S) is a fully exclusive factorizable set system over S.*
4. *For any $u \in [n]$, and a separable set $\mathsf{A} \subseteq \Phi$, the set $\mathsf{P}_u \cap \mathsf{A}$ is separable.*

Proof. Lemma 2.31

1. If a subset $\mathsf{S}_1 \in (\mathsf{S})$, then it holds for any $u \in [n] \setminus \mathsf{S}$ that $\mathsf{S}_1 \in \mathsf{P}_u$; hence $\mathsf{S}_1 \in \cap_{u \in [n] \setminus \mathsf{S}} \mathsf{P}_u$. For the opposite direction, if $\mathsf{S}_2 \in \cap_{u \in [n] \setminus \mathsf{S}} \mathsf{P}_u$, then it holds that $\mathsf{S}_2 \cap ([n] \setminus \mathsf{S}) = \emptyset$; hence $\mathsf{S}_2 \subseteq \mathsf{S}$.
2. If $\mathsf{S}_1 \in \Phi \setminus \mathsf{F}(\mathsf{S})$, then it holds that there exists $u \in \mathsf{S}$ such that $u \notin \mathsf{S}_1$; hence $\mathsf{S}_1 \in \cup_{u \in \mathsf{S}} \mathsf{P}_u$. For the opposite direction, if $\mathsf{S}_2 \in \cup_{u \in \mathsf{S}} \mathsf{P}_u$, then it holds that there exists $u \in \mathsf{S}$ such that $u \notin \mathsf{S}_2$; hence $\mathsf{S}_2 \notin \mathsf{F}(S)$, i.e. $\mathsf{S}_2 \in \Phi \setminus \mathsf{F}(\mathsf{S})$.
3. It is easy to observe that (S) is fully-exclusive over the elements of S. Now consider a subset $\mathsf{S}_1 \in (\mathsf{S})$ and an atom $u \in \mathsf{S}$; we will check the set $(\mathsf{S}_1) \cap \mathsf{P}'_u$, where $\mathsf{P}'_u = (\mathsf{S}) \setminus \mathsf{F}(u)$. First if $u \notin \mathsf{S}_1$ then $(\mathsf{S}_1) \cap \mathsf{P}'_u = (\mathsf{S}_1)$ and we are done since (S_1) is ideal. Now suppose $u \in \mathsf{S}_1$. We will show that $(\mathsf{S}_1) \cap \mathsf{P}'_u = (\mathsf{S}_1) \cap \mathsf{P}_u$ where $\mathsf{P}_u = \Phi \setminus \mathsf{F}(u)$; this will establish that $(\mathsf{S}_1) \cap \mathsf{P}'_u$ is separable. If $\mathsf{S}_2 \in (\mathsf{S}_1) \cap \mathsf{P}'_u$, then it follows that $\mathsf{S}_2 \in (\mathsf{S}_1) \cap \mathsf{P}_u$ as $\mathsf{P}'_u \subseteq \mathsf{P}_u$. For the opposite direction, consider a subset $\mathsf{S}_3 \in (\mathsf{S}_1) \cap \mathsf{P}_u$, then it holds that $\mathsf{S}_3 \in (\mathsf{S}_1) \setminus \mathsf{F}(u) \subseteq \mathsf{P}'_u$; hence $\mathsf{S}_3 \in (\mathsf{S}_1) \cap \mathsf{P}'_u$.
4. Given that A is separable, by definition, the lower-maximal partition of A consists of ideals. We have $\mathsf{A} = \cup_{j=1}^{k} \mathsf{I}_j$. By Lemma 2.17 u belongs to only one of these ideals, say $\{u\} \in \mathsf{I}_s$. Thus, for any $j \neq s, 1 \leq j \leq k$, $\mathsf{I}_j \cap \mathsf{P}_u = \emptyset$. On the other hand, since Φ is factorizable, the lower maximal partition of $\mathsf{I}_s \cap \mathsf{P}_u$ consists of disjoint ideals and thus $\mathsf{P}_u \cap \mathsf{A}$ is a separable set.

■

Interestingly, the property of being factorizable has an alternative characterization that is of a more local nature:

Definition 2.32. *We say a fully-exclusive set system Φ has the diamond property if for any $\mathsf{S}_1, \mathsf{S}_2 \in \Phi$ such that $\mathsf{S}_1 \cap \mathsf{S}_2 \neq \emptyset$, then it holds that $\mathsf{S}_1 \cup \mathsf{S}_2 \in \Phi$.*

We prove the following:

Theorem 2.33. *A fully-exclusive set system Φ that is an ideal satisfies the following: Φ is factorizable if and only if Φ has the diamond property.*

Proof. Theorem 2.33 Suppose that Φ has the diamond property. We will prove that Φ is factorizable by showing that for any ideal I and any atom $u \in \mathsf{I}$, the lower set P_u inside I, i.e. $\mathsf{I} \cap \mathsf{P}_u$, is a separable set. Consider the lower-maximal partition $\langle \mathsf{M}_1, \ldots, \mathsf{M}_k \rangle$ of $\mathsf{I} \cap \mathsf{P}_u$ and suppose the converse is true, $\mathsf{I} \cap \mathsf{P}_u$

is not separable, i.e., there exists $l \in \{1,\ldots,k\}$ for which M_l is not ideal while it holds that $\mathsf{ord}(\mathsf{M}_l) = 1$. In such case M_l fails the directed property i.e., there are at least two elements a, b for which there is no upper bound, i.e., $\mathsf{maxnum}(\mathsf{M}_l) > 1$. Consider the set of maximal elements $\langle \mathtt{m}_1,\ldots,\mathtt{m}_s\rangle$, with $s = \mathsf{maxnum}(\mathsf{M}_l)$, that satisfies the properties (1-2) of Definition 2.14. Lemma 2.15 implies that there exist an index-pair i, j for which $\mathtt{m}_i$ and $\mathtt{m}_j$ share a common atom, i.e. the subsets corresponding to the maximal elements are intersecting. Denoting the subsets by S_i and S_j, we obtain $\mathsf{S} = \mathsf{S}_i \cup \mathsf{S}_j \in \Phi$ due to the diamond property. Observe now that, the node $\mathtt{m}$ corresponding to the subset S dominates exactly the atoms of $\mathtt{m}_i$ and $\mathtt{m}_j$ and hence we have $u \not\leq \mathtt{m}$; as a result $\mathtt{m} \in \mathsf{I} \cap \mathsf{P}_u$. Due to the disjointness of the lower sets in a lower maximal partition, as it is proven in Proposition 2.12, it holds that $\mathtt{m} \in \mathsf{M}_l$. However, this contradicts with the maximality of the elements $\mathtt{m}_i$ and $\mathtt{m}_j$ in M_l since it holds that $\mathtt{m}_i \leq \mathtt{m}$ and $\mathtt{m}_j \leq \mathtt{m}$. This concludes that M_l is an ideal for any $l \in \{1,\ldots,k\}$, hence $\mathsf{I} \cap \mathsf{P}_u$ turns out to be a separable set.

For the opposite direction, suppose that Φ is factorizable but does not satisfy the diamond property. There exists, then, two subsets $\mathsf{S}_1, \mathsf{S}_2$ that are intersecting and $\mathsf{S} = \mathsf{S}_1 \cup \mathsf{S}_2$ does not exist in Φ. Let us denote the nodes within the poset description corresponding to the subsets S_1 and S_2 by $\mathtt{m}_1$ and $\mathtt{m}_2$ respectively. Consider the minimal ideal I in size that contains the set of atoms dominated by $\mathtt{m}_1$ and $\mathtt{m}_2$, i.e., I is the smallest ideal (S') in size such that $(\mathtt{m}_1 \in (\mathsf{S}') \wedge \mathtt{m}_2 \in (\mathsf{S}'))$; denote the principal element of I by $\mathtt{m}$. Since $\mathsf{S} \notin \Phi$, there exists an atom $u \leq \mathtt{m}$ for which we have $u \not\leq \mathtt{m}_1$ and $u \not\leq \mathtt{m}_2$. On the other hand, due to factorizability, $\mathsf{I} \cap \mathsf{P}_u$ is separable, i.e. the lower maximal partition $\langle \mathsf{I}_1,\ldots,\mathsf{I}_s\rangle$, for some $s \in \mathbb{Z}$ of $\mathsf{I} \cap \mathsf{P}_u$ consists of ideals that are strict subsets of I. Recall that the sets in the above lower-maximal partition are disjoint and their union covers the set $\mathsf{I} \cap \mathsf{P}_u$, (see Proposition 2.12); hence given that $\mathsf{S}_1 \cap \mathsf{S}_2 \neq \emptyset$, the nodes $\mathtt{m}_1$ and $\mathtt{m}_2$ are contained in the same ideal I_j for some $j \in \{1,\ldots,s\}$, i.e. $\mathtt{m}_1 \in \mathsf{I}_j \wedge \mathtt{m}_2 \in \mathsf{I}_j$. This contradicts with the assumption on minimality of I. ■

Optimal Solution of Revocation for Factorizable Families.

We are now ready to describe an algorithmic solution for the revocation problem over any factorizable family Φ. Recall the reduction of the revocation problem to the `PatternCover` problem given in lemma 2.27 that was based on chopping a series of atomic filters from Φ. We next prove the following interesting result about factorizable families: the action of chopping atomic filters splits a factorizable family into ideals.

Theorem 2.34. *Given a factorizable set system Φ, let $\Phi' =$ **Chop**$(\Phi, \{\mathsf{j}_1, \mathsf{j}_2, \ldots, \mathsf{j}_r\})$ for a set of elements $\{\mathsf{j}_i\}_{i\in[r]}$ that all encode singleton subsets, i.e., j_i encodes the subset $\{\ell_i\}$ with $\ell_i \in [n]$ for $i = 1,\ldots,r$. Then, it holds that $\Phi' = \cap_{i=1}^{r} \mathsf{P}_{\ell_i}$. Futher, Φ' is separable.*

Proof. Theorem 2.34 We first note that, the set system $\Phi' =$ **Chop**$(\Phi, \{\mathsf{j}_1, \mathsf{j}_2, \ldots, \mathsf{j}_r\})$ corresponds to the partially ordered set $\cap_{i=1}^{r} P_{\ell_i}$ where P_{ℓ_i} is the complement of the atomic filter $\mathsf{F}(\ell_i)$ within the set system Φ. Indeed, if a subset S is an element of Φ', then $\mathsf{S} \cap \{\ell_1, \ldots, \ell_r\} = \emptyset$ which implies that $\mathsf{S} \in \mathsf{P}_{\ell_i}$ for any $1 \leq i \leq r$. Similarly, for any subset S of $\cap_{i=1}^{r} \mathsf{P}_{\ell_i}$ it holds that $\mathsf{S} \in \Phi'$.

We will now prove by induction on r that $\cap_{i=1}^{r} \mathsf{P}_{\ell_i}$ is a separable set. This will show that **Chop**(Φ, $\{\mathsf{j}_1, \mathsf{j}_2, \ldots, \mathsf{j}_r\}$) constitutes a separable set system. The $r = 1$ case can be proved as follows: given that Φ is factorizable, i.e. itself is separable, we obtain that the set $\mathsf{P}_{\ell_1} = \Phi \cap \mathsf{P}_{\ell_1}$ is separable as a consequence of Lemma 2.9 and 2.31(4). Consider now the induction hypothesis that for any $1 \leq s < r$ and $\ell_1, \ldots, \ell_s$, it holds that $\cap_{i=1}^{s} \mathsf{P}_{\ell_i}$ is a separable set. Now, consider r atoms over Φ.

Using the induction hypothesis, the intersection of the complement of atomic filters of the first $r - 1$ atoms will be a separable set, i.e., $\cap_{i=1}^{r-1} \mathsf{P}_{\ell_i} = \mathsf{A}$ where A is a separable set. The Lemma 2.31(4) implies that the intersection of A with P_{ℓ_r} is separable which concludes the statement of the theorem. ■

In light of the Theorems 2.29 and 2.34, the algorithm in Figure 2.9 outputs an optimal solution for the revocation problem for a factorizable set system Φ using the chopping filters operation in conjunction to the **PatternCover** algorithm for separable families.

Revoke(Φ, R)
1. let $\mathsf{R} = \{\ell_1, \ldots, \ell_r\}$ and j_i be the encoding for $\{\ell_i\}$
2. define $\Phi' = $ **Chop**(Φ, $\{\mathsf{j}_1, \ldots, \mathsf{j}_r\}$)
3. output **PatternCover**(Φ')

Fig. 2.9. Optimal Solution for the revocation problem in a factorizable set system.

Theorem 2.35. *Given that the fully-exclusive set system Φ is factorizable, the algorithm in Figure 2.9 outputs an optimal solution for the revocation problem with respect to a set of revoked users $\mathsf{R} = \{\ell_1, \ell_2, \ldots, \ell_r\}$. The number of subsets in the solution will be* $\mathsf{ord}(\cap_{i=1}^{r} \mathsf{P}_{\ell_i})$.

Proof. Theorem 2.35 The proof follows from Theorem 2.34 and the correctness of the `PatternCover` algorithm given in Figure 2.8. As shown in Theorem 2.34, **Chop**(Φ, $\{\mathsf{j}_1, \ldots, \mathsf{j}_r\}$), where j_i is the encoding for the singleton $\{\ell_i\}$, will be set of disjoint principal ideals, thus the optimal solution will consist of those principal elements. Their number will be as many as the number of ideals in $\cap_{i=1}^{r} \mathsf{P}_{\ell_i}$ which is equal to $\mathsf{ord}(\cap_{i=1}^{r} \mathsf{P}_{\ell_i})$. ■

As shown above, for a given factorizable family Φ and a set of users, $\mathsf{R} = \{\ell_1, \ell_2, \ldots, \ell_r\}$, the intersection $\cap_{i=1}^{r} \mathsf{P}_{\ell_i}$ has a lower-maximal partition consisting of disjoint ideals. Their number would equal to the transmission overhead for the ciphertext to be transmitted. We can provide an explicit upper bound for the transmission overhead by providing an upper bound on the size of the lower-maximal partition of $\mathsf{I} \cap \mathsf{P}_u$ for any ideal I and atom u of Φ in terms of the size of ideal I.

Theorem 2.36. *Suppose that a fully-exclusive set system Φ over $[n]$ is factorizable. If for any subset $\mathsf{S} \in \Phi$ and an atom u, it holds that $\mathsf{ord}((\mathsf{S}) \cap \mathsf{P}_u) \leq f$ then for any $\ell_1, \ldots, \ell_r \in [n]$, $\mathsf{ord}(\cap_{i=1}^{r} \mathsf{P}_{\ell_i}) \leq r(f-1)+1$.*

Proof. Theorem 2.36 We consider the successive chopping of filters $\mathsf{F}_{\ell_1}, \ldots, \mathsf{F}_{\ell_r}$ from Φ. Given the factorizability of the family, each chopping operation applies to a specific ideal in the lower-maximal partition. Initially this ideal is Φ, in the second step it is one of the ideals of P_{ℓ_1} and so on. Given that $\mathsf{ord}((\mathsf{S}) \cap \mathsf{P}_u) \leq f$ for any $\mathsf{S} \in \Phi$, we have that at each successive chopping, the ideal that is selected will be removed from the list and at most f ideals would be added. Thus, the total number of ideals at the end will be bounded by $f + (r-1)(f-1) = r \cdot f - r + 1$. ■

2.5 Constructions

In this section we present a series of constructions of broadcast encryption schemes in the key poset framework. In each case we give first a combinatorial description and then we provide the key poset description.

2.5.1 Complete Subtree

The Complete Subtree (CS) is a method that defines a set system over a binary tree where the users are located on the leaves of the tree, and any intermediate node defines a subset in the set system which contains the users placed on the leaves rooted at this node. It is assumed that the number of users n is a power of 2. In this way a set system Φ^{CS} is defined over a user population $[n] = \{1, \ldots, n\}$ that consists of $2n-1$ subsets each corresponding to a node in the full binary tree with n leaves.

Set system description in the KP framework.

We next provide the description of the complete subtree method in the key poset framework. Let $\mathcal{J}^{CS}$ be the set of encodings of subsets in the set system Φ^{CS} defined over the set $\mathsf{N} = \{1, \ldots, n\}$. Recall that for simplicity, we assume that $\log n$ is an integer.

An encoding $\mathsf{j} \in \mathcal{J}^{CS}$ is a binary string of length at most $\log n$. Each such encoding corresponds to an index of a node in a full binary tree where the indices are constructed in a top-down manner: the root of the binary tree is encoded by ϵ (the empty string by ϵ), an index of a left child is constructed by appending '0' to its parent index, while an index of a right child is constructed by appending '1' to its parent index.

1. *Encoding Testing:* $\mathbf{tst}(\mathsf{j})$*; return* 1 *if* $\mathsf{j} = \{0,1\}^s$ *for some* $s \in \{0,1\ldots,\log n\}$.
2. *Membership Testing:* $\mathbf{mbr}(\mathsf{j}, u)$*; if* $\mathsf{j} = \epsilon$ *or* j *is a prefix of* u*, then return 1.*
3. *Outside Selection:* $\mathbf{slo}(\mathsf{j}_1, \mathsf{j}_2, \ldots, \mathsf{j}_r)$*; if* $\mathsf{j}_i = \epsilon$ *for an* $i \le r$ *return* $\bot$*, otherwise compute the mimimal string* s*, that does not have any of* j_i*'s as a prefix. This can be done quite efficiently starting from the most significant bits of the input strings. Then pad the string* s *with* 0 *and* 1*'s arbitrarily to prepare a string* u *of length* $\log n$*; output* u.
4. *Inclusion Testing:* $\mathbf{sbs}(\mathsf{j}, \mathsf{j}')$*; if* j' *is a prefix of* j *then return 1.*
5. *Parent Finding:* $\mathbf{cvr}(\mathsf{j}, i)$*; if* $i \neq 1$ *then return* $\bot$*. Otherwise, given that* $\mathsf{j} = \mathsf{j}'b$ *for* $b \in \{0,1\}$*, output* j'.
6. *Split Finding:* $\mathbf{spt}(\mathsf{j})$*; if* $|\mathsf{j}| < \log n$ *then return the subset pair* $(\mathsf{j}0, \mathsf{j}1)$ *else return* $\bot$.

It is straightforward to see that the complete subtree family as defined above is efficient.

The key-forest for compression.

The key forest $\mathcal{F}_{CS}$ used for compression is defined trivially by having trees of size one, i.e., each node constitutes a tree by itself and thus there is no compression. Hence, the key-handling procedure of Definition 2.21 would essentially yield a information theoretical key-assignment where each subset is assigned a unique key randomly and independently. It is not hard to observe that there is no possible way to derive a better strategy in this case : indeed any upward looking tree in the complete subtree poset needs to be a single node.

The factorizability of the complete subtree set system.

We see next that the complete subtree set system satisfies the factorizability property and thus it inherits the revocation algorithm of Figure 2.9.

Proposition 2.37. *The set system* Φ^{CS} *is a factorizable set system.*

Proof. Our proof will take advantage of the alternative characterization for factorizability, that is the "diamond property" given in definition 2.32 which is shown to be equivalent with factorizability (see Theorem 2.33).

Indeed, it is immediate to see that if any two subsets in Φ^{CS} are intersecting, then one of them is actually completely containing the other and hence their union is also in the set system. ■

Since the Complete Subtree method satisfies the factorizability property the revocation algorithm given in Figure 2.9 finds the optimal cover.

Transmission Overhead

As the theorem 2.36 illustrates the transmission overhead depends on the order of the lower maximal partition of an intersection $(S) \cap \mathsf{P}_u$. For the set system Φ^{CS} we have the following:

Proposition 2.38. *For any subset* $\mathsf{S} \in \Phi^{CS}$ *and an atom* u*, it holds that* $\mathsf{ord}((\mathsf{S}) \cap \mathsf{P}_u) \leq \log |\mathsf{S}|$

Proof. In the key-poset of the complete subtree set system, $(\mathsf{S}) \cap \mathsf{P}_u$ consists of the subtrees hanging from the path from u to the node corresponding to the subset S. Hence, there would be $\log |\mathsf{S}|$ ideals in the lower-maximal partition of the intersection $(\mathsf{S}) \cap \mathsf{P}_u$. ■

The above result combined with Theorem 2.36 gives an upper bound for the transmission overhead that equals $r(\log n - 1) + 1 \leq r \log n$. We will show next a slightly more refined analysis that brings this bound further down.

Theorem 2.39. *The transmission overhead of the optimal revocation algorithm given in Figure 2.9 for the factorizable set system* Φ^{CS} *is bounded by* $r(\log n/r - 1)$ *where* r *is the number of revoked users.*

Proof. Observe that the chopped set system $\mathbf{Chop}(\Phi, \{\mathsf{j}_1, \ldots, \mathsf{j}_r\})$ is constructed by chopping the filter of the subset $\{\ell_i\}$ encoded by j_i one by one starting from $i = 1$. For each user, the chopping takes an intersection of the filter of the user with an ideal containing it (recall Theorem 2.35 for more details on how the revocation algorithm operates). In the light of proposition 2.38, a subset contributes on the size of the broadcast pattern (which is transmission overhead) as many as elements as its height. It follows that in each revocation the subset S that contains the revoked user in question contributes $\log |\mathsf{S}| - 1$ subsets in the broadcast pattern.

It remains to find the maximum size that a subset in each revocation can have. Let $i = 1, \ldots, r$ denote the revocation index and m_i be the maximum size a subset can have when revoking the i-th user. We have that $m_1 = n$, $m_2 = n/2$, $m_3 = m_4 = n/4$ and in general $m_i = n/2^l$ where $2^{l-1} < i \leq 2^l$.

Using this series, the upper bound on the broadcast pattern would then be given by the summation

$$\sum_{i=1}^{r} \log m_i - (r - 1)$$

where we subtract $r - 1$ since at each revocation we will be picking up an existing subset and substituting with the ones that result from the intersection with the subsets in the atomic filter of the user.

Let k be such that $2^k \leq r < 2^{k+1}$. We analyze the above summation to obtain the following upper bound

$$\log n + \sum_{l=1}^{k} \sum_{i=2^{l-1}+1}^{2^l} (\log n - l) + (r - 2^k)(\log n - k - 1) - (r - 1) =$$

$$= \log n + \sum_{l=1}^{k} 2^{l-1}(\log n - l) + (r - 2^k)(\log n - k - 1) - (r - 1)$$

Now based on the identities $\sum_{l=1}^{k} 2^{l-1} = 2^k - 1$ and $\sum_{l=1}^{k} l2^{l-1} = (k + 1)2^k - 2^{k+1} + 1$ we simplify the expression to

$$2^k \log n - (k - 1)2^k - r + (r - 2^k)(\log n - k - 1)$$

After the calculations and using the fact $k > \log r - 1$ we get

$$r \log n - r(k + 1) + 2^{k+1} - r \leq r \log n - r(k + 2) + 2r \leq r(\log n - \log r + 1)$$

This completes the proof. ∎

A direct revocation algorithm.

We will next discuss a direct revocation algorithm for the CS method that has the same performance as the generic algorithm that is inherited due to factorizability. Given a set of users R to be revoked, the broadcast pattern that covers $[n] \setminus \mathsf{R}$ can be determined by computing first the Steiner tree $\mathsf{Steiner}(\mathsf{R})$. Recall that the Steiner tree is the minimal subtree of the full binary tree that connects all the leaves in R. Consider now the nodes that are "hanging" from the tree $\mathsf{Steiner}(\mathsf{R})$. Assume there are m such nodes corresponding to the subsets $\mathsf{S}_1, \mathsf{S}_2, \ldots, \mathsf{S}_m$. We say a node is hanging from the Steiner tree if its sibling is in the Steiner tree while itself is not. See Figure 2.10 for the hanging nodes for a simple revocation instance in the case of 16 users; ; the nodes hanging from the Steiner Tree constitute the broadcast pattern. It holds that $[n] \setminus \mathsf{R} = \cup_{i=1}^{m} \mathsf{S}_i$; indeed for any $i \in \{1, \ldots, m\}$, S_i would not contain any revoked user. On the other hand, if $u \notin \mathsf{R}$ then, there exists some node S that is on the path from u to the root of the binary tree and hangs from the Steiner tree. It follows that the broadcast pattern that is revoking R would be $\{\mathsf{S}_1, \ldots, \mathsf{S}_m\}$. The transmission overhead of the broadcast encryption scheme that is using the CS as the underlying set system would be upper-bounded by the number of inner nodes in the Steiner tree $\mathsf{Steiner}(\mathsf{R})$. An analysis on the number of nodes in a Steiner tree with $|\mathsf{R}| = r$ leaves would yield a transmission overhead of size $r \log(n/r)$. We argue about this next.

Theorem 2.40. *The size of the broadcast pattern output resulting from the revocation algorithm outlined above is at most* $r \log(n/r)$ *where* $0 < r < n$ *is the size of the revoked set* R.

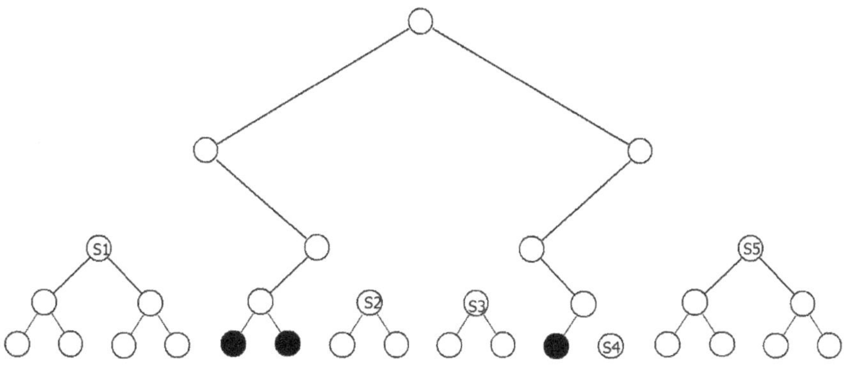

Fig. 2.10. Steiner tree that is connecting the revoked leaves.

Proof. Observe that the number of subsets hanging from the Steiner Tree Steiner(R) is exactly the number of nodes in Steiner(R) that have degree 1. We will now prove the above claim by induction on the height of the tree, i.e. induction on $\log n$.

Base Case $\log n = 1$: This case corresponds to a set system with two users only, and the claim can be easily seen to hold for any r, $r = 1, 2$.

Induction Assumption for $\log n = s$: Suppose that the number of subsets hanging from the Steiner Tree Steiner(R) is at most $r(s - \log r)$ for any subset $\mathsf{R} \subseteq \mathsf{N}$ with $|\mathsf{R}| = r$ and $0 < r < n$.

Induction Step for $\log n = s + 1$: We have two cases: either all the revoked users are located on the same subtree of one of the children of the root, or $r = r_1 + r_2$ so that r_1 users are located on the left child of the root, and r_2 users are located on the right child.

In the first case, due to induction assumption, Steiner(R) would yield at most $r(s - \log r) + 1$ nodes of degree 1, where the extra node is because of the root, and the remaining are within the child contains all revoked users. The induction step is proven in this case since $r(s - \log r) + 1 \leq r(s + 1 - \log r)$.

In the second case, due to the induction assumption Steiner(R) would yield at most $r_1(s - \log r_1) + r_2(s - \log r_2)$ nodes of degree 1.

$$\begin{aligned} r_1(s - \log r_1) + r_2(s - \log r_2) &= rs - (r_1 \log r_1 + r_2 \log r_2) \\ &\leq rs - (-r + r \log r) \\ &= r(s + 1) - r \log r \\ &= r(s + 1 - \log r) \end{aligned}$$

The above, indeed, holds, since it holds that $r(\log r - 1) \leq r_1 \log r_1 + r_2 \log r_2$ for any possible r, r_1, r_2 with $r = r_1 + r_2$. ■

2.5.2 Subset Difference

We will next discuss the subset difference (SD) set system that outperforms the complete subtree set system in terms of transmission overhead at the expense of increasing the size of the set system. In fact the increase is such that the number of keys required to be stored by each user become uneconomical as it is linear in the number of users. This downside will be mitigated by a non-trivial application of the key compression technique of Section 2.3.3.

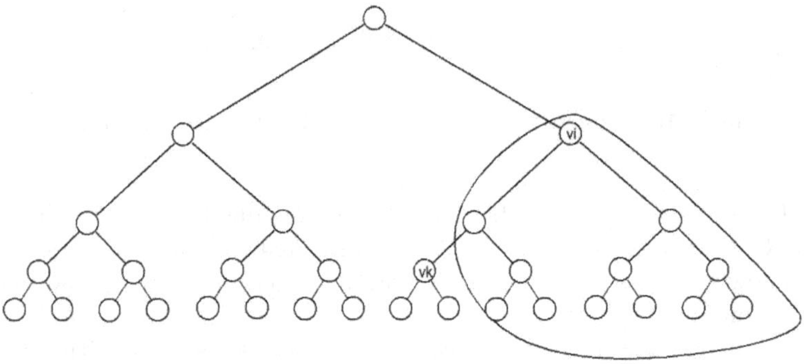

Fig. 2.11. The subset encoded by a pair of nodes (v_i, v_k) in the subset difference method.

We consider again a binary tree whose leaves correspond to the receivers in the user population $[n] = \{1, \ldots, n\}$ where n is a power of 2. A subset $\mathsf{S} \in \Phi^{SD} = \{\mathsf{S}_\mathsf{j}\}_{\mathsf{j} \in \mathcal{J}}$ can be denoted by a pair of nodes $\mathsf{j} = (v_i, v_k)$ in the binary tree where v_i is an ancestor of v_k. S_j is the set of all leaves in the subtree rooted at v_i excluding the leaves in the subtree rooted at v_k. See Figure 2.11 for an example description of a subset.

Set system description in the KP framework.

The key poset of the subset difference method is, as expected, more complex compared to the complete subtree set system. We refer reader to the Figure 2.12 for a depiction of the key poset of SD method for 8 users.

Let $\mathcal{J}^{SD}$ be the set of encodings of subsets in the set system Φ^{SD} defined over a set $[n]$. An element in $\mathcal{J}^{SD}$ is a pair of binary strings so that the sum of their length is less than or equal to $\log n$. Recall that for the sake of simplicity we assume that $\log n$ is an integer.

We define an index for each node in the binary tree in a top-down manner similar indexing as in the complete subtree set system : the root of the binary tree is encoded by ϵ, the index of a left child is constructed by appending '0' to its parent's index while index of a right child is constructed by appending '1' to its parent's index. An encoding $\mathsf{j} \in \mathcal{J}^{SD}$ now is a *pair* of strings (L, R)

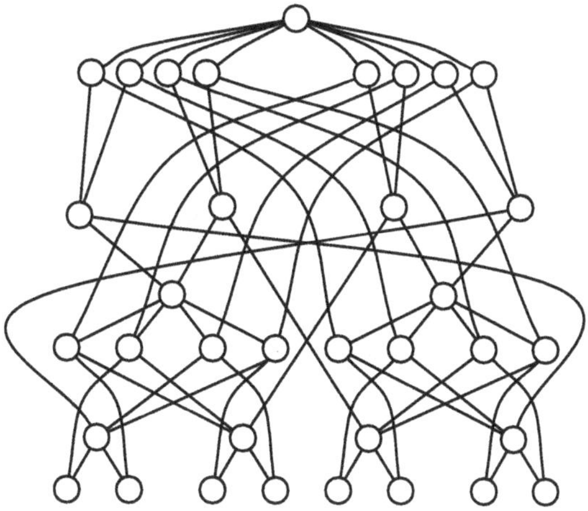

Fig. 2.12. A graphical depiction of the subset difference key poset for 8 users.

where the concatenated string LR has a length at most $\log n$. We refer reader to the Figure 2.13 for the computational specification of Subset Difference in the KP framework.

The key-forest for compression.

Consider the set of trees of the following form : let $L \in \{0,1\}^x$ with $0 \leq x \leq \log n - 1$ and $b \in \{0,1\}$. We have that F_{Lb} is a binary tree constructed as follows: it includes as root the node that corresponds to the subset j where $\mathsf{j} = (L, b)$. In addition, F_{Lb} includes all the nodes that can be added recursively following this rule : for any node j' in F_{Lb}, the first child of j' is $\mathbf{cvr}(\mathsf{j}', 2)$ and the second child of j' is $\mathbf{cvr}(\mathsf{j}', 3)$ (see Figure 2.13 for computational specification of the Subset Difference). The subset encoded by ϵ that contains the whole user population also forms a tree by itself as a single node that is denoted by F_{ε}. The family of trees is denoted by $\mathcal{F}_{SD}$.

Proposition 2.41. *The set* $\mathcal{F}_{SD} = \{\mathsf{F}_s \mid s \in \{0,1\}^x, x = 0, \ldots, \log n\}$ *is a key-forest of the set system* Φ^{SD} *with degree* 3.

Proof. Due to the definition of F_{Lb} for any $L \in \{0,1\}^x$ with $0 \leq x \leq \log n - 1$ and $b \in \{0,1\}$, it is easy to observe that the tree edges follow the superset relation, i.e. it holds that a parent of a node is a subset of that node. Now consider any four nodes in the tree F_{Lb} denoted by $(L_1, R_1), (L_2, R_2), (L_3, R_3), (L_4, R_4)$ for which it holds that R_1 is a prefix of R_2, R_3 and R_2, R_3 are both prefixes of R_4. While this condition is necessary for a cycle (albeit not sufficient) it also suggests that R_2, R_3 must satisfy that one is a prefix of the other and thus the four nodes cannot be in a cycle.

Computational Specification of Subset Difference in the KP Framework.

1. Encoding Testing: $\mathbf{tst}(\mathsf{j})$; if $\mathsf{j} = \epsilon$ return 1, otherwise parse j as $(\{0,1\}^x, \{0,1\}^y)$. If $x + y \leq \log n$ provided that $y \geq 1$, then return 1.
2. Membership Testing: $\mathbf{mbr}(\mathsf{j}, u)$; let $\mathsf{j} = (L, R)$ and $u \in \{0,1\}^{\log n}$. if L is a prefix of u whereas LR is not, then return 1.
3. Outside Selection: $\mathbf{slo}(\mathsf{j}_1, \mathsf{j}_2, \ldots, \mathsf{j}_r)$; if $\mathsf{j}_i = \epsilon$ for any $i \leq r$ then return $\perp$. Let $\mathsf{j}_i = (L_i, R_i)$ for $i = 1, \ldots, r$. We have two possible cases:
   (i) $\{s \in \{0,1\}^{\log n} \mid \exists i \in [r], R \text{ s.t. } s = L_i R\} \neq \{0,1\}^{\log n}$; this case implies that there exists a $u \in \{0,1\}^{\log n}$ such that none of L_i's are prefix of u; in this case return u. This string can be determined easily by computing the tree connecting the nodes corresponding to strings L_i.
   (ii) $\{s \in \{0,1\}^{\log n} \mid \exists i \in [r] \text{ s.t. } s = L_i R\} = \{0,1\}^{\log n}$; observe that for any u that is selected outside the subsets encoded by $\{\mathsf{j}_1, \ldots, \mathsf{j}_r\}$, it holds that if L_i is a prefix of u for any $i \leq r$ then $L_i R_i$ is also a prefix of u. We will compute such u, if it exists, in the following way: for all $i = 1, \ldots, r$, set $p = L_i R_i$ and test whether it holds that for all $j \neq i$, either $L_j R_j$ is a prefix of p or L_j is not a prefix of p. If such an i is found, $p = L_i R_i$ is padded arbitrarily to length $\log n$ to obtain a string u and return it. Otherwise return $\perp$.
4. Inclusion Testing: $\mathbf{sbs}(\mathsf{j}, \mathsf{j}')$; Let $\mathsf{j} = (L, R), \mathsf{j}' = (L', R')$, if L' is not prefix of L then return 0. We have two possible cases:
   (i) L is a prefix of $L'R'$: if LR is also prefix of $L'R'$ return 1, otherwise return 0.
   (ii) L is not prefix of $L'R'$: if $L'R'$ is prefix of L then return 0; else return 1.
5. Parent Finding: $\mathbf{cvr}(\mathsf{j}, i)$; We define for $i = 1, 2, 3, 4 = \mathbf{cvm}$.
   $i = 1$: if j is defined such that $\mathsf{j} = (Lb, R)$, where $b \in \{0,1\}$ and $|L| \geq 0$, then return (L, bR); otherwise return $\perp$.
   $i = 2$: if j is defined such that $\mathsf{j} = (L, R)$, where $|LR| < \log n$, then return $(L, R0)$; otherwise return $\perp$
   $i = 3$: if j is defined such that $\mathsf{j} = (L, R)$, where $|LR| < \log n$, then return $(L, R1)$; otherwise return $\perp$
   $i = 4$: if j is defined such that $\mathsf{j} = (Lb, R)$, where $b \in \{0,1\}$ and $|LbR| = \log n$, then return $(L, \bar{b})$; otherwise return $\perp$
6. Split Finding: $\mathbf{spt}(\mathsf{j})$; if j is defined such that $\mathsf{j} = (L, bR)$, where $b \in \{0,1\}$ and $|R| > 0$, then return $\{(L, b), (Lb, R)\}$; otherwise if $R = \epsilon$ then return $\{(L\bar{b}, 0), (L\bar{b}, 1)\}$ where $\bar{b} = 1 - b$.

Fig. 2.13. The computational specification of subset difference set system in the Key-Poset framework.

Regarding the coverage of the set family by the trees, consider a subset encoded as $\mathsf{j} = (L, R)$ where R is a string of length at least 1 starting with $b \in \{0,1\}$. It is easy to see that this node is located in the binary tree F_{Lb} and not in any other binary tree.

Finally, the degree of the key-forest is 3 since the key forest consists of only binary trees. ∎

Since the above key-forest has a degree of three, we can apply the key-assignment of Definition 2.21 by employing 3-fold key extender $\mathsf{f}_3 : \mathsf{K} \mapsto \mathsf{K}^3$.

It is easy to see that each of trees in the forest has height less than $\log n$ and hence the computation overhead for key decompression would be bounded by $\log n$. The key storage for a user u is the number of trees in the forest $|\mathcal{F}_{SD} \cap \mathsf{F}(u)|$ where $\mathsf{F}(u)$ refers to the filter of the user u in the key-poset (see Figure 2.14 for graphical illustration). Recall that user u is given a local value for the root of each tree in the intersection forest $|\mathcal{F}_{SD} \cap \mathsf{F}(u)|$. In order to find the number of trees in the intersection forest, we need to consider for each $L \in \{0,1\}^x, b \in \{0,1\}$ the number of trees that are produced when intersecting the tree F_{Lb} with the nodes of the filter $\mathsf{F}(u)$. We will denote this forest by $\mathsf{F}_{Lb} \cap \mathsf{F}(u)$. We distinguish the following three cases.

Case 1: if L is not a prefix of u; then $\mathsf{F}_{Lb} \cap \mathsf{F}(u)$ is empty.

Case 2: if L is a prefix of u, but Lb is not; then the intersection $\mathsf{F}_{Lb} \cap \mathsf{F}(u)$ is the tree F_{Lb} itself, meaningly all nodes in that tree is already included in the filter.

Case 3: If Lb is a prefix of u; then the intersection would have $\log n - |Lb|$ disjoint trees.

The second case happens for $\log n$ different choices of L as a prefix of u, (L can not be equal to u). The third case also happens for $\log n$ different choices of Lb as a prefix of u, with each case resulting $\log n - |Lb|$ disjoint trees. Also the user would need the one key for the unit-size tree F_ϵ. Based on the above, the key storage required by a user would be equal to

$$1 + \log n + \sum_{i=1}^{\log n} (\log n - i) = 1 + \frac{\log n \cdot (\log n + 1)}{2}$$

Factorizability of the subset difference set system.

We now prove that the subset difference set system satisfies the factorizability property and hence it inherits the optimal revocation algorithm of Figure 2.9.

Proposition 2.42. *The set system Φ^{SD} is a factorizable set system.*

Proof. Our proof will take advantage of the alternative characterization for factorizability, the diamond property given in definition 2.32 which is shown to be equivalent with factorizability (see Theorem 2.33).

Consider two subsets encoded by $\mathsf{j}_1 = (L_1, R_1)$ and $\mathsf{j}_2 = (L_2, R_2)$ that are intersecting. We will have to show that their union is in the set system. Since

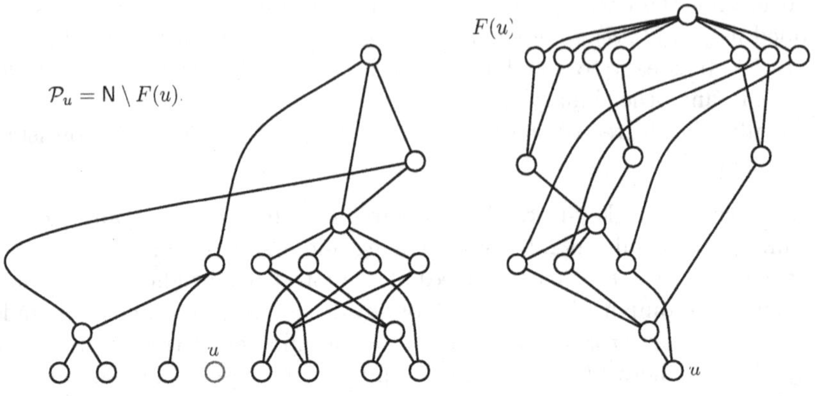

Fig. 2.14. The $\mathsf{P}(u)$ and $\mathsf{F}(u)$ sets for a user u in the subset difference key poset for 8 receivers.

they are intersecting there is a common element u for which it holds that L_1 and L_2 are prefixes of u. If $L_1 = L_2$, then it is easy to see that either of the following cases holds : (i) one is covering the other entirely, (ii) their union is equal to the subset $(M, \bar{b})$ where $L_1 = L_2 = Mb$ and $|b| = 1$, (iii) their union is equal to the subset of all users. In all three cases the union belongs to the set systems.

In the other case we assume without loss of generality that $|L_1| < |L_2|$. Then it holds that L_1 is a prefix of L_2. Moreover, $\mathbf{mbr}(\mathsf{j}_1, u) = 1$ implies that L_1R_1 is not a prefix of u while L_2 is a prefix of u, hence L_1R_1 can not be a prefix of L_2. Then we have two cases: (i) either the common prefix of L_1R_1 and L_2 is shorter than L_2, or (ii) L_2 is prefix of L_1R_1.

For case (i), since L_1R_1 is not a prefix of L_2, this case implies that the common prefix is also shorter than L_1R_1. Observe now that for any user u that satisfies $\mathbf{mbr}(\mathsf{j}_2, u) = 1$, it also holds that $\mathbf{mbr}(\mathsf{j}_1, u) = 1$. Hence one is covering the other, and their union, the superset among the two, is included in the set system.

For case (ii) observe that for any user u with a prefix L_1 either satisfies $\mathbf{mbr}(\mathsf{j}_1, u) = 1$ or satisfies $\mathbf{mbr}(\mathsf{j}_2, u) = 1$. Hence, the union of these two subsets would either correspond to the subset $(M, \bar{b})$ where $L_1 = Mb$ with $|b| = 1$ or the set of all users if $L_1 = \epsilon$. ∎

Given that the subset difference set system satisfies the factorizability property, the revocation algorithm given in Figure 2.9 provides the optimal solution.

Transmission overhead.

As the theorem 2.36 illustrates the transmission overhead depends on the order of the lower maximal partition of an intersection $(S) \cap P_u$. The superiority of the set system Φ^{SD} compared to the complete subtree is mainly in that it satisfies the following:

Proposition 2.43. *For any subset* $\mathsf{S} \in \Phi^{SD}$ *and an atom* u, *it holds that* $\mathsf{ord}((\mathsf{S}) \cap P_u) \leq 3$.

Proof. Suppose S has the encoding $\mathsf{j} = (L, R)$. If $\mathtt{mbr}(\mathsf{j}, u) = 0$, then the intersection itself equals to the ideal (S), hence the proposition holds. If not, then L would be a prefix of u while LR is not a prefix of u. Then we can write $u = LL'bU$ where LL' is the longest common prefix of LR and u so that $LR = LL'\bar{b}R'$ and $|LL'bU| = \log N$ for some U, R'. Observe that $b \in \{0, 1\}$ necessarily exists, but U and R' may possibly be empty strings.

Consider now the subsets, $\mathsf{j}_1 = (L, L'), \mathsf{j}_2 = (LL'b, U), \mathsf{j}_3 = (LL'\bar{b}, R')$ where $\mathsf{j}_2, \mathsf{j}_3$ are well defined in case U, R' exist respectively. It is easy to observe that none of these subsets are intersecting. Indeed if $\mathtt{mbr}(\mathsf{j}_1, v) = 1$ for some v, then it holds that LL' is not a prefix of v, so $\mathtt{mbr}(\mathsf{j}_2, v) = \mathtt{mbr}(\mathsf{j}_3, v) = 0$. Similarly, if $\mathtt{mbr}(\mathsf{j}_2, v) = 1$, then it holds that $LL'b$ is a prefix of v so $LL'\bar{b}$ not while v is explicitly excluded from j_1; the same reasoning applies to j_3.

On the other hand, it is easy to verify that any $v \in \mathsf{S} \setminus \{u\}$ would be included in one of the above subsets. Indeed, $v \in \mathsf{S}$ implies that L is a prefix of v while LR is not. There are two mutually exclusive cases : (i) either LL' is not a prefix of v or (ii) $LL'c$ is a prefix of v for some $c \in \{0, 1\}$:

Case (i) implies that $\mathtt{mbr}(\mathsf{j}_1, v) = 1$. On the other hand, for case (ii) if $c = b$, then it holds that $\mathtt{mbr}(\mathsf{j}_2, v) = 1$; otherwise it holds that $\mathtt{mbr}(\mathsf{j}_3, v) = 1$.

Next we observe that for $\mathsf{j}' \in \{\mathsf{j}_1, \mathsf{j}_2, \mathsf{j}_3\}$ and $i = 1, 2, 3, 4$, it holds that $\mathtt{cvr}(\mathsf{j}', i)$ would either contain u or are outside (S). This establishes the fact that the above subsets correspond to the principal ideals of the lower-maximal partition of $(\mathsf{S}) \cap P_u$. ∎

Applying Theorem 2.36 provides an upper bound on the transmission overhead for the subset difference set system, resulting in an overhead of $2r + 1$. A simple observation would refine this bound: in particular if S is the subset for whole receiver population, i.e. the encoding of S is ϵ, then j_2 and j_3 would not exist in the above formulation, in such case the first chopping for Theorem 2.36 will result a lower-maximal partition of order 1. Hence, the overall transmission overhead will amount to $2r - 1$.

A direct revocation algorithm.

We also describe a direct revocation algorithm for the subset difference set system that has the same performance as the generic algorithm described above. This is useful for historical reasons and in order to provide further intuition for the way the set system works. The algorithm utilizes the Steiner Tree induced by the set of revoked users R and the root as well. In this case, $\mathsf{Steiner}(\mathsf{R})$ is the minimal subtree that connects all the leaves corresponding the user set R. We compute the "broadcast pattern" that is covering the users in $[n]\setminus\mathsf{R}$ iteratively by modifying the Steiner Tree at each step. We set initially $\mathsf{T} = \mathsf{Steiner}(\mathsf{R})$ and repeat the following until the tree is empty.

1. Find a node v in the tree T that has two children v_L and v_R with each one being an ancestor of a single leaf. Denote the leaf that is a descendent of v_L by v_i and the leaf that is a descendent of v_R by v_j. If no such node exists, i.e., there is only one leaf left in the tree, then set the nodes $v_i = v_j$ to the leaf, set v to be the root and $v_L = v_R = v$.
2. If $v_L \neq v_i$, then add the subset $\mathsf{S}_{\mathsf{j}_1}$ with encoding $\mathsf{j}_1 = (v_L, v_i)$ to the broadcast pattern. Likewise, if $v_R \neq v_j$, then add the subset $\mathsf{S}_{\mathsf{j}_2}$ with encoding $\mathsf{j}_2 = (v_R, v_j)$ to the broadcast pattern.
3. Remove from T all the descendents of v and make v a leaf.

We next show that the the size of the broadcast pattern is at most $2r - 1$ in the worst case scenario and $1.38r$ in the average case.

Theorem 2.44. *The size of the broadcast pattern output by the above revocation algorithm is at most $2r - 1$ and $1.38r$ on average where r is the size of the revoked set* R.

Proof. In each step of the above algorithm, the number of leaves is decreasing by 1. Indeed, v_i and v_j are replaced by a single node v, and at most two new subsets are included in the broadcast pattern. This continues until the last leaf which yields a single subset. Hence, it is quite easy to observe that the transmission overhead is bounded by $2(r - 1) + 1 = 2r - 1$.

Note that it is possible that v_i is left child of v, or v_j is right child of v. These cases do not generate a subset to be included in the broadcast pattern. As a result the transmission overhead can be much smaller than $2r - 1$.

We will now discuss the average-case for randomly chosen r users to be revoked, i.e. the expected number of subsets generated by the above revocation algorithm. First, we mark the nodes that are set as leaves during the revocation algorithm. As mentioned before, in each step two leaves are revoked and an ancestral node is set as a new leaf. Hence, there are $r - 1$ of those nodes that are marked and both left and right children of these nodes are included in the $\mathsf{Steiner}(\mathsf{R})$. Denoting the children of the marked leaves as $v_1, \ldots, v_{2r-2}$, a possible subset is generated for each of them depending on how the revoked users are located beneath each node v_i, for $i = 1, \ldots, 2r - 2$.

If v_i has an outdegree 2 in the Steiner Tree, then no subset will be generated, otherwise, if the outdegree is 1, a single subset will be generated. Assuming that there are k_i revoked users rooted at this node the probability that a subset is generated is $1/2^{k_i - 1}$. This comes from the event that the users are either placed all on the left subtree of the node or on the right subtree of the node. The expected number of subsets over the values of k_i is thus given by the summation:

$$\sum_{i=1}^{2r-2} \frac{1}{2^{k_i - 1}}$$

We next observe that $|\{i : k_i = x\}| \leq \frac{r}{x}$, for $x \in \{1, \ldots, r\}$. This observation enables the following upper bound:

$$\sum_{x=1}^{r} \frac{r}{x} \cdot \frac{1}{2^{x-1}} \leq 2r \sum_{x=1}^{\infty} \frac{1}{k} \cdot \frac{1}{2^k} \leq 2r \ln 2 \approx 1.38 \cdot r$$

This completes the proof. ■

2.5.3 Key Chain Tree

In this section we will describe the key-chain tree set system Φ^{KCT}. Consider again a binary tree whose leaves correspond to the receivers in the user population $[n] = \{1, \ldots, n\}$ where n is considered a power of 2. For each internal node v_i of the binary tree, consider the sequence of consecutive leaves of the tree rooted at v_i. Any consecutive sequence starting from the leftmost or rightmost leaf of the tree rooted at v_i amounts to a subset in the set system. See the figure 2.15 for two examples of subsets in the set system. With this description, it is not hard to observe that there are lists of leaves in the binary tree starting from the leftmost (resp. rightmost) leaf of an intermediate node v_i that will also yield a subset due to the node v_j if v_j is a left (resp. right) child of v_i. Hence, each subset is being considered more than once depending on the geometry of its leaves, which results an unnecessary increase in key-storage unless some special care is taken.

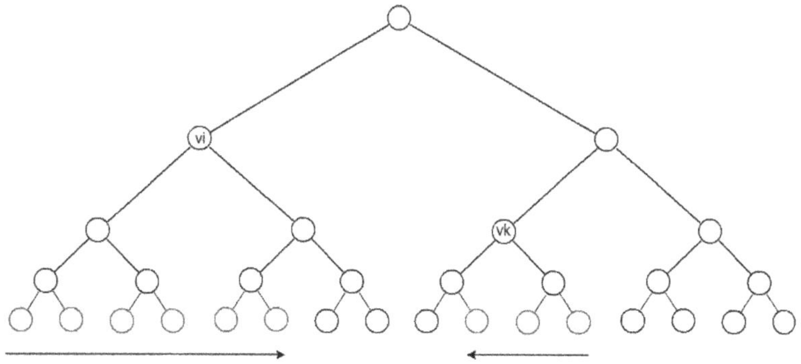

Fig. 2.15. An example of a subset in the Key Chain Tree method.

For the sake of avoiding the extra counting we define the following notion: we say a a pair of nodes (u_1, u_2) is *related* to an intermediate node v if the following hold: (i) v is the least-common ancestor of u_1 and u_2 and (ii) it holds that either u_1 is the leftmost leaf or u_2 is the rightmost leaf of the tree rooted at node v. We consider the pairs that can be related to an intermediate node as the subsets of the Key Chain Tree. This will be suffice to count each subset once.

Set System Description in the KP Framework

Let $\mathcal{J}^{KCT}$ be the set of encodings of subsets in the set system Φ^{KCT} defined over a set $[n] = \{1, \ldots, n\}$. An element in $\mathcal{J}^{KCT}$ is a pair of binary strings so that the sum of their length is equal to $\log n$. The algorithms, mostly, will be based on the integer representation of the encoding, hence we denote the procedure to convert a string into an integer by str2int; specifically $\mathsf{str2int}(b_k \ldots b_0) = 1 + \sum_{i=0}^{k} 2^i \cdot b_i$. We also use the inverse function int2str. As mentioned already, for the sake of simplicity, we assume that $\log n$ is an integer.

Regardless of the description of the set system, we can picture the key-poset of the basic set system in Figure 2.16. The figure reflects the the consecutive lists of users present in the set system as the long chains of nodes; especially observe the left and right sides of the triangle-looking key poset.

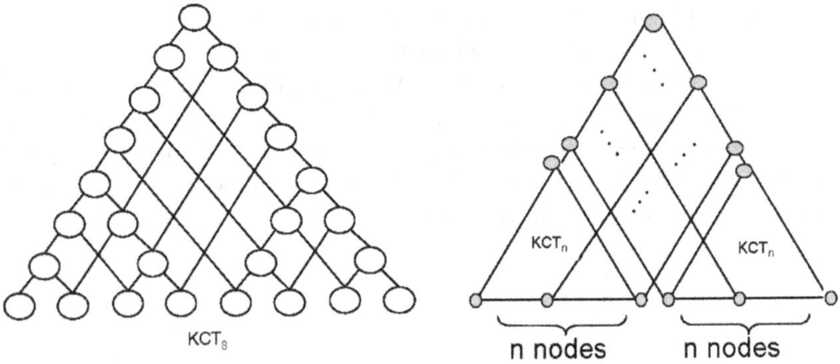

Fig. 2.16. (left) the key-poset of the key-chain tree method for 8 users. (right) the recursive definition of the key-poset for the key-chain tree for $2n$ users.

We define an index for each node in the binary tree in a top-down manner similar to the indexing of the complete subtree method: the root of the binary tree is encoded by ϵ (the empty string) and subsequently the index of a left child is constructed by appending '0' to its parent's index while the index of a right child is constructed by appending '1' to its parent's index. We denote the node corresponding to the string z by v_z for any $z \in \{0,1\}^i$ such that $0 \leq i \leq \log n$. An encoding $\mathsf{j} \in \mathcal{J}^{KCT}$ is a pair of strings $\mathsf{j} = (L, R)$ with $|L| + |R| = \log n$. The value L is the encoding of the root of the subtree that $\mathsf{S_j}$ is contained, i.e. the least common ancestor of all leaves in $\mathsf{S_j}$ will be the node v_L. In case $L = \epsilon$ then the least common ancestor of the leaves of the subset is the root of the binary tree; in case $|L| = \log n$ then the subset contains a single leaf corresponding to the encoding L. In case $0 < |L| < \log n$, observe that the value R is of the suitable length to identify a leaf in the subtree rooted by v_x. We determine the sequence of leaves that are in $\mathsf{S_j}$ as follows: (i) if R starts with 1 then S_j contains the sequence of leaves of the subtree rooted at v_x that start with the leftmost leaf and continue up to and including the leaf encoded by LR. (ii) if R starts with 0 then S_j contains the sequence of leaves of the subtree rooted at v_x that start with the rightmost leaf and continue towards the left up to and including the leaf encoded by LR.

The encoding that we put forth above is convenient as can be seen from the following facts. Given $\mathsf{j} = (L, 1R)$ we can represent the set $\mathsf{S_j}$ in the following way. Suppose that $a = \mathsf{str2int}(L0^{|R|})$ and $b = \mathsf{str2int}(L1R)$ then it holds that $\mathsf{S_j} = \{a, a+1, \ldots, b\}$. On the other hand, if $\mathsf{j} = (L, 0R)$, suppose that $c = \mathsf{str2int}(L0R)$ and $d = \mathsf{str2int}(L1^{|R|})$ then it holds that $\mathsf{S_j} = \{c, c{+}1, \ldots, d\}$.

Observe that the encoding scheme would cover all subsets of Φ^{KCT} exactly once with the only exception being the subsets that consist of the complete sets of leaves that are rooted at a node in the binary tree. These sets of leaves will be counted twice. For example, $(\epsilon, 0^{\log n})$ and $(\epsilon, 1^{\log n})$ are both referring to the set $\{1, \ldots, n\}$. For this reason, for any L with $|L| < \log n$, we will consider invalid as encoding the pair $\mathsf{j} = (L, R)$ with $R = b^{\log n - |L|}$ where b is the last bit of L (and say $b = 0$ if $L = \epsilon$). In this way any $\mathsf{S} \in \Phi^{KCT}$ uniquely corresponds to an encoding $\mathsf{j} \in \mathcal{J}^{KCT}$.

To summarize the above for any L, R with $|L| + |R| + 1 = \log n$ we have

$$\mathsf{S}_{(L,0R)} = \{\mathsf{str2int}(L0R), \ldots, \mathsf{str2int}(L1^{|R|+1})\}$$

and

$$\mathsf{S}_{(L,1R)} = \{\mathsf{str2int}(L0^{|R|+1}), \ldots, \mathsf{str2int}(L1R)\}$$

while note that $\mathsf{S}_{(Lb, b^{\log n - |L| - 1})}$ and $\mathsf{S}_{(\epsilon, 0^{\log n})}$ are undefined.

The key forest for compression.

Let $L \in \{0,1\}^x$ with $0 \le x \le \log n - 2$. We define F_{L0} (resp. F_{L1}) as a chain of length $2^{\log n - x - 1} - 1$ which consists of subsets that are of the following form: a subset is included in chain F_{L0} (resp. F_{L1}) if it is a consecutive set of leaves rooted at node v_{L0} (resp. v_{L1}) including the rightmost (resp. leftmost) leaf rooted at node v_{L0} (resp. v_{L1}).

Observe that the leaf encoded by $(Lb\bar{b}^{\log n - x - 1}, \epsilon)$ with $\bar{b} =_{df} 1 - b$ for $b \in \{0,1\}$ either amounts to the rightmost leaf of the subtree rooted at v_{Lb} in case $b = 0$ or the leftmost leaf in case $b = 1$. The chain F_{Lb} can be formally described as follows: it contains the leaf that corresponds to the encoding $\mathsf{j} = (Lb\bar{b}^{\log n - x - 1}, \epsilon)$, and includes all the nodes in a chain recursively following this rule : for any node j' in F_{Lb}, if it holds that $\mathbf{cvr}(\mathsf{j}', 2) \neq (Lb, \bar{b}^{\log n - x - 1})$ (refer to the Figure 2.17 for the computational key assignment of Key Chain Tree) the next node (as a child of j') is assigned $\mathbf{cvr}(\mathsf{j}', 2)$, otherwise the chain ends as it reaches its maximum of length $2^{\log n - x - 1} - 1$.

In addition, we define F_{fl} to be the chain starting from $\mathsf{j} = (0^{\log n}, \epsilon)$ and F_{fr} be the chain starting from $\mathsf{j} = (1^{\log n}, \epsilon)$. In such case, the chain covers the consecutive set of leaves defined for the root of the Figure 2.15.

Computational Specification of Key Chain Tree in the KP Framework.

1. Encoding Testing: **tst**(j); Let the encoding j be (L, R) such that $|LR| = \log n$. Denote the last bit of L by $b \in \{0,1\}$, define $b = 0$ if $L = \epsilon$. If $R = b^{\log n - |L|}$ and $|x| < \log n$ then return 0 otherwise return 1.
2. Membership Testing: **mbr**(j, u); Let j be a valid encoding (L, bR) such that $|LbR| = \log n$, $b \in \{0,1\}$ and $u \in \{0,1\}^{\log n}$. Return 1 if and only if $\mathsf{str2int}(u) \in \mathsf{S}_\mathsf{j}$.
3. Outside Selection: **slo**($\mathsf{j}_1, \mathsf{j}_2, \ldots, \mathsf{j}_r$). Choose the smallest integer that lies outside the set $\mathsf{S}_{\mathsf{j}_1} \cup \ldots \cup \mathsf{S}_{\mathsf{j}_r}$ and if no such integer exists return $\perp$.
4. Inclusion Testing: **sbs**(j, j′); return 1 if and only if $\mathsf{S}_\mathsf{j} \subseteq \mathsf{S}_{j'}$.
5. Parent Finding: **cvr**(j, i), where $1 \le i \le$ **cvm** $= 2$.
   - $i = 1$: Let j be encoded by (L, bR) such that $|LbR| = \log n$ and $b \in \{0,1\}$. If $L = L' b \bar{b}^x$ for some L', x, then return $(L', b\bar{b}^x bR)$. Recall $\bar{b} =_{df} 1 - b$. Return $\perp$ if j is not of the form required.
   - $i = 2$: If $\mathsf{j} = (Lbb', \epsilon)$, then return $(Lb, \bar{b})$. Otherwise, let j be encoded by (L, bR) such that $|LbR| = \log n$ and $b \in \{0,1\}$: (i) $b = 0$; if $\mathsf{str2int}(bR) > 2$ then return (L, bR') such that $\mathsf{str2int}(bR') = \mathsf{str2int}(bR) - 1$, otherwise if $\mathsf{str2int}(bR) = 2$, return $(L'a, \bar{a}^{\log n - |L|})$ where $L = L'a$ for some $a \in \{0,1\}$ (return $\perp$ in case $L = \epsilon$), otherwise if $\mathsf{str2int}(bR) = 1$, we have that $bR = 0^{\log n - |L|}$ (and hence by the validity of encoding it holds that $L = L'1$) return $(L', 01^{\log n - |L|})$.
     (ii) $b = 1$; if $\mathsf{str2int}(bR) < 2^{|bR|} - 1$ then return (L, bR') such that $\mathsf{str2int}(bR') = \mathsf{str2int}(bR) + 1$, otherwise if $\mathsf{str2int}(bR) = 2^{|bR|} - 1$, return $(L'a, \bar{a}^{\log n - |L|})$ where $L = L'a$ for some $a \in \{0,1\}$ (return $(\epsilon, 1^{\log n})$ in case $L = \epsilon$), otherwise if $\mathsf{str2int}(bR) = 2^{|bR|}$, we have $bR = 1^{\log n - |L|}$ (and hence by the validity of encoding it holds that either $L = L'0$ or $L = \epsilon$) return $(L', 10^{\log n - |L|})$ if $|L| > 0$ and $\perp$ otherwise.
6. Split Finding: **spt**(j); There are two cases:
   (i) Let j be encoded by $(L, 0R)$ such that $|L0R| = \log n$. Suppose $R = 1^x 0 R'$, then output $\{(L01^x, 0R'), (L1, 0^{|R|})\}$.
   (ii) Let j be encoded by $(L, 1R)$ such that $|L1R| = \log n$. Suppose $R = 0^x 1 R'$, then output $\{(L10^x, 1R'), (L0, 1^{|R|})\}$.

Fig. 2.17. The computational specification of the key chain tree set system in the Key-Poset framework.

As an illustration, let us write the chains for the key forest of a key chain tree with 8 users given in Figure 2.16, i.e. the case $\log n = 3$.

$\mathsf{F}_{00} = (001, \epsilon)$	$: \{2\}$
$\mathsf{F}_{01} = (010, \epsilon)$	$: \{3\}$
$\mathsf{F}_{10} = (101, \epsilon)$	$: \{6\}$
$\mathsf{F}_{11} = (110, \epsilon)$	$: \{7\}$
$\mathsf{F}_{0} \ = (011, \epsilon) \rightarrow (01, 0) \rightarrow (0, 01)$	$: \{4\} \rightarrow \{4,3\} \rightarrow \{4,3,2\}$
$\mathsf{F}_{1} \ = (100, \epsilon) \rightarrow (10, 1) \rightarrow (1, 10)$	$: \{5\} \rightarrow \{5,6\} \rightarrow \{5,6,7\}$
$\mathsf{F}_{fl} = (000, \epsilon) \rightarrow (00, 1) \rightarrow (0, 10) \rightarrow (0, 11)$	$: \{1\} \rightarrow \{1,2\} \rightarrow \{1,2,3\}$
$\rightarrow (\epsilon, 100) \rightarrow (\epsilon, 101) \rightarrow (\epsilon, 110) \rightarrow (\epsilon, 111)$	$\rightarrow \{1, \ldots, 4\} \rightarrow \ldots \rightarrow \{1, \ldots, 8\}$
$\mathsf{F}_{fr} = (111, \epsilon) \rightarrow (11, 0) \rightarrow (1, 01) \rightarrow (1, 00)$	$: \{8\} \rightarrow \{7,8\} \rightarrow \{6,7,8\}$
$\rightarrow (\epsilon, 011) \rightarrow (\epsilon, 010) \rightarrow (\epsilon, 001)$	$\rightarrow \{5, \ldots, 8\} \rightarrow \ldots \rightarrow \{2, \ldots, 8\}$

Proposition 2.45. *The set* $\mathcal{F}_{KCT} = \{\mathsf{F}_s \mid s \in \{fl, fr, \{0,1\}^x\}, x = 0, \ldots, \log(n-2)\}$ *is a key-forest of the set system* Φ^{KCT} *with degree* 2.

Proof. Due to the definition of the sets F_{Lb} it is easy to observe that the key-forest consists of "upward" looking trees in the poset, i.e. it holds that a parent of a node is a subset of that node.

Consider now a subset $\mathsf{j} = (L, bR)$ for any $b \in \{0,1\}$ where $|LbR| = \log n$. We have two cases: (i) $L = \epsilon$; if $b = 0$ then S_j exists in the chain F_{fr}, if $b = 1$ then S_j exists in the chain F_{fl}.

(ii) Suppose that $L = L'\bar{b}^x$ for some $x \geq 0$ so that L' is either ϵ or ends with b. In case $L' = \epsilon$ holds, it is easy to see that the subset exists in the chain F_{fr} if $b = 0$ and it exists in the chain F_{fl} otherwise. We next claim that if $L' \neq \epsilon$, this subset belongs to the chain $\mathsf{F}_{L'}$ and not in any other chain. To prove the claim, we recall the following two facts:

- $\mathsf{F}_{L'}$ is a chain that starts with a leaf encoded by $(L'\bar{b}^{\log n - |L'|}, \epsilon)$ and grows one-by-one until all leaves are covered (except one) located in the subtree rooted at $v_{L'}$ in the following direction: (i) if $b = 0$ then from right to left, starting from $(L'1^{\log n - |L'|}, \epsilon)$ adding leaves whose string-indices represent smaller numbers. (ii) if $b = 1$ then from left to right, starting from $(L'0^{\log n - |L'|}, \epsilon)$ adding leaves whose string-indices represent larger numbers.
- Recall that $\mathsf{j} = (L, bR)$ is an encoding of a subset $\mathsf{S}_j = \{c, c+1, \ldots, d\}$ where (i) if $b = 0$ then $c = \mathsf{str2int}(LbR)$ and $d = \mathsf{str2int}(L1^{\log n - |L|}) = \mathsf{str2int}(L'1^{\log n - |L'|})$.
  (ii) if $b = 1$ then $c = \mathsf{str2int}(L0^{\log n - |L|}) = \mathsf{str2int}(L'0^{\log n - |L'|})$ and $d = \mathsf{str2int}(LbR)$.

Hence, we obtain the fact that the subset encoded as $\mathsf{j} = (L, bR)$ is contained in the tree $\mathsf{F}_{L'}$. Furthermore it can be easily verified that any other chain cannot contain j. The degree of the key-forest is 2 since the key-forest consists of chains. ∎

Since the above key-forest has a degree of two, we can apply the key-assignment of Definition 2.21 by employing a 2-fold key extender $\mathsf{f}_2 : \mathsf{K} \mapsto \mathsf{K}^2$.

Observe that the trees with a maximum chain-length are F_{fl} and F_{fr}, hence the computation overhead is bounded by n function evaluations. The key storage for a user u is the number of trees in the forest $|\mathcal{F}_{KCT} \cap \mathsf{F}(u)|$ where $\mathsf{F}(u)$ refers to the filter of the user u in the key-poset. Recall that user u is given the label of the root of each tree in the intersection $|\mathcal{F}_{KCT} \cap \mathsf{F}(u)|$. We will count the number of trees by counting over each intersection $\mathsf{F}_{Lb} \cap \mathsf{F}(u)$:

1. if Lb is not a prefix of u; then $\mathsf{F}_{Lb} \cap \mathsf{F}(u)$ is empty.
2. if Lb is a prefix of u, then the intersection $\mathsf{F}_{Lb} \cap \mathsf{F}(u)$ is a subchain of F_{Lb}.

The second case happens for $\log n - 1$ different choices of $Lb \neq \epsilon$ as a prefix of u, (Lb can not be equal to u). Including also the subchains from F_{fl} and F_{fr}, the total key storage of a user would be $1 + \log n$.

Factorizability of the KCT set system.

We next show that the key chain tree set system satisfies the factorizability property and thus we ensure the existence of an efficient revocation algorithm.

Proposition 2.46. *The set system Φ^{KCT} is a factorizable set system.*

Proof. Our proof will take advantage of the alternative characterization for factorizability, the diamond property, given in definition 2.32 which is shown to be equivalent with factorizability (see Theorem 2.33)

Now consider two subsets $\mathrm{j}_1 = (L_1, b_1R_1)$ and $\mathrm{j}_2 = (L_2, b_2R_2)$ that are intersecting. We show that their union is in the set system. Since they are intersecting there is a common element u for which it holds that L_1 and L_2 are prefixes of u. If $L_1 = L_2$, then it is obvious that either one is covering the other in case $b_1 = b_2$, or their union corresponds to a subset in Φ^{KCT} that is containing all leaves rooted at node v_{L_1} in case $b_1 \neq b_2$.

Otherwise, without loss of generality say $|L_1| < |L_2|$ and we have that L_1 is a prefix of L_2. We have two cases: either (1) L_1b_1 is not a prefix of L_2 or (2) L_1b_1 is a prefix of L_2.

(1) This case implies that all leaves in the subtree rooted at v_{L_2} are included in the subset encoded by j_1, hence one is j_1 covers j_2.

(2) Suppose that L_1b_1 is a prefix of L_2. We consider the cases (a) L_2 is a prefix of $L1b_1R_1$ and (b) L_2 is not a prefix of $L_1b_1R_1$.

- Case (a) : The union of $\mathrm{j}_1, \mathrm{j}_2$ can be expressed as the set (L_1, b_1R') where R' is defined by requiring that (L_1b_1R', ϵ) to be respectively the rightmost ($b_1 = 1$) or leftmost ($b_1 = 0$) leaf of the sets $\mathrm{j}_1, \mathrm{j}_2$.
- Case (b) : The only feasible arrangement of the sets $\mathrm{j}_1, \mathrm{j}_2$ is that j_2 is entirely contained in j_1.

With the above we showed that the union of the two subsets is always in the family. ∎

Since the set system of Key Chain Tree method satisfies the factorizability property, our revocation algorithm given in Figure 2.9 applies and is optimal.

Transmission Overhead

Recall from the theorem 2.36 that the transmission overhead depends on the order of the lower maximal partition of an intersection $(S) \cap P_u$. The set system Φ^{KCT} satisfies the following:

Proposition 2.47. *For any subset* $\mathsf{S} \in \Phi^{KCT}$ *and an atom* u*, it holds that* $\mathsf{ord}((\mathsf{S}) \cap \mathsf{P}_u) \leq 3$.

Proof. First we give some intuition: any subset S encoded as $\mathsf{j} = (L, bR)$ corresponds to a consecutive sequence of leaves and will be splitted into two parts after removing a complement of an atomic filter P_u. One of the parts will contain the end leaf of the subset S, i.e., the leaf (LbR, ϵ), while the other part can be described as a union of two subsets in the set system. Totally, the ideal (S) will end-up with at most 3 ideals after removing the complement of an atomic filter. Let us see next a more detailed analysis of this.

Let S have an encoding $\mathsf{j} = (L, bR)$, if $\mathbf{mbr}(\mathsf{j}, u) = 0$, then the intersection $(\mathsf{S}) \cap \mathcal{P}_u$ itself equals to the ideal (S), hence the proposition holds. If not, then L would be a prefix of u. We have two cases: either (i) Lb is a prefix of u or (ii) Lb is not a prefix of u. In both of these cases, we will construct disjoint subsets $\mathsf{j}_1, \mathsf{j}_2, \mathsf{j}_3$ that are covering all the atoms in the intersection $(\mathsf{S}) \cap \mathsf{P}_u$, further it will be easy to observe that these subsets can not grow further, i.e. $\mathbf{cvr}(\mathsf{j}', i)$ would either contain u or goes outside the range of (S) for $\mathsf{j}' \in \{\mathsf{j}_1, \mathsf{j}_2, \mathsf{j}_3\}$ and $i = 1, 2$.

(i) In this case it holds that the leaves corresponding to u and (LbR, ϵ) are on the same half of the subtree rooted at v_L. Denote the longest common prefix of the string that encodes u and LbR by LbP where $P \in \{0, 1\}^x$ for some $x \geq 0$. Given that u belongs to (L, bR) it will hold that $LbP\bar{b}$ is prefix of u while $LbPb$ is prefix of LbR.

Suppose first that $b = 1$. Provided that u is not the leftmost leaf in the subtree rooted at v_L, the subset $\mathsf{S}_{\mathsf{j}_1} = \{\mathsf{str2int}(s_1), \ldots, u - 1\}$ (with $s_1 = L0^{\log n - |L|}$) contains all leaves located on the left of the leaf corresponding to u. To cover the remaining leaves we define the subsets $\mathsf{S}_{\mathsf{j}_2} = \{\mathsf{str2int}(s_2), \ldots, \mathsf{str2int}(L1R)\}$ where $s_2 = L1P10^{\log n - |LP| - 2})$ and $\mathsf{S}_{\mathsf{j}_3} = \{u + 1, \ldots, \mathsf{str2int}(s_3)\}$ where $s_3 = L1P01^{\log n - |LP| - 2}$. It is easy to verify that the subsets are not intersecting, they are members of the set systems and cover all leaves of (L, bR) except u. Note that it is possible that some of these subsets are empty; in such case there less than three subsets are needed to cover the leaves.

The case $b = 0$ is symmetric. Provided that u is not the rightmost leaf in the subtree rooted at v_L, the subset $\mathsf{S}_{\mathsf{j}_1}$ equal to $\{u + 1, \mathsf{str2int}(s_1)\}$ where $s_1 = L1^{\log n - |L|}$, contains all leaves located on the right of the leaf encoded by u. To cover the remaining leaves we define the subsets $\mathsf{S}_{\mathsf{j}_2} = \{\mathsf{str2int}(L0R), \ldots \mathsf{str2int}(s_2)\}$ where $s_2 = L0P01^{\log n - |LP| - 2}$ and $\mathsf{S}_{\mathsf{j}_3} = \{\mathsf{str2int}(s_3), \ldots, u - 1\}$ where $s_3 = L0P10^{\log n - |LP| - 2}$. As before it is easy to verify that these subsets are disjoint and cover all leaves of (L, bR) except u.

(ii) In this case it holds that the leaves corresponds to the indices u and LbR are on the different half of the subtree rooted at v_L.

Suppose first that $b = 1$. If u is not the leftmost leaf in the subtree rooted at v_L, the subset $\mathsf{S}_{\mathsf{j}_1}$ with an interval $[\mathsf{str2int}(s_1), u-1]$ (with $s_1 = L0^{\log n - |L|}$) contains all leaves located on the left of the leaf encoded by u. If $u+1$ has a prefix of $L1$ then the subset $\mathsf{S}_{\mathsf{j}_2} = \{\mathsf{str2int}(s_2), \ldots \mathsf{str2int}(LbR)\}$ where $s_2 = L10^{\log n - |L| - 1}$, will be enough to cover all remaining atoms in the intersection $(\mathsf{S}) \cap \mathsf{P}_u$. Otherwise we also define the subset $\mathsf{S}_{\mathsf{j}_3} = \{u+1, \mathsf{str2int}(s_3)\}$ where $s_3 = L01^{\log n - |L| - 1}$. We observe that none of these three subsets are intersecting and they all belong to the set system.

The case $b = 0$ is symmetric. If u is not the rightmost leaf in the subtree rooted at v_L, the subset $\mathsf{S}_{\mathsf{j}_1} = \{u+1, \ldots, \mathsf{str2int}(s_1)\}$ where $s_1 = L1^{\log n - |L|}$, contains all leaves located on the right of the leaf encoded by u. If $u - 1$ has a prefix of $L0$ then the subset $\mathsf{S}_{\mathsf{j}_2} = \{\mathsf{str2int}(LbR), \ldots \mathsf{str2int}(s_2)\}$ where $s_2 = L01^{\log n - |L| - 1}$, will be enough to cover all remaining atoms in the intersection $(\mathsf{S}) \cap \mathsf{P}_u$. Otherwise we also define the subset $\mathsf{S}_{\mathsf{j}_3} = \{\mathsf{str2int}(s_3), \ldots, u-1\}$ where $s_3 = L10^{\log n - |L| - 1}$. As before it is easy to see that none of these three subsets are intersecting and that they all belong to the set system. ■

Applying Theorem 2.36 gives an upper bound on the transmission overhead for the key chain tree method, which yields an overhead of $2r + 1$.

A direct revocation algorithm.

An direct revocation algorithm is also possible as follows. First we determine the contiguous sets of enabled users. Given $\mathsf{R} = \{\ell_1, \ldots, \ell_r\}$, we will get at most $r + 1$ contiguous subsets of enabled users. One of them is possibly starting with the leftmost user and another one is possibly ending with the rightmost user. It is possible to cover any other consecutive set of users with at most 2 subsets of the key-chain tree set system. To see this consider a set of consecutive users $\mathsf{S} = \{u_1, \ldots, u_t\}$, and denote the least common ancestor of u_1 and u_t by node v of the binary tree of the set system. If u_1 is leftmost leaf or u_t is rightmost leaf of the subtree rooted at v, then it is already the case that S belongs to the set system. Otherwise, say u_i is the rightmost leaf of the left child of the node v for some i; this is guarranteed to exist due to the choice of v. It holds that u_{i+1} will be the leftmost leaf of the right-child of the node v. Hence, both $\{u_1, \ldots, u_i\}$ and $\{u_{i+1}, \ldots, u_t\}$ belong to the set system and they cover the initial subset S. This revocation algorithm yields a broadcast pattern with size at most $2r$.

2.6 Generic Transformations for Key Posets

A generic transformation for key posets is a technique of deriving a new key poset from an existing one. Such transformations have frequently the capability to improve the performance characteristics of the underlying set-systems. In this section we will see two such transformation techniques.

2.6.1 Layering Set Systems

In this section, we present a generic transformation of a set system to a new set system that supports a greater number of receivers. A k-layering of a set system over d receivers is a transformation that produces a set system over d^k receivers where k is an positive integer parameter. While the new set system supports an exponential in k increase in the number of receivers, the transmission overhead and the key storage will increase by a factor of only k while the computation overheadfor key decompression will remain the same. Such a change in efficiency parameters has different net effects depending on the underlying basic set system and may yield advantageous trade-offs between the transmission and computation overheads and the key storage needed at the receiver side.

Provided that the computation overhead for copmression of the basic set system is linear in number of receivers, the transformation results in a set-system such that the computation overhead is reduced by a $1/k$ root. Provided that transmission overhead and/or the key storage is linear in number of revoked users the parameters in the transformed system would increase by a multiplicative factor of k; in case the dependency is logarithmic in the number of receivers there would be no change. The usefulness of the transformation can be immediately evidenced by applying the transformation over the key chain tree set system of the previous section. This will yield a non-trivial trade-off between the transmission overhead and the computation overhead. Recall that the key chain tree set system enjoys a logarithmic key-storage and a transmission overhead that is linear in number of revoked receivers while it suffers from a computation overhead that is linear in number of receivers. The resulting set system would decrease the computation overhead by an $1/k$-th root while sacrificing somewhat the transmission overhead which will bear an increase by a multiplicative factor of k.

We describe the transformation in detail next. Let Φ^{BS_d} be the basic set system defined over a set $[d] = \{1, \ldots, d\}$ on which we apply the transformation. The k-layering of the basic set system is constructed by generating $\frac{d^k-1}{d-1}$ copies of the basic set system and connecting them in a top-down manner by merging a leaf of an upper-level set system with the root of a lower-level set system. We formally, define the transformation as follows:

Definition 2.48. *The transformation* k-**LTrans**, *given a key-poset of set system* Φ^{BS_d} *over* $[d] = \{1, \ldots, d\}$, *outputs a new key-poset of a set system over a set* $[d^k] = \{1, \ldots, d^k\}$. *The construction for the new key-poset will be as follows:*

1. *Generate* $\frac{d^k-1}{d-1}$ *copies of* Φ^{BS_d}, *and label each one with a string* $s \in \{1, \ldots, d\}^x$ *where* $0 \leq x \leq k-1$. *We denote the copy with a label* s *by* $\Phi_s^{BS_d}$.

2. *Replace the i-th leaf of the set system $\Phi_s^{BS_d}$ that corresponds to the user-index $i \in [d]$, for $s \in \{1, \ldots, d\}^x$, $0 \leq x \leq k-1$, with the top subset of the set system $\Phi_{si}^{BS_d}$.*

We denote the output of k-layering by $\mathbf{LTrans}^k(BS_d)$.

It is very intuitive in the key-poset framework to reflect the above transformation as depicted in the Figure 2.18.

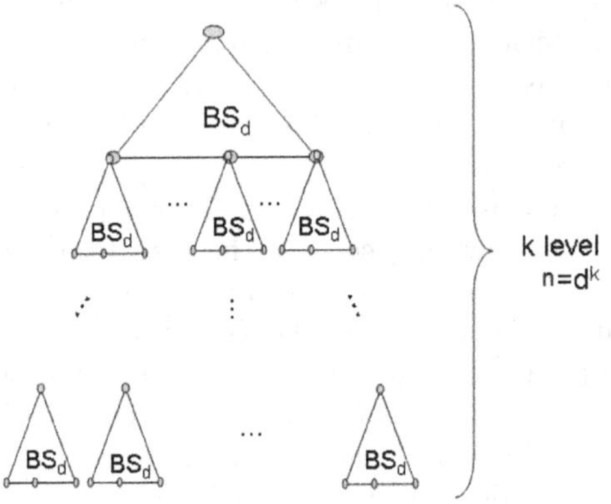

Fig. 2.18. Graphical depiction of the key-poset of the k-layering of a basic set system BS for d users.

The computational specification of the new set system $\mathbf{LTrans}^k(\Phi^{BS_d})$ in the KP framework can be defined based on the specification of the basic set system BS_d. Recall that $\mathbf{LTrans}^k(\Phi^{BS_d})$ consists of $\frac{d^k-1}{d-1}$ copies of the set system Φ^{BS_d}. The labeling of each copy can be comprehensible in the construction figure 2.18 by traversing the set systems top-down: the root set system of the figure is labeled by ϵ, the label of an i-th child set system is constructed by appending i to its parent's label. An encoding for the set system $\mathbf{LTrans}^k(\Phi^{BS_d})$ is a pair (s, j) where $\mathrm{j} \in \mathcal{J}^{BS_d}$ and $s \in \{1, \ldots, d\}^x$, $0 \leq x \leq k-1$, is the label of the set system the subset corresponding to the encoding (s, j) is located in. The algorithmic specification of the set system $\mathbf{LTrans}^k(BS_d)$ can be defined based on the specification of Φ^{BS_d} by taking the labels of the encodings into account: If the labels of two encodings are comparable, i.e. one is strict prefix of another, then the subset with longer label contains the other; if the labels are same, then whatever rules within the basic set system hold would be effective; if the labels are not comparable then the subsets corresponding to the encodings are disjoint. Since all six algorithms that we require in Definition 2.18 can be constructed without much effort, we will not explicitly state the descriptions in here and leave them as an exercise for the reader.

Similar to the algorithmic specification, the key-forest of the new set system can trivially be constructed by retrieving the key-forests of the set systems $\Phi_s^{BS_d}$ for $s \in \{1, \ldots, d\}^x$ with $0 \leq x \leq k-1$. The union of all these key forests constitutes the key forest of the new set system $\mathbf{LTrans}^k(BS_d)$.

Factorizability of the layering transformation.

Provided that the set system Φ^{BS_d} is factorizable, the layering transformation preserves the factorizability property for $n = d^k$ receivers. Hence, the new set system is accompanied with an efficient and optimal revocation algorithm due to the Theorem 2.35. We prove this in the next theorem.

Theorem 2.49. *Given that the fully exclusive set system Φ^{BS_d} defined over $\{1, \ldots, d\}$ is factorizable, then the transformation* **LTrans** *described in Definition 2.48 preserves the factorizability, i.e.* $\mathbf{LTrans}^k(\Phi^{BS_d})$ *is a factorizable set system defined over $\{1, \ldots, d^k\}$.*

Proof of Theorem 2.49: We will prove that $\mathbf{LTrans}^k(\Phi^{BS_d})$ is a factorizable set system by showing that it satisfies the diamond property, i.e. given any two intersecting subsets we will show that their union is in the new set system. Our proof will be based on the location of subsets that are intersecting:

Suppose, now, we have two subsets $\mathsf{S}_1 \in \mathbf{LTrans}^k(\Phi^{BS_d})$ and $\mathsf{S}_2 \in \mathbf{LTrans}^k(\Phi^{BS_d})$ so that $\mathsf{S}_1 \cap \mathsf{S}_2 \neq \emptyset$. If S_1 and S_2 are located in the same set system $\Phi_s^{BS_d}$ for some string $s \in \{1, \ldots, d\}^x$ with $0 \leq x \leq k-1$, then it will hold that $(\mathsf{S}_1 \cup \mathsf{S}_2) \in \mathbf{LTrans}^k(\Phi^{BS_d})$ due to the factorizability of the set system $\Phi_s^{BS_d}$. Otherwise, given that they are overlapping, it must be the case that one is covering the other and hence again their union is in the set system. ■

Efficiency parameters of the transformation.

We now come to the point to discuss the transmission overhead of a set system constructed by the layering transformation. Even though the transformation defines a new set system that increases by an exponential factor of k the size of the receiver population, it turns out that it increases the transmission overhead and the key storage by only a multiplicative factor of k. This will be observed in the following theorem that bounds the order of a lower-maximal partition for the intersection of any ideal with the complement of an atomic-filter. In the same theorem we also argue that the storage overhead will only suffer a multilplicative factor of k independently of the method that is used to assign the keys.

Theorem 2.50. *Suppose that a fully-exclusive set system Φ defined over a set $[d] = \{1, \ldots, d\}$ is factorizable.*

(i) If for any subset $\mathsf{S} \in \Phi$ and an atom $u \in \Phi$ it satisfies that $\mathsf{ord}((\mathsf{S}) \cap \mathsf{P}_u) \leq \mathsf{t}(d)$ within the poset Φ for some function $\mathsf{t}(\cdot)$, then it holds that

*$\mathsf{ord}((\mathsf{S}') \cap \mathsf{P}_{u'}) \leq k \cdot \mathsf{t}(d)$ for any $\mathsf{S}' \in$ **LTrans**$^k(\Phi)$ and any atom $u' \in$ **LTrans**$^k(\Phi)$.*

(ii) if there exists a key-assignment technique for Φ such that the key-storage for each user is bounded by $\mathsf{s}(d)$ for some function $\mathsf{s}(\cdot)$ and the computation overhead is bounded by $\mathsf{c}(d)$ for some function $\mathsf{c}(\cdot)$, then there is a key-assignment technique that the key-storage in **LTrans**(Φ) *is bounded by $k \cdot \mathsf{s}(d)$ and computation overhead is bounded by $\mathsf{c}(d)$.*

Proof of Theorem 2.50: (i) If $u' \notin \mathsf{S}'$, then the proof is straightforward since $(\mathsf{S}') \cap \mathsf{P}_{u'} = (\mathsf{S}')$. Otherwise, consider the leaf-to-root path from u' to the root of the key-poset of the set system **LTrans**(Φ). This path passes over a sequence of nodes that are at the leaf level of the component set systems, i.e., given that $u' \in [d^k]$ can be represented by a string $b_1 b_2 \ldots b_k$ with $b_i \in \{1, \ldots, d\}$ for $i \in [k]$, the path passes through the set systems $\Phi_{s_0}, \Phi_{s_1}, \ldots, \Phi_{s_{k-1}}$ where $s_0 = \epsilon$ and $s_i = b_1 \ldots b_i$ is a substring of the d-digit representation of u' with length i. It holds that S' belongs to Φ_{s_j} for some $j \in \{0, \ldots, k-1\}$. We observe next that the lower maximal partition of the intersection $(\mathsf{S}') \cap \mathsf{P}_{u'}$ will include $\mathsf{t}(d)$ sets for each one of the $k-j$ levels starting from the j-th level and going to the lowest one for a total of $(k-j) \cdot \mathsf{t}(d)$. This completes the proof of item (i).

(ii) The key-assignment for the new set system can be done by employing the key-assignment independently for each underlying set system. This will yield a key-storage for a user to be $k \cdot \mathsf{s}(d)$ since a user $u \in [d^k]$ with a d-digit representation of length k is related to k basic set systems in the new key-poset. On the other hand, the computation time will be same as if the set system is Φ, since the key of a subset is derivable within the basic set system that contains this subset. ∎

Applying the layering transformation to the KCT set system.

We next give an example for the application of the layering transformation. The set system based on Key Chain Tree enjoys a transmission overhead that is same as the transmission overhead for the Subset Difference along with a logarithmic key storage while the Subset Difference method has a log-square key storage. On the other hand the Key Chain Tree method suffers from the computation overhead in the worst case which is linear in number of receivers.

Consider the set system Φ^{KCT} of key chain tree for d receivers. The transformation described in definition 2.48 will yield factorizable set systems over exponentially growing receiver populations that satisfy the statement of the theorem 2.50.

2.6.2 X-Transformation

In this section we describe another transformation of set systems that also preserves the factorizability property and has superior performance characteristics compared to the layering transformation. The transformation has no parameters and requires a certain property from the underlying set system, called the $\mathrm{X}-$ property, that we will define herein. The number of users in the resulting set system equals the square of the number of users of the underlying set system while the transmission overhead increases by a constant amount while the storage approximately doubles. The transformation preserves a logarithmic computation overhead, i.e. given that the computation overhead of the basic set system is logarithmic in the number of receivers, the new computation overhead remains logaritmic in the new size of the receiver population.

In order to understand the transformation it will be helpful to think of the set system as the graph corresponding to the transitive reduction diagram of the corresponding poset. The X-property that is required by the basic set system is crucial in curbing the increase in the parameters of the set system while squaring the number of receivers. More formally, the property is defined as follows.

Definition 2.51. *We say a fully-exclusive set system $(\Phi, \subseteq)$ defined over a set $\mathsf{M} = \{1, \ldots, 2^m\}$ satisfies the* $\mathrm{X}-$ property *if*

1. There exist two elements $\mathsf{S}_1, \mathsf{S}_2 \in \Phi$ so that $\mathsf{F}(\mathsf{S}_1)$ and $\mathsf{F}(\mathsf{S}_2)$ are disjoint full binary trees of height $m-1$. We denote them by F_Φ^1 and F_Φ^2 respectively.

2. For each user $u \in \mathsf{M}$, the complement of the atomic filter $\mathsf{F}(u)$ intersects with the above binary trees on a single path of length m; i.e. $\mathsf{P}_u \cap (\mathsf{F}(\mathsf{S}_1) \cup \mathsf{F}(\mathsf{S}_2)) = \{\mathrm{u}_p^1, \ldots, \mathrm{u}_p^m\}$ where u_p^i is a node in the key poset of the set system Φ that is a parent of u^{i-1} for $i = 2, \ldots, m$.

Observe that due to the structure imposed by the $\mathrm{X}-$ property the top leaves of the binary tree filters $\mathsf{F}(\mathsf{S}_1)$ and $\mathsf{F}(\mathsf{S}_2)$ will be as many as the number of receivers in the set system. The second requirement of the $\mathrm{X}-$ property ensures that each leaf is uniquely related to an atom, and further it will hold that the leaves represent the subsets of the form $\mathsf{C}_u =_{df} \mathsf{M} \setminus \{u\}$.

The goal of the transformation is to expand the receiver population covered by the set system in a non-trivial way. This will be again through generating many copies of the basic set system and combining them in a non-trivial way. The first requirement in the $\mathrm{X}-$ property gives a way to combine a set system with an upper level copy and connecting non-trivial edges between those two set systems. Recall that the k-layering transformation doesn't support such interaction between the copies. The second requirement not only helps in supporting edge-transitions between upper and lower level copies but also makes it easier to employ the computational key assignment discussed in Definition 2.21. Such employment will make the transformation keep the computation overhead logarithmic while giving a reasonable increase in key storage. We next define the transformation formally.

Definition 2.52. *The transformation* **XTrans** *is a mapping over set systems that satisfy the* $\mathrm{X}-$ property. *The transformation takes the key-poset of a set system Φ over $\mathsf{M} = \{1, \ldots, 2^m\}$ and outputs a new key-poset of a set system* *over* $\mathsf{M}' = \{1, \ldots, 2^{2m}\}$*. The construction for the new key-poset will be as follows:*

1. Generate 2^m *copies of* Φ*. We enumerate and denote the copies by* $\Phi_1, \Phi_2, \ldots, \Phi_{2^m}$*. We say* Φ_i *is defined over the set* $\mathsf{M}_i = \{(i-1)2^m+1, \ldots, (i-1)2^m + 2^m\}$ *while* Φ *will be called as the 'body' of the transformation.*

2. For $i = 1, \ldots, 2^m$ *generate a copy of* $\mathsf{F}^1_{\Phi_i}$ *and* $\mathsf{F}^2_{\Phi_i}$*, and denote them by* F^1_i *and* F^2_i *respectively. These collections should be thought as graphs, while their subset content will be determined in the remaining steps of the transformation.*

Constructing the 'feet' of the transformation:

3. Replace the leaf $\{v\} \in \Phi$ *that corresponds to the user* $v \in \mathsf{M}$ *with the leading subset of the set system* Φ_v*. We will name these parts as the feet of the new set system.*

Constructing the 'head' of the transformation:

4. Remove the edges outgoing from the leading subset of Φ*.*

5. For any $v \in \mathsf{M}$*, add edges* $\mathsf{C}_v \subset \mathsf{F}^1_v$ *and* $\mathsf{C}_v \subset \mathsf{F}^2_v$*. (here* F^1_v *and* F^2_v *represent the roots of the corresponding binary trees)*

6. Connect the leading subset of Φ *with the leaves of binary tree* F^b_v *for all* $v \in \mathsf{M}$ *and* $b \in \{1, 2\}$*.*

Finally :

7. For any $v \in \mathsf{M}$ *and* $b \in \{1, 2\}$*, add an edge between* S *and* S' *where* $\mathsf{S}' \in \mathsf{F}^b_v$ *is the copy of the subset* $\mathsf{S} \in \mathsf{F}^b_{\Phi_v}$*. Recall that* F^b_v *and* $\mathsf{F}^b_{\Phi_v}$ *are isomorphic to each other.*

We denote the output of the X-Transformation by $\mathbf{XTrans}(\Phi)$*.*

The above transformation is illustrated in Figure 2.19. Note that the depiction lacks the representation of step 7 (as the inclusion would make it rather hard to read - for a complete example the reader is referred to the example in the end of this section).

We will now prove that the transformation preserves the $\mathrm{X-property}$.

Theorem 2.53. *The transformation* **XTrans** *described in definition 2.52 preserves the* $\mathrm{X-property}$.

Proof of Theorem 2.53: To begin with, it is easy to observe that the new set system Φ' is defined over the set $\mathsf{M}' = \{1, 2, \ldots, 2^{2m}\}$ and it is fully-exclusive; indeed, the new key poset is connected and for each $u \in \mathsf{M}'$ there exists a corresponding node in the key poset. It also holds that the subsets in the head of the new key poset are valid subsets in the new set system since each has an incoming edge from a subset in the feet of the key poset.

We prove next that the new key-poset satisfies the two properties required in Definition 2.51. We will use the following argument: if a subset S in the has incoming edges from s different subsets $\mathsf{S}_1, \ldots, \mathsf{S}_s$, then it holds that $\mathsf{S} = \bigcup_{i=1}^{s} \mathsf{S}_i$.

1. Recall that there exist two elements $\mathsf{S}_1 \in \Phi$ and $\mathsf{S}_2 \in \Phi$ such that $\mathsf{F}(\mathsf{S}_1)$ and $\mathsf{F}(\mathsf{S}_2)$ are disjoint full binary trees of height $m-1$ so that C_v is a leaf of one of these binary trees for any $v \in \mathsf{M}$ (this is ensured by the second

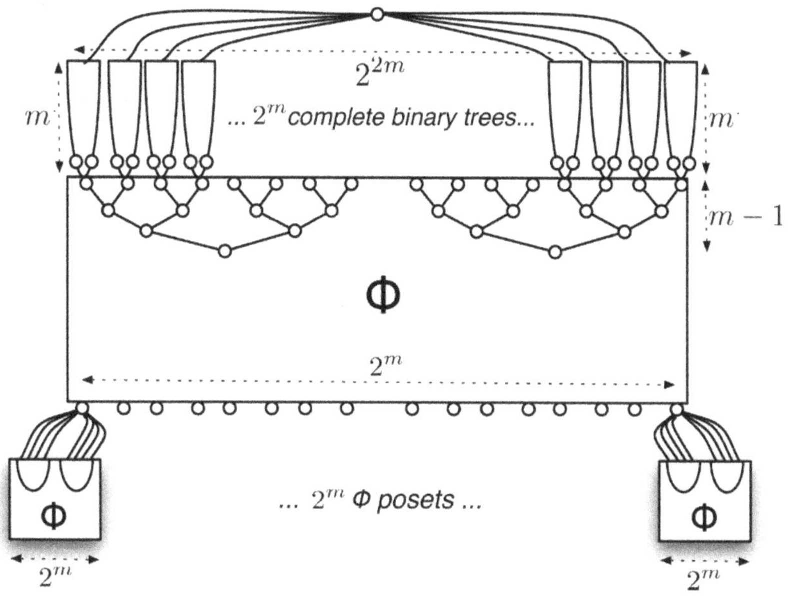

Fig. 2.19. The transformation of definition 2.52 (note that the illustration does not include the connections described in step number 7).

requirement of the X – property of the set system Φ). We will show that the filters of the same subsets are the required filters we need to demonstrate their existence of for the set system Φ'. It is easy to see that $\mathsf{F}(\mathsf{S}_1)$ and $\mathsf{F}(\mathsf{S}_2)$ within the new set system Φ' are full binary trees of height $2m-1$. This is true as for each $v \in \mathsf{M}$, the node $\mathsf{C}_v \in \Phi_b$ was connected (see the 5-th step of the transformation) to two full binary trees of height $m-1$; it follows that $\mathsf{F}(\mathsf{S}_1)$ and $\mathsf{F}(\mathsf{S}_2)$ within Φ' are binary trees of height $m-1+1+m-1 = 2m-1$.

2. For any index $u \in \mathsf{M}'$, there exists an integer $v \in \{1, \ldots, 2^m\}$ so that $u \in \mathsf{M}_v$. Since Φ_v satisfies the X – property, there is a unique path $\{u_v^1, \ldots, u_v^{m-1}\}$ not including the atom u that is intersecting with the either the filter $\mathsf{F}^1_{\Phi_v}$ or $\mathsf{F}^2_{\Phi_v}$. Since those filters that are structurally upward full binary trees are copied (refer to the second step of transformation) to the head of the resulting set system we can discover an isomorphic copy of this path that we denote by $\{u_{v*}^1, \ldots, u_{v*}^m\}$. Note that by definition the subsets corresponding to u_{v*}^i for $i = 1, \ldots, m$ exclude the atom u.

Recall now that $v \in \mathsf{M}$, hence there exists a unique path within one of the two filters of the body set system Φ. The subsets corresponding to the nodes over this path do not contain the node v which is atomic in the body while it is the leading subset of the lower level set system Φ_v. Hence, this path does not contain the receiver indexed by $u \in \mathsf{M}'$. Moreover, the path ends with the node corresponding to the subset $\mathsf{C}_v = \mathsf{M} \setminus \{v\}$. Recall that in the 5-th step of the transformation, we connected the set C_v with the filters F_v^1 and F_v^2. Observe now that the path within the body that excludes v and the path in the extension (the one denoted by $\{u_{v*}^1, \ldots, u_{v*}^m\}$) on the head are connected and all corresponding subsets exclude u. This results to a unique path of length $2m$ in the transformed set system. ■

The computational specification of the resulting set system **XTrans**(Φ) in the KP framework can be described based on the specifications of the basic set system Φ defined over $\{1, \ldots, 2^m\}$. Recall that **XTrans**(Φ) generates 2^m copies of the set system Φ. An encoding for the set system **XTrans**(Φ) is a triple (b, s, j) where $\mathsf{j} \in \mathcal{J}^\Phi$ and $s \in \{\epsilon\} \cup \{0,1\}^m$ is the label of the set system the node corresponding to the encoding j is located in while $b \in \{0,1\}$. In case, $b = 0$ then the subset j is located in one of the set systems $\Phi, \Phi_1, \ldots, \Phi_{2^m}$, while in case $b = 1$ then the subset encoded by $\mathsf{j} \in \mathcal{J}^\Phi$ is a copy of a subset in the filter and it is located on the head of the transformed set system. Note that not all triples (b, s, j) correspond to a legal subset. The algorithmic specification of the set system **XTrans**(Φ) can be defined based on the specification of Φ by taking the labels of the encodings into account. Since all six algorithms we require in Definition 2.18 can be constructed without so much effort, we will not explicitly state the algorithms in here and leave this task as an exercise for the reader.

An important characteristic of X transformation is that, it is respecting the key-forest key compression approach as it was defined in Section 2.3.3. Given that the underlying set system Φ has a key-forest F_Φ, the key forest of the set system $\Phi' =$ **XTrans**(Φ) is the union of the key-forests of the underlying building set systems while the binary trees on the head can be appended to corresponding trees of the key-forest defined for the body of the extended family Φ'. This means that it is possible to maintain a small overall number of trees in the key-forest as the transformation is applied repetitively. For an example of this the reader is referred to the explicit instantiation of an X-transformation shown in the end of this section.

Factorizability of the X-Transformation.

We will prove next that the transformation described in definition 2.52 preserves the factorizability of the underlying set system.

Theorem 2.54. *Given that the fully exclusive set system Φ defined over $\{1, \ldots, 2^m\}$ is factorizable and further satisfies the* X – property, *then it holds that the set system* **XTrans**(Φ) *defined over $\{1, \ldots, 2^{2m}\}$ is also factorizable.*

Proof of Theorem 2.54: We will prove that **XTrans**(Φ) is a factorizable set system by showing that it satisfies the diamond property, i.e. given any two intersecting subsets we will show that their union is in the new set system. Our proof will be based on the location of subsets that are intersecting:

Suppose, now, we have two subsets $\mathsf{S}_1 \in \mathbf{XTrans}(\Phi)$ and $\mathsf{S}_2 \in \mathbf{XTrans}(\Phi)$ so that $\mathsf{S}_1 \cap \mathsf{S}_2 \neq \emptyset$. If S_1 and S_2 are in the same Φ component of the new key-poset, it will hold that $(\mathsf{S}_1 \cup \mathsf{S}_2) \in \mathbf{XTrans}(\Phi)$ due to the factorizability of the set system Φ. Otherwise, we have three cases:

1. S_1 is located on the head, and S_2 is located in the body. It holds that S_1 extends $\mathsf{C}_i \in \Phi$ for some $i \in \{1, \ldots, 2^m\}$. Let S_2^* be the subset of Φ that corresponds to S_2. If $i \in \mathsf{S}_2^*$, this means that S_2 contains all atoms of Φ_i while on the other hand S_1 contains all other atoms (as it extends C_i). It follows that $\mathsf{S}_1 \cup \mathsf{S}_2 = \mathsf{M}'$, hence their union is the top subset of the set system which belongs to $\mathbf{XTrans}(\Phi)$. On the other hand, if $i \notin \mathsf{S}_2^*$ then it holds that $\mathsf{S}_2 \subset \mathsf{S}_1$.

2. S_1 is located on the head, and S_2 is located on the feet. It holds that S_1 is in a binary tree that extends $\mathsf{C}_i \in \Phi$ for some $i \in \{1, \ldots, 2^m\}$. If $\mathsf{S}_2 \in \Phi_i$, then there is a corresponding copy of S_1 within Φ_i say called $\mathsf{S}_3 \in \Phi_i$. It is easy to see that $\mathsf{S}_2, \mathsf{S}_3$ are also intersecting and hence the union of $\mathsf{S}_3 \cup \mathsf{S}_2$ exists within Φ_i. The union is also in the filter of S_3, hence it holds that there would be a corresponding element of the union-subset on the head of new key-poset $\mathbf{XTrans}(\Phi)$ that will contain S_1. On the other hand, if S_2 is located on the set system $\Phi_{i'}$ for some leaf $i' \neq i$, then it holds that $\mathsf{S}_2 \subset \mathsf{S}_1$.

3. S_1 is located in the body, and S_2 is located on the feet: it holds that S_2 is located on the set system Φ_i for some leaf $\{i\} \in \Phi$. Let S_1^* be the subset of Φ that corresponds to S_1. Since $\mathsf{S}_1 \cap \mathsf{S}_2 \neq \emptyset$ then it holds that $i \in \mathsf{S}_1^*$. This suggests that $\mathsf{S}_2 \subset \mathsf{S}_1$. ∎

Efficiency parameters of the transformation.

We now come to the point to discuss the transmission overhead of the set system constructed by the X-transformation. Provided that the set system satisfies the $\mathrm{X}-$property, even though the transformation defines a new set system that squares the size of the receiver population, it increases the transmission overhead by a constant factor only. This can be observed by the following theorem on bounding the order of a lower-maximal partition for the intersection of any ideal with the complement of an atomic-filter. At the same time we show how the key storage and computation overhead are affected by the transformation.

Theorem 2.55. *Suppose that a fully-exclusive set system Φ defined over a set $\mathsf{M} = \{1, \ldots, 2^m\}$ is factorizable and further satisfies the $\mathrm{X}-$property.*

(i) If for any subset $\mathsf{S} \in \Phi$ and an atom $u \in \Phi$ it holds that $\mathsf{ord}((\mathsf{S}) \cap \mathsf{P}_u) \leq \mathsf{t}(m)$ within the poset Φ for some function $\mathsf{t}(\cdot)$, then it holds that $\mathsf{ord}((\mathsf{S}') \cap \mathsf{P}_{u'}) \leq \mathsf{t}(m) + 2$ for any $\mathsf{S}' \in \mathbf{XTrans}(\Phi)$ and any atom $u' \in \mathbf{XTrans}(\Phi)$.

(ii) If there exists a key-assignment technique for Φ such that the key-storage for each user is bounded by $\mathsf{s}(m)$ for some function $\mathsf{s}(\cdot)$ and the computation overhead is bounded by $\mathsf{c}(m)$ for some function $\mathsf{c}(\cdot)$, then there is a key-assignment technique so that the key-storage in $\mathbf{XTrans}(\Phi)$ is bounded by $2\mathsf{s}(m) + m$ and computation overhead is bounded by $\max(\mathsf{c}(m), m)$.

Proof of Theorem 2.55: (i) On transmission overhead of the transformation:

For any leaf $u' \in \mathbf{XTrans}(\Phi)$ there exists a leaf v' in the body which is replaced with the set system $\Phi_{v'}$ that satisfies $(v'-1)2^m + 1 \leq u' \leq v' \cdot 2^m$. Denote the leading subset of $\Phi_{v'}$ by (v'). First recall that the subset $\mathsf{C}_{u'}^{v'} =_{df} (v')\setminus\{u'\}$ exists in the set system $\Phi_{v'}$ located in the feet of the transformation. We have three cases depending on the location of $\mathsf{S}' \in \mathbf{XTrans}(\Phi)$:

1. S' is located on the head: it holds that S' is in a binary tree extending $\mathsf{C}_v \in \Phi$ for some $v \in \{1,\ldots,2^m\}$, recall that we define $\mathsf{C}_v = \mathsf{M} \setminus \{v\}$ and S' is corresponded to a subset in Φ_v; we will denote its corresponding subset by S'^{*}. We have two subcases:
(i) if $v = v'$: Consider now the lower-maximal partition $\langle \mathsf{I}_1,\ldots,\mathsf{I}_o\rangle$ of $(\mathsf{S}'^{*}) \cap \mathsf{P}_{u'}$ within the set system $\Phi_{v'}$ (here $\mathsf{P}_{u'}$ is the complement of the atomic filter u' in key-poset $\Phi_{v'}$); due to the factorizability of the set system and the theorem's statement it holds that the lower maximal partition satisfies $o \leq \mathsf{t}(m)$. Consider now the intersection $(\mathsf{S}') \cap \mathsf{P}_{u'}$ within the set system $\mathbf{XTrans}(\Phi)$; it will hold that the users of $(\mathsf{S}') \cap \mathsf{P}_{u'}$ can be covered in the worst case by $\mathsf{C}_v \cup (\cup_{j=1}^{o} \mathsf{I}_j)$ (it might be possible that $\mathsf{C}_v \cup \mathsf{I}_j$ exists in the new set system for some j something that would give an even smaller cover). In any case, $\mathsf{ord}((\mathsf{S}') \cap \mathsf{P}_{v'}) \leq \mathsf{t}(m) + 1$.
(ii) if $v \neq v'$: The users of the set $(\mathsf{S}') \cap \mathsf{P}_{u'}$ can be covered by the sets $\mathsf{S}'^{*} \cup \mathsf{C}_{u'}^{v'}$ as well as the users in the intersection $(\mathsf{C}_v \cap \mathsf{P}_{v'})$; note that the latter intersection is taken within the body of the transformation. Hence, in any case the cover of $(\mathsf{S}') \cap \mathsf{P}_{u'}$ will number at most $\mathsf{ord}((\mathsf{S}') \cap \mathsf{P}_{u'}) \leq \mathsf{t}(m) + 2$ subsets.

2. S' is located in the body: Provided that $u' \in \mathsf{S}'$ (otherwise the intersection is S' itself), it holds that $v' \in \mathsf{S}'$ within the set system Φ and hence it holds that the users of $(\mathsf{S}') \cap \mathsf{P}_{u'}$ can be covered by $\mathsf{C}_{u'}^{v'} \cup (\mathsf{S}' \cap \mathsf{P}_{v'})$ where the latter intersection is taken within the body of the transformation. It follows that $\mathsf{ord}((\mathsf{S}') \cap \mathsf{P}_{u'}) \leq \mathsf{t}(m) + 1$.

3. S' is located on the feet of the transformation: Suppose S' is located in the set system Φ_v for some $v \in \{1,\ldots,2^m\}$. If $v \neq v'$ then the intersection is of the ideal (S') and the complement of the atomic filter $\mathsf{F}(u')$ would be (S') itself. Otherwise S' is located within the set system with u' for which the intersection yields a lower maximal partition of order less than or equal to $\mathsf{t}(m)$ due to the factorizability of the set system Φ.

(ii) Dealing with the body and feet part of the transformation is relatively easy. We will employ the key assignment technique of the basic set system for the set system of the body Φ as well as $\Phi_1, \Phi_2, \ldots, \Phi_{2^m}$ used in the transformation. Observe that the user would need to store exactly $2 \cdot \mathsf{s}(m)$ keys (one set of keys for the component Φ_i it belongs to and one set of keys for Φ) and in order to derive any key in the head and body part would require computation overhead bounded by $\mathsf{c}(m)$.

With respect to the subsets located on the head of the transformation no extra keys would be needed. We will use the structure of the binary trees and the computational key compression method of described in definition 2.21.

Observe that a user u is able to derive the keys for each subset $\mathsf{C}_{u'}$ in the body. Each subset C_u is the root of an upward binary tree for which the user requires all or some of the keys. Specifically, based on the X-property there is a single binary tree for which the user u requires only a subset of the keys and in fact he would need exactly m keys as it needs a key for each sibling of a node in the path that excludes u. Hence, employing a 3-fold key extender to derive the keys for all the nodes in the binary trees using the keys of the C_u sets as the locals a user needs to store m extra keys (the labels of the nodes that are siblings of the nodes in the unique path that excludes the user) and thus the computation overhead is bounded by m. It follows that the key storage is bounded by $2\mathsf{s}(m) + m$. The computation overhead is bounded by the maximum of $\mathsf{c}(m)$ and m. ■

Instantiation for X-Transformation

Theorem 2.55 proves that the X-transformation of a set system squares the size of the population, while the efficiency parameters increase only linearly. This motivates us to apply successive applications of the transformation described in Definition 2.52 over a fully-exclusive set system.

Definition 2.56. *Let $\Phi^{(d)}$ be a factorizable set system defined over a set $[d] = \{1, \ldots, d\}$ and further satisfies $\mathrm{X-property}$. We define $\mathrm{AS}^k_{\Phi(d)}$ as the fully-exclusive factorizable set system defined over a set of $n = d^{2^k}$ users where $\mathrm{AS}^j_{\Phi(d)} = \mathbf{XTrans}(\mathrm{AS}^{j-1}_{\Phi(d)})$ for $j = 1, \ldots, k$ with $\mathrm{AS}^0_{\Phi(d)} = \Phi^{(d)}$.*

Theorem 2.36 and Theorem 2.55 implies the following corollary which provides an upper bound on the transmission overhead of the set system $\mathrm{AS}^k_{\Phi(d)}$ and the efficiency of the key-assignment technique.

Corollary 2.57. *Let $n = d^{2^k}$ for some $d, k \in \mathbb{N}$ and $\Phi^{(d)}$ is a factorizable set system defined over a set of size d that satisfies the $\mathrm{X-property}$. Suppose that for any subset $\mathsf{S} \in \Phi^{(d)}$ and an atom u of $\Phi^{(d)}$ it holds that $\mathsf{ord}((\mathsf{S}) \cap \mathsf{P}_u) \leq \mathsf{t}(d)$ within the poset Φ, the key storage is bounded by $\mathsf{s}(d)$ and the computation overhead is bounded by $\mathsf{c}(d)$ for some functions $\mathsf{t}(\cdot), \mathsf{s}(\cdot)$ and $\mathsf{c}(\cdot)$. Consider now the set system $\mathrm{AS}^k_{\Phi(d)}$ over n users:*

1. If $d = O(1)$, then the transmission overhead to disable a set of r users in the set system $\mathrm{AS}^k_{\Phi(d)}$ would be $O(r(2\log\log n))$, the key storage is $O(\log\log n \cdot \log n)$ and the computation overhead would be $O(\log n)$.

2. If $k = O(1)$, then the transmission overhead to disable a set of r in the set system $\mathrm{AS}^k_{\Phi(d)}$ would be $r(2k + \mathsf{t}(d))$, the key storage is $2^k \cdot \mathsf{s}(d) + \frac{k \log n}{2}$ and the computation overhead would be $\max(\mathsf{c}(d), \log n)$.

Proof of Corollary 2.57: Due to the theorem 2.55 the order of a lower maximal partition of $(\mathsf{S} \cap \mathsf{P}_u)$ for any subset $\mathsf{S} \in \mathrm{AS}^k_{\Phi(d)}$ and any atom $u \in [d^{2^k}]$ can be bounded by incrementing $\mathsf{t}(d)$ with $2k$.

Recall that the Theorem 2.36 relates the transmission overhead of a set system with the upper bound on the lower maximal partition order for the intersection of an ideal with a complement of an atomic filter. Hence, we obtain the transmission overhead for the ciphertext revoking r users is bounded by $r(2k+\mathsf{t}(d)-1)+1$. That would conclude the case when k is a constant. While on the other hand, if d is a constant then we obtain $r(\log\log n)$.

Regarding the key storage and the computation overhead, we successively apply the bounds given in theorem 2.55 to obtain for $i = 1, \ldots, k$:

$$\mathsf{s}_i = 2\mathsf{s}_{i-1} + 2^{i-1}\log d$$

where $\mathsf{s}_0 = \mathsf{s}(d)$. By applying a telescopic sum over i values we will obtain $\mathsf{s}_k = 2^k\mathsf{s}(d) + k2^{k-1}\log d = 2^k\mathsf{s}(d) + \frac{k\log n}{2}$. That would conclude the case when k is a constant. In case d is constant we have $k = \log\log n$, hence the key storage is $O(\log\log n \cdot \log n)$. ∎

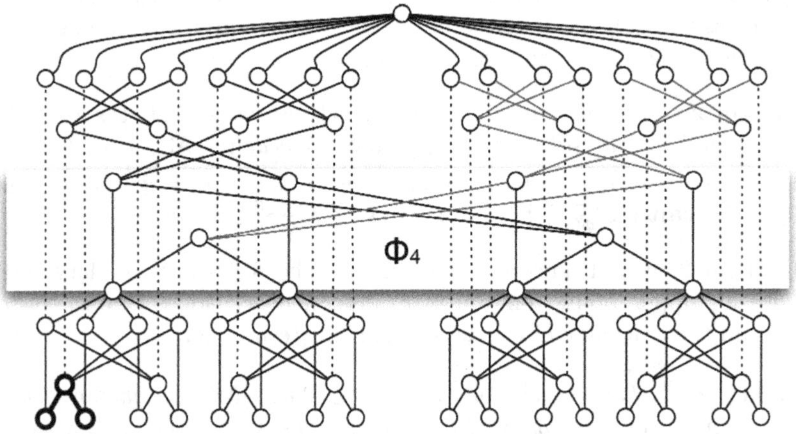

Fig. 2.20. The X-transformation over the set system $\Phi_4 = \mathrm{AS}^1_{\Phi_{\{1,2\}}}$.

We will next give an example of an AS set system and an application of the transformation technique above. We first start with a set system $\Phi_{\{1,2\}} = \{\{1,2\},\{1\},\{2\}\}$ that is the power set (without the empty set) of the set $\{1,2\}$. Observe that this basic set system satisfies the X – property and it is factorizable set system. Hence, the transformation described in definition 2.52 will yield factorizable set systems over exponentially growing receiver populations that satisfy the statement of the corollary 2.57. Observe that the resulting set system $\mathrm{AS}^2_{\Phi_{\{1,2\}}}$ is defined over a receiver population of size 16. The figure 2.20 illustrates the resulting set system after applying the transformation twice on the above simple set system.

The key-forest of the above construction is depicted in Figure 2.21. Regarding the parameters of the set system $\mathrm{AS}_{\Phi^k_{\{1,2\}}}$ that is the factorizable set sytem defined over a set of size $n = 2^{2^k}$, we have the following immediate corollary.

Corollary 2.58. *Consider the broadcast encryption scheme based on the set system* $\mathrm{AS}^k_{\Phi_{\{1,2\}}}$ *where* $k = \log\log n$*; the transmission overhead for the ciphertext revoking* r *users is* $O(r \log\log n)$*. The key-storage for each receiver is* $O(\log\log n \cdot \log n)$*, and the computation overhead for a receiver is bounded by* $\log n$*.*

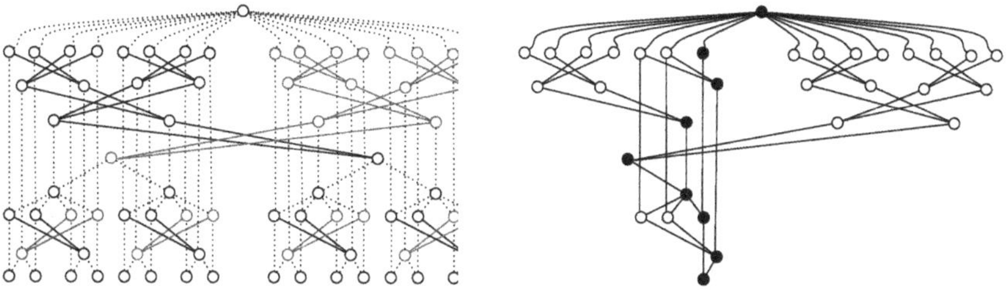

Fig. 2.21. (left) the key-forest of the set system $\mathrm{AS}^2_{\Phi_{\{1,2\}}}$. The edges define the trees in the key-forest. (right) the filter for a specific user, the black nodes represent the roots of the trees in the intersection of the key-forest and the filter.

2.7 Bibliographic notes

The concept of broadcast encryption was introduced in the work by Berkovits [10]. Combinatorial broadcast encryption schemes can be constructed by employing probabilistic techniques or with explicit combinatorial constructions. Examples of this category include the first paper [42] that introduced the first formal construction of a broadcast encryption and employed a probabilistic design as well as others such as [87, 53] that employed explicit combinatorial constructions such as the ones we focused on in this chapter. Recall that *structured* broadcast encryption schemes utilize the key-space so that it has some structure that enables the preparation of ciphertexts that are decipherable only by the enabled users. Examples of this category include schemes that are based on polynomial interpolation [90, 37] where keys are points of a polynomial over a finite field and schemes based on bilinear maps such as [18] where the discrete-logarithms of the keys over an elliptic curve group are different powers of the same base.

Given that the intended application of broadcast encryption is content distribution, it is expected that the scheme would handle large messages. This is solved in our exposition through hybrid encryption and recall that this approach requires the broadcast encryption scheme to implement a "Key Encapsulation Mechanism" (KEM). KEM is introduced by Shoup [108] in the context of public key encryption. We further require the underlying cryptographic primitive to support the CCA1 type of encryption security, or what is known as a security against lunch-time attacks [91].

Regarding combinatorial constructions the underlying key-space can be structured as an exclusive set system. Some constructions of exclusive set systems for different parameters are known [4, 117, 83] along with some existence results (see [77]) using the probabilistic method. Various tools have been used for explicit constructions including polynomials over finite fields, [49], and algebraic-geometric codes [76].

The subset cover framework introduced by Naor, Naor and Lotspiech in [87] as a wide class of exclusive set systems with some specific properties. [87] also proposed the two schemes of Complete Subtree (CS) and Subset Difference (SD). The idea in both of these schemes was to locate the receivers on the leaves of a binary tree. The CS is related to the logical key hierarchy (LKH) that was proposed independently by Wallner et al. [121] and Wong et al. [125], for the purpose of designing a key distribution algorithm for Internet multicasting.

The applicability of this framework is also evidenced by the fact that a subset cover scheme (a simple variant of the subset-difference method) is at the heart of the AACS standard [1] that is employed by high definition DVDs (Blu-Ray and HD-DVD). The Advanced Access Content System (AACS) is a standard for content distribution and digital rights management, intended to restrict access to and copying of the next generation of optical discs and DVDs. The specification was publicly released in April 2005 and the standard has been adopted as the access restriction scheme for Blu-ray (BD) discs. It is developed by AACS Licensing Administrator, LLC (AACS LA), a consortium that includes Disney, Intel, Microsoft, Matsushita (Panasonic), Warner Bros., IBM, Toshiba and Sony. In this particular application, the distribution channel is an optical disc or DVD. The decoders required to playback the content are either hardware DVD-players or software video-players. The decoders have embedded the necessary secret-key information at the manufacturing stage.

In a broadcast encryption scheme, all unlicensed receivers must be excluded in the broadcast pattern. The transmission overhead of a broadcast encryption can be further reduced in some settings when some of the unlicensed receivers are allowed to continue receiving the transmission. Abdalla et al. in [3] introduced the concept of *free riders* to capture this observation and investigate the performance gains. Ramzan and Woodruff [97] proposed an algorithm to optimally choose the set of free riders in the CS system, and Ak, Kaya and Selcuk in [5] presented a polynomial time algorithm which computes the optimal placement for a given number of free riders in an SD scheme.

After the introduction of Subset Cover Framework by Naor, Naor and Lotspiech in [87], this combinatorial framework gave rise to a diverse number of fully-exclusive set systems: Complete Subtree and Subset Difference [87], the Layered Subset Difference [53], the Key Chain Tree [122], the Stratified Subset Difference [50], the Subset Incremental Chain [6] and the class of set systems of [55] as well as that of [56, 57].

The Key Chain Tree [122], the Stratified Subset Difference [50] and the Subset Incremental Chain [6] are all employing the same set system with slight differences in their key-handling procedures. Those differences result in different efficiency parameters but still they utilize the exact same key-poset. It is quite easy to observe that [6] and [122] have the same key-poset whereas it is more involved to see the isomorphism of the set system Stratified Subset Difference ([50]) to the former two without explicitly thinking of the key-poset of [50]. We refer the reader to [105] for more information on partial ordered sets.

As a short diversion within this short set of bibliographic notes, we will show that, indeed, the key-poset of the Stratified Subset Difference is isomorphic to the key-poset of Key Chain Tree. In a nutshell, the set system Φ^{SSD} of [50] consists of subsets that are formed as follows. Consider a subset of a SD method, and denoted by S_j where $\mathsf{j} = (v_i, v_k)$ is a pair of nodes in the binary tree that has leaves the set of users. The set $\mathsf{S}_\mathsf{j}^L \in \Phi^{SSD}$ is defined as the set of nodes rooted at v_i and located on the left of the nodes rooted at v_k. The set $\mathsf{S}_\mathsf{j}^R \in \Phi^{SSD}$ is defined as the set of nodes rooted at v_i and located on the right of the nodes rooted at v_k. Observe that both subsets S_j^L and S_j^R consist of continuous nodes at the leaf level in the subtree rooted at node v_i.

Theorem 2.59. *The key poset of Stratified Subset Difference is equal to the key poset stemming from the schemes of [6, 122] that is depicted in figure 2.16.*

Proof. of Theorem 2.59 It is quite obvious that any subset described in the stratified subset difference exists in the set system of Key Chain Tree. We will, now, complete the proof by showing that for any subset $\mathsf{S}_{\mathsf{j}^k} \in \Phi^{\mathsf{KCT}}$ there exists some $\mathsf{S}_{\mathsf{j}^s} \in \Phi^{\mathsf{SSD}}$ that satisfies $\mathsf{S}_{\mathsf{j}^k} = \mathsf{S}_{\mathsf{j}^s}$:

We have two cases for the location of leaves in $\mathsf{S}_{\mathsf{j}^k} = \{u_1, \dots, u_t\}$:

(i) $\mathsf{S}_{\mathsf{j}^k}$ is set of consecutive leaves rooted at a minimal node v_1 so that u_1 is the leftmost leaf of v_1. Denote the least common ancestor of u_t and u^* by v_2 where u^* comes after the leaf u_t in the left-to-right ordering of the leaves. Consider the right child of v_2 and name it by v_3. Observe now that the subset $\mathsf{S}_{\mathsf{j}^s}^L$ for $\mathsf{j}^s = (v_1, v_3)$ contains all leaves rooted at v_1 and located on the left of the nodes rooted at v_3.

(ii) $\mathsf{S}_{\mathsf{j}^k}$ is set of consecutive leaves rooted at a minimal node v_1 so that u_t is the rightmost leaf of v_1. Denote the least common ancestor of u_1 and u^* by v_2 where u^* comes before the leaf u_1 in the right-to-left ordering of the leaves. Consider the left child of v_2 and name it by v_3. Observe now that the subset $\mathsf{S}_{\mathsf{j}^s}^R$ for $\mathsf{j}^s = (v_1, v_3)$ contains all leaves rooted at v_1 and located on the right of the nodes rooted at v_3.

Hence, in any case, there will be a corresponding subset in the Stratified Subset Difference for each subset in the Key Chain Tree. ■

In the formalization of the Key-Poset framework we introduced in this chapter, the subset cover families of [6, 50, 87, 122] are all factorizable (see Section 2.5) and thus the results we laid out provide a unified way for solving revocation efficiently and optimally in all these schemes.

The transformation we discussed in section 2.6.1 was introduced in [55] to reduce the computation overhead sacrificing some transmission and key-storage capacity. A similar technique was already discussed in [6, 50], and employed to improve the computation overhead. The generic transformation described in [55] increases the transmission overhead by a factor of k. To take the transmission back from $2kr$ to $2r$, the work [56] presented a technique that works only for the schemes based on key-chains [6, 50, 122]. This technique will result in, not suprisingly, the basic set system depicted on the left of the Figure 2.16.

In Section 2.6.2 we presented a new generic transformation that gives rise to new schemes with different efficiency parameters. We presented an instantiation of the transformation, which ignoring $\log\log n$ factors, is a scheme that simultaneously achieves communication overhead proportional to r (the number of revoked users), receiver storage $\log n$, and receiver computation proportional to $\log n$. The same efficiency parameters are exhibited by the general Layered Subset Difference (LSD) method (see ([53])), and it turns out that this instantiation is an isomorphic representation of the general LSD method (in particular when the LSD is used for the optimal depth of layering). It worth pointing out that the description of the LSD is different from the recursive application of **XTrans** presented in this chapter and it requires some effort to observe the equivalence. We leave it as an exercise to establish formally this equivalence.

Subset cover schemes that have been discussed in this chapter are designed for *stateless receivers*. A stateless receiver need not maintain state from one transmission to the next. It can go arbitrarily offline without losing its reception capability in the long run. It is also independent of changes within the receiver population, in particular, the decryption capability of receiver keys do not change if other receivers join or leave the system.

While stateless receivers are more easy to administer in a system deployment they affect the revocation capability as well as the efficiency of the system. Suppose that the revocation list of a system employing broadcast encryption scheme increases as time passes. The state-of-the-art suggests that this would yield an increase in the transmission overhead of at least linear in the number of revocations. Such increase can be unbearable for many application scenarios. For instance, systems that employ smart-card like devices can only handle limited computation and storage. Refreshing keys in a fully stateful manner has been discussed in the context of key-management protocols such as the Logical Key Hierarchy, cf. [25, 26, 107, 121, 125]. A hybrid approach is also possible, where some degree of statefulness is required and the system introduces phases or periods over which the receiver has to maintain a state, cf. [7, 37, 45, 74, 82, 90]. The notion of *long-lived broadcast encryption* introduced by Garay et al. [47] where the revoked or compromised keys of the receivers are discarded. A long-lived scheme will minimize the cost of rekeying as well as maintaining the security for enabled users even as the compromised keys are discarded.

A natural extension to the broadcast encryption setting is to allow multiple content providers to broadcast to the same receiver population. An incentive for such an extension is that it accommodates dynamically changing content providers. As a result of using the same broadcast channel for all different providers, the underlying broadcasting infrastructure will be unified and simplified, with decreased storage and equipment costs for the receiver side. However, a shared broadcast channel raises the problem of handling the private information shared between the content providers and the broadcast center as it might be the case that the broadcast channel is entirely separated from the subscription service where the receivers acquire their secret keys.

A trivial solution to that problem is to distribute the same broadcasting key to all content providers. This risks a violation of the content protection if any of the providers is corrupted. On the other hand, distributing different broadcasting keys and their corresponding user keys will isolate providers but not scale properly as the number of content providers grows. This discussion recalls the similar deficiencies of encryption in the symmetric key setting, and leads to investigating broadcast encryption in the public key setting where the content providers all share a publicly known encryption key while the receivers are given the secret decryption keys uniquely assigned to them subject to their subscription levels. A number of early works in designing broadcast encryption schemes in the public key setting include [35, 36, 37, 90].

While these works have transmission overhead dependent on the size of the revocation list, this barrier was overcome by Boneh and et al. in [18]. They presented a construction that achieves constant size transmission overhead. As the public key size is linear in number of receivers, this scheme is not particularly practical. A number of constructions (cf. [19, 33, 34, 103]) gave trade-offs between the efficiency parameters indicated above. We would like to note that all these constructions are based on pairings over elliptic curves, a technique which has received a lot interest in the design of cryptographic schemes. See [46] for an overview of pairing-based cryptography. The latter constructions also support identity-based encryption (see [106, 17]) which suggests the fact that the public key associated to the scrambling of a transmission can be any string.

3

Traitor Tracing

A three word description for what traitor tracing aims to achieve is *key leakage deterrence.* Arguably the single most important problem in the application of cryptography is key management. Keys that are lost imply loss of data and keys that are exposed imply loss of privacy. In the context of digital content distribution the problem is heavily exacerbated by the fact that cryptographic keys reside within a possibly adversarial environment.

In a setting where a transmission is aimed to many receivers and it is desired to control the recipient list, encryption comes to mind as a possible solution. Unfortunately standard encryption techniques lead to solutions that are unrealistic to implement in practice. On the one hand, using the same key throughout motivates key leakage while on the other hand using independent keys throughout leads to heavy performance loss.

In this setting traitor tracing aims to deter key leakage while maintaining performance loss to a minimum. In this chapter we will provide a formal treatment of traitor tracing, we will introduce various constructions and measure their performance characteristics.

3.1 Multiuser Encryption Schemes

Any traitor tracing scheme is based on an underlying encryption mechanism called a multiuser encryption scheme (ME).

An s-ary multiuser encryption scheme ME is a triple (**KeyDist**, **Transmit**, **Receive**) where $s \in \mathbb{N}$. The parameter of the scheme is n, the number of receivers and is associated with three sets $\mathsf{K}, \mathsf{M}, \mathsf{C}$ corresponding to the sets of keys, plaintexts and ciphertexts respectively. In case $s = 1$, we will simply call the scheme as a multiuser encryption scheme. We describe the I/O of these procedures below:

- **KeyDist**. It is a probabilistic algorithm that on input 1^n, it produces $(tk, ek, sk_1, \ldots, sk_n)$. The decryption key sk_i is to be assigned to the i-th

A. Kiayias and S. Pehlivanoglu, *Encryption for Digital Content*, Advances in Information Security 52, DOI 10.1007/978-1-4419-0044-9_3, © Springer Science+Business Media, LLC 2010

user while ek is the encryption key. The tracing key tk is some auxiliary information to be used for tracing that may be empty.

- **Transmit**. It is a probabilistic algorithm that given a vector of inputs $M = \langle m_1, \ldots, m_s \rangle \in \mathsf{M}^s$, it prepares an element $c \in \mathsf{C}$. We will write the following to denote the distribution of the output: $c \leftarrow \mathbf{Transmit}(ek, M)$
- **Receive**. It is a deterministic algorithm that on input c sampled from $\mathbf{Transmit}(ek, \langle m_1, \ldots, m_s \rangle)$ and a user-key sk_i for some $i \in [n]$ where $(tk, ek, sk_1, \ldots, sk_n) \leftarrow \mathbf{KeyDist}(1^n)$, it either outputs m_i for some $i \in \{1, \ldots, s\}$ or fails. Note that **Receive** can also be generalized to be a probabilistic algorithm but we will not take advantage of this here.

We can consider a variant of the multiuser encryption scheme that is stateful where the algorithm **Transmit** is parameterized by a set of states denoted by States. In a stateful multiuser encryption scheme, the **Transmit** algorithm prepares an element $c \in \mathsf{C}$ as a function of the current state and updates the state after each transmission. In this chapter, unless stated otherwise, we will be discussing stateless multiuser encryption schemes.

The above determine the syntax of the algorithms that define a multiuser encryption scheme ME. We expect from such a scheme to satisfy correctness in the usual sense. In particular we require that:

Definition 3.1. ***Correctness.*** *We say an s-ary multiuser encryption scheme* ME *is correct if for any* $n \in \mathbb{N}$, *for any vector of messages* $M = \langle m_1, \ldots, m_s \rangle \in \mathsf{M}^s$ *and for any* $u \in [n]$, *it holds that*

$$\mathbf{Prob}[\mathbf{Receive}(\mathbf{Transmit}(ek, M), sk_u) \in \{m_1, \ldots, m_s\}] = 1$$

where $(tk, ek, sk_1, \ldots, sk_n)$ *is distributed according to* $\mathbf{KeyDist}(1^n)$.

It is possible to use the multiuser encryption scheme as a key encapsulation mechanism that is to transmit a cryptographic key similar to the use of broadcast encryption schemes we discussed in the previous chapter. That is something that enables the usage of the above scheme in a hybrid encryption mode. The figure 3.1 is the standard security game that captures the key encapsulation we require from the multiuser encryption scheme.

Definition 3.2. *We say an s-ary multiuser encryption scheme* ME *is CCA-1* ε*-insecure if for any probabilistic polynomial time algorithm* $\mathcal{A}$, *it holds that*

$$\mathbf{Adv}_{\mathcal{A}}^{kem}(1^n) = \mathbf{Prob}[\mathbf{Exp}_{\mathcal{A}}^{kem}(1^n) = 1] - \frac{1}{2}] \leq \varepsilon$$

where the experiment $\mathbf{Exp}_{\mathcal{A}}^{kem}$ *is defined as in figure 3.1.*

We note that ε in general is not supposed to be a function of n, i.e. the security property should hold independently of the number of users present in the recipient list. It is possible to define CPA version of the above security

TransmitOracle$(m_1,\ldots,m_s)$	ReceiveOracle(c,u)
retrieve ek;	retrieve sk_u;
$c \leftarrow \mathbf{Transmit}(ek, m_1,\ldots,m_s)$;	return $\mathbf{Receive}(c, sk_u)$;
return c;	

Experiment $\mathbf{Exp}_{\mathcal{A}}^{ME}(1^n)$

$(tk, ek, sk_1,\ldots,sk_n) \leftarrow \mathbf{KeyDist}(1^n)$
$aux \leftarrow \mathcal{A}^{\mathsf{TransmitOracle}(\cdot),\mathsf{ReceiveOracle}(\cdot)}(1^n)$
$\langle m_1^0,\ldots m_s^0\rangle, \langle m_1^1,\ldots m_s^1\rangle \stackrel{R}{\leftarrow} \mathsf{M}^s$
$b \stackrel{R}{\leftarrow} \{0,1\}$; $c \leftarrow \mathbf{Transmit}(ek, \langle m_1^1,\ldots m_s^1\rangle)$
$b' \leftarrow \mathcal{A}^{\mathsf{TransmitOracle}(\cdot)}(aux, \langle m_1^b,\ldots m_s^b\rangle, c)$
return 1 if and only if $b = b'$

Fig. 3.1. The CCA-1 security game for a multi user encryption scheme.

definition/game by not letting the attacker to access the ReceiveOracle on the second line of the security game. In such case we say the multiuser encryption scheme is CPA ε-insecure, if the above condition given in the definition holds for a CPA adversary.

Note that typically key encapsulation mechanisms are defined without any input beyond the encryption key (i.e., there is no plaintext part). For convenience we take a different approach where we provide the input. In effect, we state above that the encryption mechanism of the multiuser encryption matches the syntax of regular encryption and is supposed to satisfy the security requirements of a key encapsulation mechanism.

3.2 Constructions For Multiuser Encryption Schemes

In this section we will present some multiuser encryption schemes. The basic characteristic in all these schemes is that the keys given to users are distinct. For each scheme we will provide its definition and a proof of security. The reader will observe that the key space is selected in some deliberate manner to enforce some "separability" between the users. The exact benefits of the user key space that the schemes of this section exhibit will become useful when we introduce tracing games in the next section.

3.2.1 Linear Length Multiuser Encryption Scheme

We will now, present a straightforward multiuser encryption scheme that produces a ciphertext of length linear in number of receivers. We will name this scheme by $\mathtt{ME}_L$ which will be a unary scheme that is transmitting a single encrypted message to the receivers. It is parameterized by an encryption scheme $(\mathtt{E},\mathtt{D})$.

- **KeyDist**$_L$: Given 1^n it produces a set of keys $\{k_1, \dots, k_n\} \subseteq \mathsf{K}$, sk_i is set to be the key k_i for $i = 1, \dots, n$, and sets $ek = \langle k_1, \dots, k_n \rangle$. The tracing key tk is empty.
- **Transmit**$_L$: Given a message $m \in \mathsf{M}$ and the encryption key $ek = \langle k_1, \dots, k_n \rangle$, it transmits the encryption of the message m with ek by employing the encryption scheme $(\mathtt{E}, \mathtt{D})$ as follows:

$$\langle \mathtt{E}_{k_1}(m), \dots, \mathtt{E}_{k_n}(m) \rangle$$

- **Receive**$_L$: Given the key $sk_i = k_i$ for some $i \in [n]$ and a transmission of the form $\langle c_1, \dots, c_n \rangle$, it returns $\mathtt{D}_{k_i}(c_i)$.

Theorem 3.3. *A linear length multiuser encryption scheme* $\mathtt{ME}_L$ *satisfies correctness (cf. Definition 3.1) i.e., we assume that for all* $k, m \in \mathsf{K}, \mathsf{M}$ *it holds* $\mathtt{D}_k(\mathtt{E}_k(m)) = m$. *It is, further, CCA-1* ε*-insecure in the sense of Definition 3.2 with* $\varepsilon \leq 2n \cdot \varepsilon_p$ *where the underlying encryption scheme* $(\mathtt{E}, \mathtt{D})$ *is* ε_p*-insecure in the sense of Definition 2.5.*

Proof. Theorem 3.3: Regarding correctness, for user $i \in [n]$, the input of the receive function is some c such that $c \leftarrow \mathbf{Transmit}(ek, m)$ as well as k_i. It follows that i-th user will be able to apply the key k_i to the i-th component of the ciphertext c to recover the plaintext m correctly always. Therefore correctness follows easily.

The security proof is a simpler form of the proof we provided in the proof of Theorem 2.8. We will make the argument clear in here once more so that it will be ready for future reference. Let us start writing the original game $\mathbf{Exp}_0 = \mathbf{Exp}_{\mathcal{A}}^{\mathtt{ME}_L}(1^n)$ explicitly in Figure 3.2:

TransmitOracle(m)	ReceiveOracle(c, u)
retrieve ek; $c \leftarrow \mathbf{Transmit}(ek, m)$; return c;	retrieve sk_u; return $\mathbf{Receive}(c, sk_u)$;

Experiment $\mathbf{Exp}_0(1^n)$

$(\emptyset, \{k_i\}_{i \in [n]}, k_1, \dots, k_n) \leftarrow \mathbf{KeyDist}(1^n)$;
$ek = \{k_i\}_{i \in [n]}$; $sk_i = k_i$ for $i = 1, \dots, n$
$aux \leftarrow \mathcal{A}^{\mathsf{TransmitOracle}(\cdot), \mathsf{ReceiveOracle}(\cdot)}(1^n)$
$m_0, m_1 \stackrel{R}{\leftarrow} \mathsf{M}$; $b \stackrel{R}{\leftarrow} \{0, 1\}$
$c = \langle \mathtt{E}_{k_1}(m_1), \dots, \mathtt{E}_{k_n}(m_1) \rangle \leftarrow \mathbf{Transmit}(ek, m_1)$
$b' \leftarrow \mathcal{A}(aux, m_b, c)$
return 1 if and only if $b = b'$

Fig. 3.2. The initial security game $\mathbf{Exp}_0$.

Experiment $\mathbf{Exp}_1^v$**.** This experiment, for $v = 0, \dots, n$, is identical to $\mathbf{Exp}_0$, with a slight modification in its encryption on line 4. Let an experiment of type v, $\mathbf{Exp}_1^v$, be the one where the encryption is computed so that the first v keys are over a random plaintext while the remaining keys encode the correct message. More specifically, the 4th line is replaced with:

$$c = \langle \mathtt{E}_{k_1}(R_1), \ldots, \mathtt{E}_{k_v}(R_v), E_{k_{v+1}}(m_1), \ldots, E_{k_n}(m_1) \rangle$$

where R_i is a random string of the same length as the message m_1 for $i = 1, \ldots, v$.

Let p_1^v be the probability that the experiment $\mathbf{Exp}_1^v$ returns 1 and similarly let p_0 be the probability that the experiment $\mathbf{Exp}_0$ returns 1. Observe that in the case $v \geq n$, the sequence of encryptions no longer contains any information on b, and the same is true for all other information given to the adversary. It follows that the adversary's view is independent of b and therefore it is easy to derive that $p_1^n = \frac{1}{2}$.

On the other hand, let us assume that the adversary has advantage of at least ε in being succesful on the original experiment $\mathbf{Exp}_0$, i.e. we obtain $p_0 = p_1^0 \geq \frac{1}{2} + \varepsilon$. It follows that there is a gap of ε between p_1^0 and p_1^n and by applying the triangular inequality we obtain that there must exist some $0 < v' \leq n$ such that

$$\mid p_1^{v'-1} - p_1^{v'} \mid \geq \frac{\varepsilon}{n}$$

We next claim that for any $v = 1, \ldots, n$,

$$|p_1^{v-1} - p_1^v| \leq 2\varepsilon_p$$

We prove the claim. Consider the following CCA1 key encapsulation adversary $\mathcal{B}$ with a parameter v. $\mathcal{B}$ will be able to break the symmetric encryption scheme $(\mathtt{E}, \mathtt{D})$ in the sense of Definition 2.5 with probability at least ε_p by simulating the adversary $\mathcal{A}$ and the multiuser encryption sender.

To break the security claim of the underlying symmetric encryption scheme $(\mathtt{E}, \mathtt{D})$, $\mathcal{B}$, is given access to encryption-decryption oracle of the primitive. $\mathcal{B}$ has also access to the decryption/encryption under a key k that is unknown to her. She is then challenged with plaintext-ciphertext pair (c, m) for which either $c = \mathtt{E}_k(m)$ or $c = \mathtt{E}_k(R)$ for some random string R that has the same length with m. She is asked to test if the pair is a correct plaintext-ciphertext pair.

$\mathcal{B}$ will simulate the experiment $\mathbf{Exp}_1^v$. In the initial stage, it will simulate $\mathcal{A}$ as in the experiment $\mathbf{Exp}_1^v$ by answering all queries except those that involve the key k_v that will be answered by the encryption and decryption oracle available to $\mathcal{B}$. In the second stage, $\mathcal{B}$, will be given the challenge (c, m) where either m is the proper plaintext of c or it is randomly selected. $\mathcal{B}$ will prepare a challenge for $\mathcal{A}$ in the security game $\mathbf{Exp}_1^v$ by setting the v-th location of the challenge ciphertext with c and the remaining positions from $v + 1, \ldots, n$ with the appropriate encryptions of m. The simulation of the second stage of $\mathcal{A}$ within experiment $\mathbf{Exp}_1^v$ can be carried out by $\mathcal{B}$ without problem by resorting to its encryption oracle whenever needed.

Based on the assumption on the underlying encryption scheme we have that $|\mathbf{Prob}[\mathbf{Exp}_{\mathcal{B}}^{kem}(1^n)]-1/2| \leq \varepsilon_p$. We observe that in the key encapsulation attack of $\mathcal{B}$ in the conditional space $b=0$, the adversary $\mathcal{B}^{kem}(1^n)$ operates identically to the experiment $\mathbf{Exp}_1^{v-1}$ while in the conditional space $b=1$ it operates identically to the experiment $\mathbf{Exp}_1^v$. Based on this derive the proof of the claim:

$$|\mathbf{Prob}[\mathbf{Exp}_{\mathcal{B}}^{kem}(1^n)] - 1/2| \leq \varepsilon_p$$
$$|\tfrac{1}{2}\left(\mathbf{Prob}[\mathbf{Exp}_{\mathcal{B}}^{kem}(1^n)|b=0] + \mathbf{Prob}[\mathbf{Exp}_{\mathcal{B}}^{kem}(1^n)|b=1]\right) - 1/2| \leq \varepsilon_p$$
$$|\tfrac{1}{2}\left(\mathbf{Prob}[\mathbf{Exp}_1^{v-1} = 0] + \mathbf{Prob}[\mathbf{Exp}_1^{v} = 1]\right) - 1/2| \leq \varepsilon_p$$
$$|\tfrac{1}{2}(1 - p_1^{v-1} + p_1^v) - 1/2| \leq \varepsilon_p$$
$$|p_1^{v-1} - p_1^v| \leq 2\varepsilon_p$$

We are now ready to give the proof of the theorem. First recall from our first claim that there is a $v' \in \{1,\ldots,n\}$ such that

$$|\, p_1^{v'-1} - p_1^{v'} \,| \geq \frac{\varepsilon}{n}$$

We also have $|p_1^{v'-1} - p_1^{v'}| \leq 2\varepsilon_p$. Hence, the overall security parameter of $\mathcal{A}$ satisfies $\varepsilon \leq 2n \cdot \varepsilon_p$ which completes the proof.

■

The obvious shortcoming of the above scheme is that the ciphertext length is linear in n. A nontrivial approach to reduce the transmission overhead involves the usage of fingerprinting codes. We will next present a number of multiuser encryption schemes that are based on fingerprinting codes.

3.2.2 Multiuser Encryption Schemes Based on Fingerprinting Codes

We now introduce three different encryption schemes that are all sharing the same key distribution algorithm based on fingerprinting codes. All schemes rely on an underlying encryption scheme $(\mathtt{E}, \mathtt{D})$ with plaintext space M and key space K.

The key assignment for users is done through an (ℓ, n, q) fingerprinting code over an alphabet Q of size q where n amounts to the number of users. For the sake of simplicity and without loss of generality we will assume that $Q = \{1,\ldots,q\}$.

KeyDist$_{\mathtt{F}}$: The key distribution algorithm employs a q-ary fingerprinting code $\mathtt{F} = (\mathbf{CodeGen}^{\ell}, \mathbf{Identify})$. Given 1^n, the algorithm first produces a (ℓ, n, q)-code $\mathcal{W} = \{\mathsf{w}^1,\ldots,\mathsf{w}^n\}$ where $(\mathcal{W}, ik) \leftarrow \mathbf{Codegen}^{\ell}(1^n)$ over an alphabet Q.

It, then, produces a collection of keys $\{k_{i,j}\}_{(i,j)\in[q]\times[\ell]} \subseteq \mathsf{K}$ which is also set to be transmission key ek for the encryption. The user key sk_u, for $u \in [n]$, is set to $\langle k_{\mathsf{w}_1^u,1}, k_{\mathsf{w}_2^u,2}, \ldots, k_{\mathsf{w}_\ell^u,\ell}\rangle$ where $\mathsf{w}^u = \langle \mathsf{w}_1^u, \mathsf{w}_2^u, \ldots, \mathsf{w}_\ell^u\rangle \in \mathcal{W}$. The pair $(\mathcal{W}, ik)$ is set to be the tracing key tk.

The following schemes are named due to their authors:

The Chor-Fiat-Naor Scheme

This scheme, as a unary scheme, is a non-trivial improvement on the ciphertext length of the basic linear length multiuser encryption scheme. The idea is to split the content m into ℓ shares $m_1, \ldots, m_\ell$ so that the content is the bit-wise XOR of the m_j's. We denote the XOR operation by $\oplus$ and we assume $(\mathsf{M}, \oplus)$ is an Abelian group, i.e., the operation $\oplus$ is associative, commutative, there is an identity element, and there exists the inverse of all elements in M with respect to $\oplus$. We note that these are trivially satisfied in case $\mathsf{M} = \{0,1\}^k$ and $\oplus$ stands for the bit-wise exclusive-or operation.

The encryption procedure will be applied to each share m_j, for $j = 1, \ldots, \ell$, that will be encrypted under q keys, namely $k_{i,j}$ for $i = 1, \ldots, q$. More specifically, we define the multiuser encryption scheme $\mathtt{ME}_{CFN[\mathtt{F}]}$ as follows:

- **Transmit**$_{CFN[\mathtt{F}]}$: Given a message m and the transmission key $ek = \{k_{i,j}\}_{(i,j)\in[q]\times[\ell]}$, it selects $r_1, \ldots, r_\ell$ randomly as strings of the same length with m such that $m = r_1 \oplus \ldots \oplus r_\ell$ holds. The algorithm finally transmits the encryption of the message m with ek by using a symmetric encryption scheme $(\mathtt{E}, \mathtt{D})$ as follows:

$$\begin{bmatrix} \mathtt{E}_{k_1^1}(r_1) & \mathtt{E}_{k_1^2}(r_2) & \ldots & \mathtt{E}_{k_1^\ell}(r_\ell) \\ \mathtt{E}_{k_2^1}(r_1) & \mathtt{E}_{k_2^2}(r_2) & \ldots & \mathtt{E}_{k_2^\ell}(r_\ell) \\ \vdots & \vdots & \vdots & \vdots \\ \mathtt{E}_{k_q^1}(r_1) & \mathtt{E}_{k_q^2}(r_2) & \ldots & \mathtt{E}_{k_q^\ell}(r_\ell) \end{bmatrix}$$

- **Receive**$_{CFN[\mathtt{F}]}$: Given the key-material $sk_u = \langle k_{\mathsf{w}_1^u,1}, k_{\mathsf{w}_2^u,2}, \ldots, k_{\mathsf{w}_\ell^u,\ell}\rangle$ for any $u \in [n]$ and a transmission of the form:

$$\begin{bmatrix} c_{1,1} & c_{1,2} & \ldots & c_{1,\ell} \\ c_{2,1} & c_{2,2} & \ldots & c_{2,\ell} \\ \vdots & \vdots & \vdots & \vdots \\ c_{q,1} & c_{q,2} & \ldots & c_{q,\ell} \end{bmatrix}$$

  it returns $\mathtt{D}_{k_{\mathsf{w}_1^u,1}}(c_{\mathsf{w}_1^u,1}) \oplus \mathtt{D}_{k_{\mathsf{w}_2^u,2}}(c_{\mathsf{w}_2^u,2}) \ldots \oplus \mathtt{D}_{k_{\mathsf{w}_\ell^u,\ell}}(c_{\mathsf{w}_\ell^u,\ell})$.

We now discuss the correctnes of the above scheme:

Theorem 3.4. *The multiuser encryption scheme* $\mathtt{ME}_{CFN[\mathtt{F}]}$ *satisfies the correctness property described in Definition 3.1 assuming the correctness of the underlying encryption* $(\mathtt{E}, \mathtt{D})$ *i.e., for all* $m, k \in \mathsf{M}, \mathsf{K} : \mathtt{D}_k(\mathtt{E}_k(m)) = m$.

Proof. Theorem 3.4: First, note that the Chor-Fiat-Naor scheme is a unary multiuser encryption scheme. Let $\langle tk, ek, sk_1, \ldots, sk_n \rangle$ be distributed according to $\mathbf{KeyDist}_{\mathtt{F}}$ which employs a q-ary fingerprinting code $\mathtt{F}$. We have $tk = (\mathcal{W}, ik) \leftarrow \mathbf{CodeGen}^{\ell}(1^n)$, and $ek = \{k_{i,j}\}_{(i,j)\in[q]\times[\ell]}$ so that the private key for any user-index $u \in [n]$ is defined as $sk_u = \langle k_{\mathsf{w}_1^u,1}, k_{\mathsf{w}_2^u,2}, \ldots, k_{\mathsf{w}_\ell^u,\ell} \rangle$ where $\mathsf{w}^u = \langle \mathsf{w}_1^u, \mathsf{w}_2^u, \ldots, \mathsf{w}_\ell^u \rangle \in \mathcal{W}$.

We will now prove that for any $m \in \mathsf{M}$ and any user-index $u \in [n]$ it holds that

$$\mathbf{Prob}[\mathbf{Receive}_{CFN[\mathtt{F}]}(\mathbf{Transmit}_{CFN[\mathtt{F}]}(ek, m), sk_u) = m] = 1$$

Provided that $m = r_1 \oplus \ldots \oplus r_\ell$ holds for a set of strings $r_1, \ldots, r_\ell$ of the same length with m, and the transmission is $\mathbf{Transmit}_{CFN[\mathtt{F}]}(ek, m)$ consisting of an $q \times \ell$ matrix as described above. Observe that the **Receive** algorithm on input $sk_u = \langle k_{\mathsf{w}_1^u,1}, k_{\mathsf{w}_2^u,2}, \ldots, k_{\mathsf{w}_\ell^u,\ell} \rangle$ is capable of decrypting exactly one ciphertext from each column, i.e., for any $j = 1, \ldots, \ell$ there is a $i \in \{1, 2, \ldots, q\}$ so that decryption of $\mathtt{E}_{k_{i,j}}(m_j)$ is available to that particular user with index u, which implies the availability of the share m_j. The receiver then can apply the $\oplus$ operation to all shares to calculate the plaintext m. ■

The Boneh-Naor Scheme

The mode of transmission in a unary multiuser encryption scheme that is based on fingerprinting codes can be modified to support a shorter transmission overhead. The idea is to sample a column-index $l \xleftarrow{R} \{1, \ldots, \ell\}$ and transmit $\langle \mathtt{E}_{k_{1,l}}(m), \mathtt{E}_{k_{2,l}}(m), \ldots, \mathtt{E}_{k_{q,l}}(m) \rangle$. Such modification ensures the short ciphertext during the normal transmission. We define the multiuser encryption scheme $\mathtt{ME}_{BN[\mathtt{F}]}$ as follows:

- $\mathbf{Transmit}_{BN[\mathtt{F}]}$: Given m and the encryption key $ek = \{k_{i,j}\}_{(i,j)\in[q]\times[\ell]}$, it first picks $l \xleftarrow{R} \{1, \ldots, \ell\}$ and it transmits the encryption of the message M with ek by using a symmetric encryption scheme $(\mathtt{E}, \mathtt{D})$ as follows:

$$\langle l, \mathtt{E}_{k_{1,l}}(m), \mathtt{E}_{k_{2,l}}(m), \ldots, \mathtt{E}_{k_{q,l}}(m) \rangle$$

- $\mathbf{Receive}_{BN[\mathtt{F}]}$: Given the key-material $sk_u = \langle k_{\mathsf{w}_1^u,1}, k_{\mathsf{w}_2^u,2}, \ldots, k_{\mathsf{w}_\ell^u,\ell} \rangle$ for any $u \in [n]$ and a transmission of the form:

$$\langle i, c_1, c_2, \ldots, c_q \rangle$$

it returns $\mathtt{D}_{k_{\mathsf{w}_i^u,i}}(c_{\mathsf{w}_i^u})$.

Theorem 3.5. *The multiuser encryption scheme* $\mathtt{ME}_{BN[\mathtt{F}]}$ *satisfies the correctness property described in Definition 3.1 assuming the correctness of the underlying encryption* $(\mathtt{E}, \mathtt{D})$ *i.e., for all* $m, k \in \mathsf{M}, \mathsf{K} : \mathtt{D}_k(\mathtt{E}_k(m)) = m$.

Proof. Theorem 3.5: First, note that the Boneh-Naor scheme is a unary multiuser encryption scheme. Let $\langle tk, ek, sk_1, \ldots, sk_n \rangle$ be distributed according to $\mathbf{KeyDist}_{\mathtt{F}}$ which employs a q-ary fingerprinting code. We have $tk = (\mathcal{W}, ik) \leftarrow \mathbf{CodeGen}^{\ell}(1^n)$, and $ek = \{k_{i,j}\}_{(i,j) \in [q] \times [\ell]}$ so that the private key for any user-index $u \in [n]$ is defined as $sk_u = \langle k_{\mathsf{w}_1^u,1}, k_{\mathsf{w}_2^u,2}, \ldots, k_{\mathsf{w}_\ell^u,\ell} \rangle$ where $\mathsf{w}^u = \langle \mathsf{w}_1^u, \mathsf{w}_2^u, \ldots, \mathsf{w}_\ell^u \rangle \in \mathcal{W}$.

We will now prove that for any $m \in \mathsf{M}$ and any user-index $u \in [n]$ it holds that

$$\mathbf{Prob}[\mathbf{Receive}_{BN[\mathtt{F}]}(\mathbf{Transmit}_{BN[\mathtt{F}]}(ek, m), sk_u) = m] = 1$$

Observe that the receive algorithm on input $sk_u = \langle k_{\mathsf{w}_1^u,1}, k_{\mathsf{w}_2^u,2}, \ldots, k_{\mathsf{w}_\ell^u,\ell} \rangle$ is capable of decrypting exactly one ciphertext; i.e. for each $j = 1, \ldots, \ell$ there is a $i \in \{1, 2, \ldots, q\}$ so that decryption of $\mathtt{E}_{k_{i,j}}(m)$ is available to that particular user with index u, which implies the the correct calculation of the plaintext m. ■

It is possible to define a variation of the Boneh-Naor scheme to support an q-ary multiuser encryption scheme where the transmission of the message vector $M = \langle m_1, \ldots, m_q \rangle$ will be computed as follows:

$$\langle l, \mathtt{E}_{k_{1,l}}(m_1), \mathtt{E}_{k_{2,l}}(m_2), \ldots, \mathtt{E}_{k_{q,l}}(m_q) \rangle$$

Another variant of the Boneh-Naor scheme can utilize stateful transmission, where a state $\sigma \in \mathsf{States}$ is an integer from the set $\{1, \ldots, \ell\}$ and is updated as $\sigma = (\sigma \bmod \ell) + 1$ after each transmission. The state σ plays the role of l in the transmission that is sampled randomly from the set $\{1, \ldots, \ell\}$.

The proof of correctness and the proof of security (which we will see later in this section) of these variants of the Boneh-Naor scheme is no essentially different compared to the standard version.

The Kiayias-Yung Scheme

This scheme is an binary scheme that involves a q-ary fingerprinting code $\mathtt{F}$ with a length ℓ. It is similar to the Chor-Fiat-Naor scheme but as we will see later its tracing operation applies to a much wider class of pirate decoders. As before we will assume that the plaintext space is endowed with an additive group structure, i.e., we will assume that there is a binary operation $\oplus$ that allows the addition of plaintexts and satisfies the usual group properties, i.e., it is associative, there is a neutral element (zero) and any element has an inverse with respect to addition within the group.

- $\mathbf{Transmit}_{KY[\mathtt{F}]}$: Given a vector input $M = \langle m_0, m_1 \rangle$ and the encryption key $ek = \{k_{i,j}\}_{(i,j) \in [q] \times [\ell]}$, it first samples $l \stackrel{R}{\leftarrow} \{1, \ldots, \ell\}$, $b \stackrel{R}{\leftarrow} \{0, 1\}$ and sets the parameter $s = 0$ (this parameter is only used when tracing). It, then, transmits the encryption of the message M with ek by using a symmetric encryption scheme $(\mathtt{E}, \mathtt{D})$ as follows:

$$\begin{bmatrix} \mathtt{E}_{k_1^1}(r_1) & \mathtt{E}_{k_1^2}(r_2) & \ldots & \mathtt{E}_{k_1^l}(m'_1 - \sum_{i \neq l} r_i) & \ldots & \mathtt{E}_{k_1^\ell}(r_\ell) \\ \mathtt{E}_{k_2^1}(r_1) & \mathtt{E}_{k_2^2}(r_2) & \ldots & \mathtt{E}_{k_2^l}(m'_2 - \sum_{i \neq l} r_i) & \ldots & \mathtt{E}_{k_2^\ell}(r_\ell) \\ \vdots & \vdots & \vdots & \vdots & \vdots & \vdots \\ \mathtt{E}_{k_q^1}(r_1) & \mathtt{E}_{k_q^2}(r_2) & \ldots & \mathtt{E}_{k_q^l}(m'_q - \sum_{i \neq l} r_i) & \ldots & \mathtt{E}_{k_q^\ell}(r_\ell) \end{bmatrix}$$

where $r_1, \ldots, r_{l-1}, r_{l+1}, \ldots, r_\ell$ are drawn randomly from the plaintext space, $m'_1 = \ldots = m'_s = m_{1-b}$ and $m'_{s+1} = \ldots = m'_q = m_b$. Given that $s = 0$, observe that the encryption operation entirely ignores message m_{1-b} (nevertheless m_{1-b} is also a valid message to transmit and receive). The usefulness of the parameter s will become evident when tracing.

- **Receive**$_{KY[\mathtt{F}]}$: Given the key-material $k_u = \langle k^1_{\mathtt{w}^u_1}, k^2_{\mathtt{w}^u_2}, \ldots, k^\ell_{\mathtt{w}^u_\ell} \rangle$ for some $u \in [n]$ and a transmission of the form:

$$\begin{bmatrix} c^1_1 & c^2_1 & \ldots & c^\ell_1 \\ c^1_2 & c^2_2 & \ldots & c^\ell_2 \\ \vdots & \vdots & \vdots & \vdots \\ c^1_q & c^2_q & \ldots & c^\ell_q \end{bmatrix}$$

it returns $\mathtt{D}_{k^1_{\mathtt{w}^u_1}}(c^1_{\mathtt{w}^u_1}) \oplus \mathtt{D}_{k^2_{\mathtt{w}^u_2}}(c^2_{\mathtt{w}^u_2}) \oplus \ldots \oplus \mathtt{D}_{k^\ell_{\mathtt{w}^u_\ell}}(c^\ell_{\mathtt{w}^u_\ell})$.

Theorem 3.6. *The multiuser encryption scheme* $\mathtt{ME}_{KY[\mathtt{F}]}$ *satisfies the correctness property described in Definition 3.1.*

Proof. Theorem 3.6: First, note that the Kiayias-Yung scheme is a binary multiuser encryption scheme. Let $\langle tk, ek, sk_1, \ldots, sk_n \rangle$ be distributed according to $\mathbf{KeyDist}^\ell_q$ which employs a q-ary fingerprinting code. We have $tk = (\mathcal{W}, ik) \leftarrow \mathbf{CodeGen}^\ell(1^n)$, and $ek = \{k_{i,j}\}_{(i,j) \in [q] \times [\ell]}$ so that the private key for any user-index $u \in [n]$ is defined as $sk_u = \langle k^1_{\mathtt{w}^u_1}, k^2_{\mathtt{w}^u_2}, \ldots, k^\ell_{\mathtt{w}^u_\ell} \rangle$ where $\mathtt{w}^u = \langle \mathtt{w}^u_1, \mathtt{w}^u_2, \ldots, \mathtt{w}^u_\ell \rangle \in \mathcal{W}$.

We will now prove that for any vector of input $M = \langle m_1, m_2 \rangle$ and any user-index $u \in [n]$ it holds that

$$\mathbf{Prob}[\mathbf{Receive}_{KY[\mathtt{F}]}(\mathbf{Transmit}_{KY[\mathtt{F}]}(ek, M), sk_u) \in \{m_0, m_1\}] = 1$$

Provided that $r_1, \ldots, r_\ell, m_1, m_2$ are all elements of m, the resulting transmission would be distributed as $\mathbf{Transmit}_{KY[\mathtt{F}]}(ek, m)$ consisting of an $q \times \ell$ matrix as described above. Let $l \in \{1, \ldots, \ell\}$ be the special column index sampled for the transmission, $s \in \{0, 1, \ldots, q\}$ the switching point for m_0 to m_1 (normally $s = 0$) and $b \in \{0, 1\}$. Observe that the **Receive** algorithm on input $sk_u = \langle k^1_{\mathtt{w}^u_1}, k^2_{\mathtt{w}^u_2}, \ldots, k^\ell_{\mathtt{w}^u_\ell} \rangle$ is capable of decrypting exactly one ciphertext from each column, i.e. for any $i = 1, \ldots, \ell$ there is a $j \in \{1, 2, \ldots, q\}$ so that the user will obtain the values r_i for $i \neq l$ and the value $m - \sum_{i \neq l} r_i$ where m is either m_0 or m_1. By adding all these values the user u will obtain m. This implies that the correctness requirement is satisfied. ∎

Security

Here we will discuss security of the multiuser encryption schemes based on fingerprinting codes:

Theorem 3.7. *The Chor-Fiat-Naor and Kiayias-Yung multiuser encryption schemes are CCA-1 ε-insecure in the sense of Definition 3.2 with $\varepsilon \leq 2q \cdot \varepsilon_p$ assuming the underlying encryption-decryption scheme* $(\mathtt{E}, \mathtt{D})$ *is ε_p-insecure in the sense of Definition 2.5.*

Proof. Theorem 3.7: The security proof is a variation of the proof we provided in the security proof of the linear length multiuser scheme. Here, it suffices to make the similar walking argument over a sequence of encryptions so that we obtain q different experiments. More specifically, we define the experiment $\mathbf{Exp}_1^v$, for $v = 1, \ldots, q$, that is identical to $\mathbf{Exp}_0$ with a slight modification in its challenge transmission, and apply the similar arguments over the success probabilities of winning these experiments. The transmission for experiment $\mathbf{Exp}_1^v$ is chosen as follows for each scheme:

- *Chor-Fiat-Naor Scheme:* The walking argument is over a single column, without loss of generality, say the first column. In other terms, the first v keys of the first column are over a random share while the remaining keys encode the correct share. More specifically, the transmission challenge in the security game (cf. Figure 3.1) is replaced with:

$$\begin{bmatrix} \mathtt{E}_{k_1^1}(R_1) & \mathtt{E}_{k_1^2}(r_2) & \ldots & \mathtt{E}_{k_1^\ell}(r_\ell) \\ \mathtt{E}_{k_2^1}(R_2) & \mathtt{E}_{k_2^2}(r_2) & \ldots & \mathtt{E}_{k_2^\ell}(r_\ell) \\ \vdots & \vdots & \vdots & \vdots \\ \mathtt{E}_{k_v^1}(R_v) & \mathtt{E}_{k_v^2}(r_2) & \ldots & \mathtt{E}_{k_v^\ell}(r_\ell) \\ \mathtt{E}_{k_{v+1}^1}(r_1) & \mathtt{E}_{k_{v+1}^2}(r_2) & \ldots & \mathtt{E}_{k_{v+1}^\ell}(r_\ell) \\ \vdots & \vdots & \vdots & \vdots \\ \mathtt{E}_{k_q^1}(r_1) & \mathtt{E}_{k_q^2}(r_2) & \ldots & \mathtt{E}_{k_q^\ell}(r_\ell) \end{bmatrix}$$

- *Kiayias-Yung Scheme:* Similar to the Chor-Fiat-Naor scheme the walking argument is over a single column the one preceding the randomly selected column l (allowing wraparound modulo ℓ, i.e., when $l = 1$ then the last column would be affected).

$$\begin{bmatrix} \mathtt{E}_{k_1^1}(r_1) & \ldots & \mathtt{E}_{k_1^{l-1}}(R_1) & \mathtt{E}_{k_1^l}(m_1' - \sum_{i \neq l} r_i) & \ldots & \mathtt{E}_{k_1^\ell}(r_\ell) \\ \mathtt{E}_{k_2^1}(r_1) & \ldots & \mathtt{E}_{k_2^{l-1}}(R_2) & \mathtt{E}_{k_2^l}(m_2' - \sum_{i \neq l} r_i) & \ldots & \mathtt{E}_{k_2^\ell}(r_\ell) \\ \vdots & \vdots & \vdots & \vdots & \vdots & \vdots \\ \mathtt{E}_{k_v^1}(r_1) & \ldots & \mathtt{E}_{k_v^{l-1}}(R_v) & \mathtt{E}_{k_v^l}(m_v' - \sum_{i \neq l} r_i) & \ldots & \mathtt{E}_{k_v^\ell}(r_\ell) \\ \mathtt{E}_{k_{v+1}^1}(r_1) & \ldots & \mathtt{E}_{k_{v+1}^{l-1}}(r_{l-1}) & \mathtt{E}_{k_{v+1}^l}(m_{v+1}' - \sum_{i \neq l} r_i) & \ldots & \mathtt{E}_{k_{v+1}^\ell}(r_\ell) \\ \vdots & \vdots & \vdots & \vdots & \vdots & \vdots \\ \mathtt{E}_{k_q^1}(r_1) & \ldots & \mathtt{E}_{k_q^{l-1}}(r_{l-1}) & \mathtt{E}_{k_q^l}(m_q' - \sum_{i \neq l} r_i) & \ldots & \mathtt{E}_{k_q^\ell}(r_\ell) \end{bmatrix}$$

where R_i is a random plaintext element and $m'_1 = \ldots = m'_s = m_{1-b}$ while $m'_{s+1} = \ldots = m'_q = m_b$. With the above modifications we can follow the same line of reasoning as in Theorem 3.3. In particular it is worth noting that the additive secret-sharing properties of the way the plaintext is shared among the rows of the ciphertext guarantee that it is impossible to derive any information about the plaintext when $v = q$.

On the other hand the difference between two consecutive experiments $v, v+1$ will be at most $2\epsilon_p$. This follows from the fact that the challenge of a key encapsulation mechanism attacker against key k^1_{v+1} is of the form (c^*, r^*) where r^* is a random plaintext that: either it is encrypted within c^* (dependent case) or c^* encrypts another uniformly random plaintext (independent case). Any distinguisher between the two consecutive experiments can be turned into an attack against the key encapsulation mechanism as follows. First we put c^* in the $(v+1)$-th position. Then we use r^*, in the following manner: (i) for the Chor-Fiat-Naor scheme we use r^* as the first share r_1 in the rows $v+1, \ldots, q$ of the challenge ciphertext, (ii) for the Kiayias-Yung scheme, we use r^* as the share r_{l-1} except for the case $l = 1$ where we use r^* as r_ℓ.

With the above modifications, it is easy to verify that if the challenge (c^*, r^*) is the dependent case the above procedure results to an experiment identically distributed to the v-th experiment, while if the challenge (c^*, r^*) is the independent case the above procedure results to an experiment identically distributed to the $(v+1)$-th experiment. ■

An only slightly different line of reasoning is required for the Boneh-Naor scheme. For this reason we present it separately.

Theorem 3.8. *The Boneh-Naor multiuser encryption schemes is CCA-1 ε-insecure in the sense of Definition 3.2 with $\varepsilon \leq 2\ell q \cdot \varepsilon_p$ assuming the underlying encryption-decryption scheme* $(\mathtt{E}, \mathtt{D})$ *is ε_p-insecure in the sense of Definition 2.5.*

Proof. Theorem 3.8: We would like to apply the same reasoning as in the case of theorem 3.7. The only essential obstacle is that depending on the choice of l a different key may be used in the v-th position of the challenge transmission. For this reason we apply the following approach: we let $\mathbf{A}_i$ be the event that $l = i \in \{1, \ldots, \ell\}$ is selected for the challenge transmission. It is obvious the events $\{\mathbf{A}_i\}_{i=1\ldots\ell}$ partition the space of the attack experiments and each one has likelihood $1/\ell$. In the conditional space $\mathbf{A}_i$ one may perform the same arguments as in theorem 3.7.

Specifically, when playing with an adversary that has success probability $1/2 + \epsilon$, the walking argument is over the challenge transmission where the first v keys are over a random plaintext while the remaining keys encode the correct message:

$$\langle i, \mathtt{E}_{k^i_1}(R_1), \mathtt{E}_{k^i_2}(R_2), \ldots, \mathtt{E}_{k^i_v}(R_v), E_{k^i_{v+1}}(m), \ldots, \mathtt{E}_{k^i_q}(m)\rangle$$

The essential difference is that the success probability of the case $v = 0$ is not guaranteed to be related in a predictable manner to the overall probability of success. In particular what we may argue is that in each conditional space $\mathbf{A}_i$ the success probability of the adversary in the experiment p_v^i satisfies that $p_0^i = 1/2 + \alpha_i$ for some α_i (this is without loss of generality as if an adversary drops below 1/2 in its prediction capability in a certain conditional space there exists another adversary that by flipping its answer does better than 1/2) and $p_q^i = 1/2$. The latter statement follows from the fact that when $v = q$ no information about the plaintext is transmitted to the adversary. Regarding the former, we use α_i to denote the success of the adversary in the conditional space $\mathbf{A}_i$. Regarding the α_i values we know that $\frac{1}{\ell} \cdot \sum_{i=1}^{\ell}(1/2+\alpha_i) = 1/2+\epsilon$. Based on this there must be an i_0 such that $\alpha_{i_0} \geq \epsilon/\ell$. Indeed, if $\alpha_i < \epsilon/\ell$ for all $i = 1, \ldots, \ell$ we have that the success probability would be less than $1/2 + \epsilon$, a contradiction. As a result we can find some v' for which it holds that $|p_{v'-1}^{i_0} - p_{v'}^{i_0}| \geq \epsilon/(\ell q)$. Now the proof can be completed with identical arguments to those of theorem 3.3 while operating in the conditional $\mathbf{A}_{i_0}$ space. ■

3.2.3 Boneh-Franklin Multiuser Encryption Scheme

The scheme works in conjunction to a multiplicative cyclic group $\mathcal{G}$ of large prime order over which solving the Decisional Diffie Hellman (DDH) Problem is hard (a definition will be given shortly). Vectors in $\mathbb{Z}_q^\ell$ will be denoted by $\boldsymbol{\delta} = \langle \boldsymbol{\delta}_1, \ldots, \boldsymbol{\delta}_\ell \rangle$.

A possible example for $\mathcal{G}$ can be the subgroup of order q of $\mathbb{Z}_p^*$, where $q \mid p-1$ and p, q are large primes. It is helpful to keep in mind that arithmetic in the exponents is performed in the finite field $\mathbb{Z}_q$, i.e., $g^{x+y} = g^{x+y \bmod q}$ and similarly for exponentiation $g^{a \cdot b} = g^{a \cdot b \bmod q}$.

For some $\ell \in \mathbb{N}$, let $h_0, h_1, \ldots, h_\ell$ be random elements of $\mathcal{G}$ so that $h_j =_{\mathsf{df}} g^{r_j}$ for $j = 0, \ldots, \ell$ and define the vector $\mathbf{r} =_{\mathsf{df}} \langle r_1, \ldots, r_\ell \rangle$. A representation of h_0 with respect to the base $h_1, \ldots, h_\ell$ is an ℓ-vector $\boldsymbol{\delta} =_{\mathsf{df}} \langle \delta_1, \ldots, \delta_\ell \rangle$ such that $h_0 = h_1^{\delta_1} \ldots h_\ell^{\delta_\ell}$, or equivalently $\boldsymbol{\delta} \cdot \mathbf{r} = r_0$ where $\cdot$ denotes the inner product between two vectors.

Let **Gen** be a polynomial-time algorithm that receives 1^k as input (where k is a security parameter) and it samples the description of a multiplicative group as well as of an element g inside this group. While we will avoid making the group description explicit we assume that it contains sufficient information to perform the multiplication operation as well as it contains a membership test for the group; the value q is the prime order of the cyclic subgroup generated by g. We further require that $k < \log q < k+1$ something that implies that the group $\mathcal{G}$ cannot be specified as a list of elements.

Based on **Gen**, we define the Boneh-Franklin multiuser encryption scheme with parameters $k, \ell\mathbb{N}$ as follows

- **KeyDist**$_{BF^k_\ell}$: On input 1^n, it uses $\mathbf{Gen}(1^k)$ to produce a description of a multiplicative group $\mathcal{G}$ a generator $g \in \mathcal{G}$ of prime order q where q is a k-bit prime. It also samples elements $a_0, \ldots, a_\ell \in \mathbb{Z}_q - \{0\}$ uniformly at random. The tuple $\langle a_0, \ldots, a_\ell \rangle$ constitutes the tracing key tk, whereas the public-key contains the tuple

$$H = \langle h_0 =_{\mathsf{df}} g^{a_0}, h_1 =_{\mathsf{df}} g^{a_1}, \ldots, h_\ell =_{\mathsf{df}} g^{a_\ell} \rangle$$

It, further, computes a code $\Gamma = \{\gamma^1, \ldots, \gamma^n\}$ that contains n tuples of $\mathbb{Z}_q^\ell$ as follows: first it defines a $(n - \ell) \times n$ matrix $\mathbf{M}$ so that the j-th row of $\mathbf{M}$ equals $\langle 1, 2^{j-1}, \ldots, n^{j-1} \rangle$. Now let $\boldsymbol{\beta}^1, \ldots, \boldsymbol{\beta}^\ell$ be a basis of the right kernel[1] of $\mathbf{M}$. Denoting the basis matrix by $\mathbf{B}$, $\boldsymbol{\gamma}^j$ is defined as the j-th row of the matrix $\mathbf{B}$. i.e. $\boldsymbol{\gamma}^j = \langle \boldsymbol{\beta}^1_j, \ldots, \boldsymbol{\beta}^\ell_j \rangle$. We have the following equation:

$$\begin{bmatrix} 1 & 1 & 1 & \ldots & 1 \\ 1 & 2 & 3 & \ldots & n \\ 1^2 & 2^2 & 3^2 & \ldots & n^2 \\ \vdots & \vdots & \vdots & \vdots & \vdots \\ 1^{n-\ell-2} & 2^{n-\ell-2} & 3^{n-\ell-2} & \ldots & n^{n-\ell-2} \\ 1^{n-\ell-1} & 2^{n-\ell-1} & 3^{n-\ell-1} & \ldots & n^{n-\ell-2} \end{bmatrix} \times \begin{bmatrix} | & | & | & \cdots & | \\ \boldsymbol{\beta}^1 & \boldsymbol{\beta}2 & \boldsymbol{\beta}^3 & \ldots & \boldsymbol{\beta}^\ell \\ | & | & | & \cdots & | \end{bmatrix} = 0 \quad (3.1)$$

Hence, Γ contains n codewords of each length ℓ, we note that using Lagrange interpolation we can directly construct the j-th codeword in Γ. The secret key sk_j is computed as a vector $\boldsymbol{\delta} = b_j \cdot \boldsymbol{\gamma}^j$ with $b_j = a_0(\sum_{i=1}^{\ell} a_i \gamma_i^j)^{-1}$ for $j = 1, \ldots, n$. The encryption key ek is set to the pair $\langle H, \Gamma \rangle$
- **Transmit**$_{BF^k_\ell}$: Given a message $m \in \langle g \rangle$ and the encryption key $ek = \langle H, \Gamma \rangle$, the encryption of the message is calculated similarly to ElGamal encryption as follows:

$$\langle h_0^r \cdot m, h_1^r, \ldots, h_\ell^r \rangle$$

where r is sampled randomly from $\mathbb{Z}_q - \{0\}$. Standard variations such as $\langle \mathcal{H}(h_0^r) \oplus m, h_1^r, \ldots, h_\ell^r \rangle$ where $\mathcal{H}$ is a k-bit long hash function and $m \in \{0,1\}^k$ are also possible (but will not be analyzed here).
- **Receive**$_{BF^k_\ell}$: Having access to the public key $ek = \langle H, \Gamma \rangle$ and given the key material sk_j that is the vector $\boldsymbol{\delta} = b_j \cdot \boldsymbol{\gamma}^j$, on input a transmission of the form:

$$\langle A_0, A_1, \ldots, A_\ell \rangle$$

it outputs the result of the following computation:

$$A_0(A_1^{\delta_1} \ldots A_\ell^{\delta_\ell})^{-1}$$

[1] Recall that the right kernel of a matrix $\mathbf{B}$ is the set $\{\gamma \mid \mathbf{B} \cdot \gamma = \mathbf{0}\}$.

It is worth noting in the above description, that there is no functional dependency between $a_0, \ldots, a_\ell$ and the public-vectors γ, and Γ is attached to the public-key.

Correctness. We next discuss the correctness of the scheme.

Theorem 3.9. *The Boneh-Franklin scheme satisfies the correctness in the sense of definition 3.1.*

Proof. First note that the Boneh-Franklin scheme is a unary multiuser encryption scheme. Let $\langle tk, ek, sk_1, \ldots sk_n \rangle$ be distributed according to the process $\mathbf{KeyDist}_{BF_\ell^k}(1^n)$ where $tk = \langle a_0, a_1, \ldots, a_\ell \rangle$ and $ek = \langle H, \Gamma \rangle$ with $H = (g^{a_0}, \ldots, g^{a_\ell})$. Here Γ is an (ℓ, n, q)-code over an alphabet $\mathbb{Z}_q$ for some k bit prime number q and $g \in \mathcal{G}$ where $\mathcal{G}$ is a group whose description has been produced by $\mathbf{Gen}(1^k)$. The secret key sk_u is computed as a vector $\boldsymbol{\delta} = b_j \cdot \boldsymbol{\gamma}^j$ with $b_j = a_0 (\sum_{i=1}^{\ell} a_i \gamma_i^j)^{-1}$ for $j = 1, \ldots, n$.

We will now prove that for any $m \in \mathsf{M} = \langle g \rangle$ and any user $u \in [n]$ it holds that

$$\mathbf{Prob}[\mathbf{Receive}_{BF_\ell^k}(\mathbf{Transmit}_{BF_k^\ell}(ek, m), sk_u) = m] = 1$$

Let the transmission $\langle h_0^r \cdot m, h_1^r, \ldots, h_\ell^r \rangle$ sampled by the distribution $\mathbf{Transmit}_{BF_k^\ell}(ek, m)$ for some r randomly chosen from $\mathbb{Z}_q - \{0\}$. The receiver with index u has access to the key material $sk_u = \boldsymbol{\delta}$ which is equal to $b_u \cdot \boldsymbol{\gamma}^u$. Denoting the vector by $\langle \boldsymbol{\delta}_1, \ldots, \boldsymbol{\delta}_\ell \rangle$, the receiver outputs

$$h_0^r \cdot m \cdot (h_1^{r\boldsymbol{\delta}_1} \ldots h_\ell^{r\boldsymbol{\delta}_\ell})^{-1}$$

We will prove that $\boldsymbol{\delta} = b_u \cdot \boldsymbol{\gamma}^u$ is a representation of h_0 base $h_1, \ldots, h_\ell$ for any $u \in [n]$. In other terms, we will show that $h_0 = h_1^{\boldsymbol{\delta}_1} h_2^{\boldsymbol{\delta}_2} \ldots h_\ell^{\boldsymbol{\delta}_\ell}$. Indeed, by substituting $\boldsymbol{\delta}_i = b_u \cdot \gamma_i^u$ and $h_i = g^{a_i}$ for any $i \in \{1, \ldots, \ell\}$ we obtain:

$$\begin{aligned} h_0 &= \left(g^{a_1 \gamma_1^u} \cdot g^{a_2 \gamma_2^u} \ldots g^{a_\ell \gamma_\ell^u}\right)^{b_u} \\ &= \left(g^{a_1 \gamma_1^u} \cdot g^{a_2 \gamma_2^u} \ldots g^{a_\ell \gamma_\ell^u}\right)^{a_0 (\sum_{i=1}^{\ell} a_i \gamma_i^u)^{-1}} \\ &= g^{a_0} \end{aligned}$$

Hence the output of the receiving algorithm for any user with index $u \in [n]$ is the message m. This proves the correctness of the Boneh-Franklin scheme. ∎

Security. We, next, show that the Boneh-Franklin scheme is CPA insecure in the sense of Definition 3.2. The security proof is based on the DDH assumption which we state below:

Definition 3.10. DDH. *Let $\mathcal{G}, g, q$ be a description of a group, and an element $g \in \mathcal{G}$ of order q as produced by* $\mathbf{Gen}(1^k)$ *for some $k \in \mathbb{N}$. Consider now the random variable* $\mathtt{R}$ *that equals to $\langle \mathcal{G}, q, g, g^a, g^b, g^c \rangle$ where a, b, c*

are uniformly random from $\mathbb{Z}_q$ *and the random variable* D *that equals to* $\langle \mathcal{G}, q, g, g^a, g^b, g^{ab} \rangle$ *where* a, b *are uniformly random from* $\mathbb{Z}_q$*. A polynomial time algorithm solves the DDH problem with advantage* α *if it can distinguish* D *from* R *with probability at least* $1/2 + \alpha$*.*

The DDH-Assumption *with* ε*-insecurity with respect to* **Gen** *suggests that any algorithm that solves the DDH problem with advantage* α *satisfies* $\alpha \leq \varepsilon$*.*

Having defined the necessary computational assumption we prove the security of the Boneh-Franklin scheme.

Theorem 3.11. *The Boneh-Franklin scheme* BF_ℓ^k *is a public-key scheme that is CPA* ε*-insecure in the sense of Definition 3.2 assuming the DDH-Assumption with* ε*-insecurity holds with respect to* **Gen***.*

Proof. (of theorem 3.11) Let $\mathcal{A}$ be a CPA attacker in the sense of Definition 3.2. we rewrite the original game $\mathbf{Exp}_0 = \mathbf{Exp}_{\mathcal{A}}^{BF_\ell^k}(1^n)$ explicitly in Figure 3.3.

Experiment $\mathbf{Exp}_{\mathcal{A}}^{BF_\ell^k}(1^n)$
- $(tk, ek, sk_1, \ldots, sk_n) \leftarrow \mathbf{KeyDist}(1^n)$
- $aux \leftarrow \mathcal{A}(ek)$
- $m_0, m_1 \xleftarrow{R} \mathsf{M}$
- $b \xleftarrow{R} \{0, 1\}$; $c \leftarrow \mathbf{Transmit}(ek, m_1)$
- $b' \leftarrow \mathcal{A}(aux, ek, m_b, c)$
- return 1 if and only if $b = b'$

Fig. 3.3. The CPA security game for the Boneh-Franklin scheme.

Experiment $\mathbf{Exp}_1$. This experiment is identical to $\mathbf{Exp}_0$, with a slight modification in its encryption on line 4. Let the experiment $\mathbf{Exp}_1$, be the one where the transmission is computed as an encryption of a random message that is neither m_0 nor m_1. More specifically, the 4th line is replaced with:

$$c \leftarrow \mathbf{Transmit}(ek, m_R)$$

where m_R is a random string of the same length as the message m_0 and m_1.

Let p_1 be the probability that the experiment $\mathbf{Exp}_1$ returns 1 and similarly let p_0 be the probability that the experiment $\mathbf{Exp}_0$ returns 1. Observe that in $\mathbf{Exp}_1$, the encryption is no longer associated to m_0, m_1. Given that m_0, m_1 are identically distributed it follows that the adversary's view is independent of b and therefore $p_1 = \frac{1}{2}$.

On the other hand, let us assume that the adversary $\mathcal{A}$ has advantage of at least ε' in being successful on the original experiment $\mathbf{Exp}_0$, i.e. we obtain $p_0 \geq \frac{1}{2} + \varepsilon'$.

We next claim that,

$$|p_1 - p_0| \leq \varepsilon$$

We prove the claim by constructing a DDH distinguishing algorithm $\mathcal{B}$. The algorithm $\mathcal{B}$ on input a challenge for the DDH assumption $\langle \mathcal{G}, q, g, A, B, C \rangle$ constructs a public-key as follows: $h_0 = A, h_1 = g^{a_1}, h_2 = g^{a_2}, \ldots, h_\ell = g^{a_\ell}$, with $a_1, a_2, \ldots, a_\ell$ selected uniformly at random from $\mathbb{Z}_q$.

The challenge messages $m_0, m_1 \xleftarrow{R} \mathsf{M} = \langle g \rangle$ and $b \xleftarrow{R} \{0, 1\}$ are selected uniformly at random. $\mathcal{B}$ forms the encryption $\langle C \cdot m_1, (B)^{a_1}, (B)^{a_2}, \ldots, (B')^{a_\ell} \rangle$. Finally, it simulates the adversary $\mathcal{A}$ with the pair

$$(\langle C \cdot m_1, (B)^{a_1}, (B)^{a_2}, \ldots, (B)^{a_\ell} \rangle, m_b)$$

Observe that if $\langle \mathcal{G}, q, g, A, B, C \rangle$ is distributed following the $\mathtt{D}$ random variable, it holds that

$$\langle C \cdot m_1, (B)^{a_1}, (B)^{a_2}, \ldots, (B)^{a_\ell} \rangle = \langle g^{ab} \cdot m_1, g^{a_1 b}, g^{a_2 b}, \ldots, g^{a_\ell b} \rangle$$

where a, b are uniformly distributed over $\mathbb{Z}_q$, is a valid encryption of m_1 using the public-key $\langle g^a, g^{a_1}, g^{a_2}, \ldots, g^{a_\ell} \rangle$. This is the case where $\mathcal{B}$ operates identically to the experiment $\mathbf{Exp}_0$.

On the other hand, if $\langle \mathcal{G}, q, g, A, B, C \rangle$ is distributed following the $\mathtt{R}$ random variable, it holds that

$$\langle C \cdot m_1, (B)^{a_1}, (B)^{a_2}, \ldots, (B)^{a_\ell} \rangle = \langle g^{c} \cdot m_1, g^{a_1 b}, g^{a_2 b}, \ldots, g^{a_\ell b} \rangle$$

where a, b, c are uniformly distributed over $\mathbb{Z}_q$, leaks no information about m_0 or m_1. In fact it is identically distributed to the encryption of some random message m_R under the public-key $\langle g^a, g^{a_1}, g^{a_2}, \ldots, g^{a_\ell} \rangle$. This follows from the fact that we can find a unique c for each message m_R to satisfy the equation $g^{ab} m_R = g^c m_1$. It follows that in such case $\mathcal{B}$ operates identically to the experiment $\mathbf{Exp}_1$.

Based on the above and the DDH-assumption we conclude that $|p_1 - p_0| \leq \varepsilon$ and as a result we have that $\varepsilon' \leq \varepsilon$ which concludes the proof. ∎

3.3 Tracing Game: Definitions

We define the property that is the characteristic of a traitor tracing scheme. We first introduce the concept of the tracing game.

Definition 3.12. *A* tracing game *is specified by any triple* $\langle \mathbf{KeyDist}, \mathcal{Q}, \mathcal{R} \rangle$, *where* **KeyDist** *is a probabilistic algorithm that on input* 1^n, *it produces a tuple* $(tk, ek, sk_1, \ldots, sk_n)$, $\mathcal{R}$ *is a predicate and* $\mathcal{Q}$ *is a set of random variables.*

We now explain the meaning of the tracing game. A tracing game is an interaction between two parties: the adversary and the tracer. The tracer has at its disposal the encryption and the tracing key (resp. tk, ek) while the adversary has a set of user keys, that is a subsequence of $sk_1, \ldots, sk_n$. The ultimate objective of the tracer is to identify one of the keys that the adversary controls.

Next we set the general rules of engagement between the tracer and the adversary that are determined by $\mathcal{Q}, \mathcal{R}$. The essence on the constraint that we will place on the interaction is the following: as long as the tracer follows a certain query distribution as defined in $\mathcal{Q}$ the adversary is obliged to formulate its responses in a way that they will satisfy the predicate $\mathcal{R}$ with sufficient probability.

More specifically the pair $\langle \mathcal{A}, \mathcal{T} \rangle$ will be said to be σ-*admissible* according to a tracing game $\langle \textbf{KeyDist}, \mathcal{Q}, \mathcal{R} \rangle$ with a parameter t provided that $\mathcal{A}, \mathcal{T}$ follow the proper rules of engagement. More specifically, σ-admissible would be a pair of interacting algorithms that when $\mathcal{T}$ sends some message to $\mathcal{A}$ that follows a random variable of $\mathcal{Q}$ then $\mathcal{A}$ has to provide a response that satisfies the predicate $\mathcal{R}$. Formally we have the following definition.

Definition 3.13. *Let $\langle \mathcal{A}, \mathcal{T} \rangle$ be a pair of interacting algorithms (the adversary and the tracer) and let $\langle \textbf{KeyDist}, \mathcal{Q}, \mathcal{R} \rangle$ be a tracing game. Fix $n \in \mathbb{N}$ and a $\mathsf{C} \subseteq [n]$. We assume the following regarding the interaction of $\langle \mathcal{A}, \mathcal{T} \rangle$:*

- *Initialization. The tuple $(tk, ek, sk_1, \ldots, sk_n) \leftarrow \textbf{KeyDist}(1^n)$ is sampled and the adversary $\mathcal{A}$ is given input $\{sk_j\}_{j \in \mathsf{C}}$ while the tracer $\mathcal{T}$ is given tk, ek.*
- *Round actions. $\mathcal{A}$ and $\mathcal{T}$ exchange messages in rounds until the tracer $\mathcal{T}$ terminates. In the i-th round, $\mathcal{T}$ goes first transmitting a value q_i and then party $\mathcal{A}$ responds by a value a_i. In case $\mathcal{A}$ produces no output at a certain round i, the value a_i is defined to be $\perp$.*

*We say the pair $\langle \mathcal{A}, \mathcal{T} \rangle$ is σ-*admissible *for the game $\langle \textbf{KeyDist}, \mathcal{Q}, \mathcal{R} \rangle$ for t-coalitions, where $t \in \mathbb{N}$ if for any $n \in \mathbb{N}, \mathsf{C} \subseteq [n]$, in case q_i is distributed according to some member of $\mathcal{Q}$ it holds that for any $\mathsf{C} \subseteq [n]$ with $|\mathsf{C}| \leq t$,*

$$\textbf{Prob}[\mathcal{R}(\mathsf{C}, tk, ek, sk_1, \ldots, sk_n, q_i, a_i) = 1] \geq \sigma$$

where a_i is the response of $\mathcal{A}$ to the query q_i on input $\{sk_j\}_{j \in \mathsf{C}}$. We denote the random variable that is the output of the tracer $\mathcal{T}$ after interacting with $\mathcal{A}$ by $\langle \mathcal{A}, \mathcal{T} \rangle (tk, ek, sk_1, \ldots, sk_n, \mathsf{C})$. We denote the maximum number of rounds that take place before $\mathcal{T}$ terminates the protocol by $r_{\langle \mathcal{A}, \mathcal{T} \rangle}$.

The definition of σ-admissibility in plain words it says that as long as the tracer $\mathcal{T}$ follows some of the specified valid moves in $\mathcal{Q}$ the party $\mathcal{A}$ has to oblige and satisfy with its response the predicate $\mathcal{R}$ with probability σ. We observe that the predicate $\mathcal{R}$ takes into account the total information that is available to both players and thus it is not something that the tracer $\mathcal{T}$

is necessarily capable of computing by itself. In the coming section we will formulate various tracing games that are resulting from interactions based on multiuser encryption schemes.

We will also condider the following variations of the definition:

1. *Stateful Tracing.* Consider the set $\{\mathcal{Q}_h\}_{h\in\{0,1\}^*}$, a collection of sets of random variables. In this specification, for the adversary to oblige and satisfy the $\mathcal{R}$ predicate we require the tracing queries of $\mathcal{T}$ to be consistent with the history of previous queries. More specifically, we define, for any $i > 0$, $h = \langle q_1, \ldots, q_{i-1}\rangle$ to be the history of the queries posed by $\mathcal{T}$ (it is empty if $i = 1$), the next query q_i should be distributed according to some member of $\mathcal{Q}_h$ in order to impose the σ lower bound in the satisfaction of the predicate $\mathcal{R}$ for $\mathcal{A}$. Note that the predicate $\mathcal{R}$ will also take the history of the queries into account while producing a result. Stateful tracing is thus placing a further possible restriction on the tracer's side as it drops any compliance requirements on the part of $\mathcal{A}$ when the tracer becomes inconsistent with the query history.
2. *Alfresco.* When tracing alfresco the tracer needs to form every query he makes to be computationally indistinguishable from members of $\mathcal{Q}$ (or from $\mathcal{Q}_h$ in case of stateful tracing) in the eyes of any user of the system. More specifically, when the tracer has submitted $h = \langle q_1, \ldots, q_{i-1}\rangle$ queries, in the i-th round it must choose a query that is indistinguishable from a member of $\mathcal{Q}$ (from a member of $\mathcal{Q}_h$ in case of stateful tracing). Note that this is a different type of restriction on the tracer $\mathcal{T}$. Without this restriction the tracer has the flexibility to provide queries to $\mathcal{T}$ that are outside of $\mathcal{Q}$; depending on the case this may carry substantial advantages for the tracer that are stripped in the case of alfresco tracing. On the plus side alfresco may allow the tracer to perform tracing while honest participants are also listening to the tracing channel (without disrupting their correct operation).
3. *Tracing with Resetting.* The adversary $\mathcal{A}$ is not allowed to maintain state from one round to the next, i.e., in each round the tracer can "reset" the adversary. This model weakens the adversary $\mathcal{A}$ as it is prohibited from keeping knowledge of previous queries. This can be taken advantage of by the tracer $\mathcal{T}$. Alternatively, when the adversary maintains state across rounds (i.e., the default in the definition above) we say we deal with *history-recording* adversaries.
4. *Abrupt adversaries.* This is a strengthening of the adversarial model that enables $\mathcal{A}$ to finish the game at a moment of its choosing. This means that $\mathcal{A}$ may produce a special symbol as a response. Given such symbol the tracer $\mathcal{T}$ is not allowed to submit any further queries. We note that this is not in violation of the basic tenet of being admissible : $\mathcal{A}$ when it forms a σ-admissible pair with the adversary is still supposed to satisfy the $\mathcal{R}$ with probability at least σ. If $\mathcal{A}$ is abrupt though it may decide to stop the tracing game with probability as high as $1 - \sigma$ if given a query

from $\mathcal{Q}$ (and possibly with even higher probability when given queries from outside of this set).

Now that we have defined the rules of engagement between the two players of the tracing game we will specify when game is winnable by the tracer.

Definition 3.14. *We say that the tracing game* $\mathtt{TG} = \langle \mathbf{KeyDist}, \mathcal{Q}, \mathcal{R} \rangle$ *is* winnable *by a tracer* $\mathcal{T}$ *with probability* α *for* σ*-threshold and* t*-coalitions if for all* $\mathcal{A}$ *for which the pair* $\langle \mathcal{A}, \mathcal{T} \rangle$ *is* σ*-admissible it holds that for all* $n \in \mathbb{N}$, $\mathsf{C} \subseteq [n]$, $|\mathsf{C}| \leq t$,

$$\mathbf{Prob}[\emptyset \neq \langle \mathcal{A}, \mathcal{T} \rangle (tk, ek, sk_1, \ldots, sk_n, \mathsf{C}) \subseteq \mathsf{C}] \geq \alpha$$

where $(tk, ek, sk_1, \ldots, sk_n)$ *is distributed according to* $\mathbf{KeyDist}(1^n)$.

Provided that $\mathtt{TG}$ *is winnable by a tracer* $\mathcal{T}$*, we define the tracing overhead* $\mathsf{trover}[\mathtt{TG}, \mathcal{T}]$ *of the tracing game* $\mathtt{TG}$ *as the supremum of all* $r_{\langle \mathcal{A}, \mathcal{T} \rangle}$*; note that* $\mathsf{trover}[\mathtt{TG}, \mathcal{T}]$ *is a function of* t, σ *and possibly of other parameters as well.*

Note that in the notation $\mathsf{trover}[\mathtt{TG}, \mathcal{T}]$ we may omit $\mathcal{T}$ and write simply $\mathsf{trover}[\mathtt{TG}]$ if it is clear from the context to which tracer $\mathcal{T}$ we refer to.

It is interesting to note that the tracing game can be thought of as a privacy game if we flip the semantics of what side is adversarial. In this alternative interpretation, the good side is sitting on the adversary side and attempts to output some data that meet some "usefulness criterion" determined by $\mathcal{R}$ and are based on the private information of the users. On the other hand, the adversary is sitting on the tracer side and attempts to violate the privacy of the users. We do not pursue this parallel further here.

3.4 Types of Tracing Games

In this section we will define two basic types of tracing games that will be the focus of the chapter. Recall that a tracing game is a triple $\langle \mathbf{KeyDist}, \mathcal{Q}, \mathcal{R} \rangle$ and is defined with respect to an s-ary multiuser encryption scheme $\mathtt{ME} = (\mathbf{KeyDist}, \mathbf{Transmit}, \mathbf{Receive})$.

3.4.1 Non-Black Box Tracing Game.

In this setting, the adversary is considered to be a pirate decoder that is capable of receiving the transmission through some key material that is made out of traitor keys. The non-black box tracing game refers to the case where the response of the adversary is defined to be the key material that makes the decoder succesful. This response is not necessarily a real reaction of the adversary but rather an abstract notion that in reality may include physical tampering on behalf of the tracer. In many settings by "reverse-engineering" a decoder, it might be possible to retrieve the key employed within. We note that a decryption key from the key-space K should be available to the tracer because of the unlikelihood of performing decryption without a key.

We first define the set of key material $\mathsf{K}_{ek} \subseteq \mathsf{K}$ that is useful in decrypting the transmission of any vector of message $M = \langle m_1, \ldots, m_s \rangle \in \mathsf{M}^s$ in an s-ary multiuser encryption scheme (**KeyDist**, **Transmit**, **Receive**) as follows:

$$\begin{aligned} \mathsf{K}_{ek} = \{k \in \mathsf{K} \mid \forall M = \langle m_1, \ldots, m_s \rangle \in \mathsf{M}^s \\ \mathbf{Prob}[\mathbf{Receive}(\mathbf{Transmit}(ek, M), k) \in \{m_1, \ldots, m_s\}] = 1\} \end{aligned} \quad (3.2)$$

where $(tk, ek, sk_1, \ldots, sk_n)$ is distributed according to $\mathbf{KeyDist}(1^n)$. Note that the above can be relaxed by requiring only probabilistic correctness.

We define the tracing game in the non-black box model by specializing the predicate $\mathcal{R}$ as follows.

Definition 3.15. *We say that a multiuser encryption scheme* (**KeyDist**, **Transmit**, **Receive**) *is a non-black box traitor tracing scheme for t-coalitions with success probability α against σ-pirates if there exists a tracer $\mathcal{T}$ such that the tracing game $\langle$***KeyDist**, $\mathcal{Q}^{\mathrm{NB}}, \mathcal{R}^{\mathrm{NB}}\rangle$ *is winnable by $\mathcal{T}$ with probability α for σ-threshold and t-coalitions where $\mathcal{R}^{\mathrm{NB}}(tk, ek, sk_1, \ldots, sk_n, q, a) = 1$ holds if and only if $a \in \mathsf{K}_{ek}$ and $\mathcal{Q}^{\mathrm{NB}} = \{\mathsf{open}\}$.*

According to the above formulation, an adversary is allowed to respond with the same exact key material for each query. Hence, without loss of generality, we will consider only the case that the number of rounds $r_{\langle \mathcal{A}, \mathcal{T} \rangle}$ equals to 1. The design of a multiuser encryption scheme with capability of non-black box traitor tracing should be feasible so that the tracer $\mathcal{T}$ is able to output a traitor identity having access to only one response from the adversary $\mathcal{A}$.

3.4.2 Black-Box Tracing Game.

In many settings the non-black box approach is inapplicable. Reverse engineering can be expensive and can be possibly deterred through obfuscation techniques. Thus, it is important to consider the case whether the tracing procedure can be *black-box*. This allows tracing to work successfully using merely black-box access to the pirate decoder. Black-box traitor tracing reduces tracing costs significantly as there is no need to "reverse-engineer" the pirate decoder and may in some cases even allow tracing to be performed remotely without the physical availability of the pirate decoder.

The major challenge in the black-box traitor setting is to extract information regarding the original keys utilised in the construction of the pirate decoder. The tracer will communicate with the pirate decoder using a set of specially crafted queries. These queries will not be necessarily normal transmissions as the tracing center is allowed to communicate with the decoder in an arbitrary way. The response of the decoder may be equal to the decrypted plaintext, or be simply of binary form, essentially "yes", in case of returning the content in the cleartext form, or "no", in case of responding arbitrarily or jamming.

In our exposition, we will use the threshold σ to impose the adversarial constraint related to the success probability of the pirate decoder in decrypting regular transmissions. This is of particular importance, since tracing would be impossible against a pirate decoder that is not required to operate correctly at least some of the time.

Definition 3.16. *For some $s \in \mathbb{N}$, an s-ary multiuser encryption scheme* $\mathtt{ME} = (\mathbf{KeyDist}, \mathbf{Transmit}, \mathbf{Receive})$ *is a* black box traitor tracing scheme for t-coalitions with success probability α against σ-pirates *if there exists a tracer $\mathcal{T}$ such that the tracing game* $\mathtt{TG} = \langle \mathbf{KeyDist}, \mathcal{Q}^{\mathrm{BB}}, \mathcal{R}^{\mathrm{BB}} \rangle$ *against t-coalitions is winnable by $\mathcal{T}$ with probability α against σ-adversaries.*

Here $\mathcal{Q}^{\mathrm{BB}}$, contains all random variables $\mathbf{Transmit}(ek, M)$ *for any $M \in \mathsf{M}^s$ where $(tk, ek, sk_1, \ldots, sk_n) \leftarrow$* $\mathbf{KeyDist}(1^n)$. *In case the scheme* $\mathtt{ME}$ *is stateful over a set of* States, *$\mathcal{Q}^{\mathrm{BB}}$ is parameterized with* States *as well. On the other hand, $\mathcal{R}^{\mathrm{BB}}(\mathsf{C}, tk, ek, sk_1, \ldots, sk_n, q, a)$ is equal to 1 if and only if $a \in M$ whenever q is sampled from* $\mathbf{Transmit}(ek, M)$ *where M is selected from M^s.*

Note that for simplicity in the above definition we defined $\mathcal{Q}^{\mathrm{BB}}$ to contain random variables for each fixed $M \in \mathsf{M}^s$ but depending on the occasion we may consider more general plaintext distributions; this is consistent with the fact that the intention here is to define $\mathcal{Q}^{\mathrm{BB}}$ as capturing the *normal system operation* and occasionally we may be able to take advantage of the way a system operates to facilitate our tracing procedures.

As stated above, one may also consider a more general view of the black box tracing model, that is related to the case that the pirate decoder is a tamper resistant box, such as a music player and the response of the decoder is not the exact decryption of the transmission but rather the actual rendering of the cleartext transmission on a display device. In such case, the tracer can still extract useful information by observing whether the given ciphertext results in music being played or not. It is possible to address such definitions in our framework by having $\mathcal{R}$ determine exactly what input should be given to the tracer (as opposed to disclosing a).

Among the different variations of the tracing game described in Definition 3.12, tracing with resetting and tracing against abrupt adversaries are relevant to black-box tracing as they are defining the capabilities of the pirate decoder the tracer has access to. We would like to motivate these cases briefly in the following paragraphs for the context of the present section.

A pirate decoder is said to be resettable if the tracer has the capability to reset the pirate decoder to its initial state and the decoder is available for a new query. This gives the tracer the advantage of asking queries that will be handled independently during the tracing process, i.e., effectively preventing the decoder from using previous querying information submitted by the tracer in order to decide its present action.

Resettable pirate decoders constitute a natural model for black-box traitor tracing since they can be encountered in a number of settings, mainly:

- Software pirate decoders. If the tracer possesses a software pirate decoder, evidently we can assume that such a decoder is resettable, since the tracer may restart the decoder at each trial using a previously stored copy.
- A hardware pirate decoder may be resettable as well if e.g., the tracer can flood its internal memory with data so that history recording between two probings is assumed to be eliminated. Of course note that this implies some understanding of the internals of the decoder.

In contrast, a *history recording* pirate decoder "remembers" the previous queries made by the tracer and because the tracing procedure is public, the history recording capability can be used by the decoder to evade tracing. History-recording pirate decoders can also be encountered in a number of settings such as:

- A software pirate decoder that is only remotely accessible by the tracer, e.g. the decoder runs in some server connected to the Internet and the tracer may only probe it remotely.
- Hardware pirate decoders in general.

A decoder is said to be available if it lacks a self-defensive mechanism, i.e, even if it realizes some abnormality in the content-transmission it is incapable of halting the tracer process. On the other occasion the decoder is called abrupt. Abrupt pirate decoders are those devices that may take some counter-actions against the tracing process which can be "defensive" or "aggressive" in their nature. More specifically, by a defensive action we will refer to a shutting down mechanism, a process by which the pirate decoder erases all internal key information, thus making tracing impossible (and rendering itself useless at the same time). Such defensive actions are mechanisms that can be implemented successfully only in hardware devices. On the other hand, an aggressive action (more suitable for software decoders) could be crashing the host system, or releasing a virus. Note that aggressive counter-actions may not entirely prohibit tracing but they may substantially increase its cost. In any case the assumption here is that the occurrence of any such reaction is immediately detectable by the tracer and tracing will cease after it is triggered. It should be noted that the pirate decoder does not want such a mechanism to be triggered during normal operation. Since it is not possible to force the pirate decoder not to use such reaction mechanisms if they are available, what is needed to be shown is that there are systems where the usage of such mechanisms is detrimental to the pirate decoder itself (i.e. the triggering of the mechanism leaks some information about the traitor keys or it significantly interferes with the decoder's data reception capabilities).

Regarding alfresco tracing, observe that the way $\mathcal{Q}^{\mathsf{BB}}$ is defined suggests that in case we have an alfresco tracer we may be able to perform tracing in the presence of honest subscribers (i.e., using the same channel as the one used to transmit to all users) without disrupting their operation : the tracer will submit the tracing ciphertexts to the pirate decoder while the other participants will be decrypting them correctly.

Observe that the combination of alfresco tracing with a history-recording adversary yields a very powerful tracing mechanism. Indeed, it permits the tracing to be performed in the presence of honest users while the receiving decoder is history-recording. This setting enables us to tackle a scenario that is known as pirate rebroadcasting. In this scenario, the adversary first decrypts the content by using its traitor key material and then once it is in clear text form, it rebroadcasts the content.

3.5 Traceability of Multiuser Encryption Schemes

In this section, we will discuss traceability of the multiuser encryption schemes of Section 3.2.

3.5.1 Traceability of Linear Length Multiuser Encryption Scheme

We will now show that the linear length multiuser encryption scheme $\mathtt{ME}_L$ described in Section 3.2 is a black box traitor tracing scheme against resettable pirate decoders. Recall that resettable pirate decoders allow the tracer to reset the adversary and to receive fresh responses forgetful of the history of the interaction. This is the key fact in our choice of tracing queries; in particular we will deviate from the normal set of random variables $\mathcal{Q}^{\mathsf{BB}}$ and query the decoder with some special tracing ciphertexts that will yield the identification of a traitor involved in piracy.

Recall that the linear length multiuser encryption scheme $\mathtt{ME}_L$ transmits a vector of ciphertext $\langle \mathtt{E}_{k_1}(m), \ldots, \mathtt{E}_{k_n}(m)\rangle$ where $(\mathtt{E}, \mathtt{D})$ is the underlying symmetric encryption scheme of $\mathtt{ME}_L$ and the key k_i is available to the i-th receiver. We will, now, decribe the special tracing queries of a particular tracer, denoted by $\mathcal{T}_S$, that is interacting with $\mathcal{A}$. The tracing queries consist of the special transmission $\mathbf{Transmit}_L^s(ek, m)$ for $s = 0, 1, \ldots, n$ by substituting the first s ciphertexts with random strings.

$$\mathbf{Transmit}_L^s(ek, m) = \langle \mathtt{E}_{k_1}(R_1), \mathtt{E}_{k_2}(R_2), \ldots \mathtt{E}_{k_s}(R_s), \mathtt{E}_{k_{s+1}}(m), \ldots \mathtt{E}_{k_n}(m)\rangle \tag{3.3}$$

where R_i, for $i = 1, \ldots, s$, is a random string of the same length as the message m. Given that the adversary-tracer pair is σ-admissible the adversary will be required to respond the queries of type $\mathbf{Transmit}_L^0(ek, m)$ such that the predicate $\mathcal{R}^{\mathsf{BB}}$ is satisfied with probability at least σ. On the other hand note that the predicate necessarily fails with overwhelming probability for queries of type $\mathbf{Transmit}_L^n(ek, m)$. This suggests that the tracer can progressively randomize the pattern of the ciphertext until a position is identified that the pirate-box fails to decrypt successfully whenever it queries the tracing ciphertext.

The soundness of the above argumentation is supported by the following lemma:

Lemma 3.17. *Assuming that* $s \notin \mathsf{C}$*, any probabilistic polynomial time adversary* $\mathcal{A}$*, given* $\{k_i\}_{i \in \mathsf{C}}$*, distinguishes the distributions* $\mathbf{Transmit}_L^{s-1}(ek, m)$ *and* $\mathbf{Transmit}_L^{s}(ek, m)$ *with probability at most* $2\varepsilon_p$ *where it holds* $(tk, ek, sk_1, \ldots, sk_n) \leftarrow \mathbf{KeyDist}(1^n)$ *assuming that the underlying encryption scheme* $(\mathtt{E}, \mathtt{D})$ *is* ε_p*-insecure in the sense of Definition 2.5.*

Proof. Consider the following CCA1 key encapsulation adversary $\mathcal{B}$ that will be able to break the symmetric encryption scheme $(\mathtt{E}, \mathtt{D})$ in the sense of Definition 2.5 with probability at least ε_p by simulating the adversary $\mathcal{A}$ and the multiuser encryption center.

To break the security claim of the underlying symmetric encryption scheme $(\mathtt{E}, \mathtt{D})$, $\mathcal{B}$, is given access to encryption-decryption oracle of the primitive. $\mathcal{B}$ has also access to the decryption/encryption under a key k that is unknown to her. She is then challenged with plaintext-ciphertext pair (c, m) for which either $c = \mathtt{E}_k(m)$ or $c = \mathtt{E}_k(R)$ for some random string R that has the same length with m. She is asked to test if the pair is a correct plaintext-ciphertext pair.

$\mathcal{B}$ will simulate the distribution $\mathbf{Transmit}_L^{s}(ek, m)$. Let $\mathcal{B}$ be given the challenge (c, m) where either m is the proper plaintext of c or it is randomly selected. $\mathcal{B}$ will prepare a transmission for $\mathcal{A}$ by setting the s-th location of the challenge transmission with c and the remaining positions from $s+1, \ldots, n$ with the appropriate encryptions of m.

Based on the assumption on the underlying encryption scheme we have that $|\mathbf{Prob}[\mathbf{Exp}_{\mathcal{B}}^{kem}(1^n)] - 1/2| \le \varepsilon_p$. We observe that in the key encapsulation attack of $\mathcal{B}$ in the conditional space $b = 0$, the adversary $\mathcal{B}^{kem}(1^n)$ operates identically to the distribution $\mathbf{Transmit}_L^{s-1}(ek, m)$ while in the conditional space $b = 1$ it operates identically to the distribution $\mathbf{Transmit}_L^{s}(ek, m)$. Based on this derive the proof of the statement given in the lemma. ∎

Let us define p_s as the probability that the box decodes the special tracing ciphertext $\mathbf{Transmit}_L^{s}(ek, m)$. Suppose, now, that the key k_s is not available to the adversary. As we show in lemma 3.17 it holds that the pirate decoder can distinguish between the random variables $\mathbf{Transmit}_L^{s}(ek, m)$ and $\mathbf{Transmit}_L^{s-1}(ek, m)$ only with small probability that is related to the insecurity of the underlying encryption scheme $\mathtt{E}(\cdot)$. As a result, it holds that $|p_{s-1} - p_s|$ is relatively small assuming that the advantage ε_p in being successful in security game of the underlying encryption primitive is also small.

On the other hand, for a pirate decoder we postulate that it holds that $p_0 \ge \sigma$ due to the constraint placed on $\mathcal{A}$ as detailed in the tracing game. On the other hand it is relatively straightforward to see that $p_n \leq \frac{1}{|\mathsf{M}|}$ (recall that M denotes the plaintext space). Hence there must be at least one $0 < s \leq n$ for which $|p_{s-1} - p_s| \geq \frac{\sigma - 1/|\mathsf{M}|}{n}$ by the triangular inequality. Now if the parameters have been chosen so that $\frac{\sigma-1/|\mathsf{M}|}{n} > 10\varepsilon_p$, this can lead to the accusation of the user possessing k_s.

We will discuss this in the following basic lemma, which we will also refer to it as the *tracing lemma.*

Lemma 3.18. *For $N, K \in \mathbb{N}$, consider a sequence of $N+1$ independent experiments each one repeated K times. Let p_i the probability of success of the i-th experiment for $i \in \{0, \ldots, N\}$ and $\rho_i \in \{0, \ldots, K\}$ the number of times the i-th experiment succeeds. Then, with probability $1-\varepsilon$, there is an $s \in \{1, \ldots, N\}$ for which it holds $|\rho_s - \rho_{s-1}| \geq \frac{3}{5} \cdot K(p_0 - p_N)/N$ and the smallest such s satisfies that $|p_s - p_{s-1}| \geq \frac{1}{5} \cdot (p_0 - p_N)/N$ provided that $K \geq 75 \cdot N^2 \ln(8/\varepsilon)(p_0 - p_N)^{-2}$.*

Proof. Note that the case $p_0 \leq p_N$ is trivial thus we will only consider the proof of the lemma for $p_0 > p_N$.

Let $\mu_i = K \cdot p_i$ for $i = 1, \ldots, N$, i.e., μ_i is the expected number of successes of the i-th experiment. We apply a two-tailed Chernoff bound due to Equation 1.2 for any $i = 0, \ldots, N$ and for $0 < \delta$ we have:

$$\mathbf{Prob}[|\rho_i - \mu_i| \geq \delta\mu_i] \leq 2e^{-\mu_i\delta^2/(2+\delta)}$$

Substituting $\delta = \frac{\gamma}{\mu_i}$ for some γ and $\mu_i = K \cdot p_i$, we obtain:

$$\begin{aligned}\mathbf{Prob}[|\rho_i - \mu_i| \geq \gamma] &\leq 2e^{-\gamma^2/(2\mu_i+\gamma)} \\ &\leq 2e^{-\gamma^2/(2Kp_i+\gamma)} \\ &\leq 2e^{-\gamma^2/3K}\end{aligned}$$

where the last inequality follows from $p_i \leq 1$ and $\gamma \leq K$. Substituting $\gamma = \frac{K(p_0-p_N)}{5N}$ to the inequality we obtain:

$$\begin{aligned}2e^{-\gamma^2/3K} &= 2e^{-\frac{K^2(p_0-p_N)^2}{25N^2}\cdot\frac{1}{3K}} \\ &\leq 2e^{-\frac{75N^2\cdot\ln(8/\varepsilon)}{(p_0-p_N)^2}\cdot\frac{(p_0-p_N)^2}{75N^2}} \\ &\leq 2e^{-\ln(8/\varepsilon)} \\ &\leq \frac{\varepsilon}{4}\end{aligned}$$

The above analysis shows that for any $i \in \{0, 1, \ldots, N\}$, we have $|\rho_i - \mu_i| \leq \gamma$ with probability at least $1 - \varepsilon/4$.

Claim 1. consider any $s \in \{1, \ldots, N\}$ for which it holds that $|\rho_s - \rho_{s-1}| \geq \frac{3}{5} \cdot K(p_0 - p_N)/N$. We will prove that with probability at least $1 - \varepsilon/2$ it holds that $|p_{s-1} - p_s| \geq (p_0 - p_N)/5N$.

By applying the triangular inequality for the equations $|\mu_{s-1} - \rho_{s-1}| \leq \gamma$ and $|\mu_s - \rho_s| \leq \gamma$, we have that it holds:

$$|\mu_{s-1} - \mu_s| \geq |\rho_{s-1} - \rho_s| - 2\gamma$$

with probability at least $(1 - \varepsilon/4)^2 \geq 1 - \varepsilon/2$. Given that we have $\gamma = \frac{K(p_0 - p_N)}{5N}$ we obtain that with probability at least $1 - \varepsilon/2$ it holds that:

$$|p_{s-1} - p_s| \geq \frac{p_0 - p_N}{5N}$$

This completes the proof of claim 1.

Claim 2. We next claim that there is an $s \in \{1, \ldots, N\}$ for which it holds $|\rho_s - \rho_{s-1}| \geq \frac{3}{5} \cdot K(p_0 - p_N)/N$ with probability at least $1 - \varepsilon/2$.

Observe that there exists an $s \in \{1, \ldots, N\}$ for which it holds $|p_s - p_{s-1}| \geq (p_0 - p_N)/N$. Indeed otherwise for any s it holds $|p_s - p_{s-1}| < (p_0 - p_N)/N$ and thus $|p_0 - p_N| \leq \sum_{s=1}^{N} |p_s - p_{s-1}| < N|p_0 - p_N|/N = |p_0 - p_N|$, a contradiction.

For this s we will show that $|\rho_s - \rho_{s-1}| \geq \frac{3}{5} \cdot K(p_0 - p_N)/N$. We know that $|\mu_s - \mu_{s-1}| \geq K(p_0 - p_N)/N$. As before we know that with probability $1 - \varepsilon/2$ we will have $|\mu_{s-1} - \rho_{s-1}| \leq \gamma$ and $|\mu_s - \rho_s| \leq \gamma$, as a result $|\rho_s - \rho_{s-1}| \geq |\mu_s - \mu_{s-1}| - 2\gamma$.

We conclude that with probability $1 - \varepsilon/2$ there exists some $s \in \{1, \ldots, N\}$ for which it holds $|\rho_s - \rho_{s-1}| \geq \frac{3}{5} \cdot K(p_0 - p_N)/N$. This completes the proof of claim 2.

By combining the two claims we obtain the statement of the lemma. ■

Following the above reasoning, we are, now, ready to prove that the $\mathtt{ME}_L$ is a black-box traitor tracing scheme for which the corresponding tracing game for n-coalitions is winnable by the tracer $\mathcal{T}_S$ against any probabilistic polynomial time adversarial algorithm $\mathcal{A}$. As we have specified at the beginning of this section, the tracer $\mathcal{T}_S$ will queriy the special transmission of the form $\mathbf{Transmit}_L^s(ek, m)$ for $s = 0, 1, \ldots, n$ where m is uniformly distributed.

Theorem 3.19. *Consider a multiuser encryption scheme* $\mathtt{ME}_L$ *that employs a symmetric encryption scheme that is* ε_p*-insecure in the sense of Definition 2.5. For any* $n \in \mathbb{N}, \epsilon > 0$*, the scheme* $\mathtt{ME}_L$ *is a black box traitor tracing scheme for* n*-coalitions with success probability* $1 - \varepsilon$ *against resettable* σ*-pirates with* $\sigma > 10n\varepsilon_p + \frac{1}{|\mathsf{M}|}$. *It further holds that* $\mathsf{trover}[\mathtt{ME}_L] = O(\frac{n^3 \cdot \ln(1/\varepsilon)}{(\sigma - 1/|\mathsf{M}|)^2})$.

Proof. Consider an adversary $\mathcal{A}$ that is given access to the key material $\{sk_j\}_{j \in \mathsf{C}}$ for some subset $\mathsf{C} \subseteq [n]$ where $(tk, ek, sk_1, \ldots, sk_n)$ is distributed according to $\mathbf{KeyDist}_L(1^n)$.

The tracer $\mathcal{T}_S$ will interact with $\mathcal{A}$ by submitting suitable queries. A query of type i will correspond to $\mathbf{Transmit}_L^i(ek, m)$ as defined in Equation 3.3 for $i \in \{0, \ldots, n\}$. The tracer will reset the adversary after each query. Each query q of type i together with the response a of $\mathcal{A}$ can be thought as an experiment of type i. The experiment is said to be successful if

$$\mathcal{R}^{\mathsf{BB}}(\mathsf{C}, tk, ek, sk_1, \ldots, sk_n, q, a) = 1$$

Let p_i the probability of success of an experiment of type i and ρ_i the number of successes of the i-th experiment. The tracer will perform K experiments of each type for a parameter K to be determined. After performing all experiments the tracer will output the smallest $s \in [n]$ that satisfies $|\rho_{s-1} - \rho_s| \geq \frac{3}{5} \cdot K \frac{\sigma - 1/|\mathsf{M}|}{n}$ or it fails if such value s does not exist.

We will now prove by setting $K \geq \frac{75n^2 \cdot \ln(8/\varepsilon)}{(\sigma - 1/|\mathsf{M}|)^2}$, that the tracer $\mathcal{T}_S$ satisfies the following: For all resettable adversaries $\mathcal{A}$ that make the $\langle \mathcal{A}, \mathcal{T}_S \rangle$ pair σ-admissible, assuming $\sigma > 10n\varepsilon_p + \frac{1}{|\mathsf{M}|}$, it holds that for any $\mathsf{C} \subseteq [n]$,

$$\mathbf{Prob}[\emptyset \neq \langle \mathcal{A}, \mathcal{T}_S \rangle (tk, ek, sk_1, \ldots, sk_n, \mathsf{C}) \subseteq \mathsf{C}] \geq 1 - \varepsilon$$

In other words we will show that the tracer will output an index from the set $[n]$ that corresponds to a traitor with probability $1 - \epsilon$.

We observe that due to the allowed resettability the experiments performed by the tracer are independent. By applying lemma 3.18 we deduce that the tracer will output an index s with probability $1 - \varepsilon$ that satisfies

$$|p_s - p_{s-1}| \geq \frac{1}{5} \cdot \frac{\sigma - 1/|\mathsf{M}|}{n} > 2\varepsilon_p$$

where the final inequality follows from the bound on σ required in the theorem's statement. By Lemma 3.17 this means that $s \in \mathsf{C}$ which completes the argument that the tracer succeeds. The bound on the number of rounds comes directly from the lower bound on K and the fact that $n+1$ experiments need to be performed. ■

It should be noted that the above argumentation is oblivious to the number of corrupted users thus it is possible to trace any number of traitors by employing $\mathtt{ME}_L$. Unfortunately, this incurs a high transmission overhead. It should also be observed that the the tracing overhead is quite high. There are various strategies to reduce such costs. For example, one can employ multiuser encryption schemes based on fingerprinting codes to trace against a bounded size traitor-coalition. We will discuss this further in the following section.

3.5.2 Traceability of Schemes Based on Fingerprinting Codes

Let us first revisit the key distribution algorithm that is common for each of the schemes based on fingerprinting codes.

KeyDist$_{\mathsf{F}}$: The key distribution algorithm employs a q-ary fingerprinting code $\mathsf{F} = (\mathbf{CodeGen}^{\ell}, \mathbf{Identify})$. Given 1^n, the algorithm first produces a (ℓ, n, q)-code $\mathcal{W} = \{\mathsf{w}^1, \ldots, \mathsf{w}^n\}$ where $(\mathcal{W}, ik) \leftarrow \mathbf{Codegen}^{\ell}(1^n)$ over an alphabet Q.
It, then, produces a collection of keys $\{k_{i,j}\}_{(i,j) \in [q] \times [\ell]} \subseteq \mathsf{K}$ which is also set to be the transmission key ek for encryption. The user key sk_u, for $u \in [n]$, is set to $\langle k_{\mathsf{w}_1^u,1}, k_{\mathsf{w}_2^u,2}, \ldots, k_{\mathsf{w}_\ell^u,\ell} \rangle$ where $\mathsf{w}^u = \langle \mathsf{w}_1^u, \mathsf{w}_2^u, \ldots, \mathsf{w}_\ell^u \rangle \in \mathcal{W}$. The pair $(\mathcal{W}, ik)$ is set to be the tracing key tk.

Traceability of the Chor-Fiat-Naor and Boneh-Naor Schemes

Following a similar argumentation to the case of the linear length multiuser encryption scheme, we will prove in this section that Chor-Fiat-Naor and Boneh-Naor schemes are black box traitor tracing schemes against resettable decoders. The tracer will query the decoder with special tracing ciphertexts defined separately for both of the schemes. After each query the tracer resets the adversary and continues querying new tracing ciphertexts. Resetting plays a crucial role in the tracing strategy as the pirate decoder might be capable of distinguishing the "abnormal" ciphertexts by observing the history of previous transmissions.

We note that a decoder with sufficient success probability would be required to use a sequence of ℓ secret keys each one selected from the column of the code. The purpose of the special tracing ciphertexts is to expose the secret keys used and effectively reconstruct the "pirate codeword" that corresponds to the pattern of keys that are manifested in the adversarial decoder.

We next provide the special tracing ciphertexts that will be used as queries by the tracer for both schemes:

- *Chor-Fiat-Naor Scheme:* The tracer $\mathcal{T}_{CFN}$ queries the special tracing ciphertext $\mathbf{Transmit}^{i,j}_{CFN[\mathsf{F}]}(ek, m)$, for $(i, j) \in \{0, 1, \ldots, q\} \times \{1, \ldots, \ell\}$, randomizes the first i rows of the share encrypted in the j-th column. Let $r_1, \ldots, r_\ell$ be the random strings of the same length with m that satisfy $m = r_1 \oplus \ldots \oplus r_\ell$. We define $\mathbf{Transmit}^{i,j}_{CFN[\mathsf{F}]}(ek, m)$ as:

$$\begin{bmatrix} \mathsf{E}_{k_1^1}(r_1) & \mathsf{E}_{k_1^2}(r_2) & \ldots & \mathsf{E}_{k_1^j}(R_1) & \ldots & \mathsf{E}_{k_1^\ell}(r_\ell) \\ \mathsf{E}_{k_2^1}(r_1) & \mathsf{E}_{k_2^2}(r_2) & \ldots & \mathsf{E}_{k_2^j}(R_2) & \ldots & \mathsf{E}_{k_2^\ell}(r_\ell) \\ \vdots & \vdots & \vdots & \vdots & \vdots & \vdots \\ \mathsf{E}_{k_i^1}(r_1) & \mathsf{E}_{k_i^2}(r_2) & \ldots & \mathsf{E}_{k_i^j}(R_i) & \ldots & \mathsf{E}_{k_i^\ell}(r_\ell) \\ \mathsf{E}_{k_{i+1}^1}(r_1) & \mathsf{E}_{k_{i+1}^2}(r_2) & \ldots & \mathsf{E}_{k_{i+1}^j}(r_j) & \ldots & \mathsf{E}_{k_{i+1}^\ell}(r_\ell) \\ \vdots & \vdots & \vdots & \vdots & \vdots & \vdots \\ \mathsf{E}_{k_q^1}(r_1) & \mathsf{E}_{k_q^2}(r_2) & \ldots & \mathsf{E}_{k_q^j}(r_j) & \ldots & \mathsf{E}_{k_q^\ell}(r_\ell) \end{bmatrix} \quad (3.4)$$

  where $R_1, R_2, \ldots, R_i$ is a set of random strings of length equal to the length of the shares $r_1, \ldots, r_\ell$.
- *Boneh-Naor Scheme:* The tracer $\mathcal{T}_{BN}$ queries the special tracing ciphertext $\mathbf{Transmit}^{i,j}_{BN[\mathsf{F}]}(ek, m)$, for $(i, j) \in \{0, 1, \ldots, q\} \times \{1, \ldots, \ell\}$, substitutes the first i encryptions with random strings for each type of transmission based on the choice of j. We define $\mathbf{Transmit}^{i,j}_{BN[\mathsf{F}]}(ek, m)$ as:

$$\langle j, \mathsf{E}_{k_1^j}(R_1), \mathsf{E}_{k_2^j}(R_2), \ldots, \mathsf{E}_{k_i^j}(R_i), E_{k_{i+1}^j}(m), \ldots, \mathsf{E}_{k_q^j}(m) \rangle \quad (3.5)$$

  where $R_1, R_2, \ldots, R_i$ is a set of random strings of length similar to the share m.

We start the analysis of the traceability of these two schemes by a lemma in the style of lemma 3.17.

Lemma 3.20. *Given a fingerprinting code* $\mathtt{F} = (\mathbf{CodeGen}^{\ell}, \mathbf{Identify})$, *consider* $(tk, ek, sk_1, \ldots, sk_n) \leftarrow \mathbf{KeyDist}_{\mathtt{F}}(1^n)$ *such that* $tk = (\mathcal{W}, ik) \leftarrow \mathbf{CodeGen}^{\ell}(1^n)$, $ek = \{k_{i,j}\}_{(i,j)\in[q]\times[\ell]}$ *and* $sk_u = \langle k_{\mathsf{w}_1^u,1}, k_{\mathsf{w}_2^u,2}, \ldots, k_{\mathsf{w}_\ell^u,\ell}\rangle$ *where* $\mathsf{w}^u = \langle \mathsf{w}_1^u, \mathsf{w}_2^u, \ldots, \mathsf{w}_\ell^u\rangle \in \mathcal{W}$ *for* $u \in [n]$.

Assuming that $k_{i,j} \notin \{k_{\mathsf{w}_j^u,j} \mid u \in \mathsf{C}\}$, *any probabilistic polynomial time adversary* $\mathcal{A}$, *given* $\{sk_u\}_{u\in\mathsf{C}}$, *distinguishes the following distributions*

- $\mathbf{Transmit}^{i,j-1}_{CFN[\mathtt{F}]}(ek, m)$ *from* $\mathbf{Transmit}^{i,j}_{CFN[\mathtt{F}]}(ek, m)$
- $\mathbf{Transmit}^{i,j-1}_{BN[\mathtt{F}]}(ek, m)$ *from* $\mathbf{Transmit}^{i,j}_{BN[\mathtt{F}]}(ek, m)$

with probability at most $2\varepsilon_p$ *where the underlying encryption scheme* $(\mathtt{E}, \mathtt{D})$ *is* ε_p*-insecure in the sense of Definition 2.5.*

Proof. The proof of the lemma is nearly identical to the proof of lemma 3.17, hence we skip it and leave it as an exercise for the reader. ■

The plan for the tracer design is as follows. The tracer will query the adversary with the tracing ciphertexts of the above form. An adversary that is sufficiently successful (we will make this requirement explicit later in the statements of the theorems) in both of these schemes would be using a key $k_{w_j,j}$ for each j where $w_j \in \{1, 2, \ldots, q\}$. The goal of the tracer is to deduce the key $k_{w_j,j}$ by using a walking argument over each column similar to the procedure used in the linear length scheme of the previous subsection. Finally, we will be able to construct a pirate codeword $\mathsf{w} = \langle w_1, \ldots, w_\ell\rangle$ from the keys deduced at each column. The **Identify** algorithm of the underlying fingerprinting code will then be used to output a traitor as long as the traitor coalition is bounded by t with sufficiently large success probability.

With the above brief summary of the tracer strategy, we will discuss the traceability of both schemes separately as the constraint placed on the adversary is different for the two schemes. On the one hand, the advantage of the Boneh-Naor scheme is its short transmission length (which can even be constant if the alphabet size q is taken to be constant). On the downside it will support traceability against pirates with higher success rates. The Chor-Fiat-Naor scheme, on the other hand, is successful in tracing pirates with smaller σ probabilities at the price of requiring from the transmission length to be a function of n; the exact relationship depends on the choice of the length function ℓ of the underlying code.

We first discuss traceability of the Chor-Fiat-Naor scheme. We define $p_{i,j}$ to be the probability that the pirate decoder decrypts the special ciphertext $\mathbf{Transmit}^{i,j}_{CFN[\mathtt{F}]}(ek, m)$. Suppose, now, that the key $k_{i,j}$ is not available to the adversary; in this case, it holds that the pirate decoder can distinguish between the random variables $\mathbf{Transmit}^{i-1,j}_{CFN[\mathtt{F}]}(ek, m)$ and $\mathbf{Transmit}^{i,j}_{CFN[\mathtt{F}]}(ek, m)$

only with small probability that is related to the insecurity of the underlying encryption scheme $\mathtt{E}(\cdot)$ as Lemma 3.20 suggests.

On the other hand, the σ-admissibility of the tracer adversary pair implies that a pirate decoder decrypts the ciphertext $\mathbf{Transmit}_{CFN[\mathsf{F}]}(ek, m) = \mathbf{Transmit}^{0,j}_{CFN[\mathsf{F}]}(ek, m)$ with probability at least σ for $j = 1, \ldots, \ell$, i.e. $p_{0,j} \geq \sigma$. On the other hand, $p_{q,j}$ can be at most $\frac{1}{|\mathsf{M}|}$ since the share m_j is entirely replaced by a sequence of random values. Hence, by applying the triangular inequality, there must be some $w_j \in \{1, \ldots, q\}$ such that $|p_{w_j-1,j} - p_{w_j,j}| > \frac{\sigma - 1/|\mathsf{M}|}{q}$. Along similar lines to the analysis of the linear length multiuser encryption scheme, the tracer will be able to locate such value with small failure probability for a slightly shorter probability difference. This same experiment will be run over each $j = 1, \ldots, \ell$ individually to identify the traitor key for the j-th column that is manifested by the pirate decoder.

Theorem 3.21. *Consider the multiuser encryption scheme* $\mathtt{ME}_{CFN[\mathsf{F}]}$ *that employs a symmetric encryption scheme that is* ε_p*-insecure in the sense of Definition 2.5 and an* (ℓ, n, q) *fingerprinting code* F *that is* (ε_f, t)*-identifier.*

For any $n \in \mathbb{N}$, $\epsilon > 0$, *the* $\mathtt{ME}_{CFN[\mathsf{F}]}$ *is a black box traitor tracing scheme for t-coalitions with success probability* $1 - \varepsilon - \varepsilon_f$ *against resettable* σ*-pirates where* $\sigma > 10q\varepsilon_p + \frac{1}{|\mathsf{M}|}$. *It further holds that* $\mathsf{trover}[\mathtt{ME}_{CFN[\mathsf{F}]}] = O(\frac{\ell q^3 \cdot \log(\ell/\varepsilon)}{(\sigma - 1/|\mathsf{M}|)^2})$.

Proof. Consider an adversary $\mathcal{A}$ that is given access to the key material $\{sk_u\}_{u \in \mathsf{C}}$ for some subset $\mathsf{C} \subseteq [n]$ where $(tk, ek, sk_1, \ldots, sk_n)$ is distributed according to $\mathbf{KeyDist}_{\mathsf{F}}(1^n)$.

The tracer $\mathcal{T}_{CFN}$ is a variant of the tracer $\mathcal{T}_S$ of Theorem 3.19. The tracer will interact with the adversary by submitting suitable queries. A query of type (i, j), for $i = 0, 1, \ldots, q$ and $j = 1, \ldots, \ell$, would correspond to $\mathbf{Transmit}^{i,j}_{CFN[\mathsf{F}]}(ek, m)$ as defined in Equation 3.4. The tracer will reset the adversary after each query. Each query q together with the response a of the adversary is thought of as an experiment of type (i, j) that is successful provided that : $\mathcal{R}^{\mathsf{BB}}(\mathsf{C}, tk, ek, sk_1, \ldots, sk_n, q, a) = 1$.

Let $p_{i,j}$ be the success probability of the experiment of type (i, j). Each experiment type will be repeated K times where K is a parameter that will be determined below. We define $\rho_{i,j} \in \{0, \ldots, K\}$ the number of successes of all the experiments of type (i, j).

For each $j = 1, \ldots, \ell$, the tracer finds the smallest $s \in [q]$ that satisfies $|\rho_{s-1,j} - \rho_{s,j}| \geq \frac{3}{5} \cdot K \frac{\sigma - 1/|\mathsf{M}|}{q}$. Then, the tracer sets $w_j = s$. The tracer will fail if such s does not exist for some j. Finally, the tracer constructs a codeword $\mathsf{p} = \langle w_1, \ldots, w_\ell \rangle$. It then outputs $\mathbf{Identify}(tk, \mathsf{p})$ where $\mathsf{F} = (\mathbf{CodeGen}, \mathbf{Identify})$. Consider, now, the following arguments:

1. Using lemma 3.18 the choice $K \geq \frac{75q^2 \cdot \ln(8\ell/\varepsilon)}{(\sigma - 1/|\mathsf{M}|)^2}$ suffices to locate a value $w_j \in \{1, \ldots, q\}$, for all $j = 1, \ldots, \ell$, such that $|p_{w_j-1,j} - p_{w_j,j}| \geq \frac{\sigma - 1/|\mathsf{M}|}{5q}$ holds with probability $1 - \varepsilon$.

2. Provided that $\sigma > 10q\varepsilon_p + \frac{1}{|\mathsf{M}|}$, lemma 3.20 implies that the key material $k_{w_j,j}$ belongs to the traitor coalition.
3. Assuming that the codeword $\mathsf{p} = \langle w_1, \ldots, w_\ell \rangle$ is in the descendant set of the traitor coalition it holds that **Identify**$(tk, \mathsf{p}) \in \mathsf{C}$ with probability at least $1 - \varepsilon_f$.

The traceability proof of the statement follows directly from the above arguments. Regarding the tracing overhead the result follows easily by the fact that K experiments need to be performed for each of the q symbols along the whole length of the code ℓ. ■

A slightly different line of reasoning is required for the Boneh-Naor scheme since depending on the choice of $l \leftarrow \{1, \ldots, \ell\}$, the decoder possibly decrypts the transmission with different success rates. One simple way to deal with this problem is to boost the required σ bound for the adversary to be above $\frac{\ell-1}{\ell}$ (it is worth noting that there are alternative - albeit more complex - strategies for dealing with this matter; the reader is referred to the bibliographic notes discussion in the end of the chapter).

Theorem 3.22. *Consider the multiuser encryption scheme* $\mathtt{ME}_{BN[\mathtt{F}]}$ *that employs a symmetric encryption scheme that is* ε_p*-insecure in the sense of Definition 2.5 and an* (ℓ, n, q) *fingerprinting code* $\mathtt{F}$ *that is* (ε_f, t)*-identifier.*

For any $n \in \mathbb{N}, \epsilon > 0$, $\mathtt{ME}_{BN[\mathtt{F}]}$ *is a black box traitor tracing scheme for* t*-coalitions with success probability* $1 - \varepsilon - \varepsilon_f$ *against resettable* σ*-pirates with* $\sigma > \frac{1}{\ell}(\ell - 1 + 10q\varepsilon_p + \frac{1}{|\mathsf{M}|})$. *It further holds that* $\mathsf{trover}[\mathtt{ME}_{BN[\mathtt{F}]}] = O(\frac{\ell q^3 \cdot \ln(\ell/\varepsilon)}{(\ell\sigma - \ell + 1 - 1/|\mathsf{M}|)^2})$.

Proof. We apply the same reasoning as in the case of Theorem 3.21. The only obstacle is to find a lower bound on the success probability of the adversary's decryption success in queries that are sampled from $\mathbf{Transmit}^{0,j}_{BN[\mathsf{F}]}(ek, m)$ for each $j \in \{1, \ldots, \ell\}$ (note that such issue did not arise in the case of Theorem 3.21 as that bound was trivially σ).

Towards computing the lower bound we let $\mathbf{A}_j$ be the event that $j \in \{1,, \ldots, \ell\}$ is selected for transmission. It is immediate that the events $\{\mathbf{A}_j\}_{j=1,\ldots,\ell}$ partition the space of the normal transmissions and each one has likelihood $1/\ell$. Considering the success probabilities σ_j of the adversary that are conditional to the events $\mathbf{A}_j$ we have that $\frac{1}{\ell} \sum_{j \in [\ell]} \sigma_j = \sigma$. This implies that for all j, $\sum_{j \in [\ell]} \sigma_j > \ell - 1 + 10q\epsilon_p + \frac{1}{|\mathsf{M}|}$, which implies that for all $j \in [\ell]$, $\sigma_j > 10q\epsilon_p + \frac{1}{|\mathsf{M}|}$.

Now, we can apply the same reasoning as in Theorem 3.21 within each conditional space to locate a value $w_j \in \{0, 1, \ldots, q\}$, for any $j = 1, \ldots, \ell$, such that $|p_{w_j-1,j} - p_{w_j,j}| \geq \frac{\sigma_j - 1/|\mathsf{M}|}{5q}$ holds with probability at least $1 - \varepsilon$ where $p_{i,j}$ is the probability that the predicate $\mathcal{R}^{\mathsf{B}}$ returns true on the response of the adversary when it receives a query of type (i, j).

Recall that given $\sigma_j > 10q\varepsilon_p + \frac{1}{|\mathsf{M}|}$, Lemma 3.20 implies that the key material $k_{w_j,j}$ belongs to the traitor coalition. Following lemma 3.18, the number of tracing queries for each symbol needs to be at least $\frac{75q^2 \cdot \ln(8\ell/\varepsilon)}{(\sigma_j - 1/|\mathsf{M}|)^2}$ to succeed with probability $1 - \varepsilon/\ell$. Finally, the codeword $\mathsf{p} = \langle w_1, \ldots, w_\ell \rangle$ is in the descendant set of the traitor coalition with probability at least $1 - \varepsilon$, and it holds that **Identify**$(tk, \mathsf{p}) \in \mathsf{C}$ with probability at least $1 - \varepsilon_f$.

To give an upper bound on tracing overhead we consider the following: since $\frac{1}{\ell} \sum_{j \in [\ell]} \sigma_j = \sigma$, we also have $\sigma_j \geq \ell\sigma - \ell + 1$. Hence we obtain the following upper bound:

$$\sum_{j=1}^{\ell} \frac{75(q+1)q^2 \cdot \ln(8\ell/\varepsilon)}{(\sigma_j - 1/|\mathsf{M}|)^2} = O(\frac{\ell q^3 \cdot \ln(\ell/\varepsilon)}{(\ell\sigma - \ell + 1 - 1/|\mathsf{M}|)^2})$$

This completes the proof of the theorem. ∎

Traceability of Kiayias-Yung Scheme

We next consider the Kiayias-Yung scheme $\mathtt{ME}_{KY[\mathtt{F}]}$ where $\mathtt{F} = ($**CodeGen**, **Identify**$)$ is a q-ary fingerprinting code that produces an (ℓ, n, q) code. The scheme is a binary multiuser encryption scheme, i.e., each receiver is capable of receiving a single message from the transmission of the input-vector $M = \langle m_0, m_1 \rangle$. Recall that the transmission, by using a symmetric encryption scheme $(\mathtt{E}, \mathtt{D})$, is of the following form:

$$\begin{bmatrix} \mathtt{E}_{k_1^1}(r_1) & \mathtt{E}_{k_1^2}(r_2) & \ldots & \mathtt{E}_{k_1^l}(m_1' - \sum_{i \neq l} r_i) & \ldots & \mathtt{E}_{k_1^\ell}(r_\ell) \\ \mathtt{E}_{k_2^1}(r_1) & \mathtt{E}_{k_2^2}(r_2) & \ldots & \mathtt{E}_{k_2^l}(m_2' - \sum_{i \neq l} r_i) & \ldots & \mathtt{E}_{k_2^\ell}(r_\ell) \\ \vdots & \vdots & \vdots & \vdots & \vdots & \vdots \\ \mathtt{E}_{k_q^1}(r_1) & \mathtt{E}_{k_q^2}(r_2) & \ldots & \mathtt{E}_{k_q^l}(m_q' - \sum_{i \neq l} r_i) & \ldots & \mathtt{E}_{k_q^\ell}(r_\ell) \end{bmatrix}$$

where $r_1, \ldots, r_\ell$ are drawn from the plaintext space, $m_1' = \ldots = m_s' = m_{1-b}$, $m_{s+1}' = \ldots = m_q' = m_b$, while (l, s) is sampled from the set $\{1, \ldots, \ell\} \times \{0\}$ randomly and $b \stackrel{R}{\leftarrow} \{0, 1\}$. During tracing the transmissions will be modified : in particular the tracer will variate $s \in \{0, 1, \ldots, q\}$. Note that this means that the ciphertexts will be potentially decrypted differently by different users (but still this does not violate correctness in a binary scheme).

For the objectives of tracing we will further put forth the following notion.

Definition 3.23. *For a $q \in \mathbb{N}$ and plaintext space M a q-ary plaintext distribution $\widetilde{\mathsf{M}}$ with* limited crossover *$\gamma \in (0, 1)$ over M^q satisfies that for any $\mathcal{A}$ and any $i' \in \{1, \ldots, q\}$, it holds that the probability $\mathcal{A}^{\widetilde{\mathsf{M}}}(\{m_i\}_{i \neq i'}) = m_{i'}$ is at most γ, where $\langle m_1, \ldots, m_q \rangle$ is sampled from $\widetilde{\mathsf{M}}$.*

We will assume that the plaintexts used follow a plaintext distribution with limited crossover. This is a reasonable assumption that for example is trivially satisfied by the distribution of cryptographic keys.

The tracer will variate the parameter $s \in \{0, 1, \ldots, q\}$ effectively causing a certain set of users to switch from decrypting plaintext m_0 to plaintext m_1 depending on the set of keys that a user has in the column l that is used for variating the plaintext. At this moment it should be noted that for any single user of the system the ciphertexts that are produced during tracing are computationally indistinguishable from ciphertexts transmitted during normal system operation. This suggests that tracing in the Kiayias-Yung scheme is alfresco.

After a sufficient number of queries, it will be feasible for the tracer to deduce a key from each column. This will enable the tracer to construct the pirate codeword that is consisting of the keys used by the adversary. Provided that F is (ε_f, t)-identifier, the **Identify** algorithm of the underlying fingerprinting code will output a traitor with a small error probability as long as the traitor coalition is bounded by t.

We next prove the traceability of the construction.

Theorem 3.24. *Consider the binary multiuser encryption scheme* $\mathtt{ME}_{KY[\mathtt{F}]}$ *that employs a symmetric encryption scheme that is* ε_p*-insecure in the sense of Definition 2.5 and an* (ℓ, n, q) *fingerprinting code* F *that is* (ε_f, t)*-identifier. Also consider a plaintext distribution over* M^2 *with limited crossover* γ.

For any $n \in \mathbb{N}$, $\epsilon > 0$, $\mathtt{ME}_{KY[\mathtt{F}]}$ *is an alfresco black-box traitor tracing scheme for t-coalitions with success probability* $1 - \varepsilon - \varepsilon_f$ *against resettable* σ*-pirates with* $\sigma > 10q\varepsilon_p + 2\gamma$. *It further holds that* $\mathsf{trover}[\mathtt{ME}_{BN[\mathtt{F}]}] = O(\frac{\ell q^3 \cdot \log(\ell/\varepsilon)}{(\sigma - 2\gamma)^2})$.

Proof. Consider an adversary $\mathcal{A}$ that is given access to the key material $\{sk_u\}_{u \in \mathsf{C}}$ for some subset $\mathsf{C} \subseteq [n]$ where $(tk, ek, sk_1, \ldots, sk_n)$ is distributed according to $\mathbf{KeyDist}_{\mathtt{F}}(1^n)$.

The tracing party $\mathcal{T}_{KY}$ interacts with $\mathcal{A}$ in the following fashion. $\mathcal{T}_{KY}$ will submit queries to the adversary that are regular transmissions where $l \in \{1, \ldots, \ell\}$ and $s \in \{0, 1, \ldots, q\}$. We consider each transmission q together with the response of the adversary a to be an experiment that is successful if it holds that the adversary's response is equal to the plaintext m_b (i.e., the plaintext that is selected to be the only one transmitted in the case the parameter $s = 0$). Each experiment type (l, s) will be repeated K times where K is a parameter to be determined later.

Now we define $p_{s,l}$ the probability that the experiment at column l and symbol location s is successful. In the sequence of experiments that the tracer performs we then denote by $\rho_{s,l}$ as the number of times in $\{0, \ldots, K\}$ that the experiment was successful.

Now observe that for any $l \in \{1, \ldots, \ell\}$ it holds that $p_{0,l} \geq \sigma - \gamma$ since the ciphertexts submitted by the tracer are identical to those in normal system transmission, the adversary has to decrypt correctly with probability σ. Note that the scheme is binary so the alternative plaintext can also be returned but due to the limited crossover we have that the probability drop in the experiment can be at most γ. On the other hand, observe that for all $l \in \{1, \ldots, \ell\}$ it holds that $p_{q,l} \leq \gamma$. This is because the ciphertexts transmitted in this case are entirely hiding the plaintext that is needed to return in order for the experiment to succeed. Based on the limited crossover probability we have that it can only happen with probability at most γ that the adversary recovers this other plaintext.

We continue now with the description of the tracer. For each l, the tracer finds the smallest $s \in [q]$ for which it holds that $|\rho_{s-1,j} - \rho_{s,j}| \geq K(\sigma - 2\gamma)/5q$ and sets $w_j = s$. Finally the tracer constructs a codeword $\mathsf{p} = \langle w_1, \ldots, w_\ell \rangle$. It then outputs **Identify**(tk, p) where $\mathsf{F} = $ (**CodeGen**, **Identify**).

Now using lemma 3.18 we have that the choice $K \geq \frac{75q^2 \cdot \ln(8\ell/\varepsilon)}{(\sigma-2\gamma)^2}$ suffices to locate a value $w_j \in \{1, \ldots, q\}$, for all $j = 1, \ldots, \ell$, such that $|p_{w_j-1,j} - p_{w_j,j}| \geq \frac{\sigma-2\gamma}{5q}$ holds with probability $1 - \varepsilon$. Via the reasoning of Lemma 3.20 it holds that the key material $k_{w_j,j}$ belongs to the traitor coalition for $j = 1, \ldots, \ell$ if the adversary succeeds in decrypting with probability $\sigma > 10q\varepsilon_p + 2\gamma$. Finally for the codeword $\mathsf{p} = \langle w_1, \ldots, w_\ell \rangle$ it holds that **Identify**$(tk, \mathsf{p}) \in \mathsf{C}$ with probability at least $1 - \varepsilon_f$.

This completes the proof of the theorem. ∎

Alfresco Tracing Against History-Recording Decoders

We may consider a variant of the Kiayias-Yung scheme that supports alfresco tracing against history recording decoders for the price of increasing the success probability σ that is required of the adversary. That lower bound on the success probability emerges in a similar way as in the traceability arguments of the Boneh-Naor scheme earlier in this chapter. Without detailed analysis we will describe the scheme as follows: we consider the q-ary version of the Kiayias-Yung scheme where on input vector $\langle m_1, \ldots, m_q \rangle$ the transmission is prepared so that $m'_i = m_i$ holds for $i = 1, \ldots, q$ in the l-th column (which is sampled randomly from the set $\{1, \ldots, \ell\}$). We assume the plaintexts following the distribution M^q with limited crossover γ. By choosing σ sufficiently high, each transmission will have to be decrypted correctly by the adversary with some probability that is a function of σ and ℓ so that the adversary outputs a plaintext value for the chosen column.

In order to achieve traceability in the history-recording setting, the tracer will refrain from interfering with the way regular transmissions are formed and it will wait to receive a sufficient number of responses from all columns (recall that the column used for variating the plaintext is randomly selected at each step). The number of queries needed to span all columns can be computed as an instance of coupon-collector problem, lemma 1.3.

In order to complete tracing the tracer needs to collect a sufficient number of responses from each column l. Thinking of columns as coupons, the failure probability would be the event that more than λ sample trials are needed to collect all ℓ coupons. Considering the coupon collector lemma with ℓ coupons and $\beta = 1 + \frac{\ln 1/\varepsilon'}{\ln \ell}$ we have that the probability of the event of failing to collect all coupons in at least $\beta\ell\ln\ell = \ell\ln\ell/\varepsilon'$ trials is at most

$$(\ell)^{1-\beta} = (\ell)^{-\frac{\ln 1/\varepsilon'}{\ln \ell}} = (\ell)^{-\log_\ell 1/\varepsilon'} = \varepsilon'$$

Hence a number $\lambda \geq \ell\log\ell/\varepsilon'$ of transmissions will be sufficient to receive a response from all ℓ columns with probability $1-\varepsilon'$. Let $\tilde{m}^1, \tilde{m}^2, \ldots \tilde{m}^\lambda$ be the responses of the adversary in all these transmissions where a certain $\tilde{m}^j$ might also be $\perp$ standing for a refusal to decrypt or decrypting incorrectly. Given a sufficiently high σ and limited crossover with γ we can derive that with high probability all the responses are consistent with the traitor coalition keys and thus we identify a unique traitor key for each column. Subsequently the fingerprinting code identification algorithm will provide a traitor identity. Hence, we argue that it is possible to identify a traitor with failure probability bounded by $\varepsilon_f + \varepsilon'$.

In the next chapter in Section 4.3 we discuss a trace and revoke scheme with a similar relation to the choice of γ and σ. We refer the reader there for more insights in formulating the precise number of transmissions that are required in terms of the bounds γ and σ.

3.5.3 Traceability of the Boneh-Franklin Scheme

We will first revisit the key space of the Boneh-Franklin scheme to elaborate on the set of key material that is useful for decryption of a transmission.

Recall that the scheme is based on group generation algorithm **Gen** that on input 1^k produces $\mathcal{G}, q, g$ where $g \in \mathcal{G}$ is an element of order q where q is a k-bit prime. The public-key of the scheme as sampled by **KeyDist** is an object of the form $\mathcal{G}^{\ell+1} \times \mathbb{Z}_q^{n\times\ell}$. The space of secret-keys contains objects of the form $\mathbb{Z}_q^{\ell+1}$. Finally, K_{ek} contains elements of $\mathbb{Z}_q^\ell$ that satisfy the following: if the tracing-key is $tk = \langle a_0, a_1, \ldots, a_\ell\rangle$ and the encryption key is $ek = \langle H, \Gamma\rangle$ with $H = \langle g^{a_0}, \ldots, g^{a_\ell}\rangle$, it holds that $\boldsymbol{\delta} \in \mathsf{K}_{sk}$ if and only if $a_0 = \boldsymbol{\delta} \cdot \langle a_1, \ldots, a_\ell\rangle$ (where "$\cdot$" here stands for the inner product over $\mathbb{Z}_q^\ell$ vectors).

We next consider what are the capabilities of an adversary to produce new key material in K_{ek} while in possession of some keys in K_{ek}. In particular we show that any probabilistic a lgorithm that is polynomial-time bounded and is given a number of decryption keys cannot produce a new decryption-key that is not a linear combination of the given keys. This restricts the search space of possible keys that a tracer needs to take into account when trying to win the tracing game.

Lemma 3.25. *Let $n \in \mathbb{N}$, and $\langle tk, ek, sk_1, \ldots sk_n\rangle$ be distributed according to $\mathbf{KeyDist}_{BF_\ell^k}(1^n)$ where $tk = \langle a_0, a_1, \ldots, a_\ell\rangle$ and $ek = \langle H, \Gamma\rangle$ with $H = (g^{a_0}, \ldots, g^{a_\ell})$ where $g \in \mathcal{G}$ and $(\mathcal{G}, q, g) \leftarrow \mathbf{Gen}(1^k)$. Here Γ is an (ℓ, n, q)-code over an alphabet $\mathbb{Z}_q$ for some k-bit prime number q. The secret key sk_u is computed as a vector $\boldsymbol{\delta}^u = b_u \cdot \gamma^u$ with $b_u = a_0(\sum_{i=1}^{\ell} a_i\gamma_i^u)^{-1}$ for $u = 1, \ldots, n$.*

Assume there exists $\mathcal{A}$, a probabilistic polynomial time algorithm that takes as input the public-key and the secret-keys $sk_{i_1}, \ldots, sk_{i_t}$ with $t \leq \ell - 1$ and returns a vector $\boldsymbol{\delta} \in \mathbb{Z}_q^\ell$ so that (i) $\boldsymbol{\delta}$ is a representation of h_0 base $h_1, \ldots, h_\ell$, and (ii) $\boldsymbol{\delta}$ is not a linear combination of $sk_{i_1} = b_{i_1}\gamma^{i_1}, \ldots, sk_{i_t} = b_{i_t}\gamma^{i_t}$. Then the discrete logarithm problem over $\langle g \rangle$ is solvable in polynomial-time.

Proof. (of Lemma 3.25) Let $g, h \in \langle g \rangle$ be an instance of the discrete-logarithm problem in the group $\mathcal{G}$. We construct a modified public-key as follows: suppose $a_0, \ldots, a_\ell$ are selected as specified by $\mathbf{KeyDist}_{BF_\ell^k}(1^n)$; then we set the modified public-key to be the vector $\langle h_0, h_1, \ldots, h_\ell \rangle$ where $h_0 = g^{a_0}$ and $h_1 = g^{a_1}h^{b_1}, \ldots, h_\ell = g^{a_\ell}h^{b_\ell}$ where $\mathbf{b} = \langle b_1, \ldots, b_v \rangle$ is selected so that (i) $\boldsymbol{\delta}^{i_v} \cdot \mathbf{b} = 0$ for all $v = 1, \ldots, t$, and (ii) $\mathbf{b} \neq \mathbf{0}$. Note that these conditions suggest that $\mathbf{b}$ is a non-trivial solution to a homogenous system of t linear equations. Such a $\mathbf{b}$ can be found by computing the kernel of the matrix of the system and picking an arbitrary non-zero element in it; we note that the condition of the lemma that $t \leq \ell - 1$ is critical for finding such a non-zero $\mathbf{b}$ vector.

Next, we simulate $\mathcal{A}$ on $H, \Gamma, sk_{i_1}, \ldots, sk_{i_t}$ to obtain the vector $\boldsymbol{\delta}$. Since $\boldsymbol{\delta}$ is not a linear combination of $\boldsymbol{\delta}^{\mathbf{i_1}}, \ldots, \boldsymbol{\delta}^{\mathbf{i_t}}$ it follows that $\boldsymbol{\delta} \cdot \mathbf{b} \neq 0$ with probability at least $1 - 1/q$. This happens because conditioning on the public-key the vector $\mathbf{b}$ has at least one remaining degree of freedom from the point of view of the adversarial procedure $\mathcal{A}$. From this it follows that $\log_g h = (\boldsymbol{\delta} \cdot \mathbf{b})^{-1}(a_0 - \boldsymbol{\delta} \cdot \mathbf{a})$ where $\mathbf{a} = \langle a_1, \ldots, a_\ell \rangle$. ∎

We next recall the construction of the user keys in the Boneh-Franklin scheme and motivate the choice of the matrix $\mathbf{M}$.

Lemma 3.26. *Consider the $(n-\ell) \times n$ matrix $\mathbf{M}$ that is constructed by defining the j-th column as a vector $\langle 1, 2^{j-1}, \ldots, n^{j-1} \rangle$. For such matrix we have the following:*

1. *Any vector in the span of the rows of $\mathbf{M}$ (also called the* rowspan*) corresponds to a polynomial in $\mathbb{Z}_q[x]$ of degree at most $n - \ell - 1$ evaluated at the points $1, \ldots, \ell$.*
2. *The rowspan of $\mathbf{M}$ is a linear code that is efficiently decodable for up to $\frac{\ell}{2}$ errors. Specifically given any vector $\mathbb{Z}_q^n$ that differs in at most $\ell/2$ positions from a vector in the rowspan it is possible to recover such vector by a polynomial-time algorithm.*

Proof. Regarding the first item of the lemma, let $\mathsf{w} = \langle \mathsf{w}_1, \ldots, \mathsf{w}_n \rangle$ be a vector in the span of the rows of the matrix $\mathbf{M}$, i.e. there exists a set of coefficients $\{\mu_0, \mu_1, \ldots, \mu_{n-\ell-1}\}$ such that $\mathsf{w}_v = \sum_{i=0}^{n-\ell-1} \mu_i v^i$. Observe that the value w_v corresponds to the evaluation of v on the polynomial $\mathsf{f}(x) = \mu_0 + \mu_1 x + \mu_2 x^2 + \ldots + \mu_{n-\ell-1}x^{n-\ell_1}$.

Regarding the second item, let $\nu \in \mathbb{Z}_q^n$ be a vector that differs from a vector w in the rowspan of the matrix $\mathbf{M}$ in up to $\frac{\ell}{2}$ locations. Provided that

f is the polynomial corresponding to the vector w, we will now provide an efficient algorithm that on input ν it computes the polynomial f (and hence the vector w).

Let g be a polynomial of degree at most $\ell/2$ such that $\mathsf{g}(i) = 0$ for all $i = 1, \ldots, n$ for which $\mathsf{f}(i) \neq \nu_i$ (where ν_i is the i-th component of ν). Then we know that for all $i = 1, \ldots, n$ we have $\mathsf{f}(i) \cdot \mathsf{g}(i) = \mathsf{g}(i) \cdot \nu_i$ (in $\mathbb{Z}_q$). The polynomial fg has degree at most $n - \ell/2 - 1$. Hence, we get n equations (for each $i = 1, \ldots, n$) in n variables (the variables are the coefficients of the polynomials fg and g; where the leading coefficient of g is 1.) Let h and g be a solution where g is a non-zero polynomial: h is a polynomial of degree at most $n - \ell/2 - 1$ and g is of degree at most $\ell/2$. We know that whenever $\mathsf{w}_i = \nu_i$ (i.e. at $n - \ell/2$ points i) we have $\mathsf{h}(i) = \mathsf{g}(i)\nu_i = \mathsf{g}(i)\mathsf{f}(i)$. It follows that $\mathsf{f} = \mathsf{h}/\mathsf{g}$. ■

We are now ready to prove that $\mathtt{ME}_{BF_\ell^k}$ is a non-black box traitor tracing scheme, i.e., there exists a tracer that makes the corresponding tracing game for $\ell/2$-coalitions winnable against any probabilistic polynomial time adversary $\mathcal{A}$.

Theorem 3.27. *The Boneh-Franklin multiuser encryption scheme* $\mathtt{ME}_{BF_\ell^k}$ *is a non-black box traitor tracing scheme for* $\frac{\ell}{2}$*-coalitions with success probability* α *against* σ*-pirate for any choice of* σ, α *that satisfies* $\sigma \geq \alpha$.

Proof. We need to present a tracing party $\mathcal{T}$ that works for any adversary $\mathcal{A}$ and allows the recovery of any traitor set S that is fed to $\mathcal{A}$. Let $u_1, \ldots, u_t \in \{1, \ldots, N\}$ be a set of rows S of $\mathbf{B}$ (that correspond to the keys of the traitors). Based on Lemma 3.25 and the fact that $\mathcal{A}$ is polynomial-time we know that the output of $\mathcal{A}$ on the keys of the traitors must be of the form $\boldsymbol{\eta} = \sum_{i=1}^{t} \mu_i \boldsymbol{\delta}^{u_i}$, where $\mu_1, \ldots, \mu_t \in \mathbb{Z}_q$, assuming that $t \leq \ell - 1$.

By the definition of $\boldsymbol{\eta}$ it holds that there exists a vector $\boldsymbol{\nu} = \langle \nu_1, \ldots, \nu_n \rangle$ with $\nu_{u_v} = \mu_v$ for all $v = 1, \ldots, t$ and $\nu_i = 0$ for $i \notin \{u_1, \ldots, u_t\}$, with the property $\langle \nu_1, \ldots, \nu_n \rangle \cdot \mathbf{B} = \boldsymbol{\eta}$.

The tracing algorithm proceeds as follows: first it computes an arbitrary vector $\boldsymbol{\xi} \in \mathbb{Z}_q^v$ that satisfies the system of equations $\boldsymbol{\xi} \cdot \mathbf{B} = \boldsymbol{\eta}$. Note that such $\boldsymbol{\xi}$ can be found easily since $\boldsymbol{\xi} \cdot \mathbf{B} = \boldsymbol{\eta}$ is a system of ℓ equations with n unknowns, $n > \ell$, and $\mathbf{B}$ contains a minor of size ℓ (due to the fact that *the matrix* $\mathbf{B}$ *is of full rank*). It is easy to verify that the vector $\mathbf{w} =_{\mathsf{df}} \boldsymbol{\xi} - \boldsymbol{\nu}$ belongs to the linear code $\mathbf{M}$: indeed, $\mathbf{w} \cdot \mathbf{B} = \boldsymbol{\xi} \cdot \mathbf{B} - \boldsymbol{\nu} \cdot \mathbf{B} = \boldsymbol{\eta} - \boldsymbol{\eta} = \mathbf{0}$. As a result the vector $\boldsymbol{\xi}$ can be expressed as $\boldsymbol{\xi} = \mathbf{w} + \boldsymbol{\nu}$.

Provided that $t \leq \frac{\ell}{2}$ it holds that the Hamming weight of $\boldsymbol{\nu}$ is less or equal to $\ell/2$ and as a result $\boldsymbol{\xi}$ is a n-vector that differs in at most $\frac{\ell}{2}$ positions from the vector $\mathbf{w}$ that belongs in $\mathbf{M}$. Due to the lemma 3.26 the linear code $\mathbf{M}$ is efficiently decodable i.e., it holds that $\mathbf{w}$ can be recovered efficiently if we feed $\boldsymbol{\xi}$ to the decoding procedure for $\mathbf{M}$. The recovery of $\mathbf{w}$, immediately will result in the recovery of $\boldsymbol{\nu} = \boldsymbol{\xi} - \mathbf{w}$. The set S can be thus recovered efficiently by observing the non-zero entries of $\boldsymbol{\nu}$.

The above can be executed whenever $\mathcal{A}$ produces a key $\boldsymbol{\delta}$; it follows immediately that if $\mathcal{A}$ produces such key with probability σ then we can recover successfully the corresponding identities of the traitors. ∎

3.6 Bibliographic Notes

Traitor tracing, as a piracy detection mechanism, was proposed by Chor, Fiat and Naor [28] as a possible solution to the threats that broadcast encryption [42] faced in terms of key leakage. In this chapter we provided a formalization of the notion of tracing as a two player game between the tracer and the adversary. The goal of the tracer is to perform identification of one of the traitor users while the goal of the adversary is to prevent this from happening while still maintaining a level of required functionality. We also put emphasis in the complexity of this process that is expressed as a function of the required level of functionality that is required by the adversary as well as other parameters. Of independent interest is the fact that this formalization of tracing is the flip side of a class of privacy related interactions considered in [38]; there the adversary is in the tracer side and wishes to violate the privacy of the users.

Given that the intended application of traitor tracing schemes is to handle encryption of large messages, we envisioned the security of the constructions in this chapter as key encapsulation mechanisms similar to the broadcast encryption chapter, i.e. cryptographically strong keys are transmitted using the multiuser encryption scheme and the actual message is encrypted by the transmitted key. Such hybrid type of encryption provides an asymptotically constant rate for long messages (given that the transmission overhead of the underlying scheme is negligible compared to the length of the message), where rate is measured as the ratio of ciphertext length to plaintext length. Achieving constant transmission rate overall in the basic encryption setting was studied by Kiayias and Yung [70] and others [27, 39].

Putting aside the traceability, multiuser encryption schemes fall into two categories: first we consider the *combinatorial* constructions, for which the key assignment is made through some combinatorial distribution from a pool of cryptographic keys. This follows the seminal work of Chor Fiat Naor [28] and subsequent works [29, 110, 111, 100, 113, 114, 89, 9, 13] including the Boneh-Naor [21] and Kiayias-Yung [67] schemes should all be considered in this class of multiuser encryption.

The second category of multiuser encryption schemes, are *structured* similar to broadcast encryption, and assumes that the key space is endowed with some structure so that either (i) it enables the preparation of tracing ciphertexts that makes the corresponding tracing game winnable as e.g., in [22] or (ii) any possible pirate key created from traitor keys carries enough information to trace back to one of its traitor keys as in [16, 78].

The Kurosawa-Desmedt scheme[78] is based on a public key technique, in particular on a variant of ElGamal encryption. Stinson and Wei in [114] and Boneh and Franklin in [16] pointed out that the arguments behind the traceability algorithm of [78] were problematic (in particular it was possible for traitors to foil the the tracing algorithm). Boneh and Franklin presented a different variant of ElGamal encryption and they provided the first provably robust traitor tracing procedure that could recover all traitors efficiently. This tracing procedure was suitable for the non black-box setting where it is assumed that the tracer has access to the internals of the pirate decoder. For the black-box setting (where the tracing is done based solely on input-output interaction with the pirate device), they also introduced a technique called "black-box confirmation" that can only deal with a logarithmic number of traitors. Subsequently in [68] it was shown that such public key systems cannot efficiently support a black-box traitor tracing procedure for a super-logarithmic number of traitors, thus showing that the black-box traitor tracing procedure of confirmation presented in [16] was essentially tight for their scheme for the black-box setting and could not be further improved. Later Kurosawa and Yoshida [79] worked on black-box traitor tracing of the scheme of [78]; they showed that the scheme also accepts black-box confirmation, and thus any logarithmic number of traitors can be recovered as well in this scheme (for black-box tracing). Extending these results, in [118] it was shown that linear codes based schemes can support also revocation and in [119] a relation between cover free families and ElGamal public-key traitor tracing was explored.

An extended type of ElGamal encryption is introduced by Kiayias and Yung in [71] that classifies the previous work in public key traitor tracing as those of [78] and [16]. In this type of encryption which we term ExEG for "extended ElGamal" the key of each user is a representation of an exponent. Given that the key structure of the Kurosawa-Desmedt key space has the form of a Generalized Reed-Solomon code that is efficiently decodable, it is shown in [71] that the traceability of [78] can be extended to superlogarithmic coalitions by calibrating the ciphertext size appropriately in the non black-box setting (beyond what is possible in the black-box case). The notion of a traitor tracing scheme with unbounded enrollment is also introduced in [71] to suggest that group of users can grow indefinitely and that the system administrator need not know at the start of the system's operation a (polynomial) upper bound on the number of users as it is the case with the schemes in this chapter.

The decodability of Boneh-Franklin scheme we have provided in the proof of Lemma 3.26 is based on the Berlekamp-Welch algorithm (patented in [11]). An improvement on the efficiency of decoding is given in [61] by using the Berlekamp-Massey algorithm instead. Using the list-decoding techniques of Guruswami and Sudan [51] the size of the traitor coalition for which the schemes based on extended ElGamal type encryption may resist can be increased but at a high cost.

It should be noted that these schemes share a bound on the number of the size of the traitor coalition. A notable construction is due to Boneh, Shai and Waters [22] as the scheme is fully-collusion resistant against any number of traitors at the expense of increasing the transmission overhead, i.e. proportional to the square root of the number of receivers.

We have identified three types of tracing methods in this chapter: (i) non-black box traitor tracing, (ii) black-box traitor tracing and (iii) tracing pirate rebroadcasts which requires tracing alfresco in the case of history-recording (stateful tracing alfresco also satisfies this). The Boneh-Franklin [16] (see section 3.2) and Kurosawa-Desmedt [78] and other variants we have cited above are examples of schemes that are tracable in the non-black box setting.

Regarding the black-box traitor tracing, the power of an adversary plays an important role in the design of the scheme. We have discussed a categorization over the pirate decoders given by Kiayias and Yung [67] in Section 3.4.2. According to this categorization we have proved the traceability of the linear length multiuser encryption scheme, Chor-Fiat-Naor[28] and Boneh-Naor [21] schemes for resettable and available decoders only. An abrupt decoder will be able to deploy a self-defensive mechanism while querying special ciphertexts over any column. This foils the tracing process as stops the reconstruction of the pirate codeword. A solution can be designed similar to the case in pirate rebroadcasting with variating the message through watermarking and tracing alfresco as if the decoders are history-recording.

In general, tracing abrupt decoders, in the absence of watermarking, is not an easy task and requires some care in designing schemes. The first non-trivial proposal for tracing unambiguously abrupt decoders was presented by Matsushita and Imai [84]. Their scheme aimed at producing a ciphertext of length $\sqrt{n}$ and identify one traitor explicitly (i.e., the "suspect list" contained merely a single member, the guilty receiver). It is based on an extension of ElGamal encryption that divides the receivers into groups. Each group is assigned a polynomial and each receiver obtains as secret-key the evaluation of the group's polynomial on a certain value. The key-point of the scheme is that the polynomials can share a lot of coefficients without compromising security and thus it is possible to compact the ciphertexts in the scheme so that the total communication complexity becomes sublinear. However, this scheme was broken by [80] and by [63] (a partial repair of the scheme is given in [63] that puts a limitation on the way the corruption of traitor occurs).

An important aspect of traitor tracing schemes is the number of rounds (tracing overhead as we defined in this work) of interaction that are required between the tracing authority (or simply the tracer) and a rogue device in order for the tracer to establish the desired identities. The majority of schemes share the same tracing strategy that can be summarized in the following fashion : divide the users in N subsets of a certain size and perform a "walking procedure" of N steps that utilizes partially corrupted ciphertexts and identifies which one of the N subsets is overlapping with the corrupted users. Then repeat the procedure with a different set of subsets. In the end combine all the results to infer a corrupted user identity. In its most basic form, the subsets can be singletons, i.e., the users themselves and it is only needed to perform a single such walking procedure (cf. [70]).

Referring to this ubiquitous tracing strategy as "linear tracing"; it was utilized in the majority of the works cited above and in this work as well. Two other tracing strategies based on a similar walking argument were put forth in [88] called "binary search tracing" and "noisy binary search tracing" (the latter being an improvement inspired by [40]). The authors of this work presented in [66] a new tracing strategy that has an improved tracing overhead. It relies on an application of fingerprinting codes superimposed on the tracing process.

The Kiayias-Yung scheme [67] gives a way to play the tracing game alfresco and win. Hence it can be used as a black-box tracing scheme against resettable or history-recording pirate decoders.(cf. the analysis in Theorem 3.24 for resettable case). In a similar vein can also be used in the setting of pirate rebroadcasting. Pirate rebroadcasting as an attack concept was introduced by Fiat and Tassa [43] that also introduced combinatorial constructions for solving the problem assuming broadcast encryption as an underlying building block.

In general a solution for pirate rebroadcasting would require the employment of watermarking embeddings (see [30]). The availability of the embeddings would enable the content to become varied over the user population. Here we abstracted away this need by introducing plaintext distributions with limited crossover. In practice one way to achieve such limited crossover is through watermarking. In this case the crossover probability models the capability of the adversary to manipulate the watermark and fool the reading algorithm to return an incorrect value (cf. Definition 1.6).

There are essentially two techniques known in the literature for obtaining non-trivial solutions for dealing with pirate rebroadcasting: one is dynamic traitor tracing [43] and the other is sequential traitor tracing [58, 60, 99, 102]. The idea in both cases is similar: the center will induce a marking of content and by observing the feedback from the pirate rebroadcast we will identify the traitors. The two methods differ in the following way: in the former, after each transmission the center obtains the feedback and tries to refine the suspect list by reassigning the marks adaptively. The number of traitors is not known beforehand and the system adjusts itself after each feedback. In the latter setting, the assignment of marks to the variations is predetermined, and hence the transmission mechanism is not adaptive to the feedback. Depending on the parameters used, it may take a number of transmissions until the system converges and identifies one traitor. A hybrid approach due to the authors of this text is given in [64] that is capable of supporting revocation while tracing unlimited number of traitors.

Fingerprinting codes play a crucial role in all of the above schemes [58, 60, 64, 99, 102] that were proposed for solving the pirate rebroadcasting problem. As a short diversion within this bibliographic notes we would like to describe the multiuser encryption scheme of [99] (cf. the extended version of this work in [102]) as an example of another scheme based on fingerprinting codes. It is a q-ary multiuser encryption scheme that is stateful; the Boneh-Naor scheme that came afterwards [21] is very similar in principle to this scheme. The security and the correctness of this scheme as well as its traceability can be analyzed as a combination to the analysis given in Theorem 3.22 and 3.24 for the Boneh-Naor and Kiayias-Yung schemes respectively and is a worthy exercise for the reader. The transmission and the decryption are defined as follows. Note that the encryption is stateful over a set $\mathsf{States} = [\ell]$.

- **Transmit**$_{SQ[\mathtt{F}]}$: Given a vector of input $M = \langle m_1, \ldots, m_q \rangle$ and the encryption key $ek = \{k_{i,j}\}_{(i,j)\in[q]\times[\ell]}$, it first retrieves the state $\sigma \in \{1, \ldots, \ell\}$ from the set States and then transmits the encryption of the message M with ek by using a symmetric encryption scheme $(\mathtt{E}, \mathtt{D})$ as follows:

$$\langle \sigma, \mathtt{E}_{k_{1,\sigma}}(m_1), \mathtt{E}_{k_{2,\sigma}}(m_2), \ldots, \mathtt{E}_{k_{q,\sigma}}(m_q) \rangle$$

  The state σ is finally updated to $(\sigma \bmod \ell) + 1$.
- **Receive**$_{SQ[\mathtt{F}]}$: Given the key-material $sk_u = \langle k_{\mathsf{w}_1^u,1}, k_{\mathsf{w}_2^u,2}, \ldots, k_{\mathsf{w}_\ell^u,\ell} \rangle$ for any $u \in [n]$ and a transmission of the form:

$$\langle i, c_1, c_2, \ldots, c_q \rangle$$

  it returns $\mathtt{D}_{k_{\mathsf{w}_i^u,i}}(c_{\mathsf{w}_i^u})$.

A final note is due regarding the important issue of designing piracy detection mechanism so that the incrimination mechanism becomes legally binding. In all the traitor tracing mechanisms we have presented in this chapter the distributor is capable of framing innocent receivers by using the (known to it) receiver's copy of the content/key information. In this light, it is also possible for a malicious user to deny being implicated to a certain key-leakage or pirate rebroadcasting incident. Non-repudiation is the concept that a receiver cannot repudiate its implication or refute the validity of the evidence presented by the distributor.

This problem was recognized as a fundamental for any traitor tracing system and led to the introduction of asymmetric fingerprinting in [95]; this was further discussed in [12, 94, 96]. The initial solutions for asymmetric traitor tracing were based on generic secure function evaluation and thus they were not very practical. Two very efficient schemes were presented in the context of public-key traitor tracing schemes by Watanabe et.al [123] and Komaki et.al [75]. These two schemes were subsequently broken by Kiayias and Yung in [69]. In this latter work, the first provable asymmetric public-key traitor tracing scheme was presented.

4

Trace and Revoke Schemes

Broadcast encryption of Chapter 2 deals with the problem of revocation for stateless receivers; the general context is a "sender to many receivers" transmission system that offers the ability for the sender to exclude a subset of the receivers from a certain transmission on demand. The statelessness of the receivers refers to the fact that receivers need not maintain state from one transmission to the next (and this enables them to go arbitrarily off-line without loosing their reception capability in the long run).

A shortcoming of broadcast encryption schemes is the possibility that some receivers can compromise the decryption boxes given to them and subsequently use the extracted key data to construct and distribute a decryption device that is also capable receiving the content. The sender may want to restrict this type of behavior, since this enables receivers to introduce additional unauthorized receivers in the system. This problem was discussed independently in Chapter 3 with the notion of a traitor tracing scheme.

Clearly it would be beneficial if the two features of tracing and revocation would be combined in a single scheme, a "trace and revoke" scheme. In such a scheme, every receiver possesses a decryption key that is capable of inverting the content encryption mechanism while at the same time the following defining characteristics are offered: (i) *revocation*: the sender can encrypt content under a "broadcast pattern" in such a way so that the decryption capability of any subset of the receiver population can be disabled, (ii) *tracing*: given a rogue decryption device (also called a pirate decoder) that was produced using the keys of a number of receivers (also called traitors in such case) it is possible to render such device useless from all future transmissions. This may be done by identifying the traitors and revoking them or in some other fashion (that may or may not involve the direct identification of a traitor).

In this chapter we study formally trace and revoke schemes and discuss how they can be applied to various adversarial settings.

A. Kiayias and S. Pehlivanoglu, *Encryption for Digital Content*, Advances in Information Security 52, DOI 10.1007/978-1-4419-0044-9_4,

4.1 Revocation Game: Definitions

A trace and revoke scheme is based on a broadcast encryption scheme $\mathsf{BE} = \langle \mathbf{KeyGen}, \mathbf{Encrypt}, \mathbf{Decrypt} \rangle$ that supports revocation over a set of receivers denoted by $[n] = \{1, \ldots, n\}$. Referring the reader to Section 2.1 for the basic definition of broadcast encryption, here we will consider the notion of s-ary broadcast encryptions in general for which the **Encrypt** algorithm prepares a ciphertext c on input a vector of messages $M = \langle m_1, \ldots, m_s \rangle \in \mathsf{M}^s$. The correctness given in Definition 2.1 can be enhanced to capture the case of input-vector as in the Definition 3.1 of correctness for multiuser encryption schemes. The security requirements can be discussed in a similar fashion with the only difference in the security game the involvement of the input-vector instead of a single message-input.

The objectives of tracing in a trace and revoke scheme are different than in the case of traitor tracing. In the context of such a scheme our objective is to disable the adversary in decrypting the transmission i.e., achieve the revocation of the decryption algorithm that is represented by the adversary. This may or may not necessarily require the identification of one of the traitors. In order to capture this we will introduce a new type of game, called the revocation game. As in the case of a tracing game it is an interaction between two parties: the adversary and the tracer. The tracer has at its disposal the encryption and the tracing key while the adversary has a set of corrupted user keys. The ultimate objective of the tracer is to disable the decryption algorithm that is represented by the adversary.

We recall the Definition 3.12 of a tracing game. In the revocation game setting, we will specialize the set of random variables $\mathcal{Q}$ as well as the way the predicate $\mathcal{R}$ responds on queries. Specifically, the game will be parameterized by a revocation instruction ψ, and adhere to the following:

- The random variable $\mathcal{Q}_\psi^{\mathbf{Encrypt}}$ represents all ways to encrypt the plaintexts with a pattern ψ from the language $\mathcal{L}$ of the broadcast encryption scheme. This means that $\mathcal{Q}_\psi^{\mathbf{Encrypt}}$ contains the random variables $\mathbf{Encrypt}(ek, M, \psi)$ for any $M = \langle m_1, \ldots, m_s \rangle \in \mathsf{M}^s$.
- $\mathcal{R}^{\mathbf{Encrypt}}$ is a predicate that on input $ek, sk_1, \ldots, sk_n, q, a$, where q is distributed according to $\mathcal{Q}_\psi^{\mathbf{Encrypt}}$, it returns 1 if and only if $a \in M$ where $q = \mathbf{Encrypt}(ek, M, \psi)$.

Based on the above, the revocation game is a triple $\langle \mathbf{KeyGen}, \mathcal{Q}_\psi^{\mathbf{Encrypt}}, \mathcal{R}^{\mathbf{Encrypt}} \rangle$ for t-coalitions against σ-pirates with rules of engagement that are as in the case of a tracing game, Definition 3.12 and 3.13. We also define the pair $\langle \mathcal{A}, \mathcal{T} \rangle$ to be admissible for a revocation game in the same way that admissibility is defined for tracing games.

Recall that an adversary in a broadcast encryption scheme is a decryption algorithm represented by the adversary that has access to a set of corrupted user keys $\{sk_u\}_{u \in \mathsf{T}}$. This adversary, in principle, is capable (but not obliged) to decrypt ciphertexts that are encrypted with revocation instructions encoded from the set:

$$\mathcal{L}_{\mathsf{T}} = \{\psi \in \mathcal{L} \mid \psi \textit{ encodes } \mathsf{R} \textit{ s.t. } \mathsf{T} \not\subseteq \mathsf{R}\}$$

Revocation of the rogue decoders that follow the code of that adversary amounts to finding an encoding from the language $\mathcal{L}$ of the broadcast encryption scheme for which all legitimate receivers can decode correctly, nevertheless if the decoder is invoked on that ciphertext it is incapable of decrypting it. Such an encoding can be determined easily if we are able to recover the whole traitor coalition and include it in the set of revoked receivers. However, the rogue decoder might be constructed in such a way that it does not reveal all information about the traitor identities, i.e. the decoder might work only for particular choices from the sublanguage $\mathcal{L}_{\mathsf{T}}$. Therefore, it follows that without making strong assumptions regarding the construction specifics of the rogue decoder or restricting ourselves to specific broadcast schemes, one cannot rely on identifying all traitors as the means to successful revocation.

This puts forth the basic question : if finding the identities of the traitors is not the primary target of the tracer in the revocation game what else can it be? We will formalize the goal of a tracer, that has input a revocation instruction, as the discovery of an *improved* revocation instruction that reveals more information on the traitor coalition compared to the given instruction. This means that the tracer may actually walk over all possible revocation instructions until a suitable one is discovered by playing a sequence of revocation games successively.

This successive improvement approach calls for an ordering between the encodings in $\mathcal{L}$ that is based on the traitor coalition. For now it suffices to say that we have a partial order $\preceq$ over the Cartesian product $\Psi = 2^{[n]} \times \mathcal{L}$. Given such partial order $\preceq$ the goal of the tracer would be to improve with respect to the ordering. We are now ready to formalize the notion of winning a revocation game.

Definition 4.1. *For a broadcast encryption scheme* $\mathsf{BE} = \langle \mathbf{KeyGen}, \mathbf{Encrypt}, \mathbf{Decrypt} \rangle$*, for* $n \in \mathbb{N}$ *and* $\psi \in \mathcal{L}$ *we say that the revocation game* $\mathsf{RG}_{\psi}^{\mathsf{BE}} = \langle \mathbf{KeyGen}, \mathcal{Q}_{\psi}^{\mathbf{Encrypt}}, \mathcal{R}^{\mathbf{Encrypt}} \rangle$ *is winnable by a tracer* $\mathcal{T}$ *for* t*-coalitions with respect to* $(\Psi, \preceq)$ *with probability* α *for* σ*-adversaries if for all* $\mathcal{A}$ *that make the pair* $\langle \mathcal{A}, \mathcal{T} \rangle$ σ*-admissible the following holds. For any* $\mathsf{C} \subseteq [n]$*,* $|\mathsf{C}| \leq t$ *and* $(ek, sk_1, \ldots, sk_n)$ *distributed according to* $\mathbf{KeyGen}(1^n)$*,*

- *The output of the game* $\psi' \neq \psi$*, that is distributed according to* $\langle \mathcal{A}, \mathcal{T} \rangle(ek, sk_1, \ldots, sk_n, \mathsf{C})$*, satisfies* $(\mathsf{C}, \psi) \preceq (\mathsf{C}, \psi')$ *with probability at least* α*.*
- *Suppose* $c = \mathbf{Encrypt}(ek, m, \psi')$ *for some* $m \in \mathsf{M}$*. For all* $u \in [n] \setminus (\mathsf{R} \cup \mathsf{C})$ *it holds that* $\mathbf{Decrypt}(sk_u, c) = m$ *where* $\mathsf{R} \subseteq [n]$ *is the revocation subset that is encoded by* ψ*.*

Provided that $\mathsf{RG}_{\psi}^{\mathsf{BE}}$ *is winnable by a tracer* $\mathcal{T}$*, we define the revocation overhead* $\mathsf{rvover}[\mathsf{RG}_{\psi}^{\mathsf{BE}}, \mathcal{T}]$ *of the revocation game* $\mathsf{RG}_{\psi}^{\mathsf{BE}}$ *as the supremum of all*

$r_{\langle \mathcal{A},\mathcal{T}\rangle}$ where $r_{\langle \mathcal{A},\mathcal{T}\rangle}$ is the maximum number of rounds needed to win the game; note that $\mathsf{rvover}[\mathsf{RG}^{\mathsf{BE}}_{\psi}, \mathcal{T}]$ *is a function of t, σ and possibly of other parameters as well.*

As in the case of traitor tracing we will consider a number of variations for the revocation game:

1. *Stateful revocation.* Similarly to the case of stateful tracing in stateful revocation the tracer has to choose its queries in a way that is dependent with the history of previous queries from a set $\mathcal{Q}^{\mathbf{Encrypt}}_{\psi,h}$. Similarly, the adversary also has to oblige and satisfy the $\mathcal{R}^{\mathbf{Encrypt}}$ predicate that now also takes the history of the queries into account while producing a result. As in the case of tracing, stateful revocation is a mechanism to place a further restriction on the tracer's side as it drops any compliance requirements on the part of the adversary when the tracer becomes inconsistent with the query history.
2. *Alfresco revocation.* As in the case of tracing alfresco, the tracer needs to form every query he makes statistically indistinguishable from members of $\mathcal{Q}^{\mathbf{Encrypt}}_{\psi}$ (or from $\mathcal{Q}^{\mathbf{Encrypt}}_{\psi,h}$ in case of stateful revocation). More specifically, when the tracer has submitted a history of $h = \langle q_1, \ldots, q_{i-1}\rangle$ queries, in the i-th round it must choose a query that is statistically indistinguishable from a member of $\mathcal{Q}^{\mathbf{Encrypt}}_{\psi}$ (from a member of $\mathcal{Q}^{\mathbf{Encrypt}}_{h,\psi}$ in case of stateful revocation).
3. *Revocation with resetting.* The adversary $\mathcal{A}$ is not allowed to maintain state from one round to the next, i.e., in each round the tracer can "reset" the adversary. As in the case of tracing the decoder can be in software and thus it can be tested independently across rounds till the tracer produces the revocation instruction that is better with respect to the partial order. When the adversary maintains state across rounds we can also say that we are performing revocation against history-recording decoders.

The following observations are in place for the above definition. Conceptually, the revocation game becomes an extension of the revocation algorithm starting with the encoding ψ as the initial point: the tracer through interacting with the adversary produces a new encoding ψ' that is then used as the advice to the algorithm of encryption to produce a ciphertext that all honest users can decode correctly, while on the other hand, ψ' is intended to reveal some more information on the identities of the traitors compared to the original encoding ψ (this gradual improvement is relying on the properties of the ordering $\preceq$).

The perspective here is to view the revocation game as a step towards the goal of disabling of the decryption algorithm represented by the adversary. The idea is to repeatitively play the revocation game. The tracer should be able to win the game for each encoding that is the result of the previous game. At some point, it will happen that the tracer-adversary pair would be no σ-admissible any more; the resulting revocation game for which σ admissibility fails points to the revocation instruction that disables the rogue decoder (which cannot reach the required threshold σ).

This suggests that the revocation game should be defined on suitable posets over $\Psi = 2^{[n]} \times \mathcal{L}$. In particular we would be interested in partial orders $\preceq$ for which any maximal element (C, ψ) in the poset satisfies that ψ encodes an instruction that revokes a set R that satisfies $\mathsf{C} \subseteq \mathsf{R}$. In such a case, when a topmost (C, ψ) is reached, it is easy to see that the adversary $\mathcal{A}$, given the key materials of the corrupted parties $\{sk_u\}_{u \in \mathsf{C}}$, can recognize whether the pair (m, c) is a valid plaintext-ciphertext pair, where c is distributed according to $\mathbf{Encrypt}(ek, \cdot, \psi)$, with probability less than ε where the broadcast encryption scheme BE is ε-insecure in the sense of Definition 2.2. We next define the condition imposed on $\preceq$ as follows:

Definition 4.2. *A partial order relation over $\Psi = 2^{[n]} \times \mathcal{L}$, where $\mathcal{L}$ is a language encoding subsets from $2^{[n]}$, is* revocation-suitable, *if (i) for any $\mathsf{C} \in 2^{[n]}$ and for any $\psi \in \mathcal{L}$, (C, ψ) is a maximal element in $\preceq$ implies that ψ encodes some subset R such that $\mathsf{C} \subseteq \mathsf{R}$, (ii) elements of the form $(\mathsf{C}, \psi), (\mathsf{C}', \psi')$ for $\mathsf{C} \neq \mathsf{C}'$ are incomparable, and (iii) all chains in $\preceq$ are finite.*

Based on this notion we define next a trace and revoke scheme in a generic way and discuss two variants of the definition afterwards:

Definition 4.3. *We say a broadcast encryption scheme BE = ($\mathbf{KeyGen}$, $\mathbf{Encrypt}, \mathbf{Decrypt}$) for t-coalitions is a trace and revoke scheme with probability α for σ-adversaries if there exists a tracer $\mathcal{T}$ and a revocation-suitable relation $\preceq$ over $\Psi = 2^{[n]} \times \mathcal{L}$ for which the following holds:*

For any number of users $n \in \mathbb{N}$ and revocation instruction $\psi \in \mathcal{L}$, the revocation game $\mathsf{RG}_{\psi}^{\mathsf{BE}} = \langle \mathbf{KeyGen}, \mathcal{Q}_{\psi}^{\mathbf{Encrypt}}, \mathcal{R}^{\mathbf{Encrypt}} \rangle$ for t coalitions is winnable by $\mathcal{T}$ with respect to $(\Psi, \preceq)$ with probability α against σ-adversaries.

We define the revocation overhead $\mathsf{rvover}[\mathsf{BE}, \mathcal{T}]$ *of the broadcast encryption as the supremum of all* $\mathsf{rvover}[\mathsf{RG}_{\psi}^{\mathsf{BE}}, \mathcal{T}]$.

We will now discuss how to use a trace and revoke scheme BE = ($\mathbf{KeyGen}$, $\mathbf{Encrypt}, \mathbf{Decrypt}$) as defined above to disable an actual decryption algorithm represented by the adversary. An adversary, corrupting a set of traitors $\mathsf{T} \subseteq [n]$, constructs a decryption algorithm using the key materials of the traitors. More specifically, a pirate decryption algorithm B is any polynomial-time bounded algorithm that receives as input a ciphertext and is successful at decrypting it for at least some broadcast pattern $\psi \in \mathcal{L}_{\mathsf{T}}$, i.e. B satisfies $\mathbf{Prob}[\mathsf{B}(\mathbf{Encrypt}(ek, m, \psi)) = m] \geq \sigma$ where σ is a lower bound for the success probability of decryption, i.e. the admissibility requirement of the tracer-adversary pair (below that bound no decoder is deemed useful for the application at hand; this parameter in practice would be depending on the application domain). We associate to each decryption algorithm the collection of patterns from $\mathcal{L}_{\mathsf{T}}$ that the decoder is decrypting with probability at least σ. Note that the language $\mathcal{L}_{\mathsf{T}}$ has an efficient probabilistic membership test.

Consider a broadcast pattern $\psi \in \mathcal{L}$ for which the decoder is successful with probability at least σ in decrypting the ciphertext of the form **Encrypt**(ek, m, ψ). This essentially means that the decoder constitutes a σ-admissible pair along with the tracer of the underlying revocation game $\langle$**KeyGen**, $\mathcal{Q}_{\psi}^{\mathbf{Encrypt}}, \mathcal{R}^{\mathbf{Encrypt}}\rangle$. Since the broadcast encryption scheme is a trace and revoke scheme, the output of the revocation game advances the pair (T, ψ) to (T, ψ') for which we have $(\mathsf{T}, \psi) \preceq (\mathsf{T}, \psi')$ on the partial order Ψ. For the new revocation instruction ψ' it either holds that the decoder is no more a σ adversary, i.e. the decoder is disabled, or it decrypts the ciphertexts sampled from $\mathcal{Q}_{\psi'}^{\mathbf{Encrypt}}$. For the second case we continue playing the revocation game until the decoder is disabled or we hit a maximal element in the partial order. Recall that the maximal elements in the partial order with a revocation-suitable relation satisfy the following fact: the broadcast pattern revokes the traitor coalition entirely. Hence, the goal of a tracer is to disable the pirate decoder by advancing along the order $\preceq$ using this methodology. A high level algorithmic description of the above procedure is given in Figure 4.1 where the **Revocation**$(\psi, \mathsf{B}, \sigma)$ stands for the output of the tracer in the revocation game $\langle$**KeyGen**, $\mathcal{Q}_{\psi}^{\mathbf{Encrypt}}, \mathcal{R}^{\mathbf{Encrypt}}\rangle$ against the σ-adversary B. We note that the experiment at line 3 may fail with probability ϵ and the condition of line 2 requires statistical testing that may be turn out to be incorrect with negligible probability; for simplicity we omit direct handling of those issues in the below pseudocode.

GenDisable(pattern ψ, pirate box B, σ)
1. repeat
2.   if **Prob**[B(**Encrypt**$(ek, m, \psi)) = m] < \sigma$ then break
3. $\psi =$ **Revocation**$(\psi, \mathsf{B}, \sigma)$
4. until break
5. output ψ /* ψ is a pattern that disables B */

Fig. 4.1. The generic algorithm to disable a pirate decoder.

The termination of the generic **GenDisable** algorithm is ensured by the fact that, the winnable revocation game returns a better encoding with respect to a revocation-suitable relation $\preceq$ over the poset $\Psi = 2^{[n]} \times \mathcal{L}$. After sufficient number of repetitions, the algorithm will either return a broadcast pattern that disables the pirate box, or it will output a revocation instruction that encodes the traitor coalition to be revoked. That is indeed, correct, since the revocation-suitable property of the relation implies such an upper bound with each **Revocation** game (note that the underlying poset is finite).

Here we would like to note that it might be possible to consider a different algorithm disabling the given pirate decoder other than the one given in Figure 4.1. In general, we will refer to a more general procedure by **Disable** where the inputs are ψ, B and σ and the output is some ψ' for which the adversarial decoder is not capable of decrypting while any other legitimate receiver is not revoked.

Disabling in Parallel

We denote the successive applications of any **Disable** algorithm to a sequence $\mathsf{B}_1, \ldots, \mathsf{B}_v$ of pirate decoders by $\mathbf{Disable}(\psi, \langle \mathsf{B}_1, \ldots, \mathsf{B}_v \rangle, \sigma)$. This notation implies the following: we first start with invocation of $\mathbf{Disable}(\psi, \mathsf{B}_1, \sigma)$ that returns ψ_1 and continue with $\psi_{i+1} = \mathbf{Disable}(\psi_i, \mathsf{B}_{i+1}, \sigma)$ for $i \geq 1$. After invoking the process for each decoder once, we continue in a circular fashion from the beginning, as it might be the case that the decoder B_1 becomes active for the revocation instruction ψ_v. The algorithm **Disable** terminates after observing no change for v invocations of the **Disable** algorithm.

Pattern Optimization

The structural properties of the set system may allow operating on ψ to improve its performance as a revocation instruction. This step if available would replace line 5 of Figure 4.1. In particular there will be an operation $\psi = \mathbf{Compact}(\psi, aux)$ where **Compact** is the optimization operation and aux is some auxiliary information extracted from the tracing operation (in case such extra information is useful for optimization). While there is not a generic technique to perform optimization, techniques for specific schemes will be discussed later in the chapter.

We note that one has to be careful with the exit condition of the **Disable** algorithm when using an optimization as depending on the setting it may be the case that the algorithm **Compact** affects the success rate of the adversarial decoders.

4.2 Tracing and Revoking in the Subset Cover Framework

We will now show that the broadcast encryption scheme $\mathtt{BE} = \langle \mathbf{KeyGen}, \mathbf{Encrypt}, \mathbf{Decrypt} \rangle$ based on a subset cover set system Φ that fits the template of Figure 2.2 is a trace and revoke scheme against resettable pirate decoders. As we do not put any constraint on the type of queries the tracer is allowed, we may consider the whole operation in the black-box setting. Recall that resettable pirate decoders allow the tracer to reset the adversary and to receive fresh responses that are oblivious to the history of the tracer-adversary interaction. This is a key fact in our choice of tracing queries; in particular we will deviate from the normal set of random variables $\mathcal{Q}_\psi^{\mathbf{Encrypt}}$ and query the decoder with some special tracing ciphertexts as we have done in Chapter 3 for traitor tracing. However, this time the output of a similar interaction will be a subset in the revocation instruction ψ that contains a traitor involved in piracy.

Recall that the broadcast encryption scheme BE based on a subset cover set system Φ and transmits a vector of ciphertexts $\langle \mathtt{E}_{k_{j_1}}(m), \ldots, \mathtt{E}_{k_{j_s}}(m) \rangle$ where $(\mathtt{E}, \mathtt{D})$ is the underlying symmetric encryption scheme of BE and the key k_{j_i} is the key that corresponds to the subset S_{j_i}. We denote the tracer by $\mathcal{T}_{SC}$ who queries the transmissions of the form $\mathbf{Encrypt}_v(ek, m, \psi)$ for $v = 0, 1, \ldots, s$ for which it holds that we have substituted the first v plaintexts with random strings. Specifically,

$$\mathbf{Encrypt}_v(ek, m, \psi) = \langle j_1, \ldots, j_s, \mathtt{E}_{k_{j_1}}(R_1), \ldots, \mathtt{E}_{k_{j_v}}(R_v), \mathtt{E}_{k_{j_1}}(m), \ldots, \mathtt{E}_{k_{j_s}}(m) \rangle \tag{4.1}$$

where R_i is a random string of the same length as the message m. Given that the adversary-tracer pair is σ-admissible the adversary will be required to respond to the queries of type $\mathbf{Encrypt}_0(ek, m, \psi)$ such that the predicate $\mathcal{R}^{\mathbf{Encrypt}}$ is satisfied with probability at least σ. On the other hand note that the predicate necessarily fails with overwhelming probability for queries of type $\mathbf{Encrypt}_s(ek, m, \psi)$. This suggests that the tracer can progressively randomize the pattern of the ciphertext until a position is identified that the pirate-box fails to decrypt successfully whenever it queries the tracing ciphertext. In other words we can locate a subset that intersects with the traitor coalition in this fashion.

The soundness of the above argumentation is supported by the following lemma (which is similar to Lemma 3.17):

Lemma 4.4. *Let* $\psi = \{\mathsf{S}_{j_1}, \ldots, \mathsf{S}_{j_s}\}$. *Assuming that* $\mathsf{C} \cap \mathsf{S}_{j_v} = \emptyset$, *any probabilistic polynomial-time adversary* $\mathcal{A}$, *given* $\{sk_u\}_{u \in \mathsf{C}}$, *distinguishes the distributions* $\mathbf{Encrypt}_{v-1}(ek, m, \psi)$ *and* $\mathbf{Encrypt}_v(ek, m, \psi)$ *with probability at most* $2\varepsilon_p$ *where* $(ek, sk_1, \ldots, sk_n) \leftarrow \mathbf{KeyDist}(1^n)$ *and the underlying encryption scheme* $(\mathtt{E}, \mathtt{D})$ *is* ε_p*-insecure in the sense of Definition 2.5.*

Proof. Consider the following CCA1 key encapsulation adversary $\mathcal{B}$ that will be able to break the symmetric encryption scheme $(\mathtt{E}, \mathtt{D})$ in the sense of Definition 2.5 with probability at least ε_p by simulating the adversary $\mathcal{A}$.

To break the security claim of the underlying symmetric encryption scheme $(\mathtt{E}, \mathtt{D})$, $\mathcal{B}$, is given access to encryption-decryption oracle of the primitive. $\mathcal{B}$ has also access to the decryption/encryption under a key k that is unknown to her. She is then challenged with a plaintext-ciphertext pair (c, m) for which either $c = \mathtt{E}_k(m)$ or $c = \mathtt{E}_k(R)$ for some random string R that has the same length with m. She is asked to decide if the pair is a correct plaintext-ciphertext pair.

$\mathcal{B}$ will simulate the distribution $\mathbf{Encrypt}_v(ek, m, \psi)$ in a suitable way. Let $\mathcal{B}$ be given the challenge (c, m) where either m is the proper plaintext of c or it is randomly selected. $\mathcal{B}$ will prepare a ciphertext for $\mathcal{A}$ by setting the v-th location of the challenge ciphertext with c and the remaining positions from $v + 1, \ldots, s$ with encryptions of m.

Based on the assumption on the underlying encryption scheme we have that $|\mathbf{Prob}[\mathbf{Exp}_{\mathcal{B}}^{kem}(1^n)] - 1/2| \leq \varepsilon_p$. We observe that in the key encapsulation attack of $\mathcal{B}$ in the conditional space $b = 0$, the adversary $\mathcal{B}^{kem}(1^n)$ operates identically to the distribution $\mathbf{Encrypt}_{v-1}(ek, m, \psi)$ while in the conditional space $b = 1$ it operates identically to the distribution $\mathbf{Encrypt}_{v}(ek, m, \psi)$. Based on this we easily derive the proof of the statement of the lemma. ■

Let us denote by p_v the probability that the decoder box decodes the special tracing ciphertext $\mathbf{Encrypt}_{v}(ek, m, \psi)$. Suppose, now, that the key k_{j_v} is not available to the adversary. As we show in Lemma 4.4 it holds that the pirate decoder distinguishs between the random variables $\mathbf{Encrypt}_{v-1}(ek, m, \psi)$ and $\mathbf{Encrypt}_{v}(ek, m, \psi)$ only with small probability that is related to the insecurity of the underlying encryption scheme E. As a result, it holds that $|p_{s-1} - p_s|$ is relatively small assuming that the advantage ε_p of breaking the security of the underlying encryption primitive is also small.

On the other hand, for a pirate decoder we postulate that it holds that $p_0 \geq \sigma$ due to the constraint placed on $\mathcal{A}$ as detailed in the revocation game. It is relatively straightforward to see that $p_s \leq \frac{1}{|\mathsf{M}|}$ (recall that M denotes the plaintext space and we assume a random plaintext distribution). Hence there must be at least one $0 < v \leq s$ for which $|p_{v-1} - p_v| \geq \frac{\sigma - 1/|\mathsf{M}|}{s}$ by the triangular inequality. Similar to the traceability of linear length scheme of Chapter 3, we now can find such index v under some specific conditions that we will see later.

Recall that the output of the revocation game $\mathsf{RG}^{\mathsf{BE}}_{\psi} = \langle \mathbf{KeyGen}, \mathcal{Q}^{\mathbf{Encrypt}}_{\psi}, \mathcal{R}^{\mathbf{Encrypt}} \rangle$ needs to be a revocation instruction ψ' that satisfies the conditions given in Definition 4.1 for some revocation-suitable relation $\preceq$ over $\Psi = 2^{[n]} \times \mathcal{L}$. Jumping ahead, an algorithmic description of the tracer can be found in Figure 4.2. In this description we have a step (line 4) that approximates the pirate box decoding capability: this abstracts the standard statistical test of querrying the decoder with the tracing ciphertexts many times by resetting the pirate decoder to locate the subset containing a traitor. The procedure uses the threshold parameter σ as determined by the σ-admissibility property.

The Lemma 4.4 ensures that the set S of line 7 in figure 4.2 contains a traitor. The revocation algorithm then splits this subset and updates the revocation instruction to include the split-pair while removing the original subset from the broadcast pattern. The resulting pattern produced by this process should be better with respect to a revocation-suitable relation defined over the key poset $\Psi = 2^{[n]} \times \mathcal{L}$ which we will define accordingly.

Here, it should be noted that the efficiency of the tracing algorithm given in Figure 4.1 depends on how the function $spt(\cdot)$ operates on a subset. Relatively evenly balanced splits will result to a better convergence.

We return now to introduce a revocation-suitable relation $\preceq_{SC}$ (SC stands for Subset Cover as the following relation is very specific to subset cover schemes with bifurcation property) over $\Psi = 2^{[n]} \times \mathcal{L}$. We have $\Psi = 2^{[n]} \times \mathcal{L}$ with the set of revocation instructions $\mathcal{L}$ sampled from $\mathbf{KeyGen}(1^n)$ based on a set system Φ that fits the template of Figure 2.2. Specifically, consider two elements of the set Ψ, i.e. (C, ψ) and (C', ψ'). We define $\psi[u]$ as the

Revocation(pattern ψ, pirate box B, σ)
Let $\psi = \{\mathsf{S}_{j_1}, \mathsf{S}_{j_2}, \ldots, \mathsf{S}_{j_s}\}$
if $\mathbf{Prob}[\mathsf{B}(\mathbf{Encrypt}(ek, m, \psi)) = m] < \sigma$ then return $\emptyset$
else
  for $i = 0$ to s approximate
    $p_i \approx \mathbf{Prob}[\mathsf{B}(\mathbf{Encrypt}_i(ek, m, \psi)) = m]$
  for $i = 1$ to s
    if $|p_{i-1} - p_i| \geq \frac{\sigma - 1/|\mathsf{M}|}{s}$ then set $\mathsf{S} = \mathsf{S}_{j_i}$ and break
  $\psi' = \psi \setminus \mathsf{S}$
  If $|\mathsf{S}| > 1$ then $(\mathsf{S}_1, \mathsf{S}_2) = \Phi.\mathbf{spt}(\mathsf{S})$
    $\psi' = \psi' \cup \{\mathsf{S}_1, \mathsf{S}_2\}$
  return ψ'

Fig. 4.2. The algorithmic description of the tracer (cf. Theorem 4.8) that makes the revocation game for subset cover schemes winnable.

element in the broadcast pattern ψ that contains u, i.e. $\psi[u] \in \psi$ such that $u \in \psi[u]$; if such element does not exist then we say $\psi[u] = \emptyset$. We now define $(\mathsf{C}, \psi) \preceq_{SC} (\mathsf{C}', \psi')$ if and only if the following hold: (i) $\mathsf{C} = \mathsf{C}'$, (ii) for all $u \in \mathsf{C}$ we have $\psi'[u] \subseteq \psi[u]$.

We next show that the relation is revocation-suitable.

Lemma 4.5. *The relation $\preceq_{SC}$ over $\Psi = 2^{[n]} \times \mathcal{L}$, as defined above, is revocation-suitable.*

Proof. Suppose that $\preceq_{SC}$ does not satisfy property (i) of revocation-suitable relation, i.e., there is a C corresponding to a set of corrupted users and a ψ so that (C, ψ) is a maximal element of the relation $\preceq_{SC}$ but ψ encodes some subset R for which it holds that $\mathsf{C} \not\subseteq \mathsf{R}$, i.e., there is a $u \in \mathsf{C} \setminus \mathsf{R}$. Observe that this also implies that $\psi[u] \neq \emptyset$. Now consider the pair (C, ψ') where ψ' is defined in the same way as ψ, but it holds that the element $\psi[u]$ of ψ is substituted in ψ' with a sequence of elements that covers $\psi[u] \setminus \{u\}$ (and as a result $\psi'[u] = \emptyset$). The existence of this sequence is based on the exclusive property of the underlying family Φ. It is easy to see that $(\mathsf{C}, \psi) \preceq_{SC} (\mathsf{C}, \psi')$ thus contradicting the maximality of (C, ψ). Properties (ii), (iii) are easy to follow from the definition of the relation and the fact that Φ is a finite set system. ■

We will, now, prove formally that a broadcast encryption scheme based on any exclusive set system is a trace and revoke schemes with respect to the relation $\preceq_{SC}$.

Theorem 4.6. *Let* BE *be a broadcast encryption scheme based on an (n, r, s)-exclusive set system Φ that fits the template of Figure 2.2.* BE *is a trace and revoke scheme for n-coalitions with probability $1 - \varepsilon$ against resettable σ-adversaries with $\sigma > 4n\varepsilon_p + \frac{1}{|\mathsf{M}|}$.*

Furthermore it holds that $\mathsf{rvover}[\mathsf{BE}, \mathcal{T}_{SC}] \leq O(\frac{s^3 \cdot \ln(1/\varepsilon)}{(\sigma - 1/|\mathsf{M}|)^2})$.

Proof. Fixing an encoding $\psi = \{\mathsf{S}_{\mathsf{j}_1}, \ldots, \mathsf{S}_{\mathsf{j}_s}\}$, we will argue that the related revocation game is winnable by the tracer $\mathcal{T}_{SC}$ with the parameters given in the theorem for the revocation-suitable relation $\preceq_{SC}$. (i) Based on an almost similar argument of the proof of Theorem 3.19, it is left as an exercise for the reader to see that the given parameters suffice to locate a subset $\mathsf{S}_{\mathsf{j}_w}$, for $w \leq s$, containing a traitor.

The tracer then splits the subset $\mathsf{S}_{\mathsf{j}_w}$; we denote the output by $(\mathsf{S}_{\mathsf{j}_l}, \mathsf{S}_{\mathsf{j}_r}) = \mathbf{spt}(\mathsf{S}_{\mathsf{j}_w})$; the tracer then returns the broadcast pattern $\psi' = \{\mathsf{S}_{\mathsf{j}_1}, \ldots, \mathsf{S}_{\mathsf{j}_{w-1}}, \mathsf{S}_{\mathsf{j}_l}, \mathsf{S}_{\mathsf{j}_r}, \mathsf{S}_{\mathsf{j}_{w+1}}, \ldots, \mathsf{S}_{\mathsf{j}_s}\}$. It is easy to observe that for any $u \in [n] \setminus (\mathsf{R} \cup \mathsf{C})$ it holds that $\mathbf{Decrypt}(sk_u, c) = m$ where $c \leftarrow \mathbf{Encrypt}(ek, m, \psi')$ and ψ encodes the set R to be revoked. It further holds that $(\mathsf{C}, \psi) \preceq_{SC} (\mathsf{C}, \psi')$ which completes the proof of the theorem.

■

4.3 Tracing and Revoking Pirate Rebroadcasts

In this section, we consider a stronger scenario for tracing and revoking : when the tracing needs to be performed alfresco against history recording adversaries. This is important in the setting of pirate rebroadcasting : in such case, it is not feasible for the tracer to privately experiment with the rogue decoder. The tracer collects feedback from the pirate rebroadcasts but is incapable of experimenting with the pirate decoder in a way that hurts correctness for legitimate receivers.

To deal with this problem we will introduce a special class of stateful q-ary broadcast encryption schemes. Each such scheme is parameterized by a fingerprinting code $\mathsf{F} = (\mathbf{CodeGen}, \mathbf{Identify})$ and is denoted by $\mathtt{BE}_{\mathsf{F},q}$. The state $\sigma \in States$ of the scheme $\mathtt{BE}_{\mathsf{F},q}$ is a pair $\langle \mathcal{W}, l \rangle$ where $\mathcal{W}$ is an instance of the fingerprinting code that is sampled by the $\mathbf{CodeGen}^{\ell}$ algorithm on input $q \in [n]$, and l is an integer that satisfies $0 < l \leq \ell$. We also allow $\mathcal{W}$ to be empty in which case $l = 0$. We define the three algorithms associated with the scheme as follows.

- $\mathbf{KeyGen}_{\mathsf{F}}$. Given 1^n it chooses an (n, r, t)-exclusive set system $\Phi = \{\mathsf{S}_{\mathsf{j}}\}_{\mathsf{j} \in \mathcal{J}}$. The algorithm then generates a collection of keys $\{k_{\mathsf{j}}\}_{\mathsf{j} \in \mathcal{J}} \subseteq \mathsf{K}$. For any $u \in [n]$, define $\mathcal{J}_u := \{\mathsf{j} \mid u \in \mathsf{S}_{\mathsf{j}}\}$ and $\mathsf{K}_u = \{k_{\mathsf{j}} \mid \mathsf{j} \in \mathcal{J}_u\}$. It sets $ek = \langle \Phi, \{k_{\mathsf{j}}\}_{\mathsf{j} \in \mathcal{J}} \rangle$ and $sk_u = (\mathcal{J}_u, \mathsf{K}_u)$ for any $u \in [n]$.
  The language $\mathcal{L}$ consists of the descriptions of those elements of 2^{Φ} such that $\mathcal{P} = \{\mathsf{S}_{\mathsf{j}_1}, \ldots, \mathsf{S}_{\mathsf{j}_s}\} \in \mathcal{L}$ if and only if $s \leq t$ and the set $\mathsf{R} = [n] \setminus \cup_{i=1}^{s} \mathsf{S}_{\mathsf{j}_i}$ satisfies $|\mathsf{R}| \leq r$; in such case we say that $\mathcal{P}$ encodes R.
  The initial state σ_0 is set to be $\langle \perp, 0 \rangle$.
- $\mathbf{Encrypt}_{\mathsf{F}}$. Given $\psi \in \mathcal{L}$ and a vector of input $M = \langle m_1, \ldots, m_q \rangle$, say $\psi = \{\mathsf{S}_{\mathsf{j}_1}, \ldots, \mathsf{S}_{\mathsf{j}_s}\}$ where $\mathsf{j}_i \in \mathcal{J}$ for $i \in \{1, \ldots, s\}$. The set of keys $\{k_{\mathsf{j}} \mid \mathsf{j} \in \mathcal{J}$ and $\mathsf{S}_{\mathsf{j}} \in \psi\}$ is retrieved from $\{k_{\mathsf{j}}\}_{\mathsf{j} \in \mathcal{J}}$.

In case the state is $\langle \perp, 0 \rangle$, then $\mathcal{W} = \{\mathsf{w}^1, \ldots, \mathsf{w}^s\}$, with $s = |\psi|$ is sampled by running $\mathbf{CodeGen}^{\ell}(1^s)$ and l is set to be 1. Otherwise let the state be $\sigma = \langle \mathcal{W}, l \rangle$.
By employing the encryption scheme $(\mathtt{E}, \mathtt{D})$ the ciphertext is computed as follows:

$$c \leftarrow \langle \mathsf{j}_1, \ldots, \mathsf{j}_s, \mathtt{E}_{k_{\mathsf{j}_1}}(m_{\mathsf{w}_l^1}), \ldots, \mathtt{E}_{k_{\mathsf{j}_s}}(m_{\mathsf{w}_l^s}) \rangle$$

Finally, the state index is updated to be $l = (l \bmod \ell) + 1$.

- **Decrypt**$_{\mathtt{F}}$. Given the key-pair $sk_u = (\mathcal{J}_u, \mathsf{K}_u)$ for some $u \in [n]$ and a ciphertext of the form

$$c = \langle \mathsf{j}_1, \ldots, \mathsf{j}_s, c_1, \ldots, c_s \rangle$$

it first searches for an encoding j_i that satisfies $\mathsf{j}_i \in \mathcal{J}_u$ and then returns $\mathtt{D}_{k_{\mathsf{j}_i}}(c_i)$. If no such encoding is found it returns $\perp$.

The scheme is a simple extension of the original broadcast encryption to support transmitting an input vector in a stateful manner. Hence its correctness and security can be proven in a similar fashion with the analysis as given in Theorem 2.8.

Given that there is a state involved now some comments are in place with respect to the way the state is relevant in the security definition 2.2. We assume that the state is initialized with the first encryption query that is made by the adversary and the state advances in the prescribed fashion as in the definition of the scheme. The adversary will receive the challenge at the particular state that it chooses to terminate its initial stage of her experimentation.

Theorem 4.7. *The q-ary broadcast encryption scheme defined above satisfies correctness (cf. Definition 2.1) and it is secure with the same parameters of the Theorem 2.8.*

Proof. The proof is very similar to the proof of Theorem 2.8 and is left as an exercise for the reader. It should be noted that the scheme is q-ary therefore the challenge plaintext will use plaintext vectors of length q (this differs from Theorem 2.8 where the underlying scheme is unary). ■

We next claim that the above broadcast encryption, for the choice of a subset cover scheme Φ, is in fact an alfresco trace and revoke scheme. As we are now in the domain of alfresco revocation games we need to prepare tracer queries that are statistically indistinguishable from regular transmissions. The tracing queries will make use of the underlying fingerprinting code as in the case of traceability of multiuser encryption schemes based on fingerprinting that we have discussed in Chapter 3.

Jumping ahead, we describe how tracing works for a given revocation isntruction ψ: only one of the message from the input vector is made available to each subset in the encoding ψ through the fingerprinting code that is retrieved

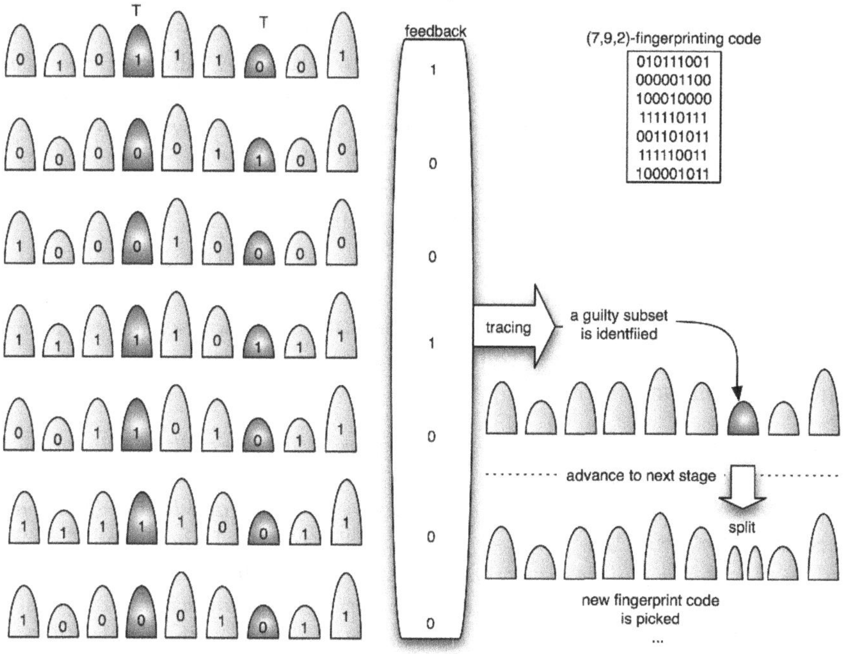

Fig. 4.3. Illustration of tracing and revoking a pirate rebroadcast. In this example, the revocation instruction ψ has 9 subsets and a code of length 7 is used over a binary alphabet.

from the state. After a sufficient number of transmissions (that matches the length of the code) the sequence of pirate rebroadcasts will form a pirate codeword and by applying the identify algorithm of the fingerprinting code on it we will identify a subset that contains at least one traitor. This is because of the fact that the codewords of $\mathtt{F}$ are assigned to subsets of receivers, i.e., the detection of a "traitor" from the **Identify** algorithm is now equivalent to finding a subset that contains a traitor. This constitutes the progress that is necessary for winning the revocation game. Moreover observe that this subset may be split into 2 subsets or more depending on the properties of the underlying subset cover scheme and the process be repeated. The updated set of users, i.e the subsets in the new partition, will be reassigned new codewords from possibly a fresh fingerprinting code. Observe that the **Identify** algorithm of the fingerprinting code substitutes the "walking" argument that was employed in the previous section that progressively randomized the pattern ciphertext untill a position is identified that the adversary fails to decrypt successfully. This mechanism was the the basic procedure which tests a pirate box that is successful in decrypting with a given pattern by using some special tracing ciphertexts to output a subset containing a traitor. We note that such walking arguments cannot be used in tracing pirate rebroadcasts since they would require transmitting "garbage" to a subset of legitimate receivers, something that is unacceptable in the alfresco setting. An illustration of this process is presented in figure 4.3 where each subset shown in the figure is a valid subset in the collection Φ of the underlying Subset Cover Scheme.

We, again, consider the revocation-suitable relation $\preceq_{SC}$ over $\Psi = 2^{[n]} \times \mathcal{L}$ of the previous section. We will argue that for any $\psi \in \mathcal{L}$ the revocation game $\langle \mathbf{KeyGen}_{\mathtt{F}}, \mathcal{Q}_{\psi}^{\mathbf{Encrypt}_{\mathtt{F}}}, \mathcal{R}^{\mathbf{Encrypt}_{\mathtt{F}}} \rangle$ is winnable with respect to $(\Psi, \preceq_{SC})$ for suitable parameters. Recall we have $\Psi = 2^{[n]} \times \mathcal{L}$ with the set of revocation instructions $\mathcal{L}$ sampled from $\mathbf{KeyGen}_{\mathtt{F}}$.

We will next prove that the q-ary broadcast encryption scheme as defined above is a trace and revoke scheme with respect to the relation $\preceq_{SC}$ with an alfresco tracing and revocation process.

Theorem 4.8. *Consider the stateful q-ary broadcast encryption scheme $\mathtt{BE}_{\mathtt{F},q}$ parameterized by the fingerprinting code $\mathtt{F}$ that is (ε_f, w)-identifier. Let Φ, the underlying set system of $\mathtt{BE}_{\mathtt{F},q}$, be a subset cover scheme and let the underlying encryption scheme $(\mathtt{E}, \mathtt{D})$ be ε_p-insecure in the sense of Definition 2.5. We finally consider a plaintext distribution over M^q with limited crossover γ.*

For any $n \in \mathbb{N}, \varepsilon > 0$, the q-ary broadcast ecnryption scheme $\mathtt{BE}_{\mathtt{F},q}$ is an alfresco stateful trace and revoke scheme for w-coalitions with probability $1-\varepsilon_f$ against σ adversaries with $\sigma > \frac{1}{\ell}(\ell-1+2n\varepsilon_p)$ and $\gamma^{-1} = \Omega(\frac{\ell}{\varepsilon}\log\frac{\ell}{\varepsilon}\sigma_0^{-1})$ where $\sigma_0 = \ell\sigma - \ell + 1 - 2n\varepsilon_p$. It also holds,

$$\mathsf{rvover}[\mathtt{BE}_{\mathtt{F},q}] = O(\ell\sigma_0^{-1}\log(\ell\varepsilon^{-1}))$$

Proof. Fixing an encoding $\psi = \{\mathsf{S}_{\mathrm{j}_1}, \ldots, \mathsf{S}_{\mathrm{j}_s}\}$ we will argue that the related revocation game is winnable with the parameters given in the theorem for the revocation-suitable relation $\preceq_{SC}$.

Starting from the state $state_0 = (\perp, 0)$, the tracer will first sample a code $\mathcal{W}$ of length ℓ from the code generation algorithm of the fingerprinting code $\mathtt{F}$. The tracer will then query the transmissions prepared for state $state_i = (\mathcal{W}, i)$, for $i = 1, \ldots, \ell$, similar to the regular transmission in a stateful manner. For each i, the response $\tilde{m}^i$ of the adversary will either be a valid message (which is likely to reveal the key available to the adversary for that column) or $\perp$ standing for a refusal to decrypt or decrypting incorrectly.

We can repeat the above series of transmissions, a number of λ' times to ensure that we have collected a sufficient number of executions to have a non $\perp$ decoding value for each column. We can define the value w_j^i that corresponds to the symbol in $\{1, \ldots, q\} \cup \{\perp\}$ that was returned as a j-th column response in the i-th execution. We define by w_j any non-$\perp$ symbol in $\{1, \ldots, q\}$ that appears the most times among $w_j^1, \ldots, w_j^{\lambda'}$ for all $j \in [\ell]$; if w_j cannot be defined for some j the tracing procedure will fail. The implication we would like to make is that for all $j = 1, \ldots, \ell$ the key material $k_{w_j,j}$ belongs to the traitor coalition.

First we need to ensure that there is sufficient number of executions performed such that w_j becomes well-defined (i.e. we have non-$\perp$ symbols among the w_j^i's). Recall that it is possible that the success probability of the adversary may differ for each column, for example the success probability σ_i of the adversary conditional to the transmission for state column i may not be necessarily σ. Assuming now a lower bound σ_l for the adversary to return a correct decryption for the choice of l in transmission, let V_l be the number of symbols that are non $\perp$. Now without loss of generality we can assume that in each transmission all symbols in the l-th column other than those that correspond to the keys that are owned to the adversary substituted by a value that is not in the plaintext space (random values can be used for only a slight change of the argument below). This ensures that any other plaintext is inaccessible to the adversary per the security of the underlying encryption; via a standard hybrid argument and the reasoning of Lemma 3.20 it is easy to show that the success probability of the adversary in each experiment can change by at most $2n\varepsilon_p$ given that $|\psi| \leq n$, i.e. the success probability bound will be at least $\sigma_{l,0} = \sigma_l - 2n\varepsilon_p$. On the other hand, based on the assumption placed on σ and following the same reasoning in Theorem 3.22 it is easy to show that the probability of obtaining a non $\perp$ decoding value for each column that belongs to the coalition will be at least $\sigma_0 = \ell\sigma - \ell + 1 - 2n\varepsilon_p \leq \min_l \sigma_l - 2n\varepsilon_p$.

Our intent now is to apply the identify algorithm of the fingerprinting code on the string $w_1, \ldots, w_\ell$. Nevertheless, to apply this algorithm we need to argue that the marking assumption is satisfied, i.e., the pirate codeword $\mathsf{p} = \langle w_1, \ldots, w_\ell \rangle$ is in the descendant set of the traitor coalition.

For a single column the probability of obtaining a non-$\perp$ value for a column is at least σ_0. Given that we repeat this λ' times we have that the probability of failing all of them is at most $(1-\sigma_0)^{\lambda'} \leq e^{-\lambda' \cdot \sigma_0}$. By setting $\lambda' = \lceil k \cdot \sigma_0^{-1} \rceil$ the failure probability in obtaining a well-defined symbol is at most e^{-k}. Applying this logic to ℓ columns we have that they are all well defined with probability $(1 - e^{-k}) \geq 1 - \ell e^{-k}$.

Now given that the crossover of the plaintext distribution is γ it follows that with probability $1 - \lambda'\ell \cdot \gamma$ we will have no crossover in any of the ℓ columns. To summarize in order to bound the probability of failure by ε we require in each column we have at least one symbol well-defined (an event that fails with probability ℓe^{-k}) and all ℓ symbols represent traitors, an event that fails with probability $\lambda'\ell \cdot \gamma$. We need to achieve $1 - \varepsilon \leq 1 - \ell e^{-k} - \lambda'\ell \cdot \gamma$ that can be satisfied by setting $k \geq \ln \frac{2\ell}{\varepsilon}$ and $\gamma \leq \varepsilon/(2\lambda'\ell)$.

It follows that we can choose $k = \lceil \ln \frac{2\ell}{\varepsilon} \rceil$. This will force the number of experiments to satisfy $\lambda' = O(\sigma_0^{-1} \ln(\ell\varepsilon^{-1}))$. Observe that the condition $\gamma \leq \varepsilon/(2\lambda'\ell)$ is then trivially satisfied based on the assumption placed on γ in the statement of the theorem. Hence, the overall failure probability in constructing a pirate codeword from the descendant set of traitor coalition is bounded by ε in $O(\ell\sigma_0^{-1} \ln(\ell\varepsilon^{-1}))$ rounds.

Upon constructing the pirate codeword as described above, the underlying identification algorithm returns an index $w \in [s]$. The tracer then splits the subset $\mathsf{S}_{\mathsf{j}_w}$, denoting the output by $(\mathsf{S}_{\mathsf{j}_l}, \mathsf{S}_{\mathsf{j}_r}) = \mathbf{spt}(\mathsf{S}_{\mathsf{j}_w})$, returns the broadcast pattern $\psi' = \{\mathsf{S}_{\mathsf{j}_1}, \ldots, \mathsf{S}_{\mathsf{j}_{w-1}}, \mathsf{S}_{\mathsf{j}_l}, \mathsf{S}_{\mathsf{j}_r}, \mathsf{S}_{\mathsf{j}_{w+1}}, \ldots, \mathsf{S}_{\mathsf{j}_s}\}$. It is easy to observe that for any $u \in [n] \setminus (\mathsf{R} \cup \mathsf{C})$ it holds that $\mathbf{Decrypt}(sk_u, c) = M$ where $c \leftarrow \mathbf{Encrypt}(ek, M, \psi')$ and ψ encodes the set R to be revoked. It further holds that $(\mathsf{C}, \psi) \preceq_{SC} (\mathsf{C}, \psi')$ which completes the proof of the theorem. ■

Picking a Fingerprinting Code.

The choice of the underlying fingerprinting code is flexible. It is even possible to pick totally different codes in a series of tracing transmissions, i.e., the broadcast encryption scheme is not necessarily attached to a single type of fingerprinting. Moreover, this choice will be reflected in the deciphering process within the content transmission, hence the choice of fingerprinting code is independent from the keys stored by the receiver. The code is used to simply restructure the marking-assignment logically, by reassigning a subset to a new codeword.

A crucial difference regarding the selection of the fingerprinting code in the present section when compared to other applications of fingerprinting codes we have seen earlier is that in the present section we only need codes with a number of codewords proportional to the number of revoked users and active traitors as opposed to the whole population. Due to this important characteristic, one can employ fingerprinting codes that allow for arbitrary traitor collusions such as Boneh-Shaw and Tardos codes presented in Chapter 1 without hurting the efficiency of the above scheme and thus an unbounded number of traitors can be traced.

Recall that the basic process given in the revocation game will be repeated recursively until all the traitors are identified or the rebroadcast ceases. It is worth noting here that our formulation of tracing and revoking pirate rebroadcasts (as it is the case for trace and revoke schemes in Section 4.1) only suggests that the tracer does progress towards the ultimate revocation of the traitor coalition. We refer the reader to figure 4.4 for an illustration of how the above scheme works in combination with the subset-difference method.

4.4 On the effectiveness of Trace and Revoke schemes

Given that Definition 4.3 does not suggest the immediate revocation of the pirate decoder it is important to consider how eventually the traitors are revoked in such schemes. Based on the formulation, the tracer will progress and walk along a chain of the relation $\preceq$ changing revocation instructions till it reaches a maximal point (or the pirate decoder stops working). Given that the end points of all chains ensure that the traitors are revoked, the formulation of traceability ensures that the tracer advances to the right direction. As

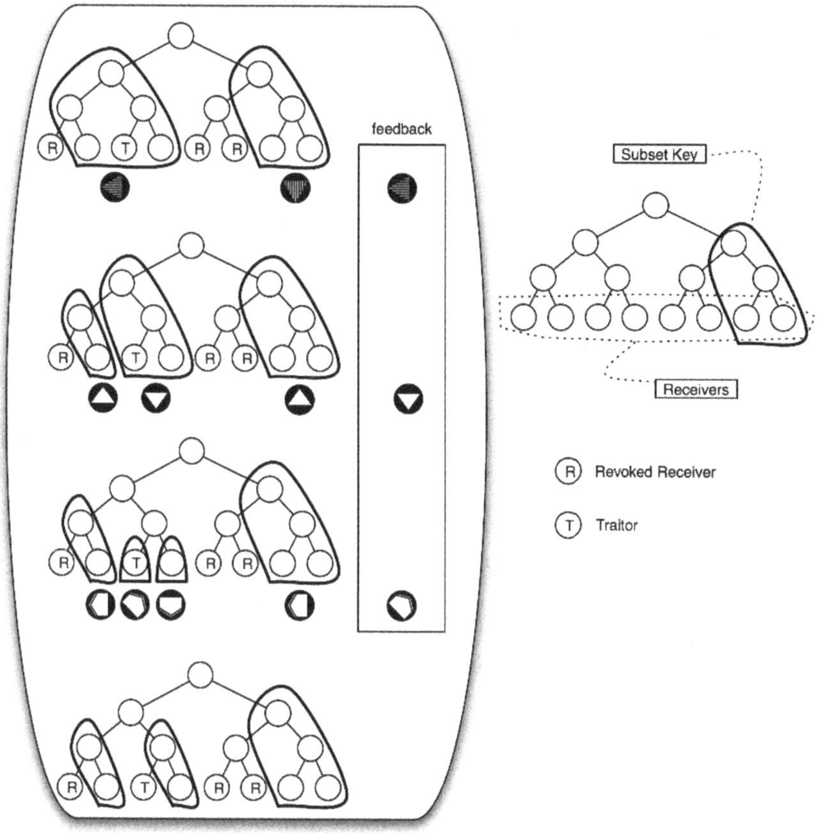

Fig. 4.4. Depiction of tracing a traitor following a pirate rebroadcast it produces while employing the Subset-Difference method for key assignment.

long as the adversary remains functional, i.e., the tracer-adversary pair is σ-admissible, then the tracer will improve the current state of the system to a revocation instruction that is more suitable for disabling the pirate decoder.

Given the above it is obvious that an adversary may choose to manipulate the content distribution system so as to choose the longest chain over $\preceq$ possible and force the tracer to use all its intermediate points till it reaches the maximal element. This type of adversarial behavior relates to the concept of pirate evolution that will be discussed in the next chapter.

4.5 Bibliographic Notes

Trace and revoke schemes conceptually are a combination of two cryptographic primitives that have been originally suggested and studied independently: revocation (broadcast encryption) and traitor tracing. Combining these two functionalities of tracing and revoking in a single system is not straightforward. This was identified in [90] and explored further in [37].

The trace and revoke schemes for stateless receivers proposed by Naor, Naor and Lotspiech [87] were the first efficient constructions that are capable of dealing with the problem of disabling pirate decoders while supporting unbounded revocation. In this work the subset cover framework was put forth, that we laid out in Chapter 2; a large number of works, including [53, 122, 50, 6, 55, 56, 57], can be described within this framework.

Regarding the overall effectiveness of the revocation game, a relevant property is "bifurcation". It was put forth in [87] and suggests that splitting any subset $\mathsf{S} \in \Phi$ can be done in two roughly equal sets. In the terminology of this chapter, bifurcation enables one to bound the length of the longest chain in the partial order of revocation instructions $\preceq_{SC}$ to be logarithmic in the number of users. It is worth noting that one may trade bifurcation for weaker, more unbalanced splits, to increase other efficiency parameters of a scheme. This behavior is exhibited for example by the layered Subset Difference method of [53].

Regarding the public-key setting, Dodis and Fazio[35] showed how the subset cover framework can be used to make efficient public-key schemes. A more recent trace and revoke scheme in the public key setting was proposed by Boneh et al. in [24], and further improved by Furukawa and Attrapadung in [44].

All the above schemes were designed for tracing in the black-box setting and it is not straightforward how to add revocation on top of known traitor tracing schemes for pirate rebroadcasting. To see why the straightforward approach fails suppose one decides to combine a broadcast encryption at the decoder level with, say, a traitor tracing scheme pirate for rebroadcasting by combining the two encryption functions (e.g., via a 2-out-of-2 secret-sharing scheme[1]). This means that legitimate decoders will have to possess independent sets of keys from both schemes, i.e., one set of keys for the encryption/decryption involved in the traitor tracing layer that binds the marked content to a receiver and one set of keys for the encryption/decryption involved in the broadcast encryption layer. It is easy to see that a pirate possessing the key material of as few as two traitor users can evade revocation at the decoder level by simply employing the keys of one user for decrypting the traitor tracing layer and the keys of the other user for decrypting the broadcast encryption layer. In this attack scenario, the traitor tracing scheme will successfully recover the identity of one of the traitors but subsequently revoking the recovered user will have absolutely no effect in the decryption capability of the pirate decoder (which will continue to operate due to the fact that it

[1] A 2-out-of-2 secret-sharing scheme enables the split of a secret to two parts so that both are needed to recover the secret and each one individually is independent from the secret.

is using the broadcast encryption keys of the second user which will remain uninidentified).

A trace and revoke scheme able to guard against pirate rebroadcasts is implemented as part of the AACS standard [1]. The scheme is presented and its security and performance analysed in Jin and Lotspiech[58], with further analysis in [64] that revealed some limitations of that construction. In [65, 64] tracing and revoking pirate rebroadcasting was formally modelled and a scheme for tracing and revoking an unlimited number of users was shown. We outlined this scheme in Section 4.3.

5

Pirate Evolution

In Chapter 4 we put forth the notion of winnable revocation games. Winning a sequence of such games implies that the adversary can be eventually disabled by the tracer. Nevertheless, the fact that the adversary can be disabled does not necessarily imply that a certain *leaking incident*, i.e., an incident where some key material of some users are exposed to the adversary, can be simultaneously contained. This is due to the fact that a leaking incident enables possibly the creation of a sequence of adversaries that may have to be successively revoked (in a succession of many revocation games). This gives rise to the notion of an evolving adversary which is the subject of this chapter.

Specifically, pirate evolution is an attack concept against a trace and revoke scheme that exploits the properties of the combined functionality of tracing and revocation in such a scheme. In a pirate evolution attack, a pirate obtains a set of traitor keys through a "key-leaking" incident. Using this set of keys the pirate produces an initial pirate decoder. When this pirate decoder is captured and revoked by the transmission system using the tracing mechanism, the pirate "evolves" the first pirate decoder by issuing a second version that succeeds in decrypting ciphertexts that the first version fails. The same step is repeated again and the pirate continues to evolve a new version of the previous decoder whenever the current version of pirate decoder becomes disabled from the system. Each version of the pirate decoder in this sense will be called a "generation" of pirate decoders (since many copies of the same decoder can be spread by the pirate).

It is worth noting that this is a different attack concept from the ones that were discussed in Chapter 2 and 3. The adversary here is not trying to evade the revocation or the traceability component. Instead it tries to remain active in the system for as long as possible in spite of the efforts of the system administrators.

In this chapter, we study pirate evolution in the subset cover framework of stateless receivers (cf. Section 2.2.2). We first formalize the concept of pirate evolution through the means of an attack game played between the evolving pirate and a challenger that verifies certain properties about the pirate

A. Kiayias and S. Pehlivanoglu, *Encryption for Digital Content*, Advances in Information Security 52, DOI 10.1007/978-1-4419-0044-9_5, © Springer Science+Business Media, LLC 2010

decoders produced by the evolving pirate. Next, we discuss how the pirate evolution can be applied to the subset cover schemes and subsequently we study pirate evolution for the complete-subtree and subset-difference exclusive set systems as described in Section 2.5. For the complete subtree method we present a pirate evolution attack that given t traitor keys, it enables an evolving pirate to produce up to $t\log(n/t)$ generations where n is the total number of users in the system. For the subset difference method we present a pirate evolution attack that given t traitor keys, it enables an evolving pirate to produce up to $t \log n$ generations of pirate decoders.

5.1 Pirate Evolution: Definitions

In this section we introduce the concept of pirate evolution. We present a game based definition that is played with the adversary which is the *evolving pirate*. Let t be the number of traitor keys in the hands of the pirate. The traitor keys are made available to the pirate through a key-leaking incident **Leaking** that somehow chooses a subset T of size t from the receiver population $\{1, \ldots, n\}$. The **Leaking** algorithm, on input the set of encodings ($\mathcal{L}$ with all possible revocation instructions, recieves the corresponding subset $\{sk_u\}_{u \in \mathsf{T}}$ of all users' private data where $(\mathcal{L}, \{sk_1, \ldots, sk_n\}) \leftarrow$ **KeyGen**(1^n). We permit **Leaking** to be also based on the current set of revoked users R. Specifically, if $\mathsf{T} =$ **Leaking**$(\mathcal{L}, t, \mathsf{R})$ then $|\mathsf{T}| = t$, $\mathsf{T} \subseteq \{u \mid u \in [n] \setminus \mathsf{R}\}$. This models the fact that the evolving pirate may be able to select the users that it corrupts. Separating the evolving pirate from the leaking incident is important though as it enables us to describe how a pirate can deal with leaking incidents that are not necessarily the most favorable. Indeed, the forms of pirate evolution that we will describe in the sequel will operate with any given leaking incident and there will be leaking incidents that are more favorable than others.

Once the leaking incident determines the private user data that will be available to the evolving pirate (i.e., the traitor key material), the evolving pirate $\mathcal{P}$ receives the keys and produces a "master" pirate box **MasterBox**. The pirate is allowed to have oracle access to an oracle **Encrypt**(ek, m, ψ) for each $\psi \in \mathcal{L}$ that returns ciphertexts distributed according to plaintext distribution that is employed by the digital content distribution system.

Given the master pirate box, an iterative process is initiated: the master pirate box spawns successively a sequence of pirate decoders $\mathsf{B}_1, \mathsf{B}_2, \ldots$ where $\mathsf{B}_\ell =$ **MasterBox**$(1^{t+\log n}, \ell)$ for $\ell = 1, 2, \ldots$. Note that we loosely think that the master box is simply the compact representation of a vector of pirate boxes; the time complexity allowed for its operation is polynomial in $t + \log n + \log \ell$. We note that this may be generalized in other contexts but is sufficient for describing a wide range of evolving pirate strategies. Each pirate box is tested whether it decrypts correctly the plaintexts that are transmitted with success probability at least σ, which is a parameter of the underlying trace and revoke scheme.

The first pirate box is tested against the 'initial' broadcast pattern ψ whereas any subsequent box is tested against **Disable**$(\psi, \langle \mathsf{B}_1, \ldots, \mathsf{B}_{i-1} \rangle, \sigma)$ which is the resulting pattern that corresponds to the conjunctive tracing of all previous pirate boxes. Here, we refer to the **Disable** algorithm of section 4.1 and an example can be considered as the generic algorithm given in Figure 4.1. The iteration stops when the master pirate box **MasterBox** is incapable of producing a pirate decoder with decryption success exceeding the threshold σ. Each iteration of the master box corresponds to a "generation" of pirate boxes. The number of successfully decoding pirate generations that the master box can spawn is the output of the game-based definition given in Figure 5.1. In the figure, the **Disable** algorithm is a procedure that disables the sequence of pirate decoders; it utilizes the tracer that is given from the fact that the revocation game winnable for any ψ.

We say that a trace and revoke scheme is immune to pirate evolution if the number of generations that an evolving pirate can produce equals the number of traitor keys that have been corrupted (i.e., the number of traitors). The number of traitors is a natural lower bound to the generations that an evolving pirate can produce: trivially, an evolving pirate can set each version it releases to be equal to the decoder of one of the traitors. Nevertheless, the number of generations that a pirate may produce can be substantially larger depending on the combinatorial properties of the underlying trace and revoke system. We call the maximum number of decoders an evolving pirate can produce, the pirate evolution bound evo of the trace and revoke scheme. Note that this bound will be a function of the number of traitors t as well as of other parameters in the system (such as the number of users).

When evo is larger than t, we say that a trace and revoke scheme is susceptible to pirate evolution. The amount of susceptibility varies with the difference between the number of generations and t; the pirate evolution bound evo is the highest number of generations any evolving pirate can produce. When evo is much larger than t, this means that an initial leaking incident can be "magnified" and be of a scale much larger than what originally expected.

Formally, we have the following:

Definition 5.1. *Consider the game of figure 5.1 given a probabilistic time adversary $\mathcal{P}$ and two probabilistic algorithms* **Leaking**, **Disable** *and parameters* $n \in \mathbb{N}, \mathsf{R} \subseteq [n],\ t,\ r = |\mathsf{R}|, \sigma$.

Let $PE^{\mathsf{R},\mathbf{Disable}}_{\mathcal{P},\mathbf{Leaking}}(t)$ be the output of the game. We say that the trace and revoke scheme TR *based on a broadcast encryption scheme* (**KeyGen**, **Encrypt**, **Decrypt**) *is immune to pirate evolution with respect to key-leaking incident* **Leaking** *if, for any probabilistic polynomial time adversary $\mathcal{P}$, any* R *and any* $t \in [n-r]$, *there exists* **Disable**$'$ *algorithm that satisfies* $PE^{\mathsf{R},\mathbf{Disable}'}_{\mathcal{P},\mathbf{Leaking}}(t) = t$.

We define the pirate evolution bound $\mathsf{evo}[\mathsf{TR}, \mathbf{Disable}]$ *of a trace and revoke scheme* TR *as the supremum of all* $PE^{\mathsf{R},\mathbf{Disable}}_{\mathcal{P},\mathbf{Leaking}}(t)$, *for any leaking incident*

$\mathcal{L}, \langle sk_1, sk_2, \cdots sk_n \rangle \leftarrow \mathbf{KeyGen}(1^n)$
$\mathsf{T} \leftarrow \mathbf{Leaking}(\mathcal{L}, t, \mathsf{R})$
$\mathbf{MasterBox} \leftarrow \mathcal{P}^{\mathbf{Encrypt}()}(\mathsf{T}, \{sk_u\}_{u \in \mathsf{T}}, \mathsf{R})$
$\ell = 0$; $\psi \in \mathcal{L}$ encodes R to be revoked
repeat $\ell = \ell + 1$
$\quad \mathsf{B}_\ell \leftarrow \mathbf{MasterBox}(1^{t+\log n}, \ell)$
$\quad$ Set $\psi' = \mathbf{Disable}(\psi, \langle \mathsf{B}_1, \ldots, \mathsf{B}_{\ell-1} \rangle, \sigma)$
until $\mathbf{Prob}[\mathsf{B}_\ell(\mathbf{Encrypt}(ek, m, \psi')) = m] < \sigma$ with $m \leftarrow \mathsf{M}$
output ℓ.

Fig. 5.1. The attack game played with an evolving pirate.

Leaking, *any set of revoked users* R *and any evolving pirate* $\mathcal{P}$*; note that* evo[TR, **Disable**] *is a function of* t *and possibly of other parameters as well (such as* n*). A scheme accompanied with* **Disable** *is* susceptible *to pirate evolution if its pirate evolution bound satisfies* evo[TR, **Disable**] $> t$.

Note that immunity against pirate evolution attacks is potentially a stringent property; even though we show that it is attainable (cf. the next section) it could be sacrificed in favor of efficiency. Naturally, using a trace and revoke scheme that is susceptible to pirate evolution with a high pirate evolution bound may put the system's managers at a perilous condition once a leaking incident occurs; and it is worth noting here that current practice has shown that leaking incidents are unavoidable.

We, now prove, in the next section that it is in fact possible to design trace and revoke schemes that are immune to pirate evolution by presenting a simple design that renders any evolving pirate incapable of producing more pirate decoders than traitors. This result (albeit not efficient as a trace and revoke scheme) shows that immunity against pirate evolution is attainable in principle.

5.2 A Trace and Revoke Scheme Immune to Pirate-Evolution

In this section we show a simple trace and revoke design using an exclusive set system that achieves immunity against pirate-evolution. The system simply encrypts the message with the unique key of each user in the system that is not revoked. It is related to the linear length multi-user encryption scheme in chapter 3. Formally it can be expressed as follows:

Definition 5.2. *Consider the set system* Φ_L *that consists of the subsets* $\mathsf{S}_{\mathsf{j}_u} = \{u\}$ *for all* $u \in [n]$*. We define the scheme* $\mathtt{BE}^{\Phi_L}_{\mathtt{basic}}$ *according to the template of Figure 2.2.*

The ciphertext c distributed according to **Encrypt**(ek, m, ψ) contains the encryption of message m with the key L_{j_u}, if it holds that $u \in [n] \setminus \mathsf{R}$ where ψ encodes a revocation instruction that excludes the set R. Observe that this scheme is equivalent to the linear length multi-user encryption scheme we discussed in the previous chapter. Since the set system Φ_L is fully exclusive and $\mathtt{BE}^{\Phi_L}_{\mathtt{basic}}$ matches the template of Figure 2.2, Theorem 4.8 suggests that the "linear length" scheme is a trace and revoke scheme. We next show that it also possesses immunity to pirate evolution.

Theorem 5.3. *The broadcast encryption scheme* $\mathtt{BE}^{\Phi_L}_{\mathtt{basic}}$ *is immune to pirate evolution, i.e. for all polynomial-time adversaries* $\mathcal{P}$ *and for any key leaking incident* **Leaking**, *the* **GenDisable** *algorithm of figure 4.1 satisfies* $PE^{\mathsf{R},\mathbf{GenDisable}}_{\mathcal{P},\mathbf{Leaking}}(t) \leq t$.

Proof of Theorem 5.3: We fix a certain $n \in \mathbb{N}$ and we will prove the claim by induction on the number of traitors, t.

Let the scheme $\mathtt{BE}^{\Phi_L}_{\mathtt{basic}} = (\mathbf{KeyGen}, \mathbf{Encrypt}, \mathbf{Decrypt})$ be the broadcast encryption scheme that matches the template of Figure 2.2 where $\Phi_L = \{\mathsf{S}_{\mathsf{j}_u}\}_{u \in [n]}$ is generated by **KeyGen** as well as $\{k_{\mathsf{j}_u}\}$ are selected randomly and independently.

(i) Base case $t = 1$: This case states that the linear length trace and revoke scheme is secure against any polynomial pirate evolution attack $\mathcal{P}$ with respect to any key leaking incident **Leaking** provided that the number of traitors is 1, i.e. $t = 1$. Let $v \in [n] \setminus \mathsf{R}$ be the traitor index.

First, observe that the ψ that encodes a set R to be revoked contains the subset $\mathsf{S}_{\mathsf{j}_u} = \{u\}$ for any $u \in [n] \setminus \mathsf{R}$. Let the **MasterBox** constructed by $\mathcal{P}$ produce a pirate decoder B_1. Since the only key available to the pirate is k_{j_v}, the broadcast pattern disabling B_1, i.e. **GenDisable**$(\psi, \mathsf{B}_1, \sigma)$, does not contain $\mathsf{S}_{\mathsf{j}_v}$. That is equivalent to saying **GenDisable**$(\psi, \mathsf{B}_1, \sigma)$ encodes the set $\mathsf{R} \cup \{v\}$ to be revoked given the fact that no legitimate user is hurt after tracing. That concludes $PE^{\mathsf{R},\mathbf{GenDisable}}_{\mathcal{P},\mathbf{Leaking}}(1) = 1$ since the security of the broadcast encryption scheme requires the traitor with index v not to recover the message unless the broadcast pattern contains $\mathsf{S}_{\mathsf{j}_v}$.

(ii) Induction hypothesis: The linear length trace and revoke scheme is secure against pirate evolution attacks for all polynomial adversary $\mathcal{P}$ and for any key leaking incident **Leaking** provided that $|\mathsf{T}| = t - 1$. i.e. $PE^{\mathsf{R},\mathbf{GenDisable}}_{\mathcal{P},\mathbf{Leaking}}(t-1) = t - 1$.

(iii) Induction step: Let the number of traitors be t. First, observe that the ψ that encodes the set R to be revoked contains the subset $\mathsf{S}_{\mathsf{j}_u}$ for any $u \in [n] \setminus \mathsf{R}$. Suppose the master box **MasterBox** constructed by $\mathcal{P}$ initially produces a pirate decoder B_1. We next compare the broadcast patterns ψ and $\psi' = \mathbf{GenDisable}(\psi, \mathsf{B}_1, \sigma)$.

The disabling process should not harm any uncorrupted user decrypting the ciphertext, i.e. for any user $\mathsf{j}_u \in [n] \setminus (\mathsf{R} \cup \mathsf{T})$ the subset $\mathsf{S}_{\mathsf{j}_u}$ is among the enabled users in both revocation instructions ψ, ψ'. Now given that all subsets in the collection are are single element sets, it should be the case that $\psi' \setminus \psi = \emptyset$. Further, $\psi \neq \psi'$ and thus $\exists \mathsf{S}_{\mathsf{j}_v} \in \psi$ such that it is missing in ψ'; this suggests that ψ' describes a set for revocation that contains $(\mathsf{R} \cup \{v\})$.

This means that after tracing B_1 the user with index v would be revoked. Using the inductive argument we can state $PE_{\mathcal{P},\mathbf{Leaking}}^{\mathsf{R}\cup\{v\},\mathbf{GenDisable}}(t-1) \leq t-1$. Thus the number of pirate decoders succeeding B_1 will be bounded by $PE_{\mathcal{P},\mathbf{Leaking}}^{\mathsf{R}\cup\{v\},\mathbf{GenDisable}}(t-1)$. The total number of pirate decoders produced by $\mathcal{P}$ with respect to **Leaking** is thus at most t. ■

5.3 Pirate Evolution for the Complete Subtree Method

In this section, we demonstrate that the trace and revoke scheme based on the complete subtree exclusive set system is susceptible to pirate evolution. Specifically, we present an evolving pirate that can produce up to $t \log n/t$ pirate boxes, given t traitor keys. Below we present some definitions that will be used throughout this section. We first recall the specifications of the Complete Subtree method from Section 2.5.1.

An encoding $\mathsf{j} \in \mathcal{J}^{CS}$ is a binary string of length at most $\log n$. Each such encoding corresponds to an index of a node in a full binary tree where the indices are constructed in a top-down manner: the root of the binary tree is encoded by ϵ (the empty string by ϵ), an index of a left child is constructed by appending '0' to its parent index, while an index of a right child is constructed by appending '1' to its parent index. We denote the root of the subtree containing the users in a subset $\mathsf{S} \in \Phi_{\mathcal{J}}$ by $\mathsf{root}(\mathsf{S})$; occasionally we may say j as opposed to $\mathsf{root}(\mathsf{S_j})$ where j is a valid encoding in $\mathcal{J}^{CS}$. We generalize the definition for the Steiner tree of Section 2.5.1 as follows: $\mathsf{Steiner}(\mathsf{T},\mathsf{S})$ is the minimal subtree of the binary tree rooted at $\mathsf{root}(\mathsf{S})$ that connects all leaves on which the users in $\mathsf{T} \cap \mathsf{S}$ are placed.

We illustrate the complete subtree over 32 users in Figure 5.2. In this figure, we picture the set of revoked users R (the black leaves) and the set of traitors $\mathsf{T} = \{T_1, T_2, T_3, T_4\}$ (the squared leaves). The gray nodes correspond to the subsets in the broadcast pattern that results by $\mathsf{Steiner}(\mathsf{R}, [n])$, or equivalently $\mathbf{Revoke}(\Phi_{CS}, \mathsf{R})$ where the algorithm **Revoke** of the set system Φ_{CS} outputs a revocation instruction that encodes the set R.

We, next, propose an evolving pirate for the Complete Subtree. First we consider the following type of pirate decoder:

Definition 5.4. *Consider a pirate decoder that uses the key associated to* $\mathsf{S_j}$ *for which* $\mathsf{root}(\mathsf{S_j}) = \mathsf{j}$ *holds. The pirate decoder denoted by* $\mathsf{CSBox_j}$, *is constructed in such a way that satisfies* $\mathsf{CSBox_j}(\mathbf{Encrypt}(ek, m, \psi)) = m$ *if and only if* $\mathsf{S_j} \in \psi$.

The description of the evolving pirate relies on a simple observation that is the following lemma:

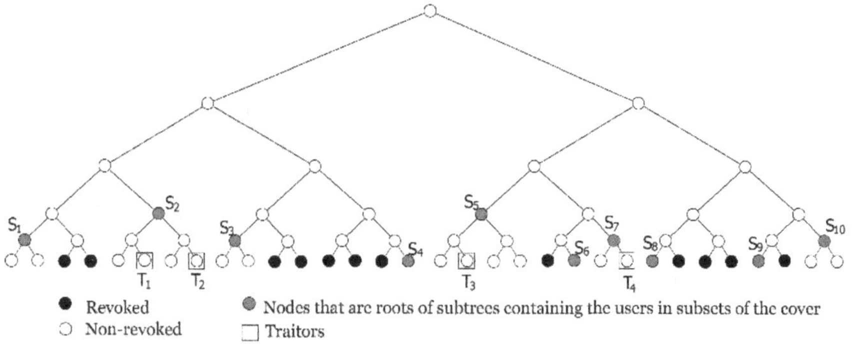

Fig. 5.2. Complete subtree method example with set cover and a set of traitors.

Lemma 5.5. *Consider an adversary using the pirate box* $\mathsf{CSBox_j}$. *Suppose* $\mathsf{S_j} = \mathsf{S_{j_l}} \cup \mathsf{S_{j_r}}$ *where the node* j_l *(resp.* j_r*) is left (resp. right) child of the node with index* j. *If* $\mathsf{S_j} \in \psi$ *then it holds that* $\mathsf{S_{j_l}} \in \mathbf{Revocation}(\psi, \mathsf{CSBox_j}, \sigma)$ *and* $\mathsf{S_{j_r}} \in \mathbf{Revocation}(\psi, \mathsf{CSBox_j}, \sigma)$ *for any* $0 < \sigma \leq 1$.

Proof of Lemma 5.5: Suppose that $\mathsf{S_j} \in \psi$. The ciphertext $\mathbf{Encrypt}(ek, \cdot, \psi)$ contains the encryption of the message by using the key associated to $\mathsf{S_j}$. The pirate box $\mathsf{B} = \mathsf{CSBox(j)}$ then, by definition, decrypts $\mathbf{Encrypt}(ek, \cdot, \psi)$ with probability meeting the threshold σ. The revocation procedure in Figure 4.2 against the box B will identify the subset $\mathsf{S_j}$ as the subset containing the traitor. The tracing algorithm will partition $\mathsf{S_j}$ into two equally-sized subsets $\mathsf{S_{j_l}}$ and $\mathsf{S_{j_r}}$ as it is the case that the split algorithm $\mathbf{spt}(\mathsf{S_j})$ of the Complete Subtree returns the children of the node corresponding to the encoding j.

The pirate box B will not be able to decrypt with the given partition $\psi' = (\psi \setminus \{\mathsf{S_j}\}) \cup \{\mathsf{S_{j_l}}, \mathsf{S_{j_r}}\}$. As a result the outcome of the winnable revocation game will be ψ' as the broadcast pattern against the pirate decoder B, i.e. $\mathbf{Revocation}(\psi, \mathsf{CSBox_j}, \sigma) = \psi'$. ■

Consider an adversary who has access to the key material sk_u for which $u \in \mathsf{S_j}$ holds. Suppose that this adversary constructs the pirate decoder $\mathsf{CSBox_j}$ and uses for illegal reception of the tranmissions. The adversary will be able to produce a new version of pirate box even though the pirate decoder $\mathsf{CSBox_j}$ is caught and disabled by the tracer. That is true due to the above lemma because the revocation instruction ψ' that disables the decoder $\mathsf{CSBox_j}$ still includes a subset that contains the traitor. Indeed, the traitor with index u is either in $\mathsf{S_{j_l}}$ or $\mathsf{S_{j_r}}$, and the pirate still will be able to produce a new box by using the key associated to $\mathsf{S_{j_l}}$(or $\mathsf{S_{j_r}}$ depends on which one contains u). The evolving pirate will be exploiting the above observation to successively generate pirate boxes.

We define the master pirate box **MasterBox** produced by the adversary $\mathcal{P}^{\mathbf{Encrypt}}(\mathsf{T}, \{sk_u\}_{u \in \mathsf{T}})$ as producing a vector of pirate boxes. **MasterBox** constructs the sequence of pirate boxes by walking on the nodes of the forest of Steiner trees $\{\mathsf{Steiner}(\mathsf{T},\mathsf{S}) \mid \mathsf{S} \in \psi\}$. More specifically, it recursively runs a procedure called `makeboxes` on each $\mathsf{Tree}_\mathsf{S} = \mathsf{Steiner}(\mathsf{T},\mathsf{S})$ which first creates a pirate box `Box` by using the unique key assigned to the node $\mathsf{root}(\mathsf{Tree}_\mathsf{S})$. It then splits the Tree_S into two trees. The splitting is needed because tracing `Box` will result in the partition of the subset S. Thus the splitting procedure is based on the partition of subset S into two equal subsets (recall that in `CS`, tracing works by splitting into the two subtrees rooted at the children of $\mathsf{root}(\mathsf{Tree}_\mathsf{S})$). The master box **MasterBox** then runs `makeboxes` independently on both of the trees resulting from the partition. Figure 5.3 is the summary of the evolving pirate strategy. The number of generations that can be produced equals the number of nodes in the forest of Steiner trees $\{\mathsf{Steiner}(\mathsf{T},\mathsf{S}) \mid \mathsf{S} \in \psi\}$.

1. For each $\mathsf{S} \in \psi$ run **makeboxes**($\mathsf{Steiner}(\mathsf{T},\mathsf{S})$) till the ℓ-th box is produced.
makeboxes(Tree)
1. Take any user u placed on a leaf of Tree
2. Retrieve the encoding j for the node of the Complete Subtree that corresponds to root(Tree).
3. Output $\mathsf{CSBox}_\mathsf{j}$ as the key for S_j is available to the pirate through sk_u
4. Let Tree_L and Tree_R be respectively the left and right subtrees of Tree.
5. run **makeboxes**(Tree_L)
6. run **makeboxes**(Tree_R)

Fig. 5.3. The master box program $\mathbf{MasterBox}(1^{t+\log n}, \ell)$ parameterized by ψ, T, sk_u for $u \in \mathsf{T}$ that is produced by the evolving pirate for the complete subtree method.

In figure 5.4, we illustrate the generations of pirate boxes for the set of traitors in the Figure 5.2. Each key assigned to a node in the forest of the trees is used to construct a pirate box. The order that the pirate boxes are released is actually the order of their construction (that is walking from top to bottom).

Theorem 5.6 is deals with the correctness of the above procedure, i.e. the next generation should be able to decrypt the message encrypted after tracing has disabled all previous boxes. This will be shown against the **GenDisable** algorithm of figure 4.1.

Theorem 5.6. *Consider the revocation instruction* $\psi = \mathbf{Revoke}(\Phi^{CS}, \mathsf{R})$ *that encodes the set* R *where* **Revoke** *is the algorithm described in Figure 2.9. Let* $0 < \sigma \leq 1$ *and* $\mathsf{B}_1, \mathsf{B}_2, \cdots, \mathsf{B}_{v+1}$ *be a sequence of pirate boxes constructed by the evolving pirate strategy described in Figure 5.3 parameterized by* ψ *and* T*. Suppose* $\psi' = \mathbf{GenDisable}(\psi, \langle \mathsf{B}_1, \ldots, \mathsf{B}_v \rangle, \sigma)$*, then it holds that*

$$\mathbf{Prob}[\mathsf{B}_{v+1}(\mathbf{Encrypt}(ek, m, \psi')) = m] \geq \sigma$$

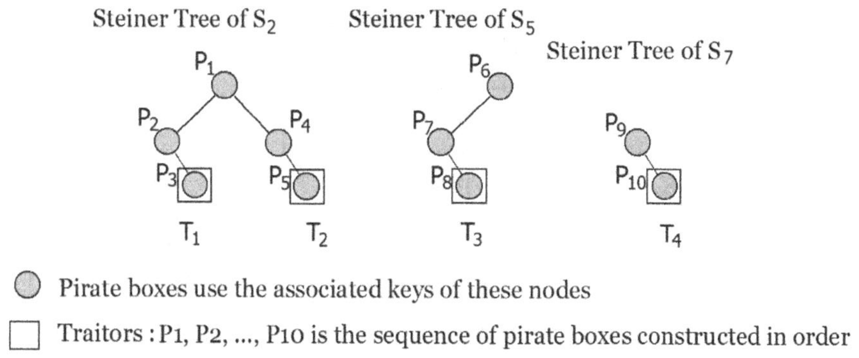

Fig. 5.4. Steiner Trees of the traitors and generation of pirate boxes (cf. figure 5.2)

provided that v is less than the number of nodes in the forest of trees $\{\mathsf{Steiner}(\mathsf{T},\mathsf{S}) \mid \mathsf{S} \in \psi\}$.

Proof of Theorem 5.6: Suppose that the pirate box B_{v+1} uses the key associated to some node j, i.e. $\mathsf{B}_{v+1} = \mathsf{CSBox}_\mathsf{j}$ holds. Due to the evolution strategy of the pirate in Figure 5.3 such node exists iff $v+1$ is less than or equal to the number of nodes in the forest of trees $\{\mathsf{Steiner}(\mathsf{T},\mathsf{S}) \mid \mathsf{S} \in \psi\}$. If it exists, then there are two cases possible on node j: j is an encoding of either (1) an internal node or leaf, or (2) a root of one of the trees in the forest $\{\mathsf{Steiner}(\mathsf{T},\mathsf{S}) \mid \mathsf{S} \in \psi\}$.

(1) Suppose j is an encoding of an internal node of $\mathsf{Steiner}(\mathsf{T},\mathsf{S})$ for some $\mathsf{S} \in \psi$. In this case, there exists a $\mathsf{B}_i = \mathsf{CSBox}_{\mathsf{j}_0}, i \le v$ such that $\mathsf{root}(\mathsf{Steiner}(\mathsf{T},\mathsf{S})) = \mathsf{root}(\mathsf{S}) = \mathsf{j}_0$ (this is obvious from the way that the evolving pirate operates). Due to the evolution strategy of Figure 5.3, we can associate the box B_k, for $i \le k \le v+1$, with a subset $\mathsf{S}_{\mathsf{j}'}$ for which $\mathsf{root}(\mathsf{S}_{\mathsf{j}'})$ is an internal node in the Steiner tree $\mathsf{Steiner}(\mathsf{T},\mathsf{S}_{\mathsf{j}_0})$. Furthermore, there exists a subsequence of pirate boxes $\mathsf{B}_i = \mathsf{B}_{i_0}, \mathsf{B}_{i_1}, \mathsf{B}_{i_2}, \cdots, \mathsf{B}_{i_s} = \mathsf{B}_{v+1}$ such that $\mathsf{root}(\mathsf{S}_{\mathsf{j}_k})$ is parent of $\mathsf{root}(\mathsf{S}_{\mathsf{j}_{k+1}})$ where we have $\mathsf{B}_{i_k} = \mathsf{CSBox}_{\mathsf{j}_k}$ for $k = 0, 1, \ldots, s-1$.

Since $\mathsf{S}_{\mathsf{j}_0} \in \psi$ ($\mathsf{S}_{\mathsf{j}_0}$ is one of the subsets forming a Steiner tree), we claim that $\mathsf{S}_{\mathsf{j}_k} \in$ **GenDisable**$(\psi, \langle \mathsf{B}_{i_0}, \mathsf{B}_{i_1}, \mathsf{B}_{i_2}, \cdots \mathsf{B}_{i_{k-1}} \rangle, \sigma)$, for $1 \le k \le s$ (*Claim 1*).

Proof of Claim 1: We will prove by induction:

(i) Base case with $k = 1$: Recall that $\mathsf{root}(\mathsf{S}_{\mathsf{j}_1})$ is a child of $\mathsf{root}(\mathsf{S}_{\mathsf{j}_0})$ and $\mathsf{B}_{i_0} = \mathsf{CSBox}_{\mathsf{j}_0}$. First, the Lemma 5.5 implies that $\mathsf{S}_{\mathsf{j}_1} \in$ **Revocation**$(\psi, \mathsf{B}_{i_0}, \sigma)$. Observe also that the **GenDisable** invokes the **Revocation** algorithm only once, hence we obtain $\mathsf{S}_{\mathsf{j}_1} \in$ **GenDisable**$(\psi, \mathsf{B}_{i_0}, \sigma)$ which completes the proof for base case.

(ii) Induction assumption: $\mathsf{S}_{\mathsf{j}_k} \in$ **GenDisable**$(\psi, \langle \mathsf{B}_i, \mathsf{B}_{i_1}, \mathsf{B}_{i_2}, \cdots \mathsf{B}_{i_{k-1}} \rangle, \sigma)$, for $1 \le k < s$.

(iii) Induction step: Let $\psi_k = \textbf{GenDisable}(\psi, \langle \mathsf{B}_i, \mathsf{B}_{i_1}, \mathsf{B}_{i_2}, \cdots \mathsf{B}_{i_{k-1}} \rangle, \sigma)$ be the the revocation instruction containing the subset $\mathsf{S}_{\mathsf{j}_k}$ as given in the induction assumption. The pirate box $\mathsf{B}_{i_k} = \mathsf{CSBox}_{\mathsf{j}_k}$ is capable of decrypting ciphertexts distributed according to $\textbf{Encrypt}(ek, \cdot, \psi_k)$ with probability greater than the threshold σ. The revocation algorithm of Figure 4.2 against the pirate box B_{i_k} with respect to ψ_k will output $\mathsf{S}_{\mathsf{j}_k}$ as the subset containing the traitor. The algorithm will then partition $\mathsf{S}_{\mathsf{j}_k}$ into two equally-sized subsets where one of it is $\mathsf{S}_{\mathsf{j}_{k+1}}$. The decoder B_{i_k} will no more be able to decrypt the encryption due to the partition in $\textbf{Revocation}(\psi_k, \mathsf{B}_{i_k}, \sigma)$. Hence, the final outcome partition that disables all boxes will satisfy following: $\mathsf{S}_{\mathsf{j}_{k+1}} \in \textbf{GenDisable}(\psi, \langle \mathsf{B}_i, \mathsf{B}_{i_1}, \mathsf{B}_{i_2}, \cdots \mathsf{B}_{i_k} \rangle, \sigma)$ as the statement of induction step.

Using the claim we now conclude that

$$S_{\mathsf{j}_s} \in \textbf{GenDisable}(\psi, \langle \mathsf{B}_i, \mathsf{B}_{i_1}, \mathsf{B}_{i_2}, \cdots \mathsf{B}_{i_{s-1}} \rangle, \sigma)$$

Given that $S_{\mathsf{j}} = \mathsf{S}_{\mathsf{j}_s}$ we have that the box B_{v+1} will be able to decrypt such revocation instructions.

Claim 2: We next claim that revoking all the other boxes in the sequence of $\{\mathsf{B}_1, \cdots \mathsf{B}_v\} \setminus \{\mathsf{B}_i, \mathsf{B}_{i_1}, \mathsf{B}_{i_2}, \cdots \mathsf{B}_{i_{s-1}}\}$ will not hurt the capability of B_{v+1} to decrypt. This would be the case as long as revoking those boxes will not result in splitting the subset S_j. The proof of claim follows easily by the fact that revoking any of those boxes does not affect S_j since each one corresponds to a subset key disjoint from S_j.

We conclude, as a consequence of the above,

$$\mathsf{S}_{\mathsf{j}_s} = \mathsf{S}_\mathsf{j} \in \textbf{GenDisable}(\psi, \langle \mathsf{B}_1, \mathsf{B}_2, \cdots \mathsf{B}_v \rangle, \sigma) = \psi'$$

Recall that $\mathsf{B}_{i_s} = \mathsf{B}_{v+1} = \mathsf{CSBox}_\mathsf{j}$, we finally obtain

$$\textbf{Prob}[\mathsf{B}_{v+1}(\textbf{Encrypt}(ek, m, \psi')) = m] \geq \sigma$$

(2) Suppose that j is an encoding of $\mathsf{root}(\mathsf{S})$ that is a root of one of the trees in the forest $\{\mathsf{Steiner}(\mathsf{T}, \mathsf{S}) \mid \mathsf{S} \in \psi\}$, i.e. it holds that $\mathsf{S} \in \psi$. Because all the Steiner trees are disjoint, with a similar argument as claim 2 before, $\mathsf{S} \in \textbf{GenDisable}(\psi, \langle \mathsf{B}_1, \mathsf{B}_2, \cdots \mathsf{B}_v \rangle, \sigma)$ since S was never split while tracing all previous boxes. From the definition of B_{v+1}, we can conclude

$$\textbf{Prob}[\mathsf{B}_{v+1}(\textbf{Encrypt}(ek, m, \psi')) = m] \geq \sigma$$

where $\psi' = \textbf{GenDisable}(\psi, \langle \mathsf{B}_1, \mathsf{B}_2, \cdots \mathsf{B}_v \rangle, \sigma)$. ■

We next study the classes of leaking incidents and the number of boxes they produce. For the polynomial time adversary $\mathcal{P}$ described in Figure 5.3, $PE^{\mathsf{R},\textbf{GenDisable}}_{\mathcal{P},\textbf{Leaking}}(t)$ is the number of nodes in the forest of the Steiner trees of the traitors. Theorem 5.7 and Theorem 5.8 give some bounds on this quantity for different leaking incidents.

Theorem 5.7. *Let $n \in \mathbb{N}$ be the number of receivers. For a given $\mathsf{R} \subseteq [n]$, any leaking incident* **Leaking** *corrupting t users in a single subset $\mathsf{S} \in$* **Revoke**$(\Phi_{CS}, \mathsf{R}) = \psi$ *enables an evolving pirate with respect to* **Leaking** *so that $PE^{\mathsf{R},\mathbf{GenDisable}}_{\mathcal{P},\mathbf{Leaking}}(t) \geq 2t - 2 + \log(|\mathsf{S}|/t)$.*

Proof of Theorem 5.7: We will count the number of nodes in the Steiner tree $\mathsf{Steiner}(\mathsf{T}, \mathsf{S})$ as it is the number of decoders $\mathcal{P}$ can construct with respect to any leaking incident **Leaking** corrupting t users in S. Denoting the number of nodes with depth i by $c_i \geq 1$ we have $PE^{\mathsf{R},\mathbf{GenDisable}}_{\mathcal{P},\mathbf{Leaking}}(t) = \sum_{i=0}^{\log|\mathsf{S}|} c_i$. It is clear that $c_i \geq \lceil c_{i+1}/2 \rceil$ and $c_{\log|\mathsf{S}|} = t$. Then it holds that $c_i \geq \lceil c_{\log|\mathsf{S}|}/2^{\log|\mathsf{S}|-i} \rceil = \lceil t/2^{\log|\mathsf{S}|-i} \rceil$, hence:

$$\sum_{i=0}^{\log|\mathsf{S}|} c_i \geq \sum_{i=0}^{\log|\mathsf{S}|} \lceil t/2^{\log|\mathsf{S}|-i} \rceil$$

Since $1 \geq \frac{t}{2^{\lceil \log t \rceil}}$ it holds that $\lceil t/2^{\log|\mathsf{S}|-i} \rceil = 1$ for all $0 \leq i \leq \log|\mathsf{S}| - \lceil \log t \rceil$.

$$PE^{\mathsf{R},\mathbf{GenDisable}}_{\mathcal{P},\mathbf{Leaking}}(t) = \sum_{i=0}^{\log|\mathsf{S}|} c_i \geq \sum_{i=\log|\mathsf{S}|-\lceil \log(t) \rceil}^{\log|\mathsf{S}|} \lceil t/2^{\log|\mathsf{S}|-i} \rceil + \sum_{i=0}^{\log|\mathsf{S}|-\lceil \log(t) \rceil - 1} 1$$

This yields the following:

$$\begin{aligned} PE^{\mathsf{R},\mathbf{GenDisable}}_{\mathcal{P},\mathbf{Leaking}}(t) &\geq t \cdot \textstyle\sum_{i=0}^{\lceil \log t \rceil} 1/2^i + \sum_{i=0}^{\log|\mathsf{S}|-\lceil \log(t) \rceil - 1} 1 \\ &\geq t \cdot (2 - 1/2^{\lceil \log t \rceil}) + \log(|\mathsf{S}|/t) - 1 \\ &\geq 2t - 2 + \log(|\mathsf{S}|/t) \end{aligned}$$

which completes the proof of the theorem. ∎

Theorem 5.8. *Let $n \in \mathbb{N}$ be the number of receivers. For a given $\mathsf{R} \subseteq [n]$, there exists a leaking incident* **Leaking** *corrupting t users in a single subset $\mathsf{S} \in$* **Revoke**$(\Phi_{CS}, \mathsf{R}) = \psi$ *so that $PE^{\mathsf{R},\mathbf{GenDisable}}_{\mathcal{P},\mathbf{Leaking}}(t) \geq t - 1 + t\log(|\mathsf{S}|/t)$.*

Proof of Theorem 5.8: It is sufficient to describe a leaking incident **Leaking** that satisfies $PE^{\mathsf{R},\mathbf{GenDisable}}_{\mathcal{P},\mathbf{Leaking}}(t) \geq 2t - 1 + t\log(|\mathsf{S}|/t)$. Consider the nodes of the Steiner tree $\mathsf{Steiner}(\mathsf{T}, \mathsf{S})$ and denote the number of nodes with depth i by c_i. We choose the leaking incident as follows: (1) any node of depth $\leq \lfloor \log t \rfloor$ is an ancestor of at least one traitor, (2) for any depth $> \lfloor \log t \rfloor$ there exist t nodes at this depth that are ancestors of a traitor. These conditions are equivalent to saying $c_i = 2^i$ for all $0 \leq i \leq \lfloor \log t \rfloor$, and $c_i = t$ otherwise. Such case can be easily constructed as the Figure 5.5 illustrates. The sum $\sum_{\log|\mathsf{S}|}^{i=0} c_i$ will give us the number of pirate decoder generations with respect to the given leaking incident:

$$PE^{\mathsf{R},\mathbf{GenDisable}}_{\mathcal{P},\mathbf{Leaking}}(t) = \sum_{\log|\mathsf{S}|}^{i=0} c_i \geq \sum_{i=0}^{\lfloor \log(t) \rfloor} 2^i + \sum_{i=\lfloor \log t \rfloor+1}^{\log|\mathsf{S}|} t$$

Arranging the sum will yield us the following statement:

$$PE^{\mathsf{R},\mathbf{GenDisable}}_{\mathcal{P},\mathbf{Leaking}}(t) \geq t - 1 + t\log(|\mathsf{S}|/t)$$

This completes the proof of the theorem. ■

We remark that if $\log t$ is an integer, then the sum will belower bounded by $2t - 1 + t\log(|\mathsf{S}|/t)$.

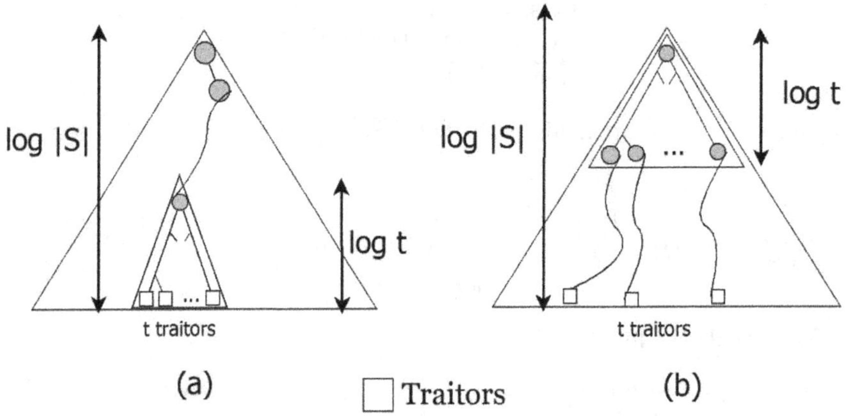

Fig. 5.5. Two leaking incidents with different pirate evolution potentials.

Figure 5.5 shows the cases where it is possible to achieve the bounds given in above two theorems. Figure 5.5(a) is yielding the bound in Theorem 3 and, Figure 5.5(b) is yielding the bound in Theorem 4. The maximum number of pirate generations can be achieved following the strategy in Figure 5.5(b) in a configuration of the system when there is no revoked user; in this case there is a single element in the partition, namely S containing n users. It follows that the pirate can produce up to $t\log(n/t)$ generations and thus:

Corollary 5.9. *The pirate evolution bound for the* CS *method satisfies*

$$\mathsf{evo}[\mathtt{CS}, \mathbf{GenDisable}] \geq t\log(n/t)$$

5.4 Pirate Evolution for the Subset Difference Method

In this section we turn our attention to the Subset Difference (SD) method (see Section 2.5.2). Compared to the Complete Subtree method, the subsets in the

SD method are represented by pairs of nodes. We, first, recall the structural definitions for the Subset Difference Method.

The receiver population corresponds to the set $[n]$ and can be thought to be placed on the leaves of a full binary tree. We define an index for each node in the binary tree in a top-down manner similar indexing as in the Complete Subtree method: the root of the binary tree is encoded by ϵ (the empty string), an index of a left child is constructed by appending '0' to its parent's index while an index of a right child is constructed by appending '1' to its parent's index. An encoding $\mathsf{j} \in \mathcal{J}^{SD}$ is a pair of strings (x, z) where the concatenated string xz has a length at most $\log n$ with the length of z is at least 1. Denoting the node corresponding to the string y by v_y for any $y \in \{0,1\}^i$ such that $0 \leq i \leq \log n$, we let $\mathsf{S_j}$ to be the set of users/leaves in the subtree rooted at v_x but not of v_{xz} where $\mathsf{j} = (x, z)$.

We next define the function

$$\mathsf{users} : \{(v_x, v_y) \mid x, y \in \{0,1\}^* \; s.t. \; |x|, |y| \leq \log n\} \to 2^{[n]}$$

such that $\mathsf{users}(v_x, v_y) = \mathsf{S}_{(x,z)}$ if there exists a string z that satisfies $y = xz$ and $|z| \geq 1$ otherwise $\mathsf{users}(v_x, v_y)$ returns emptyset. Observe that the inverse function $\mathsf{users}^{-1}(\mathsf{S_j})$, for $\mathsf{j} \in \mathcal{J}^{SD}$, returns the pair of nodes encoded by j. Since $\mathsf{S_j}$ is somehow related to a tree, we still use $\mathsf{root}(\mathsf{S_j})$ to output v_x provided that $\mathsf{j} = (x, z)$. We finally, enhance the definition of Steiner tree as follows: we say the Steiner tree $\mathsf{Steiner}(\mathsf{T}, v_x, v_y)$ is the minimal subtree of the binary tree rooted at v_x, excluding the descendants of v_y, that connects all the leaves in $\mathsf{T} \cap \mathsf{users}(v_x, v_y)$ as well as node v_y.

We illustrate the Subset Difference over 32 users in Figure 5.6. In this figure, we picture the set of revoked users R (the black leaves) and the set of traitors $\mathsf{T} = \{T_1, T_2, T_3, T_4\}$ (the squared leaves). The pair of nodes, connected with an edge, correspond to the subsets in the broadcast pattern that is resulted by $\mathsf{Steiner}(\mathsf{R}, [n])$, which equals to **Revoke**(Φ_{SD}, R) where the algorithm **Revoke** of the set system Φ_{SD} outputs the revocation instruction that encodes the set R.

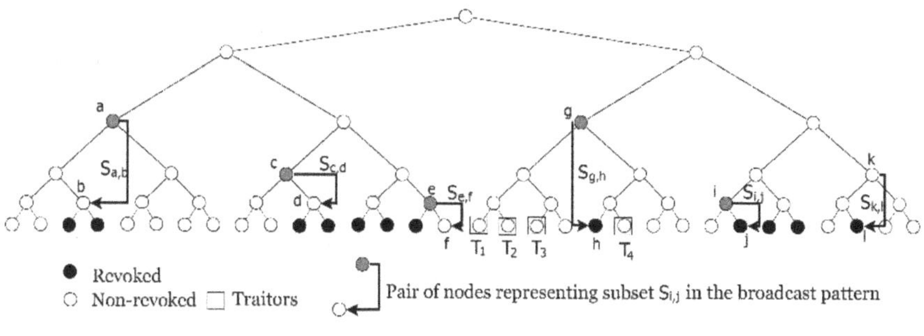

Fig. 5.6. Subset difference method example with set cover and a set of traitors.

We, next, propose an evolving pirate for the Subset Difference. First we consider the following type of pirate decoder:

Definition 5.10. *Consider a pirate decoder that uses the key associated to* $\mathsf{S_j}$ *for which* $\mathsf{users}(v_x, v_y) = \mathsf{S_j}$ *holds. Denoting the pirate box by* $\mathsf{SDBox_j}$*, it is constructed in such a way that satisfies* $\mathsf{SDBox_j}(\mathbf{Encrypt}(ek, m, \psi)) = m$ *if and only if* $\mathsf{S_j} \in \psi$*. We further use the notation* $\mathsf{SDBox_{j,u}}$ *or* $\mathsf{SDBox}(\mathsf{j}, u)$*, for* $u \in \mathsf{S_j}$*, to associate the box with a receiver index* $u \in [n]$ *whose private key* sk_u *is used in construction of the box.*

The susceptibility of the SD method to pirate evolution relies on the following simple observation regarding the revocation algorithm and the way it operates on a given pirate box:

Lemma 5.11. *Consider an adversary using the pirate box* $\mathsf{SDBox_j}$*. Let* $\mathsf{S_j} = \mathsf{users}(v_x, v_y)$ *and suppose* v_c *is the child of* v_x *that is on the path from* v_x *to* v_y*. If* $\mathsf{S_j} \in \psi$ *then it holds that* $\mathsf{users}(v_x, v_c) \in \mathbf{Revocation}(\psi, \mathsf{SDBox_j}, \sigma)$ *and* $\mathsf{users}(v_c, v_y) \in \mathbf{Revocation}(\psi, \mathsf{SDBox_j}, \sigma)$ *for any* $0 < \sigma \leq 1$.

Proof of Lemma 5.11: Suppose that $\mathsf{S_j} = \mathsf{users}(v_x, v_y) \in \psi$. The ciphertext $\mathbf{Encrypt}(ek, \cdot, \psi)$ then contains the encryption of the message by using the key associated to the $\mathsf{S_j}$ such that $\mathsf{j} = (x, z)$. The pirate box $\mathsf{B} = \mathsf{SDBox_j}$ then, by definition, decrypts $\mathbf{Encrypt}(ek, \cdot, \psi)$ with probability at least the threshold σ. Due to the revocation procedure of Figure 4.2 against the box B will identify the subset $\mathsf{users}(v_x, v_y)$ as the subset containing the traitor. The revocation procedure will then partition $\mathsf{users}(v_x, v_y)$ into two roughly equally-sized subsets $\mathsf{users}(v_x, v_c)$ *and* $\mathsf{users}(v_c, v_y)$ as it is the case that the split algorithm $\mathbf{spt}(\mathsf{S_j})$ of the Subset Difference (see Figure 2.13) returns the above pair where v_c is the child of v_x that is on the path from v_x to v_y.

The pirate box B will not be able to decrypt with the given partition $\psi' = (\psi - \{\mathsf{users}(v_x, v_y)\}) \cup \{\mathsf{users}(v_x, v_c), \mathsf{users}(v_c, v_y)\}$. As a result the outcome of the winnable revocation game will be ψ' as the broadcast pattern against the pirate decoder B, i.e. $\mathbf{Revocation}(\psi, \mathsf{SDBox_j}, \sigma) = \psi'$. This completes the proof of the statement. ∎

We will exploit the above lemma to successively generate pirate boxes. This is possible because after tracing $\mathsf{B} = \mathsf{SDBox_{j,u}}$, the traitor u is still in one of the subsets in the partition $\mathbf{Revocation}(\psi, \mathsf{B}, \sigma)$. Hence, we can design a similar evolving strategy given in Figure 5.3 with respect to the **GenDisable** algorithm that can be analyzed similarly. A different disabling algorithm for the subset difference is also known that utilizes a merging operation that compacts a broadcast pattern. We will focus on attacking this disabling algorithm here.

In fact as we will see, the merging of subsets that is suggested as a mechanism to improve the performance for the Subset Difference method turns out to be an opportunity for pirate evolution as it leads to the reuse of some nodes in different pairs, i.e. different subsets in the collection $\{\mathsf{S_j}\}_{\mathsf{j} \in \mathcal{J}}$.

To understand the way merging can be applied in the context of the subset difference method consider the following simple lemma.

Lemma 5.12. *Let* $v_x, v_{c_1}, v_{c_2}, \cdots v_{c_d}, v_y$ *be any sequence of vertices which occur in this order along some root-to-leaf path in the tree corresponding to the subset* $\mathsf{users}(v_x, v_y)$. *Then* $\mathsf{users}(v_x, v_y) = \mathsf{users}(v_x, v_{c_1}) \cup \mathsf{users}(v_{c_1}, v_{c_2}) \cup \cdots \cup \mathsf{users}(v_{c_1}, v_y)$.

Proof of Lemma 5.12: $\mathsf{users}(u, v)$ is defined as a set difference $A \setminus B$ and $\mathsf{users}(v, z)$ is defined as a set difference $B \setminus C$ for some sets of leaves that satisfy $C \subseteq B \subseteq A$. The sets are clearly disjoint, and their union is $A \setminus C$ which is the definition of $\mathsf{users}(u, z)$. Using that simple observation, one could say $\mathsf{users}(v_x, v_y) = A \setminus B$, $\mathsf{users}(v_x, v_{c_1}) = A \setminus A_1$, $\mathsf{users}(v_{c_k}, v_{c_{k+1}}) = A_k \setminus A_{k+1}$, *for* $0 < k < d$, and $\mathsf{users}(v_{c_d}, v_y) = A_d \setminus B$ such that $B \subseteq A_d \subseteq A_{d-1} \subseteq \cdots \subseteq A_1 \subseteq A$. Thus, the telescoping formula for set differences yields the desired result. ∎

Using the above, whenever the partition contains a series of subsets $\{\mathsf{users}(v_x, v_1), \mathsf{users}(v_{c_1}, v_{c_2}), \cdots, \mathsf{users}(v_{c_d}, v_y)\}$ they can potentially be merged using Lemma 5.12 into one single subset $\mathsf{users}(v_x, v_y)$. We denote the disabling algorithm, that employs a compaction algorithm to merge subsets if possible on top of **GenDisable**, by **SDDisable**. Some care is needed : in general, merging will occur whenever it is allowed based on lemma 5.12 with the following exception: S_{j_1} will not be merged if the partition contains another subset S_{j_2} such that they have resulted from a split of a single subset at an earlier iteration of the **Revocation** procedure (without this restriction the **Revocation** procedure may enter an infinite loop). More explicitly we present the algorithm in figure 5.7.

SDDisable(pattern ψ, pirate box B, σ)
repeat
  if **Prob**[B(**Encrypt**$(ek, m, \psi)) = m] < \sigma$ then break
  ψ' = **Revocation**$(\psi, \mathsf{B}, \sigma)$
  Construct new ψ by merging all subsets of ψ'
   that belong to $\psi \cap \psi'$ using lemma 5.12.
until break
output ψ /* ψ is a pattern that disables B */

Fig. 5.7. The algorithm that disables a pirate decoder applying the improvement of lemma 5.12 to the **GenDisable** algorithm of figure 4.1.

We now present an evolving pirate strategy based on the forest of Steiner trees $\{\mathsf{Steiner}(\mathsf{T}, v_x, v_y) \mid \mathsf{users}(v_x, v_y) \in \psi\}$ by walking on the paths of Steiner trees that will be predefined according to a scheduling of traitors. Unlike our evolving pirate strategy for the **GenDisable** algorithm, we are focusing on paths instead of nodes because of the inherent structure of the SD method and the way **SDDisable** works by merging subsets under the condition shown in lemma 5.12. To illustrate how evolution for SD method works, let us focus on the subset rooted at g of the Figure 5.6 that is magnified in Figure 5.8(a) and start creating pirate boxes. In this figure, the nodes are denoted by natural numbers in an arbitrary fashion for clarity of presentation (rather than using the strings that correspond to the nodes).

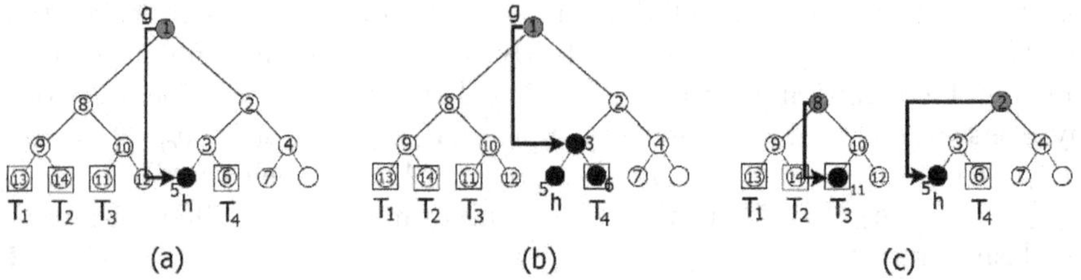

Fig. 5.8. Two different courses for pirate evolution starting from (a): in (b) T_4 is used; in (c) T_3 is used.

Suppose that the evolving pirate uses the keys of the traitor T_4 first; the sequence of pirate boxes created until T_4 is entirely revoked would be $\mathsf{B}_1 = \mathsf{SDBox}(1,5,T_4), \mathsf{B}_2 = \mathsf{SDBox}(2,5,T_4)$ and $\mathsf{B}_3 = \mathsf{SDBox}(3,5,T_4)$. Due to lemma 5.11 tracing all these boxes would end up with revoking T_4 and **GenDisable**$(\psi, \langle \mathsf{B}_1, \mathsf{B}_2, \mathsf{B}_3\rangle, \sigma) = \{\mathsf{users}(1,2), \mathsf{users}(2,3)\}$. Note that in light of lemma 5.12 the tracing algorithm will merge these two subsets to have the single subset $\mathsf{users}(1,3)$ shown in Figure 5.8(b). This reveals the possibility that an evolving pirate against the SD method may use the keys of a traitor as many times as the height of the subset it belongs to *without* necessarily restricting the same opportunity for other traitors that are scheduled to be used later. Indeed, we can execute a pirate box construction using the keys of traitor T_3 that would be as many as the height of the tree (the reader can compare this to the Complete Subtree method where this is not achievable and using the keys of one traitor strips the opportunity to use some of the keys of other traitors scheduled later). Proceeding with our example, the master pirate box **MasterBox** will now be able to create a pirate box $\mathsf{SDBox}(1,3,T_3)$ (recall that **SDDisable**$(\psi, \langle \mathsf{B}_1, \mathsf{B}_2, \mathsf{B}_3\rangle, \sigma) = \{\mathsf{users}(1,3)\}$) followed by another box $\mathsf{SDBox}(1,2,T_3)$ and so on until T_3 is entirely revoked. Even though we have the opportunity now to make more boxes per traitor compared to the complete subset method, special care is needed to choose the order with which we are expending the traitor keys as we will illustrate below. This is in sharp contrast to the complete subset method where the scheduling of traitors makes no difference in terms of the number of pirate box generations that the master box can spawn.

To see the importance of scheduling the traitors appropriately, suppose that we use the traitor T_3 first instead of T_4; then, the sequence of pirate boxes created until T_3 is entirely revoked would be $\mathsf{B}_1 = \mathsf{SDBox}(1,5,T_3)$, $\mathsf{B}_2 = \mathsf{SDBox}(1,2,T_3)$, $\mathsf{B}_3 = \mathsf{SDBox}(8,9,T_3)$ and $\mathsf{B}_4 = \mathsf{SDBox}(10,12,T_3)$ (refer to figure 5.8(b) for the node numbering). Tracing all these boxes would end up with revoking T_3 and $\mathbf{SDDisable}(\psi, \langle \mathsf{B}_1, \mathsf{B}_2, \mathsf{B}_3, \mathsf{B}_4 \rangle, \sigma) = \{\mathsf{users}(2,5), \mathsf{users}(8,10), \mathsf{users}(10,11)\}$. Note that this subset collection will also be merged by tracing algorithm, resulting to the partition given in figure 5.8(c). The pirate then will be able to create a pirate box $\mathsf{SDBox}(2,5,T_4)$ and so on until T_4 is revoked. Observe that now T_4 is isolated in its own subtree, and the master pirate box will be able to make fewer boxes using the keys of T_4. Thus, it would have been preferable to start the pirate evolution with traitor T_4.

This example shows the effect of scheduling in the number of decoders that the master pirate box can produce. In particular, it shows that the order of using the traitor keys in pirate evolution affects the number of pirate decoder generations $PE^{\mathsf{R},\mathbf{SDDisable}}_{\mathcal{P},\mathbf{Leaking}}(t)$. We observe that starting with T_4 produces more pirate boxes than T_3 because the subtree($\mathsf{users}(3,5)$) containing T_4 that is hanging off the path $1-5$ is shorter than the one corresponding T_3. This will be used as our criterion to choose which traitor to start with; applying it recursively will induce a scheduling of the traitors for the master pirate box to use that we will formalize below.

We observe that the evolving pirate strategy can be based on a representation of the Steiner tree by means of paths hanging off each other hierarchically such that each path stems from an internal node to a traitor placed on a leaf.

Each time we choose a traitor, we actually choose a path to walk on to construct pirate boxes. We observe two criteria to maximize the number of pirate decoders. (1) Once a traitor is revoked, we choose a shortest path hanging off the path containing the recently revoked traitor. (2) If there are more than one shortest paths, a path with large number of paths hanging off itself would be preferable. Choosing a traitor amounts to choosing a path according to this criteria (in a recursive way). In the next paragraphs we formalize these observations.

We next introduce a special annotation of a Steiner Tree $\mathsf{Steiner}(\mathsf{T}, u, v)$, where $\mathsf{users}(u, v)$ is one of the subsets in the partition, that will enable us to choose the best ordering of the traitors.

Definition 5.13. *A traitor annotation of a Steiner tree* $\mathsf{Steiner}(\mathsf{T}, v_x, v_y)$ *is the mapping* f *from its nodes to* $\mathsf{T} \cup \{\perp\}$ *that is defined in Figure 5.9. Observe that the annotation of* $\mathsf{parent}(v)$ *is computed symmetrically regardless of the choice of* v *or its sibling.*

We say $\mathsf{Steiner}(\mathsf{T}, v_x, v_y)$ *is annotated by* f. *Denote the parent of a node* v *by* $\mathsf{parent}(v)$, *the sibling by* $\mathsf{sibling}(v)$, *the height by* $\mathsf{height}(v)$.

We define the rank of a traitor u *given an annotation* f *as the number of nodes with 2 children that are annotated by* u. *We denote the rank of* $u \in \mathsf{T}$ *by* $\mathsf{rank}_{\mathsf{f}}(u)$.

Given a Steiner tree ST *annotated by* f*, for any* $u \in \mathsf{T}$ *the* u-$\mathsf{path}(\mathsf{ST})$ *is the path that is made out of all nodes that are annotated by* u*. Similarly, we define* $\bot$-$\mathsf{path}(\mathsf{ST})$ *and further we call it as the basic path of the tree* ST*. We denote* u-$\mathsf{path}(\mathsf{ST})$ *by a vector of nodes,* u–$\mathsf{path}(\mathsf{ST}) = \langle v_{c_1}, v_{c_2}, \cdots v_{c_s}\rangle$ *where* $v_{c_i} = \mathsf{parent}(v_{c_{i+1}})$ *for* $0 < i < s$ *and* $u = \mathsf{f}(v_{c_i})$*; we also denote* v_{c_1} *and* v_{c_s} *in this path by* $\mathsf{top_f}(u)$ *and* $\mathsf{bottom_f}(u)$ *respectively.*

annotation($\mathsf{Steiner}(\mathsf{T}, v_x, v_y)$)
Initially annotate each leaf l with its corresponding traitor $u \in \mathsf{T}$, i.e. $\mathsf{f}(l) = u$
$\mathsf{rank}(u) = 0$, for each $u \in \mathsf{T}$
$\mathsf{f}(v_y) = \bot$ and $\mathsf{rank}(\bot) = 0$.
Annotate each node from bottom to top by following rule:

$$\mathsf{f}(\mathsf{parent}(v)) = \begin{cases} \mathsf{f}(v) & \mathsf{sibling}(v) \notin \mathsf{Tree} \\ \bot & \mathsf{f}(v) = \bot \vee \mathsf{f}(\mathsf{sibling}(v)) = \bot \\ \mathsf{f}(v) & \mathsf{rank}(\mathsf{f}(v)) \geq \mathsf{rank}(\mathsf{f}(\mathsf{sibling}(v))) \\ \mathsf{f}(\mathsf{sibling}(v)) & \text{otherwise} \end{cases}$$

if $\mathsf{sibling}(v) \in \mathsf{Tree}$ then update $\mathsf{rank}(\mathsf{f}(\mathsf{parent}(v))) = \mathsf{rank}(\mathsf{f}(\mathsf{parent}(v))) + 1$
output f

Fig. 5.9. Computing the traitor annotation for a given Steiner tree.

Note that the rank of a traitor u is actually the number of paths hanging off the u-path. By a bottom-top approach as described in Figure 5.9, we make sure that any path p with length l is annotated by a traitor u that maximizes the use of length l in such a way that the number of paths hanging off u-$\mathsf{path} = p$ is maximum compared to the case another traitor v is chosen to annotate p. Figure 5.10 is illustrating the annotation of Steiner Tree $\mathsf{Steiner}(\{T_1, T_2, T_3, T_4\}, 1, 5)$ with respect to the paths dividing the tree. Note that each path is annotated with the traitor placed on the unique leaf of that path. According to this annotation the scheduling of traitors would be T_4, T_1, T_2 and T_3. This can be seen as follows: we choose the shortest path hanging off the $\bot$-path; this gives T_4 as the first traitor to be used; the next path hanging off the $\bot$-path is annotated by T_1; this gives T_1 as the second traitor to be used. After finishing T_4, T_1, all paths hanging off the $\bot$-path are expended and we move to choose the paths hanging off the previously chosen paths that are the T_4-path and T_1-path (in that order). There is no path hanging off the T_4-path, so we choose the shortest path hanging off the T_1-path; this gives T_2 as the third traitor to be used. Before describing how the master pirate box works, we will prove following lemma that will help see the rationale behind the pirate evolution attack for the SD method. This lemma tells us how the partition looks like after choosing a traitor according to the annotation, and creating pirate boxes until the chosen traitor is entirely revoked. It also defines explicitly the number of pirate decoders that the master box can spawn.

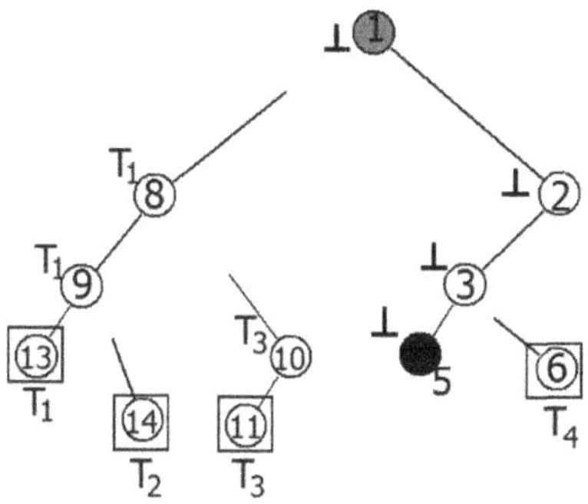

Fig. 5.10. The user paths due to the annotation given in Figure 5.9.

Lemma 5.14. *Consider the revocation instruction* $\psi = \textbf{Revoke}(\Phi^{SD}, \mathsf{R})$ *that encodes the set* R *where* **Revoke** *is the algorithm described in Figure 2.9. Let* $\mathsf{Tree} = \mathsf{Steiner}(\mathsf{T}, v_x, v_y) \in \{\mathsf{Steiner}(\mathsf{T}, g, r) \mid \mathsf{users}(g, r) \in \psi\}$ *be one of the Steiner trees for a traitor coalition* T. *Consider the annotation* f *of* Tree *given in Figure 5.9. Suppose the shortest path hanging off the* $\bot$-$\mathsf{path}(\mathsf{Tree})$ *is annotated by* u. *Let* $u_1 = \mathsf{top}_\mathsf{f}(u)$ *and* $u_s = \mathsf{bottom}_\mathsf{f}(u)$ *where* s *is the length of the* u-$\mathsf{path}(\mathsf{Tree})$. *It holds that: (1) There exists a sequence of pirate boxes* $\mathsf{B}_1, \mathsf{B}_2, \cdots \mathsf{B}_h$, *each using a private key derived from* sk_u *where* $h = \mathsf{height}(\mathsf{Tree}) + \mathsf{A}_u$ *and* $\mathsf{A}_u \in \{0, 1\}$ *such that* $\mathsf{A}_u = 1$ *if and only if* $\mathsf{sibling}(u_1)$ *has a single child in* Tree. *(2)* $\textbf{SDDisable}(\psi, \langle \mathsf{B}_1, \mathsf{B}_2, \cdots \mathsf{B}_h \rangle, \sigma) = (\psi \setminus \mathsf{users}(v_x, v_y)) \cup \{\mathsf{users}(v_x, \mathsf{parent}(u_1)), \mathsf{users}(u_1, u_s)\} \cup L_u$, *where* $L_u = \{\mathsf{users}(\mathsf{sibling}(u_1), v_y)\}$ *if* $\mathsf{A}_u = 1$ *and* $\emptyset$ *otherwise.*

Proof of Lemma 5.14: Let the $\bot$-path in $\mathsf{Tree} = \mathsf{Steiner}(\mathsf{T}, v_x, v_y)$ be the path $\langle k_1, k_2, \cdots k_m \rangle$. Note that $k_1 = v_x$ and $k_m = v_y$. The shortest path hanging off the $\bot$-path is related to the maximum l such that $\mathsf{sibling}(k_l)$ is a node in Tree, i.e. $l = \max(l : \mathsf{sibling}(k_l) \in \mathsf{Tree})$. Provided that this shortest path is annotated by u, denote the u-path by $\langle u_1, u_2, \cdots u_s \rangle$. In light of the facts that k_l and u_1 are siblings in the Tree, and u_s is a leaf, the length (in number of nodes) of the path from v_x to u_s equals to $\mathsf{height}(\mathsf{Tree}) + 1$. It follows that, $l - 1 + s = \mathsf{height}(\mathsf{Tree}) + 1$. Observe that A_u as defined in the statement of Lemma 5.14, satisfies that $\mathsf{A}_u = 0$ if $l = m$ and $\mathsf{A}_u = 1$ if $l < m$. We define the sequence of pirate boxes $\mathsf{B}_1, \mathsf{B}_2, \cdots \mathsf{B}_h$ as follows:

$$\mathsf{B}_y = \left\{ \begin{array}{ll} \mathsf{SDBox}(k_y,\ k_m,\ u) & 0 < y < l \\ \mathsf{SDBox}(k_{l-1},\ k_l,\ u) & (y = l) \wedge (\mathsf{A}_u = 1) \\ \mathsf{SDBox}(u_j,\ \mathsf{sibling}(u_{j+1}),\ u) & y = l + \mathsf{A}_u + j - 1 \text{ for } 0 < j \leq s - 1 \end{array} \right\}$$

Observe that $h = \mathsf{height}(\mathsf{Tree}) + \mathsf{A}_u$ holds. We next prove the correctness, i.e. the next generation should be able to decrypt the message encrypted after tracing has disabled all previous boxes.

For simplicity, for a given $\mathsf{B} = \mathsf{SDBox}(g, r, u)$ for a pair of nodes g, r, let us define $\mathsf{users}(\mathsf{B})$ as the set $\mathsf{users}(g, r)$. Recall that $\mathsf{users}(k_1, k_m) \in \psi$, we claim that $\mathsf{users}(\mathsf{B}_y) \in \mathbf{SDDisable}(\psi, \langle \mathsf{B}_1, \mathsf{B}_2, \cdots \mathsf{B}_{y-1}\rangle, \sigma)$ provided that $y \leq \mathsf{height}(\mathsf{Tree}) + \mathsf{A}_u$. This can be proven by induction by using the result of Lemma 5.11. The induction is similar to the induction made in the proof of Theorem 5.6. Note that the last box $\mathsf{SDBox}(u_{s-1}, \mathsf{sibling}(u_s), u)$ decrypts the ciphertext iff $\mathsf{users}(u_{s-1}, \mathsf{sibling}(u_s)) = \{u\}$ is in the partition. Tracing against all boxes would end up with revoking u entirely.

Regarding statement (2) of the lemma, we consider first the case $l < m$. It is easy to see by induction that the following two claims hold :

Claim 1. Consider $y = 2, \ldots, l-1$. Then it holds that the pattern $\mathbf{SDDisable}(\psi, \langle \mathsf{B}_1, \mathsf{B}_2, \cdots \mathsf{B}_y\rangle, \sigma)$ contains the sets

$$\mathsf{users}(k_1, k_y), \mathsf{users}(k_y, k_{y+1}), \mathsf{users}(k_{y+1}, k_m)$$

Claim 2. Consider $j = 2, \ldots, s-1$ and $y = l + j$. Then it holds that the pattern $\mathbf{SDDisable}(\psi, \langle \mathsf{B}_1, \mathsf{B}_2, \cdots \mathsf{B}_y\rangle, \sigma)$ contains the sets

$$\mathsf{users}(u_1, u_j), \mathsf{users}(u_j, u_{j+1}), \mathsf{users}(u_j, \mathsf{sibling}(u_{j+1}))$$

Based on the above it is easy to see that ψ after the tracing process, it will hold that $\mathsf{users}(v_x, v_y)$ would substituted by $\mathsf{users}(k_1, k_{l-1}), \mathsf{users}(k_l, k_m)$ and $\mathsf{users}(u_1, u_s)$.

The case of $l < m$ can be argued in exactly the same way with the only difference that there will be no "left-over" set $\mathsf{users}(k_l, k_m)$ in the pattern as we have in the case $l < m$. ■

We next describe our evolving pirate strategy against the $\mathtt{SD}$ set system. We define the master pirate box **MasterBox** produced by the adversary $\mathcal{P}^{\mathbf{Encrypt}}(\mathsf{T}, \{sk_u\}_{u \in \mathsf{T}})$ for a set of traitors T as follows: **MasterBox** recursively runs a procedure for each subset $\mathsf{users}(v_x, v_y) \in \psi$ which is called `makeboxes`, with input the traitor annotated Steiner tree $\mathsf{Tree} = \mathsf{Steiner}(\mathsf{T}, v_x, v_y)$. Observe below that whenever the recursive call is made, the annotation of Tree satisfies that the root is annotated with $\perp$. The basic procedure works as follows:

The root v_x is annotated as $\perp$. Let $u\text{-}\mathsf{path}(\mathsf{Tree}) = \langle u_1, u_2, \cdots u_s\rangle$ be the shortest path hanging off the $\perp\text{-}\mathsf{path}(\mathsf{Tree})$. The master box **MasterBox** constructs $\mathsf{SDBox}(v_x, v_y, u)$ and more pirate decoders following the way tracing works as described in lemma 5.11. After creating pirate boxes as many as the height of Tree (plus one possibly if $\mathsf{A}_u = 1$, cf. lemma 5.14), the traitor u will be entirely revoked by the system. Lemma 5.14 tells us that the partition after revoking u will include the subsets $\mathsf{users}(v_x, \mathsf{parent}(u_1))$ and $\mathsf{users}(u_1, u_s)$. We update the path $\langle u_1, u_2, \cdots u_s\rangle$ in $\mathsf{Steiner}(\mathsf{T}, u_1, u_s)$ by annotating it by $\perp$ since u is no more in $\mathsf{users}(u_1, u_s)$. The master box **MasterBox** then runs **makeboxes** independently on both of the trees $\mathsf{Steiner}(\mathsf{T}, v_x, \mathsf{parent}(u_1))$ and $\mathsf{Steiner}(\mathsf{T}, u_1, u_s)$. Refer to figure 5.11 for the detailed specification of the evolving pirate strategy.

In the following theorem we prove the correctness of the strategy, i.e. that each box will decrypt the ciphertexts that are generated assuming all previous

1. For each $set(v_x, v_y) \in \psi$
2. Compute $\mathsf{f} = \textbf{annotation}(\mathsf{Steiner}(\mathsf{T}, v_x, v_y))$
3. Run $\textbf{makeboxes}(\mathsf{Steiner}(\mathsf{T}, v_x, v_y), \mathsf{f})$ till the ℓ-th pirate box is produced (fail if there is no ℓ-th box).

makeboxes(Tree Tree, annotation f)
1. Let $\perp$-path in Tree be $\langle k_1, k_2, \cdots k_m \rangle$. Note that $k_1 = v_x$ and $k_m = v_y$
2. Choose the shortest path hanging off the $\perp$-path,
   i.e. pick $l = \max(l : \mathsf{sibling}(k_l) \in \mathsf{Tree})$.
   if no such path exists, exit.
3. Set $u = \mathsf{f}(\mathsf{sibling}(k_l))$;
4. Denote u-path by $\langle u_1, u_2, \cdots u_s \rangle$
5. Output $\mathsf{SDBox}(k_1, k_m, u), \mathsf{SDBox}(k_2, k_m, u), \cdots \mathsf{SDBox}(k_{l-1}, k_m, u)$
6. Output $\mathsf{SDBox}(k_{l-1}, k_l, u)$ iff $l < m$.
7. Output $\mathsf{SDBox}(u_1, \mathsf{sibling}(u_2), u), \mathsf{SDBox}(u_2, \mathsf{sibling}(u_3), u), \ldots,$
   $\mathsf{SDBox}(u_{s-1}, \mathsf{sibling}(u_s), u)$
8. Update $\mathsf{f}(u_i) = \perp$, for $0 < i \leq s$
9. $\textbf{makeboxes}(\mathsf{Steiner}(\mathsf{T}, u_1, u_s), \mathsf{f})$
10. $\textbf{makeboxes}(\mathsf{Steiner}(\mathsf{T}, k_1, k_{l-1}), \mathsf{f})$

Fig. 5.11. The description of master box program $\textbf{MasterBox}(1^{t+\log n}, \ell)$ parameterized by ψ, T, sk_u for $u \in \mathsf{T}$ that is produced by the evolving pirate for the subset difference method.

boxes are traced. We also show the maximum number of pirate decoders that can be created.

Theorem 5.15. *Let* $\mathsf{B}_1, \mathsf{B}_2, \cdots, \mathsf{B}_{k+1}$ *be a sequence of pirate boxes constructed by the pirate evolution strategy described in Figure 5.11 parameterized by* ψ *and* T. *Let* $0 < \sigma \leq 1$. *Suppose* $\psi_k = \textbf{SDDisable}(\psi, \langle \mathsf{B}_1, \mathsf{B}_2, \cdots, \mathsf{B}_k \rangle, \sigma)$, *then it holds that*

$$\textbf{Prob}[\mathsf{B}_{k+1}(\textbf{Encrypt}(ek, m, \psi_k)) = m] \geq \sigma$$

provided that

$$k < \sum_{\mathsf{users}(v,v') \in \psi} \left(\sum_{u \in \mathsf{T} \cap \mathsf{users}(v,v')} \mathsf{height}(\mathsf{top}_{\mathsf{f}}(u')) + \mathsf{A}_u \right) \tag{5.1}$$

where f *is the traitor annotation described in Figure 5.9 and* u' *depends on* u *as follows* u' *is the traitor (possibly* $\perp$*) such that the* u-path$(\textbf{Steiner}(\mathsf{T}, v, v'))$ *hangs off the* u'-path.

Proof of Theorem 5.15: We first prove that the **MasterBox** of Figure 5.11 on input T and ψ produces as many boxes as the number given in the equation 5.1. For a fixed subset $\mathsf{users}(v, v') \in \psi$ we next count the number of boxes the algorithm produces for this subset.

Consider the first traitor u that belongs to $\mathsf{T} \cap \mathsf{users}(v, v')$ and is selected in line 3 of Figure 5.11. We have that the number of boxes produced will equal to $l - 1 + s - 1 + \mathsf{A}_u$, where $l - 1$ is the number of nodes in the $\perp$-path from v to the junction for the u-path and s is the number of nodes in the u-path. It is immediate that the height of the node u' as defined in the theorem's statement based on u will be exactly $l + s - 2$; it follows that the number of boxes contributed by traitor u will be $\mathsf{height}(\mathsf{top}_\mathsf{f}(u')) + \mathsf{A}_u$. Based on the way the makeboxes procedure works, the same exact argumentation applies to theremaining traitors in $\mathsf{T} \cap \mathsf{users}(v, v')$.

This completes the argument on the number of boxes the **MasterBox** of Figure 5.11 produces. We denote this number by K. We next prove by induction on k that if Equation 5.1 holds, i.e. $k < K$, then we obtain:

$$\mathbf{Prob}[\mathsf{B}_{k+1}(\mathbf{Encrypt}(ek, m, \psi_k)) = m] \geq \sigma$$

where $\mathsf{B}_i \leftarrow \mathbf{MasterBox}(1^{t+\log n}, i)$ and ψ_k is the revocation instruction produced by $\mathbf{SDDisable}(\psi, \langle \mathsf{B}_1, \mathsf{B}_2, \cdots, \mathsf{B}_k, \sigma)$.

(i) Base case with $k = 0$: as there is no pirate box other than B_1 we have $\psi_0 = \psi$. Denote the first box produced by $\mathbf{makeboxes}(\mathsf{Steiner}(\mathsf{T}, v, v'), f)$ as B_1 where (v, v') is a pair of nodes such that $\mathsf{users}(v, v') \in \psi$. Since the $\perp$-path of the Steiner tree starts with v and ends with v', the box will be of the form $\mathsf{SDBox}(v, v', u)$ for the traitor u whose traitor path is the shortest path hanging off the $\perp$-path. It is immediate that $\mathbf{Prob}[\mathsf{B}_1(\mathbf{Encrypt}(ek, m, \psi_0)) = m] \geq \sigma$.

(ii) Induction assumption for some $0 \leq k < K - 1$: We assume that

$$\mathbf{Prob}[\mathsf{B}_k(\mathbf{Encrypt}(ek, m, \psi_{k-1})) = m] \geq \sigma$$

holds for $\psi_{k-1} = \mathbf{SDDisable}(\psi, \langle \mathsf{B}_1, \mathsf{B}_2, \cdots, \mathsf{B}_{k-1}, \sigma)$.

(iii) Induction step: We have two cases; either the pirate decoders B_k and B_{k+1} are generated subsequently in the same batch of a call of **makeboxes** on some Tree, or B_{k+1} is the first output of a new call while B_k is the last output of a previous call to **makeboxes**.

The first case: Suppose that B_k and B_{k+1} are produced by the key of a traitor $u \in \mathsf{T}$ whose traitor path is the shortest path hanging off the $\perp$-path of the Tree. Note that if the $\perp$-path $= \langle v_1, \ldots, v_m \rangle$ for some m, then Tree would be of the form $\mathsf{Steiner}(\mathsf{T}, v_1, v_m)$.

Let us suppose that $\mathsf{B}_k = \mathsf{SDBox}(x_1, y_1, u)$ and $\mathsf{B}_{k+1} = \mathsf{SDBox}(x_2, y_2, u)$ for some nodes x_1, y_1, x_2, y_2. The induction assumption along with the definition of SDBox yield the fact that $\mathsf{users}(x_1, y_1) \in \psi_{k-1}$. Due to the evolution strategy given in Figure 5.11 observe that the set $\mathsf{users}(x_2, y_2)$ is a subset of the set $\mathsf{users}(x_1, y_1)$ and we have that $\mathsf{users}(x_2, y_2) \in \mathbf{SDDisable}(\psi_{k-1}, \mathsf{B}_k, \sigma)$. Next we observe that $\psi_k = \mathbf{SDDisable}(\psi, \langle \mathsf{B}_1, \mathsf{B}_2, \cdots, \mathsf{B}_k, \sigma)$ is equal to $\mathbf{SDDisable}(\psi_{k-1}, \mathsf{B}_k, \sigma)$ due to the way we define the successive revocation over a sequence of pirate decoders. Hence we obtain $\mathsf{users}(x_2, y_2) \in \psi_k$. Recall that $\mathsf{B}_{k+1} = \mathsf{SDBox}(x_2, y_2, u)$, the definition of **SDBox** completes the final argument:

$$\mathbf{Prob}[\mathsf{B}_{k+1}(\mathbf{Encrypt}(ek, m, \psi_k)) = m] \geq \sigma$$

The second case: Let the box B_{k+1} be produced as the first box on a call of **makeboxes**($\mathbf{Steiner}(\mathsf{T}, x, y), \mathsf{f}$). The box then would be of the form $\mathsf{SDBox}(x, y, u)$ for some $u \in \mathsf{T}$ that is the annotation of the shortest path hanging of the $\perp$-path of the tree $\mathbf{Steiner}(\mathsf{T}, x, y)$.

The call for **makeboxes**($\mathbf{Steiner}(\mathsf{T}, x, y), \mathsf{f}$) is either a call on a set $\mathsf{users}(x, y)$ that is present in ψ (line 2 of the **MasterBox** program in Figure 5.11) or it is a call in a stack of recursive calls (lines 9-10 of the **makeboxes** procedure in Figure 5.11). The first subcase would trivially imply that $\mathsf{users}(x, y) \in \psi_k$ as no previous calls have changed the set $\mathsf{users}(x, y)$ in the original revocation instruction ψ. For the second subcase, the Lemma 5.14 ensures that the set $\mathsf{users}(x, y)$ is formed due to the parent invocation of **makeboxes**; hence again we obtain $\mathsf{users}(x, y) \in \psi_k$. In both of the cases it holds:

$$\mathbf{Prob}[\mathsf{B}_{k+1}(\mathbf{Encrypt}(ek, m, \psi_k)) = m] \geq \sigma$$

This completes the induction proof. ■

We next study classes of leaking incidents and the number of pirate generations they allow. For the polynomial time evolving pirate $\mathcal{P}$ described in Figure 5.11, the value of $PE^{\mathsf{R},\mathbf{SDDisable}}_{\mathcal{P},\mathbf{Leaking}}(t)$ follows from theorem 5.15. We next give a lower bound on this quantity by suitably constructing a class of leaking incidents in the following theorem.

Theorem 5.16. *Let $n \in \mathbb{N}$ be the number of receivers. For a given R, there exists a leaking incident* **Leaking** *corrupting t users in a single subset $\mathsf{S} \in$* $\mathbf{Revoke}(\Phi_{SD}, \mathsf{R})$ *where we assume for simplicity that S is a complete subset, and thus $\log|\mathsf{S}|$ is an integer, that enables an evolving pirate with respect to* **Leaking** *so that $K = PE^{\mathsf{R},\mathbf{SDDisable}}_{\mathcal{P},\mathbf{Leaking}}(t)$ satisfies:*

$$K = \begin{cases} t \log|\mathsf{S}| + 1, & t \leq \log|\mathsf{S}| + 1 \\ t \log(\frac{|\mathsf{S}|}{2^{s+1}}) + 2^{s+1}\log(\frac{|\mathsf{S}|}{2^{s-2}}) - \log|\mathsf{S}| - 2, & \end{cases}$$

$$t \in \left\{2^s \log(\frac{|\mathsf{S}|}{2^{s-1}}) + 1, \ldots, 2^{s+1}\log(\frac{|\mathsf{S}|}{2^s})\right\}, 0 < s < \log|\mathsf{S}|$$

Proof of Theorem 5.16:

Consider the following leaking incident **Leaking**: the first traitor is placed in an arbitrary leaf; its initial rank is 0; then, h stages follow (easing the notation we will use h in place of $\log|\mathsf{S}|$): in stage s (where $s = 0, \ldots, h-1$), a number of new traitors will be placed as follows: for each already placed traitor u that has rank 0 and path length $h - s$ we will add $h - s$ new traitors in the disjoint subtrees that are hanging off the u-path. Observe this makes

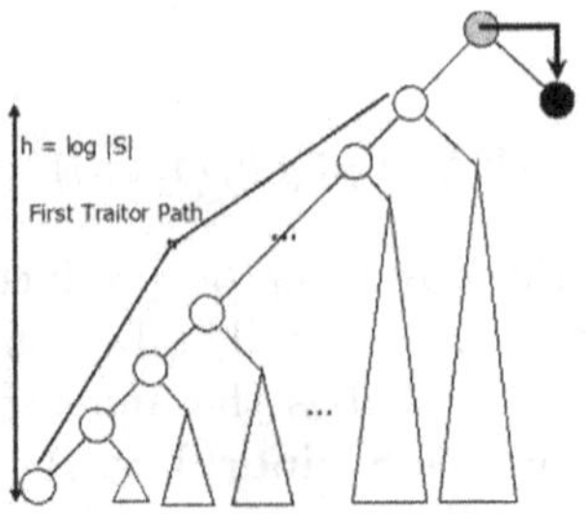

Fig. 5.12. Maximizing the number of pirate generations for the evolving pirate in the subset difference method.

the rank of traitor u maximum. We continue in this fashion until all traitors are placed.

Claim. In the beginning of stage $s > 0$, there will be exactly 2^{s-1} traitors of rank 0 each one with a traitor path of length $h - s$.

We prove this by induction; the base case of $s = 1$, is easy to see: in stage 1 there is a single traitor of traitor path length $h - 1$ (this is the traitor placed in the rightmost subtree in the illustration of figure 5.12). Now we prove the induction step. From stage 0 we have a single traitor of length h that contributes a single traitor with path length $h - s$. Similarly, from stage 1 we have a single traitor of traitor length $h - 1$ that contributes a single traitor with path length $h - s$. From stage 2 we have 2 traitors of length $h - 2$ that each one contributes a single traitor of path length $h - s$. In general in stage $m < s$ we have 2^{m-1} traitors that contribute each one a single traitor of path length $h - s$. In total we have

$$1 + \sum_{m=1}^{s-1} 2^{m-1} = 2^{s-1}$$

which completes the proof of the claim.

Based on the claim, at the end of stage $s > 0$ there will be a total of $2^{s-1}(h - s)$ new traitors placed. Therefore, the total number of traitors that will be placed by the end of stage $s > 0$ is equal to

$$1 + h + \sum_{m=1}^{s} 2^{m-1}(h - m) = 2^s(h - s + 1)$$

We, next, compute the number of decoders that can be produced by the traitors placed according to the above leaking incident. Recall that corrupting t users from $\mathsf{T} \subset \mathsf{S}$ with respect to the above leaking incident, the evolving pirate $\mathcal{P}$ annotates the traitors in Steiner tree $\mathbf{Steiner}(\mathsf{T}, \mathsf{S})$ to apply the strategy of Figure 5.11.

Define $K = PE^{\mathsf{R},\mathbf{SDDisable}}_{\mathcal{P},\mathbf{Leaking}}(t)$ is to be the summation over $\mathsf{height}(\mathsf{top}_\mathsf{f}(u')) + \mathsf{A}_u$ as stated in Theorem 5.15 where u' is defined as the traitor (possibly $\perp$)

such that the u-path(**Steiner**(T, v, v')) hangs off the u'-path. Observe that u' appears in the summation for as many traitors as its rank. We will first compute K for the choice of $t = 2^s(h-s+1)$ for $s \in \{0, 1, \ldots, h-1\}$ (we denote it by K_s for the choice of stage s):

Since the number of traitors satisfies $t = 2^s(h-s+1)$, we are at the end of the stage s for $s = 0, 1, \ldots, h-1$. We make three easy observations: (i) Other than the traitors that have path of length at least $h-s$, all the remaining traitors placed according to above leaking incident have rank 0. This is because no other traitors are placed below their path (which is shorter than $h-s$). Thus, considering the summation of Theorem 5.15, those traitors will never appear as u' in the summation. (ii) On the other hand, the traitors with non-zero rank (and their rank is the maximum possible) will appear in the summation as a u' node as many as their rank (which equals to the number of traitors hanging off the u'-path). For such traitors, except the traitor that placed first, the $\mathsf{height}(\mathsf{top}_\mathsf{f}(u'))$ equals to the length of the u'-path. (ii) Finally, $\mathsf{A}_u = 0$ always holds for each traitor u due to the way the traitors are placed (recall the definition of A_u given in Lemma 5.14).

Based on the above we can now compute K_s:

$$K_s = \sum_{u \in \mathsf{T} \cap \mathsf{S}} (\mathsf{height}(\mathsf{top}_\mathsf{f}(u')) + \mathsf{A}_u) = h + 1 + \sum_{u \in (\mathsf{T} \setminus \{v\}) \cap \mathsf{S}} |(u')\text{-path}|$$

where v is the first traitor path and u' is a function of u that equals the traitor such that the u-path hangs off the u'-path. We next arrange the above summation with respect to u', i.e. the below holds due to the relation between u' and u in the above equation:

$$K_s = h + 1 + \sum_{u' \in \mathsf{T}} \mathsf{rank}(u') \cdot |(u')\text{-path}|$$

Now due to the placement of the traitors $|(u')\text{-path}|$ equals to the rank of u' (this is implied by the observations (i) and (ii) above); thus we obtain:

$$K_s = h + 1 + \sum_{u' \in \mathsf{T} \wedge \mathsf{rank}(u') \neq 0} |(u')\text{-path}|^2$$

We now arrange the above summation over $|u'\text{-path}| = h, h-1, h-2, \ldots 1$. Recall also that if $|u'\text{-path}| < h-s$ then the rank of u' is zero and non-zero otherwise.

$$K_s = h + 1 + \sum_{m=0}^{s} |\{u' : u' \in \mathsf{T} \wedge |(u')\text{-path}| = h - m\}| \cdot (h-m)^2$$

Due to the claim we have proved above, there will be a single traitor with path of length h and 2^{m-1} traitors with path of lenght $h-m$ for $m > 0$. Thus we obtain:

$$K_s = h + 1 + h^2 + \sum_{m=1}^{s} 2^{m-1} \cdot (h-m)^2$$

Finally we obtain $K_s = 2^s(h-s+1)^2 + 2^{s+1} - h - 2$ (an easy proof by induction that is left as an exercise).

We finally argue about the formula for K given in the statement of the theorem. In the case that $t \leq h+1$, we have easily that K equals $(t-1)h + h + 1 = th + 1$ which settles the first case. Now suppose that $2^s(h-s+1) < t \leq 2^{s+1}(h-s)$ for some $s \geq 0$. We have that the number of pirate decoders will be equal to K_s plus the number of decoders that can be produced by the remaining $t - 2^s(h-s+1)$ traitors. The traitors placed in the $s+1$ contribute $h-s-1$ decoders therefore we have that the total number of decoders contributed by them is $(t - 2^s(h-s+1))(h-s-1)$. So we obtain :

$$K_s + (t - 2^s(h-s+1))(h-s-1) = 2^{s+1}(h-s+2) + t(h-s-1) - h - 2$$

This completes the proof. ∎

The maximum number of generations can be achieved following the leaking incident of Theorem 5.16 in a configuration of the system when there is no revoked user; in this case there is a single element in the partition, namely S containing n users. The corollary below follows easily from theorem 5.16.

Corollary 5.17. *The pirate evolution bound for the* SD *method satisfies*

$$\mathsf{evo}[\mathtt{SD}, \mathbf{SDDisable}] \geq t \log n$$

for $t \leq \log n$. *It also satisfies that for* $t \leq \sqrt{n} \cdot \frac{\log n}{2}$ *that*

$$\mathsf{evo}[\mathtt{SD}, \mathbf{SDDisable}] = \Omega(t \log n)$$

5.5 Bibliographic Notes

Pirate evolution, as an attack concept against trace and revoke schemes, was introduced by the authors in [62]. The susceptibility of the trace and revoke schemes of Naor, Naor and Lotspiech from [87] as it is discussed in Sections 5.3 and 5.4 of this text was also given there. Pirate evolution has practical implications. For example the advanced access content system (AACS) that is used in Blu-ray disks employs the subset difference method (SD) in clusters of $n = 2^{23}$ nodes. It follows that a leaking incident as the one described in Theorem 5.16 with t traitors enables an evolving pirate strategy to generate up to $23 \cdot t$ generations of pirate decoders. This means that key leakage incidents can be magnified, i.e., 10 traitor keys can result in up to 230 decoders and so forth. This was a "nightmare" scenario as described by the AACS implementers in [59]. The suggested proposal to deal with pirate evolution is to magnify the ciphertext overhead to reach a level of $\sqrt{n}$. While this enables only 2 generations of pirate evolution and may still be acceptable given the high capacity of Blu-ray disks it shows that the benefits of the subset difference method (its low ciphertext overhead) are entirely cancelled in practice due to pirate evolution. Going beyond, the concept of pirate evolution inspired new types of attack scenarios as the ones introduced by Billet and Phan in [14].

References

1. AACS Specifications, 2006. http://www.aacsla.com/specifications/.
2. M. Abdalla, D. Pointcheval, P.-A. Fouque, and D. Vergnaud, editors. *Applied Cryptography and Network Security, 7th International Conference, ACNS 2009, Paris-Rocquencourt, France, June 2-5, 2009. Proceedings*, volume 5536 of *Lecture Notes in Computer Science*, 2009.
3. M. Abdalla, Y. Shavitt, and A. Wool. Key management for restricted multicast using broadcast encryption. *IEEE/ACM Trans. Netw.*, 8(4):443–454, 2000.
4. W. Aiello, S. Lodha, and R. Ostrovsky. Fast digital identity revocation (extended abstract). In H. Krawczyk, editor, *CRYPTO*, volume 1462 of *Lecture Notes in Computer Science*, pages 137–152. Springer, 1998.
5. M. Ak, K. Kaya, and A. A. Selcuk. Optimal subset-difference broadcast encryption with free riders. *Information Sciences*, 2009.
6. N. Attrapadung and H. Imai. Graph-decomposition-based frameworks for subset-cover broadcast encryption and efficient instantiations. In B. K. Roy, editor, *ASIACRYPT*, volume 3788 of *Lecture Notes in Computer Science*, pages 100–120. Springer, 2005.
7. L. M. Batten and X. Yi. Efficient broadcast key distribution with dynamic revocation. *Security and Communication Networks*, 1(4):351–362, 2008.
8. M. Bellare, editor. *Advances in Cryptology - CRYPTO 2000, 20th Annual International Cryptology Conference, Santa Barbara, California, USA, August 20-24, 2000, Proceedings*, volume 1880 of *Lecture Notes in Computer Science*. Springer, 2000.
9. O. Berkman, M. Parnas, and J. Sgall. Efficient dynamic traitor tracing. In *SODA*, pages 586–595, 2000.
10. S. Berkovits. How to broadcast a secret. In *EUROCRYPT*, pages 535–541, 1991.
11. E. R. Berlekamp and L. Welch. Error correction of algebraic block codes. U.S. Patent, Number 4,633,470, 1986.
12. I. Biehl and B. Meyer. Protocols for collusion-secure asymmetric fingerprinting (extended abstract). In R. Reischuk and M. Morvan, editors, *STACS*, volume 1200 of *Lecture Notes in Computer Science*, pages 399–412. Springer, 1997.
13. O. Billet and D. H. Phan. Efficient traitor tracing from collusion secure codes. In R. Safavi-Naini, editor, *ICITS*, volume 5155 of *Lecture Notes in Computer Science*, pages 171–182. Springer, 2008.

14. O. Billet and D. H. Phan. Traitors collaborating in public: Pirates 2.0. In A. Joux, editor, *EUROCRYPT*, volume 5479 of *Lecture Notes in Computer Science*, pages 189–205. Springer, 2009.
15. G. R. Blakley, C. Meadows, and G. B. Purdy. Fingerprinting long forgiving messages. In H. C. Williams, editor, *CRYPTO*, volume 218 of *Lecture Notes in Computer Science*, pages 180–189. Springer, 1985.
16. D. Boneh and M. K. Franklin. An efficient public key traitor tracing scheme. In Wiener [124], pages 338–353.
17. D. Boneh and M. K. Franklin. Identity-based encryption from the weil pairing. In J. Kilian, editor, *CRYPTO*, volume 2139 of *Lecture Notes in Computer Science*, pages 213–229. Springer, 2001.
18. D. Boneh, C. Gentry, and B. Waters. Collusion resistant broadcast encryption with short ciphertexts and private keys. In Shoup [109], pages 258–275.
19. D. Boneh and M. Hamburg. Generalized identity based and broadcast encryption schemes. In J. Pieprzyk, editor, *ASIACRYPT*, volume 5350 of *Lecture Notes in Computer Science*, pages 455–470. Springer, 2008.
20. D. Boneh, A. Kiayias, and H. W. Montgomery. Robust fingerprinting codes : a near optimal construction. In *ACM Workshop on Digital Rights Management*, 2010.
21. D. Boneh and M. Naor. Traitor tracing with constant size ciphertext. In P. Ning, P. F. Syverson, and S. Jha, editors, *ACM Conference on Computer and Communications Security*, pages 501–510. ACM, 2008.
22. D. Boneh, A. Sahai, and B. Waters. Fully collusion resistant traitor tracing with short ciphertexts and private keys. In S. Vaudenay, editor, *EUROCRYPT*, volume 4004 of *Lecture Notes in Computer Science*, pages 573–592. Springer, 2006.
23. D. Boneh and J. Shaw. Collusion-secure fingerprinting for digital data (extended abstract). In D. Coppersmith, editor, *CRYPTO*, volume 963 of *Lecture Notes in Computer Science*, pages 452–465. Springer, 1995.
24. D. Boneh and B. Waters. A fully collusion resistant broadcast, trace, and revoke system. In A. Juels, R. N. Wright, and S. D. C. di Vimercati, editors, *ACM Conference on Computer and Communications Security*, pages 211–220. ACM, 2006.
25. R. Canetti, J. A. Garay, G. Itkis, D. Micciancio, M. Naor, and B. Pinkas. Multicast security: A taxonomy and some efficient constructions. In *INFOCOM*, pages 708–716, 1999.
26. R. Canetti, T. Malkin, and K. Nissim. Efficient communication-storage tradeoffs for multicast encryption. In *EUROCRYPT*, pages 459–474, 1999.
27. H. Chabanne, D. H. Phan, and D. Pointcheval. Public traceability in traitor tracing schemes. In Cramer [31], pages 542–558.
28. B. Chor, A. Fiat, and M. Naor. Tracing traitors. In Y. Desmedt, editor, *CRYPTO*, volume 839 of *Lecture Notes in Computer Science*, pages 257–270. Springer, 1994.
29. B. Chor, A. Fiat, M. Naor, and B. Pinkas. Tracing traitors. *IEEE Transactions on Information Theory*, 46(3):893–910, 2000.
30. I. J. Cox, J. Kilian, F. T. Leighton, and T. Shamoon. Secure spread spectrum watermarking for multimedia. *IEEE Transactions on Image Processing*, 6(12):1673–1687, 1997.

31. R. Cramer, editor. *Advances in Cryptology - EUROCRYPT 2005, 24th Annual International Conference on the Theory and Applications of Cryptographic Techniques, Aarhus, Denmark, May 22-26, 2005, Proceedings*, volume 3494 of *Lecture Notes in Computer Science*. Springer, 2005.
32. J. Daemen and V. Rijmen. *The Design of Rijndael: AES- The Advanced Encryption Standard*. Springer, New York, 2002.
33. C. Delerablée. Identity-based broadcast encryption with constant size ciphertexts and private keys. In *ASIACRYPT*, pages 200–215, 2007.
34. C. Delerablée, P. Paillier, and D. Pointcheval. Fully collusion secure dynamic broadcast encryption with constant-size ciphertexts or decryption keys. In T. Takagi, T. Okamoto, E. Okamoto, and T. Okamoto, editors, *Pairing*, volume 4575 of *Lecture Notes in Computer Science*, pages 39–59. Springer, 2007.
35. Y. Dodis and N. Fazio. Public key broadcast encryption for stateless receivers. In Feigenbaum [41], pages 61–80.
36. Y. Dodis and N. Fazio. Public key trace and revoke scheme secure against adaptive chosen ciphertext attack. In Y. Desmedt, editor, *Public Key Cryptography*, volume 2567 of *Lecture Notes in Computer Science*, pages 100–115. Springer, 2003.
37. Y. Dodis, N. Fazio, A. Kiayias, and M. Yung. Scalable public-key tracing and revoking. In *PODC*, pages 190–199, 2003.
38. C. Dwork, M. Naor, O. Reingold, G. N. Rothblum, and S. P. Vadhan. On the complexity of differentially private data release: efficient algorithms and hardness results. In M. Mitzenmacher, editor, *STOC*, pages 381–390. ACM, 2009.
39. N. Fazio, A. Nicolosi, and D. H. Phan. Traitor tracing with optimal transmission rate. In J. A. Garay, A. K. Lenstra, M. Mambo, and R. Peralta, editors, *ISC*, volume 4779 of *Lecture Notes in Computer Science*, pages 71–88. Springer, 2007.
40. U. Feige, P. Raghavan, D. Peleg, and E. Upfal. Computing with noisy information. *SIAM J. Comput.*, 23(5):1001–1018, 1994.
41. J. Feigenbaum, editor. *Security and Privacy in Digital Rights Management, ACM CCS-9 Workshop, DRM 2002, Washington, DC, USA, November 18, 2002, Revised Papers*, volume 2696 of *Lecture Notes in Computer Science*. Springer, 2003.
42. A. Fiat and M. Naor. Broadcast encryption. In Stinson [112], pages 480–491.
43. A. Fiat and T. Tassa. Dynamic traitor training. In Wiener [124], pages 354–371.
44. J. Furukawa and N. Attrapadung. Fully collusion resistant black-box traitor revocable broadcast encryption with short private keys. In L. Arge, C. Cachin, T. Jurdzinski, and A. Tarlecki, editors, *ICALP*, volume 4596 of *Lecture Notes in Computer Science*, pages 496–508. Springer, 2007.
45. E. Gafni, J. Staddon, and Y. L. Yin. Efficient methods for integrating traceability and broadcast encryption. In Wiener [124], pages 372–387.
46. S. D. Galbraith, K. G. Paterson, and N. P. Smart. Pairings for cryptographers. *Discrete Applied Mathematics*, 156(16):3113–3121, 2008.
47. J. A. Garay, J. Staddon, and A. Wool. Long-lived broadcast encryption. In Bellare [8], pages 333–352.
48. M. R. Garey, D. S. Johnson, and L. J. Stockmeyer. Some simplified np-complete problems. In *STOC*, pages 47–63, 1974.

49. C. Gentry, Z. Ramzan, and D. P. Woodruff. Explicit exclusive set systems with applications to broadcast encryption. In *FOCS*, pages 27–38. IEEE Computer Society, 2006.
50. M. T. Goodrich, J. Z. Sun, and R. Tamassia. Efficient tree-based revocation in groups of low-state devices. In M. K. Franklin, editor, *CRYPTO*, volume 3152 of *Lecture Notes in Computer Science*, pages 511–527. Springer, 2004.
51. V. Guruswami and M. Sudan. Improved decoding of reed-solomon and algebraic-geometric codes. In *FOCS*, pages 28–39, 1998.
52. H.-J. Guth and B. Pfitzmann. Error- and collusion-secure fingerprinting for digital data. In A. Pfitzmann, editor, *Information Hiding*, volume 1768 of *Lecture Notes in Computer Science*, pages 134–145. Springer, 1999.
53. D. Halevy and A. Shamir. The lsd broadcast encryption scheme. In M. Yung, editor, *CRYPTO*, volume 2442 of *Lecture Notes in Computer Science*, pages 47–60. Springer, 2002.
54. H. D. L. Hollmann, J. H. van Lint, J.-P. M. G. Linnartz, and L. M. G. M. Tolhuizen. On codes with the identifiable parent property. *J. Comb. Theory, Ser. A*, 82(2):121–133, 1998.
55. J. Y. Hwang, D. H. Lee, and J. Lim. Generic transformation for scalable broadcast encryption schemes. In Shoup [109], pages 276–292.
56. Y. H. Hwang and P. J. Lee. Efficient broadcast encryption scheme with log-key storage. In G. D. Crescenzo and A. D. Rubin, editors, *Financial Cryptography*, volume 4107 of *Lecture Notes in Computer Science*, pages 281–295. Springer, 2006.
57. N.-S. Jho, J. Y. Hwang, J. H. Cheon, M.-H. Kim, D. H. Lee, and E. S. Yoo. One-way chain based broadcast encryption schemes. In Cramer [31], pages 559–574.
58. H. Jin and J. Lotspiech. Renewable traitor tracing: A trace-revoke-trace system for anonymous attack. In J. Biskup and J. Lopez, editors, *ESORICS*, volume 4734 of *Lecture Notes in Computer Science*, pages 563–577. Springer, 2007.
59. H. Jin and J. B. Lotspiech. Defending against the pirate evolution attack. In F. Bao, H. Li, and G. Wang, editors, *ISPEC*, volume 5451 of *Lecture Notes in Computer Science*, pages 147–158. Springer, 2009.
60. H. Jin and S. Pehlivanoglu. Traitor tracing without a priori bound on the coalition size. In P. Samarati, M. Yung, F. Martinelli, and C. A. Ardagna, editors, *ISC*, volume 5735 of *Lecture Notes in Computer Science*, pages 234–241. Springer, 2009.
61. P. Junod, A. Karlov, and A. K. Lenstra. Improving the boneh-franklin traitor tracing scheme. In S. Jarecki and G. Tsudik, editors, *Public Key Cryptography*, volume 5443 of *Lecture Notes in Computer Science*, pages 88–104. Springer, 2009.
62. A. Kiayias and S. Pehlivanoglu. Pirate evolution: How to make the most of your traitor keys. In A. Menezes, editor, *CRYPTO*, volume 4622 of *Lecture Notes in Computer Science*, pages 448–465. Springer, 2007.
63. A. Kiayias and S. Pehlivanoglu. On the security of a public-key traitor tracing scheme with sublinear ciphertext size. In E. Al-Shaer, H. Jin, and G. L. Heileman, editors, *Digital Rights Management Workshop*, pages 1–10. ACM, 2009.
64. A. Kiayias and S. Pehlivanoglu. Tracing and revoking pirate rebroadcasts. In Abdalla et al. [2], pages 253–271.

65. A. Kiayias and S. Pehlivanoglu. Detecting and revoking pirate redistribution of content. U.S. Patent, Publication Number 2010/0043081, 2010.
66. A. Kiayias and S. Pehlivanoglu. Improving the round complexity of traitor tracing schemes. In J. Zhou and M. Yung, editors, *ACNS*, Lecture Notes in Computer Science, 2010.
67. A. Kiayias and M. Yung. On crafty pirates and foxy tracers. In Sander [104], pages 22–39.
68. A. Kiayias and M. Yung. Self protecting pirates and black-box traitor tracing. In Kilian [72], pages 63–79.
69. A. Kiayias and M. Yung. Breaking and repairing asymmetric public-key traitor tracing. In Feigenbaum [41], pages 32–50.
70. A. Kiayias and M. Yung. Traitor tracing with constant transmission rate. In L. R. Knudsen, editor, *EUROCRYPT*, volume 2332 of *Lecture Notes in Computer Science*, pages 450–465. Springer, 2002.
71. A. Kiayias and M. Yung. Public-key traitor tracing from efficient decoding and unbounded enrollment: extended abstract. In G. L. Heileman and M. Joye, editors, *Digital Rights Management Workshop*, pages 9–18. ACM, 2008.
72. J. Kilian, editor. *Advances in Cryptology - CRYPTO 2001, 21st Annual International Cryptology Conference, Santa Barbara, California, USA, August 19-23, 2001, Proceedings*, volume 2139 of *Lecture Notes in Computer Science*. Springer, 2001.
73. D. Kirovski and F. A. P. Petitcolas. Replacement attack on arbitrary watermarking systems. In Feigenbaum [41], pages 177–189.
74. N. Kogan, Y. Shavitt, and A. Wool. A practical revocation scheme for broadcast encryption using smart cards. In *IEEE Symposium on Security and Privacy*, pages 225–235. IEEE Computer Society, 2003.
75. H. Komaki, Y. Watanabe, G. Hanaoka, and H. Imai. Efficient asymmetric self-enforcement scheme with public traceability. In K. Kim, editor, *Public Key Cryptography*, volume 1992 of *Lecture Notes in Computer Science*, pages 225–239. Springer, 2001.
76. R. Kumar, S. Rajagopalan, and A. Sahai. Coding constructions for blacklisting problems without computational assumptions. In M. J. Wiener, editor, *CRYPTO*, volume 1666 of *Lecture Notes in Computer Science*, pages 609–623. Springer, 1999.
77. R. Kumar and A. Russell. A note on the set systems used for broadcast encryption. In *SODA*, pages 470–471, 2003.
78. K. Kurosawa and Y. Desmedt. Optimum traitor tracing and asymmetric schemes. In *EUROCRYPT*, pages 145–157, 1998.
79. K. Kurosawa and T. Yoshida. Linear code implies public-key traitor tracing. In D. Naccache and P. Paillier, editors, *Public Key Cryptography*, volume 2274 of *Lecture Notes in Computer Science*, pages 172–187. Springer, 2002.
80. M. Lee, D. Ma, and M. Seo. Breaking two k-resilient traitor tracing schemes with sublinear ciphertext size. In Abdalla et al. [2], pages 238–252.
81. T. Lindkvist. *Fingerprinting Digital Documents*. PhD thesis, Linkoping Studies in Science and Technology, 1999.
82. D. Liu, P. Ning, and K. Sun. Efficient self-healing group key distribution with revocation capability. In S. Jajodia, V. Atluri, and T. Jaeger, editors, *ACM Conference on Computer and Communications Security*, pages 231–240. ACM, 2003.

83. M. Luby and J. Staddon. Combinatorial bounds for broadcast encryption. In *EUROCRYPT*, pages 512–526, 1998.
84. T. Matsushita and H. Imai. A public-key black-box traitor tracing scheme with sublinear ciphertext size against self-defensive pirates. In P. J. Lee, editor, *ASIACRYPT*, volume 3329 of *Lecture Notes in Computer Science*, pages 260–275. Springer, 2004.
85. M. Mitzenmacher and E. Upfal. *Probability and Computing: randomized algorithms and probabilistic analysis.* Cambridge University Press, London, 2005.
86. D. Naccache, editor. *Topics in Cryptology - CT-RSA 2001, The Cryptographer's Track at RSA Conference 2001, San Francisco, CA, USA, April 8-12, 2001, Proceedings*, volume 2020 of *Lecture Notes in Computer Science.* Springer, 2001.
87. D. Naor, M. Naor, and J. Lotspiech. Revocation and tracing schemes for stateless receivers. In Kilian [72], pages 41–62.
88. D. Naor, M. Naor, and J. Lotspiech. Revocation and tracing schemes for stateless receivers. *Electronic Colloquium on Computational Complexity (ECCC)*, (043), 2002.
89. M. Naor and B. Pinkas. Threshold traitor tracing. In H. Krawczyk, editor, *CRYPTO*, volume 1462 of *Lecture Notes in Computer Science*, pages 502–517. Springer, 1998.
90. M. Naor and B. Pinkas. Efficient trace and revoke schemes. In Y. Frankel, editor, *Financial Cryptography*, volume 1962 of *Lecture Notes in Computer Science*, pages 1–20. Springer, 2000.
91. M. Naor and M. Yung. Public-key cryptosystems provably secure against chosen ciphertext attacks. In *STOC*, pages 427–437. ACM, 1990.
92. K. Nuida, M. Hagiwara, H. Watanabe, and H. Imai. Optimization of tardos's fingerprinting codes in a viewpoint of memory amount. In T. Furon, F. Cayre, G. J. Doërr, and P. Bas, editors, *Information Hiding*, volume 4567 of *Lecture Notes in Computer Science*, pages 279–293. Springer, 2007.
93. C. Peikert, A. Shelat, and A. Smith. Lower bounds for collusion-secure fingerprinting. In *SODA*, pages 472–479, 2003.
94. B. Pfitzmann. Trials of traced traitors. In R. J. Anderson, editor, *Information Hiding*, volume 1174 of *Lecture Notes in Computer Science*, pages 49–64. Springer, 1996.
95. B. Pfitzmann and M. Schunter. Asymmetric fingerprinting (extended abstract). In *EUROCRYPT*, pages 84–95, 1996.
96. B. Pfitzmann and M. Waidner. Asymmetric fingerprinting for larger collusions. In *ACM Conference on Computer and Communications Security*, pages 151–160, 1997.
97. Z. Ramzan and D. P. Woodruff. Fast algorithms for the free riders problem in broadcast encryption. In C. Dwork, editor, *CRYPTO*, volume 4117 of *Lecture Notes in Computer Science*, pages 308–325. Springer, 2006.
98. R. L. Rivest. All-or-nothing encryption and the package transform. In E. Biham, editor, *FSE*, volume 1267 of *Lecture Notes in Computer Science*, pages 210–218. Springer, 1997.
99. R. Safavi-Naini and Y. Wang. Sequential traitor tracing. In Bellare [8], pages 316–332.
100. R. Safavi-Naini and Y. Wang. New results on frame-proof codes and traceability schemes. *IEEE Transactions on Information Theory*, 47(7):3029–3033, 2001.

101. R. Safavi-Naini and Y. Wang. Traitor tracing for shortened and corrupted fingerprints. In Feigenbaum [41], pages 81–100.
102. R. Safavi-Naini and Y. Wang. Sequential traitor tracing. *IEEE Transactions on Information Theory*, 49(5):1319–1326, 2003.
103. R. Sakara and J. Furukawa. Identity-based broadcast encryption, 2007. Available at the IACR Crypto Archive http://eprint.iacr.org.
104. T. Sander, editor. *Security and Privacy in Digital Rights Management, ACM CCS-8 Workshop DRM 2001, Philadelphia, PA, USA, November 5, 2001, Revised Papers*, volume 2320 of *Lecture Notes in Computer Science*. Springer, 2002.
105. B. S. W. Schroder. *Ordered Sets: An Introduction*. Birkhauser, Boston, 2003.
106. A. Shamir. Identity-based cryptosystems and signature schemes. In *CRYPTO*, pages 47–53, 1984.
107. A. T. Sherman and D. A. McGrew. Key establishment in large dynamic groups using one-way function trees. *IEEE Trans. Software Eng.*, 29(5):444–458, 2003.
108. V. Shoup. A proposal for an iso standard for public key encryption (version 1.1), 2001.
109. V. Shoup, editor. *Advances in Cryptology - CRYPTO 2005: 25th Annual International Cryptology Conference, Santa Barbara, California, USA, August 14-18, 2005, Proceedings*, volume 3621 of *Lecture Notes in Computer Science*. Springer, 2005.
110. A. Silverberg, J. Staddon, and J. L. Walker. Efficient traitor tracing algorithms using list decoding. In C. Boyd, editor, *ASIACRYPT*, volume 2248 of *Lecture Notes in Computer Science*, pages 175–192. Springer, 2001.
111. J. Staddon, D. R. Stinson, and R. Wei. Combinatorial properties of frameproof and traceability codes. *IEEE Transactions on Information Theory*, 47(3):1042–1049, 2001.
112. D. R. Stinson, editor. *Advances in Cryptology - CRYPTO '93, 13th Annual International Cryptology Conference, Santa Barbara, California, USA, August 22-26, 1993, Proceedings*, volume 773 of *Lecture Notes in Computer Science*. Springer, 1994.
113. D. R. Stinson and R. Wei. Combinatorial properties and constructions of traceability schemes and frameproof codes. *SIAM J. Discrete Math.*, 11(1):41–53, 1998.
114. D. R. Stinson and R. Wei. Key preassigned traceability schemes for broadcast encryption. In S. E. Tavares and H. Meijer, editors, *Selected Areas in Cryptography*, volume 1556 of *Lecture Notes in Computer Science*, pages 144–156. Springer, 1998.
115. G. Tardos. Optimal probabilistic fingerprint codes. In *STOC*, pages 116–125. ACM, 2003.
116. G. Tardos. Optimal probabilistic fingerprint codes. *J. ACM*, 55(2), 2008.
117. O. Telelis and V. Zissimopoulos. Absolute o(log m) error in approximating random set covering: an average case analysis. *Inf. Process. Lett.*, 94(4):171–177, 2005.
118. V. D. Tô and R. Safavi-Naini. Linear code implies public-key traitor tracing with revocation. In H. Wang, J. Pieprzyk, and V. Varadharajan, editors, *ACISP*, volume 3108 of *Lecture Notes in Computer Science*, pages 24–35. Springer, 2004.

119. D. Tonien and R. Safavi-Naini. An efficient single-key pirates tracing scheme using cover-free families. In J. Zhou, M. Yung, and F. Bao, editors, *ACNS*, volume 3989 of *Lecture Notes in Computer Science*, pages 82–97, 2006.
120. N. R. Wagner. Fingerprinting. In *IEEE Symposium on Security and Privacy*, pages 18–22, 1983.
121. D. M. Wallner, E. J. Harder, and R. C. Agee. Key management for multicast: issues and architectures, 1999. Internet Draft.
122. P. Wang, P. Ning, and D. S. Reeves. Storage-efficient stateless group key revocation. In K. Zhang and Y. Zheng, editors, *ISC*, volume 3225 of *Lecture Notes in Computer Science*, pages 25–38. Springer, 2004.
123. Y. Watanabe, G. Hanaoka, and H. Imai. Efficient asymmetric public-key traitor tracing without trusted agents. In Naccache [86], pages 392–407.
124. M. J. Wiener, editor. *Advances in Cryptology - CRYPTO '99, 19th Annual International Cryptology Conference, Santa Barbara, California, USA, August 15-19, 1999, Proceedings*, volume 1666 of *Lecture Notes in Computer Science*. Springer, 1999.
125. C. K. Wong, M. G. Gouda, and S. S. Lam. Secure group communications using key graphs. In *SIGCOMM*, pages 68–79, 1998.
126. Y. Yacobi. Improved boneh-shaw content fingerprinting. In Naccache [86], pages 378–391.

Index